Miniature Metropolis

Miniature Metropolis

LITERATURE IN AN AGE OF
PHOTOGRAPHY AND FILM

Andreas Huyssen

 Harvard University Press

Cambridge, Massachusetts
London, England   2015

First Printing

Library of Congress Cataloging-in-Publication Data
Huyssen, Andreas.
   Miniature metropolis : literature in an age of photography and film /
Andreas Huyssen.
      pages cm
   Includes bibliographical references and index.
   ISBN 978-0-674-41672-7 (alk. paper)
   1. Cities and towns in literature.   2. City and town life in litera-
ture.   3. European prose literature—20th century—History and
criticism.   4. Feuilletons—History and criticism.   5. Literature and
photography—Europe.   6. Modernism (Literature)—Europe.   I. Title.
   PN56.C55H79 2015
   809'.93358209732—dc23

                                                       2014035332

To my students

Contents

Acknowledgments

IT TOOK MANY years of teaching modernist literature and culture in comparative perspective before I discovered the metropolitan miniature as a major and largely misrecognized mode of modernist writing. First published in the feuilletons of major European newspapers or in little magazines and always engaged with the challenges literature confronted from new media such as photography and film, the metropolitan miniature was hiding in plain sight. But its trajectory from Baudelaire to Benjamin and Musil has never attracted the historical and theoretical attention it deserves.

In retrospect, I can discern several dimensions of my earlier work that had to come together to make this book possible. From the start of my intellectual life as an academic immigrant to the United States, there was the challenge modern mass culture posed to high culture and avant-gardism, a topic that has occupied me since *After the Great Divide* (1986). Later came my immersion in urban studies, triggered by the post-1989 transformation of Berlin, which I wrote about in a number of essays in *Twilight Memories* (1995) and *Present Pasts* (2003). I then developed my interest in cities beyond the German case in the wake of a Sawyer Seminar I taught in cooperation with Columbia's program in the history and theory of architecture. This resulted in the edited volume *Other Cities, Other Worlds: Urban Imaginaries in a Globalizing World* (2008). The contemporary transformation of the modernist metropolis in an age of neoliberalism raised questions about the earlier development of the metropolis and its attendant modernisms across the world. Finally, the recent turn in literary criticism toward visual studies provided a framework that led me to ask new questions about the specificity of literature in relation to other media. A seminar on words and pictures I co-taught with Orhan Pamuk, whose literary imagination is intensely visual, increased my desire to get back from broader cultural history questions about the politics of memory in the post-1989 world to the trade I was originally trained in—close reading of literary texts, expanded of course to include historical and political context as immanent to the literary texts themselves. For me such an expanded technique of close reading remains a *sine qua non* of literary criticism and cultural history and their transmission to our students. All of this work over the decades owes a great deal to constant discussions and exchanges, academic and non-academic, with David Bathrick, Anson Rabinbach, and the late Miriam Hansen, my fellow editors at *New German Critique*.

For practical pedagogic reasons, teaching German and Austrian modernist prose to nonnative speakers always involved teaching shorter texts alongside the long novel. Fortunately there were a lot of well-known short prose texts by modernists to choose from, texts written not just by novelists but also by poets. But it was the street texts by Kracauer and Benjamin read in light of the Frankfurt School's critical theory of modernity that made me ask whether there wasn't something like a common trace that ran through this whole trajectory of short prose from Baudelaire to Musil and Benjamin. The answers this book suggests owe a lot to several cohorts of graduate students who took my seminars on the modernist novel and on the metropolitan miniature over these past ten to twelve years and whose readings, conversations, and papers have influenced the outcome in more than one way. To them I dedicate this book.

Sustained writing did not begin until a sabbatical year in 2010–11 in Paris, where four chapters, including the ones dealing with Baudelaire and Aragon were written while I was a fellow at Columbia's Reid Hall. With its inner courtyards, hedges, and sunlit rose garden, Reid Hall was an oasis of peace and quiet in the midst of bustling Montparnasse. I am grateful for the welcoming ambiance and practical help Reid Hall's staff, especially Brune Biebuyck and Nebahat (Naby)

Avcioglu, provided for me to do my work, split between Reid Hall and the new Bibliothèque Nationale. Over lunches at a nearby bistro on boulevard Raspail, I cherished the companionship and conversations about modernism with Michael Gorra, who was then writing *Portrait of a Novel*, his celebrated book on Henry James's *Portrait of a Lady*. A visit with Jay Winter to the battlefields of the Somme and the Historial de la Grande Guerre in Péronne resonated strongly with me while I was writing about Gottfried Benn in occupied Brussels. It was during that intense and rewarding year in Paris that the conceptual frame of the project solidified around the issue of literature's relationship to media and the modern metropolis.

Major thanks are due to friends and colleagues who have given me their reactions to and suggestions about earlier chapter drafts. Many conversations in Broadway bistros and cafés have gone into the mix as well. Here I thank Leslie Adelson, Mark Anderson, Stefan Andriopoulos, David Bathrick, Eric Bulson, Noam Elcott, Devin Fore, Isabel Gil, Axel Honneth, Helmut Lethen, Reinhold Martin, Johannes von Moltke, Harro Müller, Dorothea von Mücke, Anson Rabinbach, Klaus Scherpe, and Abigail Susik. I need to single out Tony Vidler and Tony Kaes, who read the whole manuscript and gave invaluable advice for major and minor revisions. Mark Anderson translated the strangely hermetic passages from Gottfried Benn's *Rönne Novellas*. My assistant Nick Fitch organized image permissions in an efficient and timely fashion. Diana Reese created the index. Bill Dellinger and Peggy Quisenberry in my department provided all kinds of help over the long haul with tasks both small and large. Special thanks also go to Matteo Galli, who invited me to the Università di Ferrara as Copernicus Visiting Scientist to teach a compact seminar in the fall of 2013. It was there under Italian skies, in that very first European city to feature a completely geometrical urban plan centuries before Kracauer's uncanny natural geometry, that I began to revise the book manuscript. Finally I must acknowledge Rosalind Krauss, who came up with the title *Miniature Metropolis*. I feel deep gratitude to all for their hidden hands in the emergence of this book.

Versions of some of the chapters were given as invited lectures at the University of Aarhus, the University at Buffalo, Cooper Union, the University of Copenhagen, Cornell University, Dartmouth College, Emory University, the Getty Research Institute, the Hammer Museum in Los Angeles, the Institute for Cultural Inquiry in Berlin, the Institute for Fine Arts in New York, the Institut für Kulturwissenschaften in Vienna, Johns Hopkins University, the University of Illinois in Urbana-Champaign's School of Architecture, the Universitá Católica in Lisbon, the Museu de Arte do Río in Río de Janeiro, the New School University, Northwestern University, Oxford University, Princeton University, the Reina Sofia in Madrid, Stanford University, Trinity College in Connecticut, Washington University, Universität Wien, and the University of Wisconsin–Madison. My gratitude goes to all of my hosts and interlocutors at these venues, friends, colleagues, and students from whose engaging comments and queries I have benefited more than I can possibly acknowledge here.

I must acknowledge an earlier essay that took a first exploratory stab at the topic of the urban miniature and was published in the *PMLA* 122:1 (January 2007): 27–42 in a special issue dedicated to cities. A much shorter version of the chapter on Benjamin and Kracauer appeared in two somewhat different versions as "Urban Miniatures and the Feuilleton in Siegfried Kracauer and Walter Benjamin," *Culture in the Anteroom: The Legacies of Siegfried Kracauer*, ed. Johannes von Moltke and Gerd Gmünden (Ann Arbor: Michigan University Press, 2012) 213–225 and as "The Urban Miniature and the Feuilleton in Kracauer and Benjamin," in *Literatur inter- und transmedial*, ed. David Bathrick and Heinz-Peter Preusser (Amsterdam, New York: Rodopi: 2012), 173–188. I am grateful for the permission to reprint parts of those last two publications, which have been incorporated in chapter 4.

Lindsay Waters at Harvard University Press, a friend of many decades going back to the early days of *New German Critique* and his editorship of the Theory and History of Literature series at the University of Minnesota Press, was the perfect editor to shepherd this project to completion. I also thank Shan Wang, Jennifer Bossert, and Kate Babbitt for their organizational help and line-editing savvy.

My deepest thanks and love remain reserved, as always, for my wife, Nina Bernstein, who was there when I first started writing in English and has never stopped editing me since then in any number of ways. To her, our sons, Daniel and David, their partners, Tara and Mary, and to our grandchildren, Benjamin and June, I owe that most special debt of gratitude that comes from lifelong love, intimacy, and commitment.

Miniature Metropolis

Introduction

The splinter in your eye is the best magnifying glass.
—Theodor W. Adorno, *Minima Moralia*

*E*VER SINCE THE publication of Carl Schorske's seminal book *Fin de siècle Vienna: Politics and Culture* (1980) or T. J. Clark's *The Painting of Modern Life: Paris in the Art of Manet and His Followers* (1984), the culture of metropolitan modernity has challenged the imagination of humanists and social scientists: the Paris of Baudelaire and Manet; the Vienna of Klimt and the Secession; the London of the Bloomsbury group; the Berlin of Taut and Höch, Brecht and Döblin; the Prague of Kafka and Brod; the Moscow of Eisenstein and Tretyakov; the New York of Zora Neale Hurston and the Harlem Renaissance. The spectrum of cities and themes has grown considerably since those earlier seminal publications to include modernist and avant-gardist circles in Oslo, Milan, St. Petersburg, Barcelona, Munich, and other cities. Questions of new media; theories of perception, visuality, and aurality in urban life; commerce and fashion; typologies of gender and sexuality; and the impact of technology and science have displaced literature, painting, architecture and even politics from the center of modernism studies to the margins. There is no question that our understanding of metropolitan cultures has greatly benefited from such an expanded vision. But so far

1

the triangular constellation of new media, the modern metropolis, and modernist literature has not been adequately explored. By focusing on what I call the metropolitan miniature as a neglected literary form hidden in plain view, this book undertakes the project of reading a selected body of texts written by major authors as a significant innovation within the trajectory of literary modernism. This book is the first analytical study that differentiates among the various uses of the miniature form by canonical writers and theorists from Baudelaire via Rilke and Kafka to Kracauer and Benjamin, Musil and Adorno. In fine-grained readings combined with broad panoramic and comparative vistas, the metropolitan miniature emerges as one of the few genuinely innovative modes of spatialized writing created by modernism. In its focus on visual perception, the rise of new media, and urban time and space, the miniature as a form also reveals the constitutive relationship between modernist literature and German critical theory, whose major figures contributed compellingly to this literary project.

Just as our own time is characterized by the conflation of lived urban space with digital interconnectedness, new media, and changing patterns of social interaction, the modernist city of the late nineteenth and early twentieth centuries is unthinkable without the rise of mass publications, new forms of print and image making, illustrated papers, photography, film, and radio. All of it contributed to a sense of an accelerating speedup of life, crystallized in the compression of time and space, as David Harvey has described it.[1] The new media of that earlier metropolitan modernity and all their related social and economic practices first challenged the status of high literature and art as it had solidified in the bourgeois age since the eighteenth century. Photography, as has often been said, replaced portraiture and certain forms of painting, with time of exposure shrinking from several minutes to the click of the camera. Film took over drama from the theater and narrative from the novel at the speed of twenty-four frames per second. The vinyl record and the radio remediated the live concert. Photography, film, and the recording of sound together challenged and even threatened the dominant culture of the book and live performance. Reciprocal porousness between media accelerated in the age of mechanical reproducibility, leaving none of the traditional arts untouched. Hybrid forms became commonplace in conjunction with cultural and social massification in the new metropolis. For many critics at the time, this was not cultural progress but undesirable contamination, if not plain decline.[2] Literary and artistic high culture kept claiming superiority and tried hard to delegitimize the new forms of mass entertainment that increasingly invaded and shaped traditional modes of high culture itself. From the mid-nineteenth century on, high culture and mass culture, united in increasingly industrialized modes of production and distribution, performed an obsessive *pas de deux*. At first the dancers still had their separate bodies. But not for long, as remediation between media and an ever-increasing interchange between high and low came to be the norm.

This is the cultural context that generated the metropolitan miniature as a paradigmatic modernist form that sought to capture the fleeting and fragmentary experiences of metropolitan life, emphasizing both their transitory variety and their simultaneous ossification. As the early work of Kafka shows, motion and its sudden arrest, standstill and its transformation into renewed motion were central aspects of the urban experience. Akin to the snapshot, the *faits divers*, and the news flash, the miniature took its cue from the new media. As a deliberately short form, it found its privileged venue in the feuilletons of large urban newspapers and magazines serving a rushed and distracted readership. Only later were such texts reassembled, reorganized, and often rewritten for book publication as we now know them. It is telling that critical theorists such as Kracauer, Benjamin, and Adorno, who in different ways wrote compellingly about photography and film, are among the major practitioners of the miniature form. Indeed, this book argues that the literary miniature, in its emphasis on visual perception and urban life, always implied a critical theory of bourgeois society. This is true not only of the interwar Marxist theorists but also of Baudelaire, Rilke, Kafka, Benn, Aragon, Jünger, Keun, and Musil, the other major figures treated in these pages. The critique manifested itself in a wide variety of textual practices and in very different politics that this book analyzes in an alternation of large panorama shots and close-up textual analysis.

Rather than resorting to traditional genre definitions such as fragment, *poème en prose*, *Denkbild*, *récit poétique*, or even short prose (*Kurzprosa*), I interrogate each of my authors in terms of their respective
contexts, influences, and intentions. I illuminate the respective narrative arc of their assemblages to throw light on the trajectory of the
metropolitan miniature as a whole, from Baudelaire in Paris to Adorno
in Los Angeles. The metropolitan miniature permits primary access
to the ways the notion of the literary was transformed from within
the literary project itself rather than from without. Novels had been
published in the newspapers in installments since the early nineteenth
century, and various new forms of feuilleton writing emerged, of
which the miniature is but one example among others such as celebrity gossip, commentary on culture and fashion, and glosses of all
kinds. It is worth noting that all feuilleton texts, rather than being
relegated to a separate cultural segment of the newspaper as they are
today, appeared on the bottom third of the newspaper's pages, separated by a printed line from the main body of reporting.

Much has been written about the late nineteenth century's pref-
erence for the small form, which seemed to be favored by urban
readers and spectators who looked for stimulation and quick consumption in line with the accelerated speed of modern life. Caba-
rets, variety shows, vaudeville, panoramas, dioramas, nickelodeons,
and revues flourished. Early silent film, the cinema of attractions with
its slapstick, melodrama, and urban scenes, satisfied the need for entertainment while at the same time training human perception in new
forms of urban life. Cinematic modes of writing using the quick cut,
the close-up, and montage editing invaded literary production. New
narrative, dramaturgical, and poetic techniques were developed that
guaranteed the legitimacy of avant-garde literature as it showed itself to be porous to the new technologies and transformations in perception that came in their wake. This was a kind of high cultural adaptation to the new, sometimes facile mimicry or fashionable
grandstanding and at other times creative and critical transformation. What I call the metropolitan miniature is central to understanding this constellation. The disorienting and exhilarating novelty of the metropolis at the end of the nineteenth century and the
immediately following decades must be recaptured and historicized

if we want to understand how that crisis of perception and experience generated the modernist miniature as part of a much broader process of what one could call the urbanization of modern literature and the creation of a modernist urban imaginary as an embodied material fact, a cognitive and somatic image of city life rather than a figment of the imagination.[3]

The term "miniature" to designate this mode of writing is not original with this book. I chose it for several reasons. More important than simply scale is the fact that "miniature" relates intensely to the visual in the history of art and that it conjures up objecthood: text as material object in the feuilleton. A main inspiration is owed to Walter Benjamin who once described the 19th-century arcade or passage as a city, "a world in miniature."[4] The literary miniature in turn opens up passages to the metropolitan world of that earlier time. It makes the metropolis both legible and visible.

The place of the restructuring of temporal and spatial perception, for which the modernist miniature, like photography and film, was an important field of experimentation, was the metropolis at a time when it was still an island of accelerating modernization in a society in which the slow pace of country and small-town life was still dominant but losing ground—the period of high modernism and the historical avant-garde. Metropolitan cities such as Vienna, Berlin, or Paris became laboratories of perception. New urban imaginaries and a whole new scientific discourse about perception itself emerged in the wake of fast changing cityscapes and scientific experiments with vision, hearing, and other sensual experiences. There was the emergence of automobile traffic, the electrification of public space, the creation of the first subways, new forms of mass housing, and the rise of modernist architecture and urban planning, all of which contributed to the creation of new visual imaginaries of urban dwelling and to the accelerated speed of urban experience.[5] The constitutive link between technological media such as cinema and radio on the one hand and automobile speed, its promises and its dangers, on the other is nowhere captured better than in the laconic introductory chapter of Ilya Ehrenburg's 1929 montage novel *10 PS*, one of the most scintillating reportage novels of European modernism.[6] Predictably, in that first chapter, the seduction of ever-accelerating speed combined with media hype in film and on radio ends in a deadly car crash.

All of this is well known. But it doesn't quite answer the question: What specifically was it that made these metropolitan feuilleton texts modernist beyond the standard tropes of fragmentation, condensation, acceleration, disjunction, estrangement, and montage? Various answers will emerge in the course of my readings, but certain features are shared by all of these texts. They all understand the urban condition as the sine qua non of modern life and experience. But they avoid realistic description, keeping their distance both from the nineteenth-century urban novel and from the urban sketch in the tradition of Louis Sébastien Mercier's 1781 *Tableau de Paris*, a mode of journalistic writing found around 1900 and after in the work of Peter Altenberg, Robert Walser, and Joseph Roth. They avoid plot, psychological development, and storytelling through fleshed-out characters, offering instead, as Musil had it, "unstorylike stories" (the subtitle of a section in his *Posthumous Papers of a Living Author*). On the positive side, they offer protocols of dreams rather than descriptions of urban sites, hallucinations rather than ekphrasis, oneiric effects linked to a cinematic imaginary, inner visions triggered by threatening urban perceptions, elusive memories rather than evidential accounts, metamorphoses of spaces in the mind. Psychic experiences are more than simply internal as they are always embodied and related to the urban environment. There is interpenetration and reciprocity between the external and the internal. The visible world is always accompanied, if not haunted by the shadow of what remains invisible. The compression of space and time that David Harvey has analyzed so compellingly is always accompanied by a simultaneous expansion of space and time in the urban imaginary. The miniature is thick with urban realities that become visible only in their poetic and narrative metamorphoses—that is, in language.

All of these writers share the obsession with sensual experience, including sound and tactility besides vision;[7] the feeling of terror and/ or exhilaration emanating from space; the loss of boundaries between private and public space, interior living space, and street space; the ever-recurring motif of *Leere* and *Hohlraum*, void and hollow space; the *Schrift-Bilder* (scriptural images or hieroglyphs) of urban advertising and their excess of legibility; the pervasive presence of dream images pointing to an urban unconscious that is fed by photography and film's impact on perceptions of urban space. I will give not one but multiple frames to my discussion, as called for by the respective texts in question. The frames will be taken as needed from photography and film, from the tradition of the emblem, from psychophysiology, from discourses about architecture and urban space, and from the post–World War I critique of anthropocentrism and its questioning of the relationship of humans to animals and things.

Literary *Eigensinn* and Remediation in Reverse

The metropolitan miniature was a mode of writing that did not simply adapt itself to the new technologies and emerging mass cultural forms. It rather insisted on the *Eigensinn* (translated as obstinacy, Negt and Kluge) of literature as medium in its "differential specificity" (Sam Weber, Rosalind Krauss) in relation to photography and film.[8] Its practitioners did not opt for hybridity, a merging of the visual and the verbal, pictures and words. Instead they recognized the constitutive thresholds between literature and the visual media. At the same time, its preferred initial place of publication was the transitory feuilleton of metropolitan papers and magazines rather than the finite form of the book. It is this fundamental contradiction of an ambitiously new mode of urban writing first published in organs of mass circulation that makes the metropolitan miniature sit like a foreign body in the feuilleton. It is no surprise that its success with readers only came at a much later time when these texts were reassembled and revised for book publication, the form in which we read them today.[9] As a major experimental mode of urban writing, the miniature articulated the aesthetic specificity of literary language in its relationship to the new media of photography and film, both of which took the city and urban life as their major subject. The miniature did not imitate photography and film but worked through both their deficiencies and achievements in representing urban life. The goal was to make these new media productive for the literary enterprise without resorting to imitation, and it is significant that none of these miniatures were ever published with photographs or other visual illustrations. The miniature never indulged in the crisis of language, which was such a pervasive theme in modernism around 1900.[10] It rather attempted to show what language could do differently and sometimes perhaps even better than photography or film. Rather than falling silent or simply trying to imitate structures and techniques of photography and film in language, the metropolitan miniature thus insisted on a notion of the literary that would absorb critically and imaginatively new ways of seeing and experiencing the city that had been generated by the new image media. This is what I call the miniature's *Eigensinn*, or its differential specificity.

This differential specificity is fundamentally linked to remediation, a phenomenon much discussed in media studies today. The term "remediation" goes back to McLuhan's *Understanding Media*.[11] McLuhan argued correctly that every medium was bound to become the content of the next and newer media technology: manuscript into print; portraiture into photography; photography and the novel into film; film into television; television, by extension beyond McLuhan, into the Internet, which increasingly threatens any differential specificity of mediums. This is what he called remediation. But it worked in one direction only, on a linear trajectory. Remediation today is seen in a more complex multidirectional sense, but the older privileging of the new has been a hard habit to kick.[12] Today it is commonly acknowledged that older media will often adapt to the newer ones. Thus the modernist novel adopted cinematic techniques of narration (Döblin); drama adopted montage (Brecht); film now uses computer graphics; contemporary prose experiments celebrate hypertext. But it is telling that Jay David Bolter and Richard Grusin's book *Remediation: Understanding New Media* chooses to call the refashioning of an older medium a retrograde remediation.[13] While there surely are retrograde uses of new media superficially in the service of marketing and updating an older medium, there will always be moments when an older medium reasserts itself by critically working through what the new medium does and does not do. This is what I will call remediation in reverse. In the metropolitan miniature, literature remediates photography and film, thus reasserting its differential specificity rather than simply clamoring for a facelift. I would further suggest that it was the prevalence of a multidirectional remediation around 1900 brought about by the increasing porousness among media that in reaction called forth the intense desire at that time for the purity and transcendence of language in literature or of vision in the painting of an emerging high modernism. But even film, in the 1920s, aspired to an absolute cinema, *un cinéma pur*, and photography too was very much concerned with its differential specificity, its *Eigensinn*. The line between the insistence on a medium's differential specificity and the delusion that purity was attainable, however, is sometimes difficult to draw.

At stake with the metropolitan miniature, then, was not a claim for the purity of language and literature as in late-nineteenth-century symbolism but instead the profound transformation of the literary project itself that challenged the disciplining borderline between language and the visual, between narrative and spatial representation, as it had been codified in the eighteenth century in Lessing's *Laokoon*.[14] The texts discussed in this book provide a wealth of examples for this largely undertheorized phenomenon within modernism, the other side of what Franco Moretti has called the modern epic as distinct from the novel.[15] Similar to the scholarly neglect or domestication of the modern epic, the miniature has been seen as a minor genre at best by comparison with the heroic efforts of the modern novel or the seminal cycle of poems. And even where it has been recognized as an important part of a given writer's oeuvre (Kafka, Jünger, and Benjamin come to mind), it is more often described summarily rather than actually read. Despite the fact that "the minor" has become such a major concern in poststructuralist theory (*petits récits* in Lyotard, *littérature mineure* in Deleuze and Guattari), the miniature has not yet found the treatment it deserves as a significant rather than a secondary or supplemental mode of modernist writing. If it is supplemental at all, then it is so only in a post-Derridean sense: the major wouldn't be the major without the minor. To put it differently: the modernist city novel looks different if seen in light of the metropolitan miniature. It is enough to compare the great city novels of the nineteenth century, including Fontane's Berlin novels, written as late as the 1880s and 1890s, with Rilke's *Notebooks of Malte Laurids Brigge* or the somewhat later modernist city novels by Joyce, Dos Passos, and Döblin to realize that something fundamental had changed in the literary representation of social space and regimes of perception in the city. A new urban imaginary took shape characterized by unstable subject positions, the breakup of plot, discontinuous narrative, hallucinatory imaginaries, and fragmented spaces of perception. Indeed, one claim of this book is that the trajectory initiated by the Baudelairean prose poem and culminating with the modernist miniature of the interwar years is one of the few genuinely novel modes of writing created by modernism in its complex and often tortured love affair with the feuilleton of European papers such as *La Presse* or *Le Figaro* in Paris, the *Neue Presse* in Vienna, the *Neue Rundschau*, the *Frankfurter Zeitung,* the *Vossische Zeitung,* and other dailies, weeklies, or monthlies in Germany, Austria, and France. Eventually, the fragmentation of experience combined with a disorientation of perception and their rendering in non- or anti-narrative form was to become part of the modernist novel itself. It was the urban miniature in which new forms of spatialized writing were first experimentally tested before they found their place in the city novels of Döblin or Keun, Joyce or Dos Passos. As a form, the miniature is firmly grounded in the micrological experience of metropolitan space, time, and life at that earlier stage of modernization when new shapes and scales of urban modernity emerged at accelerated speed but did not yet penetrate the totality of national social and political space. If the modern epic in Moretti represents something like national encyclopedias in the form of macroscopic fictional maps, then the modernist miniature in all its incredible variety represents the microscopic condensation of a metropolitan imaginary that never gels into or even aims at some encyclopedic totality.

The New Form That Could Not Be Named

The metropolitan miniature as a specific historical form tied to a stage of metropolitan developments in Europe emerges only in retrospect. Testimony about its novelty and elusiveness at the time comes from the authors themselves who engaged in the writing of miniatures. They simply did not know how to name this new mode of writing. Thus, Ernst Bloch, another contributor to the miniature with his *Spuren (Traces)* and sections of *Heritage of Our Times,* lamented in a letter to Kracauer of June 6, 1926: "If only we had a name for the new form, which is no longer a form."[16] In his diaries, Kafka spoke of his "little pieces" ("*Stückchen*") and "things" ("*Sachen*"), and in a letter to Felice Bauer he added a self-deprecating dimension and spoke of "my little prevarications" ("*meine kleinen Winkelzüge*").[17] Benjamin used a variety of terms such as "aphorisms, witticisms, dreams" ("*Aphorismen, Scherze, Träume*"); only later did he introduce the term 'thought images" ("*Denkbilder*").[18] Robert Musil in turn, in a review of Kafka's first book publication, *Betrachtung*, singled out Kafka's short prose and Robert Walser's feuilleton pieces as the prototype of a new mode of writing that was "not suitable to preside over a literary genre."[19] The new form emerged as anti-form, then, resistant to the laws of genre as much as to systemic philosophy or urban sociology, crossing the boundaries between poetry, fiction, and philosophy, between commentary and interpretation, and, centrally, between the verbal and the visual. This instability of genre, I would suggest, is owed primarily to what I call remediation in reverse.

Despite the chronological arrangement of the chapters, the point of this book is not to construct a continuous or even teleological tradition of the metropolitan miniature from Baudelaire to the interwar period in twentieth-century Europe. There never was a blueprint for a new genre, nor should it be constructed retrospectively. What interests me is the contingent constellation of new and powerful urban experiences from the mid-nineteenth century on, new modes of mass publication, and an emerging competition between print literature and visual media that created the metropolitan miniature as a major form of literary modernism. As always in such matters, there were discrete cases of influence (Baudelaire on Rilke and Benjamin, Kafka on Kracauer, the closeness between Benjamin and Kracauer), but overall there is just a felicitous juxtaposition of analogous writing projects that all preserve their differential specificity vis-à-vis each other. At the same time, the experience of the modern metropolis and the perceptual changes wrought by the new visual media appear consistently as a common denominator of these texts. So if in the end there should appear some arc spanning those decades, all the better.

One difficult question is why this new form, which as form seems less bound than the novel or the modern epic to a national culture, flourished so emphatically in German and Austrian writing after its emergence in mid-nineteenth-century Paris in the unique work of Baudelaire.[20] It may have been an effect of the exceptionally fast-paced late-nineteenth-century processes of urban growth in cities such as Vienna and Berlin compared with such older European cities as London and Paris, which, by the end of the nineteenth century, had slower growth rates than either Vienna or Berlin.[21] But it also reflected the impact of an ever more aphoristic and anti-systemic mode of writing philosophy that had emerged with Kierkegaard and Nietzsche and influenced many of the miniaturists. When it comes to the miniature in the interwar period, it surely can be related to the collapse of the German and Austrian Empires in 1918. In Germany and Austria, the losers of the Great War, urban transformations were exacerbated in the 1920s and 1930s by extreme economic instability and political volatility. After World War I, it was not uncommon to see the city described as a battlefield, a metaphor that came to be reality in the civil war–like armed conflicts in the early and late Weimar Republic. Benjamin's theory of urban shock as an aesthetic phenomenon is hardly thinkable without reference to the phenomenon of shell shock in the war which itself gave rise to the Freudian theory of trauma and accounts for the privileging of a shock aesthetic in the historical avant-garde. Specifically urban shock appears frequently in the description of car accidents, as in texts by Kafka, Brecht, and Musil. But these texts are not part of miniature collections, and the theme of shock has perhaps been overemphasized in the wake of Benjamin's writing. Benjamin's own literary miniatures after all are rather devoid of urban shock experiences.

Today the specific crisis of perception that initiated a new relationship to space and time as it is articulated in the modernist miniature has become history, if not nostalgia and cliché. All too often today the texts resulting from this crisis are simply read as anticipating postmodernism. Witness the scholarly focus on Weimar surfaces (as opposed to modernist depth), the cult of the flaneur (as opposed to bourgeois inwardness), rhizomic culture (as opposed to the teleology of modernity), minor literature (as opposed to canonical high modernism), and the culture of the spectacle (as opposed to real art). Whatever Weimar was, it was not postmodern. To read it that way is the kind of presentist appropriation and backshadowing we must resist if we are interested in the specificity and non-identity of cultural phenomena over time. It is precisely because there is some truth to the argument that something fundamental has changed in post–World War II urban modernity that we should guard against such elisions of historical difference. For since World War II, in contrast to the decades preceding it, metropolitan urbanity in the West has invaded and saturated all social space via consumerism, the automobile, extended freeway systems, air travel, and mass communications. It was a development Adorno could already observe in the larger Los Angeles area in the 1940s when he was writing his *Minima Moralia*. While short prose is still being written in various forms, we'd have to look to other media and their effects on our lives if we wanted to find out whether or not the perceptual regime of modernism has itself been altered or transformed into something new in our own time.[22] One author who still works with the legacies of the modernist miniature today is filmmaker and storyteller Alexander Kluge, but he is an exception and fast becoming historical himself in a media world in which his main media, film and story, are themselves becoming obsolete or at least appear dated. When Kluge described the storyteller as the guardian of time, he had Benjamin in mind, and his own stories from *Lebensläufe* to *Chronik der Gefühle* and beyond can be read as yet another transformation of the miniature. They differ significantly, however, from the earlier tradition in that they no longer focus as centrally on urban life as the laboratory of the new.[23] They also no longer shun the inclusion of photographs and other visual materials. By the post–World War II period, the urban condition had become all encompassing. The world now was interconnected and planetary issues were pushed ever more to the foreground in Kluge's writings. That is why with Kluge as guidepost I let the metropolitan miniature end in a coda with Adorno's *Minima Moralia*. In the second half of the twentieth century, the metropolitan city in the West becomes either invisible, as in Italo Calvino's marvelous book *Invisible Cities*, with its strong dose of nostalgia, or it assumes another kind of (in-)visibility requiring different forms of aesthetic mediation. The question of how to represent the urban in an age of digital interconnectedness, global megacities, and ever-expanding urban conglomerations clearly has entered another stage.[24]

Bilder

As remediation in reverse emerges as a major characteristic of the metropolitan miniature, we need to determine how precisely these writers approached photography and film, thus generating affinities in difference. It was the shortness of their texts, their frequent focus on a single phenomenon of metropolitan life, their shunning of extended narrative structures, and their investment of observation with philosophical and conceptual penetration that marked both affinity and difference. The careful use of metaphor as imagery in language itself guarded them from falsely opposing picture and word, image and language. Obsessed as they all were by the power of the image in its relationship to language, they considered *Bilder* as central to their writing (*"Bild"* in German means picture as well as image). This obsession was a key factor within modernism, the art and culture of a time in which new image media and new means of reproduction threatened the primacy of the original poetic word, that key pillar of bourgeois understanding of a national language-based culture. One might think mistakenly that these texts were generated as a mise-en-scène of a kind of fear of images common to book-oriented civilizations, but rather than ushering in iconoclasm, they critically articulated the constitutive dialectic between image and language.[25] Of course this dialectic has a long history through the centuries, but it entered into a new constellation with the rise of photography and film in the modern metropolis. Here radical critiques of photography and film stood side by side with utopian hopes that the new image media would be the harbingers of a new age and of social transformation. All of the writers, critics, and artists discussed in this book were keen observers and radical critics of the urban modernity that was emerging around them, but they also saw the social and political potential of the new media. Rather than embracing the rejectionist version of bourgeois *Kulturkritik*, which saw film and photography endangering high culture, their approach was dialectical to the core.

If the spread of photography and film was one of the factors that created the ground for the metropolitan miniature to emerge, developments internal to philosophy provided another important impetus. With philosophy becoming ever more literary in the aphoristic writings of such anti-systemic philosophers as Kierkegaard and Nietzsche, the Baudelairean prose poem underwent a significant shift: it became that specific kind of highly condensed short prose that self-consciously merged conceptual and metaphoric language, following Nietzsche's insight that the concept is always contaminated by metaphor. This new kind of writing has come to be known as *Denkbild* (Benjamin), *Raumbild* (Kracauer), *Wortbild* (Hofmannsthal), *Körperbild* (Jünger), or *Bewusstseinsbild* (Benn). Musil, in turn, in his *Posthumous Papers of a Living Author*, subtitled the first three sections "Pictures"; "Tempered Observations"; and "Unstorylike Stories." The writing of such *Bilder* was now a separate enterprise from the writing of the novel or, as in Rilke's case, the fictional diary of a protagonist who was learning how to see. The recourse to the visual in naming this literary form is striking, but it also poses certain problems. All these *Bilder* come in the medium of written language, never accompanied by pictures, and thus they have to be read as scripts (*Schriften*). They play off the fundamental difference between *Schrift* and *Bild*, attempting to strike sparks from their confrontation in the miniature. As *Schrift-Bilder* they draw on the tradition of the hieroglyph, as Miriam Hansen has shown in her brilliant work on hieroglyphic writing and mass cultural images in Kracauer and Adorno.[26] As such they are not easily legible. The visual dimension disturbs legibility, and the promise of linguistic transparency is denied in the complex texture of ekphrasis, metaphor, and abstraction. "*Bild*" is never meant here simply as a stand-in for *Gemälde*, or painting, another one of its German meanings, and its post-Renaissance regime of perspectival visuality. Even less is it identical to photography, often understood at the time as unmediated realism offering transparent evidence. We may want to remember here the Benjaminian distinction between "*Bild*" and "*Abbild*," with only the latter referring to simple mimetic representation as photography offers it. After all, there was a widespread skepticism about the new image media in both Viennese and Weimar culture, but it was precisely this skepticism that led to the ambitious remediation experiments on the thresholds of language and image represented in the urban miniature.

In another pragmatic register, the recourse to textual images (*Schrift-Bilder*) could of course be easily explained. As early as the later nineteenth century, the streets of the metropolis were full of them: store signs, street signs, electric advertising, neon signs, the marquis of theaters and movie palaces, *Litfasssäulen* (advertising pillars), the sandwich-board man, shop window displays, ads on trams and busses, and so forth. And then there was the medium of publication itself. Before being gathered in book form under an overarching title, most of these miniatures were first published separately in the feuilleton, an urban literary medium, which, as part of a newspaper, itself often combined text and image, though never together with the metropolitan miniatures. The popularity and mass circulation of postcards featuring urban sites accompanied by captions is but another instance of the relationship between words and pictures in the everyday metropolitan world. Panoramas, dioramas, and eventually silent cinema increased the flood of images exponentially, thus challenging the literary imagination and putting pressure on the privileged position of the written word.

But such pragmatic observations fall short of addressing the deeper question. As photos or postcards, *Bilder* are typically two-dimensional and suggest perspectival organization. It was, however, precisely perspectival viewing that metropolitan experience threw into turmoil. Time and again, texts by Hofmannsthal and Schnitzler, Kafka, Kracauer, Benn, Jünger, and Musil articulate this crisis of perspectival vision, focusing at the same time on the cacophony of urban noise and the resulting disturbance of directed perception.[27] Photomontage, cinema, and offset printing in the illustrated papers of course introduced a multiperspectivalism that was already present in Baudelaire's Paris texts. So a central question emerges: What if all these modernist miniatures, described as *Bilder*, actually were to account for a different organization of sensual and embodied perception that the metropolis generated? It seems that the advantage the *Bild* offered to these writers lay in the fact that a *Bild* in this more-than-photographic sense compresses the extensions of time and space, condenses them into an overdetermined, seemingly synchronous image that is significantly different from the photograph, just as it differs from ambling description, sequential observation, or the merely empirical urban sketch. On the one hand the miniature reflected on the prevalence of the new visual media; but on the other it recognized the visual media's mimetic insufficiency and lack, which it tried to transcend literarily in images made up of words. After all, images emerging from the miniature are never only synchronous and their mimetic indexical dimension is more mediated than that of a photographic picture. Just as temporality still lingers in the apprehension, say, of a painting when the eye scans and wanders over the canvas, the miniature in its sequential verbal composition opens up a dimension of temporality in the movement of reading itself. Its own temporality can thus support and strengthen the residual temporality that exists in proper images; that is, pictures, themselves. What results is a compression of space and time in the literary image, image here, however, as script: concise, provocative, surprising, sudden.

Architecture and a New Spatial Experience

The remediation of film and photography into the metropolitan miniature accounts for its often-haunting, ghostly, hallucinatory, and delirious qualities. In architectural discourse, the notion of remediation finds a loose analogue in the concept of *Durchdringung* (interpenetration) as it was codified by Sigfried Giedion in his seminal 1928 book *Bauen in Frankreich, Eisen, Eisenbeton.*[28]

Just as the boundaries of literature were challenged by the metropolitan miniature, Giedion's spatial interpenetration, achieved by building in steel, glass, and ferroconcrete, abolished borders between inside and outside, above and below, public and private, street and interior, fixed and fluid space. As in Italian futurism, where the notion of *compenetrazione dei piani* (interpenetration of planes) had assumed expressive and often violently dynamic dimensions, Giedion's notion of spatial interpenetration pertained both to objective built space and to the internal space of perception. But in the late 1920s, he gave the term its "new-matter-of-fact" (*neusachlich*) coding, shorn of its vitalist futurist dimension.[29] Interpenetration and relationality came to be perceptual and social categories for modernist architecture, replacing the fixed and structured separation of spaces, volumes, and planes as they had characterized an earlier architecture in stone. In this programmatic statement about the promises of modern architecture, which was extensively excerpted in Benjamin's notes for his arcades project, Giedion described a new spatial experience that opened up new forms of seeing. His major examples were the iron constructions of the Eiffel Tower in Paris and the industrial Pont Transbordeur in the harbor of Marseille, and Walter Gropius's Bauhaus building in Dessau. According to the felicitous phrasing by architectural historian Hilde Heynen, *Durchdringung* "stands for a weakening of hierarchical models on all levels—social as well as architectural."[30] What often appears as terrorizing spatial experience in the modernist miniature appears here as the liberating dimension of interpenetration and a new understanding of architectural space expanded to include traffic, rail lines, trains, stations, and urban movement in general. It opened up the closed city to the circulation of air, movement, and dynamism. Read through the miniature and its focus on interpenetrations, the openness and interpenetration Giedion, modernist architecture's ghostwriter, sought in large-scale engineering and urban plans may correlate with the microscale and fleeting contingency of the miniature. On the other hand, Giedion, like Corbusier, aimed at converting these new spatial qualities into the basis for rather epic master plans, analogous perhaps to the way Döblin deployed the fragmenting techniques of photomontage and the small form to create a modernist epic in *Berlin Alexanderplatz*.[31] The miniature, on the other hand, never aimed at such a utopian scale.

There were indeed two kinds of *Durchdringung* in the urban imaginary of the 1920s. Whereas *Durchdringung* of inside and outside, subject and object, private and public space took on entirely positive, even utopian connotations in the architectural and urban planning discourse of the 1920s, it appears in the modernist miniature in all its ambiguity both as exhilarating novelty and as *Angst-Raum* (space of anxiety) or *Angst-Traum* (nightmare). This is where Giedion's challenge to Cartesian rational space differs from Kracauer's theoretical critique of the rational urban plan as laid out in the miniatures in the lead section of *The Mass Ornament*, ironically entitled "Natural Geometry."[32] Giedion's positive coding of a new spatiality also differs from Simmel's warning that the overwhelming intensity of stimuli in city life threatens subjective culture, generating a blasé attitude and indifference in the city dweller.[33] At any rate, space had become central to cultural production and political understanding, as can also be seen in Carl Schmitt's political ruminations about geopolitics or in Ernst Cassirer's suggestion "that the problem of space may become *point de départ* for a new self-reflection of aesthetics."[34] And as we think about the spatial experiments in the projects of the Bauhaus, especially during the directorship of Làszlò Moholy-Nagy, one can easily observe how a new understanding of urban space is very much linked to experiments with photography and film.

What Giedion has in common with the writers treated in this book is the insight that all urban space is permeated by social relations and that space leaves its marks on bodies and subjectivities. There is no longer a single firm and defined standpoint from which to observe and judge. Visual and bodily disorientation abound, and at the extreme there is Jünger's dreamlike fall through a series of tin sheets, none of which can stop the ever-accelerating downward plunge ("The Horror") or Kafka's miniature from his *Diaries* in which a body is being pulled up by rope through floors and ceilings and made to disappear on the roof.[35]

While *Durchdringung* in Giedion refers exclusively to architecture and urban space, as a conceptual metaphor it resonates with those other dimensions of reciprocal border crossings and remediations that are central to my argument in this book. Key for the argument is the *Durchdringung* in the miniature of the verbal and the visual, whereby the visual media are simultaneously recognized for their expansion of human knowledge and perception and criticized for their inherent limitations. What is being questioned or even undermined is not the visual itself but the triumphalism of the visual as organized and exploited by the capitalist media. All writers discussed in this book were deeply skeptical of the unlimited promise of the new media, even when they tried to turn this promise toward political transformation. Outright political critique of the capitalist cultural apparatus and its exploitation of the image found its appropriate aesthetic form in the miniature, where literature asserted its *Eigensinn* in relation to the visual media and mass circulation. It did so in a mass medium, the newspaper feuilleton, rather than in some hermetic high-cultural isolation. The metropolitan miniature foreshortened and compressed temporal and spatial coordinates of urban experience. Subjective and objective perceptions of the metropolitan life world were condensed in the structure of language, text, and medium itself in such a way that these feuilleton texts subverted the very claims of transparency, easy understanding, and entertainment the popular press laid claim to. From its very beginning in Baudelaire all the way to Musil and Benjamin, the miniature thus performed a kind of "affirmative sabotage" of the popular press and of the image-based media that dominated the metropolitan public sphere.[36] It critically articulated the changes in perception brought by urbanization and the new visual media; it registered the move from a post-romantic individual consciousness to the psychic constitution and iteration of identity in mass society as average and statistical. It thus traced historical changes in the understanding of subjectivity. It tried to draw the consequences from its insight into urban mass society by thinking intensely about alternative uses of modern mass media and yet insisting on the critical power of literature. This is the simultaneously aesthetic and political legacy of the modernist metropolitan miniature.

The Literary Miniature and Critical Theory

My attention was originally drawn to the miniature when I realized that not only canonical modernist writers, poets and novelists alike, wrote in this mode but major critical theorists practiced it as well: not only Baudelaire, Rilke, and Kafka but Kracauer, Benjamin, and Adorno. The connection was plain to see, but it had never been explored in depth. At that point, I began to read the miniature as a literary project that pushed against the boundaries of traditional narrative forms of fictional literature while opening up the dimension of conceptual, social, and philosophical thought to aesthetic perception and vice versa. At the same time, it articulated compelling insights into the social and political transformations of the metropolis in that key period of late-nineteenth and early twentieth-century modernity and when radical political change came to be on the agenda after World War I and the Russian Revolution.

The miniature allowed me to understand modernist literature as umbilically tied to critical theory rather than theory imposed from the outside on literary texts. Indeed, the critical theories of Kracauer, Benjamin, and Adorno are themselves modernist to their core. Since Kracauer and Benjamin wrote extensively about perception and media, social stratification and experience in the metropolitan city, both in their theoretical essays and in their literary texts, I had found my focus on the metropolis. Given the fact that both writers published their miniature texts first in the feuilletons and that as critical theorists they are identified with the history of media theory and history, I had found my second focus on the relation between writing and the visual media. Their micrological approach to urban phenomena all but required the small form offered by feuilleton. In Inka Mülder-Bach's felicitous formulation, the feuilleton became the "production site of a fragmentary theory of modernity" more than simply the site of reportage that Egon Erwin Kisch in his classical reportage book described as an "unretouched snapshot of the times."[37] The German word *Zeitaufnahme*, however, also means a photograph of time itself, and in that sense Kisch's definition is pertinent here. Indeed, Kracauer and Benjamin's *Zeitaufnahmen* can be seen as chronotopes, as they add temporality to the spatiality of the snapshot and the emblem. As all the miniatures treated in this book, they are heavily retouched, subtly worked through, and given a kind of depth that the traditional form of the journalistic urban sketch and reportage lacked as much as the photograph did.

If throughout I emphasize the notion of literary *Eigensinn*, I deploy it in a more than intertextual sense that makes Rilke's miniatures different from Baudelaire's, Kracauer's from Benjamin's, Musil's from Jünger's. It is the *Eigensinn* of literary texts in their relation to other media that concerns me primarily in this book. New historicism, discourse theory, and other forms of contextualized readings of literary texts have all too often abandoned the question of what literature can do that other discourses or media fail to do. To insist on the *Eigensinn* of literature, then, is not to return to an older notion of literary closure and "intrinsic criticism." Nor do I want to resurrect a notion of the absolute autonomy of literature in relation to mass culture and other media. I rather stay with Adorno's point about the double character of art as being "both autonomous and *fait social*."[38] The miniature's main characteristic is precisely that it undercuts any notion of medial autonomy or purity in its constitutive relation to the metropolis and visual technological media. But it is by articulating this social and technological relationship that it asserts its autonomy as *Eigensinn*. This is part of the fraying of the arts that Adorno analyzed in one of his late essays of the 1960s and that was always already part of modernism itself.[39] What this book shows is that the metropolitan miniature as a specific project within the literature of modernism and as dependent on the historical context of major urban transformations suggests *Eigensinn* as a relational rather than an ontological concept, since it is always determined by a variety of media practices at a given time. Rather than only occupying the margin left to literature by the new technological media, as Friedrich Kittler had it in his influential book *Discourse Networks*, the metropolitan miniature shows that literature can do more than simply occupy an ever-shrinking margin.[40]

The analogies to our own time are striking. The reordering of perception in the metropolis of 1900 parallels the reordering of time and space in our own time by a whole new set of digital media and related new social practices.[41] Again, compression and miniaturization are at stake in different forms, and their effects on the human perceptual apparatus are the fulcrum of a wide-ranging debate about the benefits and downsides of our contemporary media culture.[42] This is where the topic of this book may serve as a template for current debates about literature. Time and again these days, literature and the book are lamented as obsolete media, if they are not happily and condescendingly written off, just as reality itself was written off in the 1990s by the triumphalists of the virtual. *Miniature Metropolis* shows in paradigmatic ways how once before literature was under siege by mass media, photography, silent film, and, somewhat later, the radio.[43] In the decades around 1900, older literary and artistic forms underwent a process of metamorphosis that we now admire as the great surge of modernist innovation. It remains to be seen if the digital age will ever produce literary and artistic innovations on a comparable scale. At any rate, there always was as much *Eigensinn* in photography and the cinema as there was in literature. In the age of the digital, analog media such as photography and film may themselves be experimenting with a remediation in reverse, insisting on their differential specificity in relation to their transformation by the digital. It is always premature to declare the obsolescence of literature or any other medium. The "death of . . ." discourse has proven wrong several times before, and obsolescence does have its own powers of revival from a grave that is never deep enough.

1

—⟨∿⟩—

Urban Spleen and the Terror of Paris in Baudelaire and Rilke

ANY DISCUSSION OF THE metropolitan miniature in German and Austrian literature in the early decades of the last century has to take account of the seminal *point de départ* for this modernist mode of feuilleton writing in the work of Charles Baudelaire. Baudelaire had begun to experiment with this new form of urban literature by the mid-1850s, searching for a more liberated form of writing the city than the one of the *Tableaux parisiens* and other poems in *Les Fleurs du mal*, first published in 1857. The seminal impact *Le Spleen de Paris: Petits poèmes en prose* had on the rise of the metropolitan miniature results from the fact that Baudelaire radically transformed the older genre of the impressionistic and discursive urban sketch in the tradition of Mercier's *Tableau de Paris*. His new kind of prose writing was equally distinct from the main genre of the nineteenth-century urban narrative à la Balzac or Dickens, and it anticipated new modes of writing the city that emerged only later in the novels of Kafka, Joyce, Aragon, Dos Passos, and Döblin. Its main long-distance aftereffects, however, both direct and indirect, are to be found in the urban miniature written by some of the major German and Austrian modernists in the years leading up to World War I, the war years themselves, and the interwar period. Rilke's novel *The Notebooks of Malte Laurids Brigge* (1911), with its explicit citations and multiple resonances of Baudelaire, occupies a mediating position between Baudelaire's short prose texts and the interwar miniature written in the first Austrian Republic and the Weimar Republic. Poetically close to Baudelaire's imagination, it already highlights the uncanny and surreal dimensions that would become dominant in the later metropolitan miniature.

While Baudelaire and Rilke's prose works have been extensively discussed in scholarship, we lack any direct comparison. The reason for this lacuna may be simple. Even though Rilke himself used the term "poems in prose" in a comment to his translator, *The Notebooks of Malte Laurids Brigge* is a novel, a novel in fragments, to be sure, but not a collection of *poèmes en prose*.[1] And yet the roughly first two dozen prose fragments with which *The Notebooks* open are unmistakably in the tradition of the urban miniature. Similar to Baudelaire's *Spleen*, with its multiple, even serial narrator positions, they feature a narrator whose intense perceptions of Paris ultimately shape his innermost metropolitan consciousness. Despite other significant differences, both texts articulate a sensual and bodily experience of the city without ever drawing on realistic description of concrete urban spaces, as the traditional urban sketch or the nineteenth-century urban novel would do. Both authors shared a visceral dislike of photography, a medium they believed threatened the integrity of the imagination and disabled poetic creativity itself. Of course, they experienced photography at a technically less developed stage than the later miniaturists, but despite their rejection of the new medium, traces of its presence abound in their work.

A selection of twenty Baudelairean miniatures was first published by Arsène Houssaye in 1862 in the feuilleton of the Parisian paper *La Presse*. They condense, displace, and juxtapose, to use the formulation from the dedication to his publisher, "the soul's lyrical movements, the undulations of reverie, the jolts of consciousness."[2] While these characterizations by no means exhaust the anonymous narrators' moods, attitudes, and strategies, the format of the miniature, with its experimental mix of genres, intense subjectivities, and roaming reflections, was picked up, appropriated, and transformed by Rilke, Benjamin, Kafka, Kracauer, Benn, Jünger, and Musil. As in Baudelaire himself, the soul's lyrical movements are juxtaposed to outright cynicism, if not male hysteria (Benn); the undulations of reverie turn into nightmare or the emptiness of ennui (Rilke, Kracauer); the jolts of consciousness escalate into terror (Rilke, Kafka, Jünger). New imaginaries of time and space are created by the short prose texts themselves, just as they provide new transitory reading experiences for the overstimulated and distracted urban reader of the feuilleton.

However, Baudelaire's miniatures did not meet with much success among the reading public. The first publication in *La Presse* was cut short after three installments, and another publication in *Le Figaro* two years later was also not completed, since, as the editor let Baudelaire know, they bored readers. While in length and reflective mode they attempted to satisfy the needs of their medium, they also remained something like a foreign body in the feuilleton, which at that time tended more toward entertainment, celebrity anecdotes, and society gossip. And yet it was in Baudelaire's feuilleton texts that Paris first became legible as a modern metropolis.[3] They responded in novel ways to the disorienting urban condition as analyzed by Georg Simmel four decades later in his seminal Berlin essay "The Metropolis and Mental Life."[4] But whereas Simmel analyzed only one typical reaction to the proliferation of stimuli in metropolitan life, the self-protective blasé attitude, Baudelaire displayed a whole gamut of reactions among which the blasé self-protection from urban stimuli would be only one, and not even the dominant one.

Baudelaire recognized that a new kind of writing the city was called forth by the city itself. Thus, in the dedication of 1862, published in an Appendix and entitled Preface in the recent English translation, he stated:

This obsessive ideal [of writing a poetic prose that was musical, subtle, and choppy, as he put it] came to life above all by frequenting enormous cities, in the intersection of their countless relationships. (129)

The choppiness of his little work is exacerbated by the fact that it has "neither head nor tail." Addressing his editor, he continued with cutting irony:

Consider, I beg you, what admirable convenience that combination offers us all, you, me, and the reader. We can cut wherever we want, I my reverie, you the manuscript, the reader his reading. (129)

As he offered the "entire serpent" (129) to his editor and the public, his hope must have been that the act of seduction would be successful. Despite the sarcastic authorial irony in this metaphoric description, it also holds a Baudelairean belief. It matches Baudelaire's concept of aesthetic creation as inevitably transitory and ephemeral, as he laid it out in his seminal essay "Le peintre de la vie moderne," which focused on the transitoriness of life, art, and fashion in the modern metropolis, from which a new kind of eternal beauty was to spring.[5] With that text about Constantin Guys, the Monsieur G of the essay, a minor figure in the visual arts of the time rather than one of its giants, Baudelaire was also the first influential theoretician of the metamorphoses of aesthetic creation and reception in an increasingly commercialized and technologized metropolitan culture. Constantin Guys published his sketches in the *Illustrated London News*, a leading European paper at the time that also had begun to publish photographs. Indeed, photography is the great unspoken dimension of the essay on Guys. We know how Baudelaire hated photography not only as mere copy but also as a sign of hateful progress and mass culture, a technological contraption that could not possibly compete with art. Thus, in "The Salon of 1859," we read:

> As the photographic industry was the refuge of every would-be painter, every painter too ill-endowed or too lazy to complete his studies, this universal infatuation bore not only the mark of a blindness, an imbecility, but had also the air of a vengeance. I do not believe, or at least do not wish to believe, in the absolute success of such a brutish conspiracy, in which, as in all others, one finds both fools and knaves; but I am convinced that the ill-applied developments of photography, like all other purely material developments of progress, have contributed much to the impoverishment of the French artistic genius, which is already so scarce.[6]

Baudelaire of course came to be the key figure in Benjamin—theorist par excellence of modern visual media of technical reproducibility and reader of Paris as the capital of the nineteenth century. In typical avant-gardist fashion of the interwar period, Benjamin also em-

phasized the link between urban writing and the feuilleton: "Literature submits to montage in the feuilleton."[7] And montage—always
associated with photography and film at the time—it is. Baudelaire's
miniature as form—creatively appropriated by Benjamin himself in
One-Way Street and *Berlin Childhood around 1900*—embodies paradigmatically what David Harvey has described as the compression
of time and space in the social world of modernity.[8] Montage is the
principle that shapes the collection of the miniatures into an open-
ended whole that can be said to represent a model of seriality before
film. The claim is not that somehow literature prophesies film; instead, the seriality of miniatures formally reflects and constructs
the very nature of urban experience. Both the theory and the practice of Baudelaire's writing the capitalist city in transition to the
modern metropolis at the time of the Baron Haussmann's radical
interventions into the older city fabric provide the perfect entry
point into that body of literature I call the metropolitan miniature.

Baudelaire's transformation of the older genre of journalistic urban
prose since Mercier, a tradition that was well and alive in many Paris
books of his time, did for Paris in the mid-nineteenth century what
the later German and Austrian writers did for metropolitan life, not
only of Paris but of Vienna and Berlin as well. Reading all these short
urban texts together allows us to focus on shared cross-national aspects of the experience of metropolitan space in major European cities
during an earlier phase of what now is called globalization. What
emerges in the modernist miniature is not some kind of literary city
guide but a reflection on the changing perceptions of city life and
the city's effects on structures of subjectivity at a time of rapid urbanization, industrialization, and the evolution of bohemian subcul-
tures. At stake was the creation of a modernist urban imaginary that
would account for historical changes in the mode of attentiveness and
reading.

Baudelaire is so crucial for this development of new city writing
since he stripped the older genre of *le tableau de Paris* of much of its
impressionistic urban description of recognizable Parisian sites, offering instead philosophical reflections and narrative or dialogic fragments mixed with extreme mood swings and contrarian states of
mind. The multiplicity of clashing perspectives, which modern

metropolitan life generated in that key phase of urban and social transformation after the bloodbath of 1848 and the Napoleonic putsch, recurs in his miniatures in a variety of moods from euphoria to lament and melancholy, from the epiphanies of reverie to the decrepitude and paralysis of the spleen, all the way to aggressiveness, sarcasm, and cynicism, with the latter becoming increasingly prevalent in the late miniatures written in the 1860s, during the twilight of Napoleon III's dictatorship.

Baudelaire's *Spleen* is also fundamentally different from a precursor he mentions explicitly in the *Preface:* the minor romantic poet Aloysius Bertrand, whose 1842 collection of prose fragments *Gaspard de la nuit: Fantaisies à la manière de Rembrandt et de Callot* presumably inspired him

> to try something similar, and to apply to the description of modern life, or rather of *one* modern and more abstract life, the procedure he [Bertrand] had applied to the depiction of ancient life, so strangely picturesque. (129)

Bertrand's *Gaspard* was indeed picturesque and descriptive, whereas Baudelaire aimed at abstraction from the picturesque. More important, Bertrand's writing was deeply visual in its execution and in its dedication to visual artists, and thus its posthumous editions always included visual representations with the prose fragments.[9] Baudelaire, however, despite his own highly visual imagination, did not include any visuals with his texts, which, given modern times, could only have been photographs of the city. The verbal and the visual had merged emblemlike in the editions of Bertrand's work, but like Benjamin later on, Baudelaire insisted on the *Eigensinn* of the literary in his miniatures. At stake, after all, was the power of language to conjure up urban scenes and create an urban imaginary.

In all of his multifaceted and heterogeneous miniatures, Baudelaire's relationship to the social and the political remains oscillating, amorphous, anarchic. Central are the intellectual's, the poet's radical mood swings. Thus, in "The Double Room," an *intérieur* is described lyrically as an aesthetic hothouse of voluptuous sensations of timelessness. Suddenly, clock time and the spleen of a banal everyday reenter the narrator's world with a vengeance, transforming what appeared as a "truly spiritual room" into "the abode of eternal ennui" (7). In a way, this fateful doubling is given an analogy in displaced form in the structure of the social world. Here the carefree world of the hated bourgeoisie is opposed to the world of poverty, deprivation, and vice with which the narrator identifies time and again, sometimes via empathy ("The Old Woman's Despair"; "Widows"; "The Old Acrobat"; "Eyes of the Poor"), other times via an aloof and disillusioning understanding ("The Cake"; "The Rope"). The collection opens with a soliloquy that establishes the narrator as perfect stranger and loner, prone to Rousseauean reverie. But it concludes with an allegory of social life, an elegy on the city's muse in which the social "double room," as it were, is allegorized in the opposition between the "good dogs, pitiful dogs, muddied dogs, those everyone shuns," just as everyone shuns paupers, poets, and prostitutes, and the

> foppish dogs, those conceited quadrupeds, Great Dane, King Charles spaniel, pug or lap dog, so enchanted with themselves, and so sure to please, that they leap indiscreetly onto the legs or knees of visitors, unruly like children, stupid like easy women, sometimes sulky and insolent like servants! (125)

Baudelaire was relentlessly critical of the society of the Second Empire, but in his later years he never embraced an explicit political position. Thus, the two prevailing readings of Baudelaire either as escapist aesthete or political radical need to be merged. Baudelaire was both—urban aesthete living on the margins of "good" society and that society's radical critic. His schizophrenic position oscillating violently between the pursuit of beauty and "the mire of the macadam" ("Loss of Halo") perhaps found its best expression when he wrote in *Mon Coeur mis à nu:* "It might perhaps be pleasant to be alternately victim and executioner."[10] Such oscillation between extreme states of mind generated by the urban environment characterize the narrating voices of the prose poems, distinguishing them quite clearly not only from that earlier tradition of writing *le tableau de Paris* (Mercier) but also from Balzac's and Zola's narrators weaving of their cyclical urban narratives in *La comédie humaine* and *Les Rougon-Macquart*. This constant doubling and shifting of perspective also requires a flexible and multiperspectival approach on the part of the reader. Reading Baudelaire straight has led to serious misunderstandings. Thus, "The Bad Glazier," with the poet's cruel and wanton treatment of the old glazier, who does not have any colored glass panes on offer, triggered the reproach that Baudelaire advocated an art for art's sake. But multiple phrasings in the text referring ironically to clichés like *"la vie en rose,"* or *"la vie en beau"* make it very clear that Baudelaire is criticizing the aestheticism of bourgeois beautification. When the poet-narrator suggests to the glazier that he should sell rose-colored panes in poor neighborhoods in order to "make life beautiful," it is hard to miss the satirical intent. This is a perfect example of affirmative sabotage, here the sabotage of a bourgeois kitsch aesthetic turned against itself, thus revealing its hidden violence. A text like that must be read anamorphically, not frontally, but from the side, as it were. Only then does it reveal its critical intent. The same is true of the much-discussed "Let's beat up the poor," which in similar close reading reveals itself as a satire of utopian socialism rather than a cynical theory of liberation as theory of insufficient oppression.

Le Spleen de Paris offers a model of writing that translates the raw energies of the city, its scandals and miseries as well as its temptations and ecstasies, into a new language. Even if some of this language remains mired in male misogyny and in a traditional catholic imaginary of evil and bliss, the satanic and the divine, its provocations to traditional literary culture secure it pride of place in the genealogy of modernist urban imaginaries. Baudelaire's miniatures are seminal in that neither the concrete spaces nor the overall social geography of the city ever appear as they would in the urban novel or the short urban sketch. Instead, Paris appears as if seen through the veil of a nervous and vulnerable consciousness that takes account of the city's aesthetic, human, political, and economic contradictions without transcending them evasively in poetry or escaping deliberately into *l'art pour l'art*. Despite Baudelaire's great admiration for Balzac's *Comédie humaine*, the urban miniature demonstrates implicitly why the coherent Balzacian narrative, held together by one omniscient narrator and the trajectory of plot, is no longer adequate to the writing of the city in the age of Haussmann's radical interventions in the city fabric. Instead we get a series of fragments, montages of different discourses even within those fragments, short pieces with ever-changing moods and outlooks. In Baudelaire's late work, Paris emerges as a fragmented and fragmenting space of the heterotopias of the imagination. It is an urban imaginary of a specific phase of metropolitan modernization later articulated in different ways by Benjamin and Kracauer and finding its perhaps last and by then already nostalgic instantiation in Italo Calvino's *Invisible Cities*. Indeed, the Paris, Vienna, or Berlin of the miniatures read in this book have become invisible in the post–World War II era.

But what of the term "prose poem" still used by many to describe a whole trajectory of short prose? As Todorov put it quite well, Baudelaire did not invent the prose poem,

> but it was he who gave it its seal of nobility, who introduced it on the horizon of his contemporaries and his successors, who made it into a model of writing.[11]

At the same time, the subtitle *petits poèmes en prose* has led many critics, including Todorov himself, to focus on genre issues and to ask whether we are dealing with poetic prose or prosaic poetry, a discussion that more often than not gets stuck in a dead end. And since many of the miniatures are not close to poems at all, critics have spoken of aesthetic failure or have even attributed perceived deficiencies to Baudelaire's worsening syphilitic condition and mental disturbance.[12] Another explanation offers itself. Ever since Mercier, the *tableau de Paris* came in the form of prose. Baudelaire turned the tables and versified it in *Les Fleurs du mal*. Once he himself turned to writing the city in prose, he needed to distinguish his miniatures from the tradition of the urban sketch, and thus he provocatively poeticized the idea of the tableau by calling it prose poem. A conscious strategy of reversal appears in both cases. Thus, ruminating about poetic prose vs. prosaic poetry, tied as it is to an unchanging notion of high Literature with capital L, whether prose or poetry, blocked more interesting historical and aesthetic questions regarding the changing function of literature under the impact of proliferating new print and visual media, something Baudelaire was not only acutely aware of but to which his texts explicitly respond.

Even though Baudelaire severely criticized the mimetic dimension of photography—something he has in common with Kracauer and Benjamin, who nevertheless also saw the potential of the new visual media—it is this relation to the popular print media that again links Baudelaire to the later writers of the urban miniature who wrote their feuilleton miniatures in explicit relation to the visual media of their day, primarily photography and film. Baudelaire, by contrast, developed his visual aesthetic by privileging the social and political drawings and sketches Constantin Guys published in the *Illustrated London News*, a paper that had also begun to publish photographs of events. Indeed, it is the link to the boulevard press of his day that makes Baudelaire's urban miniatures into a "*modèle d'écriture*" (Todorov) that is perhaps more palpable in the German and Austrian urban miniature of the interwar years in writers such as Kracauer, Musil, and Benjamin than in Baudelaire's immediate French "successors" of the *poème en prose* such as Rimbaud, Lautréamont, Mallarmé, or even the surrealists.

Baudelaire, while still writing sonnets in traditional alexandrine verse in *Les Fleurs du mal*, delved into and exploited the language of the everyday, as it appeared in *la petite presse*. He published both his poems and several installments of his *Petits poèmes en prose* in the papers before either were collected in *Les Fleurs du mal* and in *Le Spleen de Paris*; the latter appeared only posthumously in 1869 as volume IV of the *Oeuvres complètes*. As a practicing art critic since the 1840s, Baudelaire also had a very close relationship to the day-to-day cultural debates as they were played out in the Parisian papers and feuilletons. Even if a primary purpose of the prose pieces was to make some money from contributions to the feuilleton, Baudelaire took his urban miniatures very seriously. He tied them directly to *Les Fleurs du mal* when he wrote to his mother "that the fashioning of these little knick-knacks is the result of a great concentration of the spirit" and called it "a singular work, more singular, at least more headstrong than *The Flowers of Evil*."[13] And one year later he wrote to Jules Troubat: "In sum, it [the prose poems] are the *Fleurs du mal* again, but with much more freedom, detail, and mockery."[14] As usual, there are striking contradictions in Baudelaire's phrasing that should not be harmonized: "great concentration of the spirit" stands against "these little knick-knacks"; "singular work" stands against *Les Fleurs du mal* again." But it is above all the spirit of mockery that distinguishes *Le Spleen de Paris* from *Les Fleurs du mal* as a carefully crafted cycle of poems.

The German critic Karl Heinrich Biermann has perhaps best described what is indeed singular in *Le Spleen de Paris*. He has shown how the prose poems inscribe themselves in the specific media context of the Second Empire.[15] Given the strict censorship of any oppositional or politically critical press coverage after the coup of December 2, 1851, the 1850s saw a proliferation of nonpolitical and literary boulevard magazines and papers that created and saturated a depoliticized reading public that wanted to be entertained and pleased. Instead of political coverage, magazines such as *La chronique parisienne*, *La Revue anecdotique*, and *Le Boulevard* preferred genres such as narrative short prose, miniature portraits, celebrity anecdotes, brief dialogues, fictive letters, reflections, society gossip, most of them focusing on issues of private rather than public life. Rather than seeing the variety of clearly nonpoetic writing practices in the prose poems as an atrophy of Baudelaire's poetic imagination, we must read them as a strategy to appropriate and to transform the genres of *la petite presse*. His goal was to reach the broader public and convey to that audience his urban perceptions and acute sense of the threat to the poetic imagination in metropolitan modernity (particularly evident in "The Double Room" and "Loss of Halo"). After all, very few of the texts of *Le Spleen de Paris* are real prose poems in the traditional sense. "A Hemisphere in Tresses," "Twilight," and "Invitation au voyage" count among them, but they were written fairly early and do have their complements in *Les Fleurs du mal* as poems with the same title. The other miniatures offer anecdotes ("A Joker"; "The Counterfeit Coin"), dialogues ("The Stranger"), short novellas ("A Heroic Death"), portraits of social types ("Widows"; "The Old Acrobat")—all of them genres prevalent in the unpolitical entertainment press of Paris.[16] Baudelaire never commented himself in detail on his relation to the *petite presse*; he simply digested and transformed these found modes of writing. His authorial role was that of a creative rag-picker in the media world of the boulevard. But then he condensed what he found, intensifying his urban perceptions and embodying them in seemingly simple texts whose meanings are revealed only to the reader who does not read for information or transparent understanding. The figure of the narrator putting on diverse masks of urban flâneur and moralist, cynic and boulevardier, mystic and poet served him to register repressed social phenomena either by mimicry or aggression—the loneliness and solitude of widowhood and old age ("Widows"; "The Old Woman's Despair"), the artist's fall from an audience's favors ("The Old Mountebank"), the latent violence of poverty ("The Eyes of the Poor"; "Let's Beat Up the Poor"), the destructiveness of bourgeois clichés ("The Bad Glazier"), the link between art and prostitution ("Loss of Halo"). This critical mimesis of urban phenomena, rendered in a variety of genres found in the printed press of his day and then transformed into his own multilayered voice, has its analogy in those later attempts by Kracauer, Benjamin, and Musil to write the city for the feuilleton in relationship to the spread of photography and cinema in the metropolitan public sphere. Except that the role of an explicit aesthetic subjectivity, still strong after Baudelaire in Rilke and Benn, will be greatly reduced in most of these later miniatures in favor of objectivist expression, *Sachlichkeit*, and a generic, sometimes collective, or at least impersonal rather than individualizing ethos.

EVEN IF Baudelaire's critical awareness of the impact of the mass media on literary forms seems lacking in Rilke's *Notebooks*, a book that clearly inscribed itself in the tradition of high literature, traces of photography and photographic vision are hauntingly present in the protagonist's project of "learning how to see," which is transformed in the novel into a kind of serial writing of fragments.[17] The experience of Paris posed a long-lasting threat to Rilke's still postromantic poetic imagination, but it ultimately generated a new kind of poetic language in Rilke's later years. The *Notebooks* played a central role in that transformation.

The terror of metropolitan modernity resonates powerfully in Rilke's letters to Lou Andreas-Salomé and in Maltes's experiences and memories. On July 18, 1903, Rilke wrote to Lou in a kind of meta-phoric overdrive:

> I must tell you, dear Lou, that Paris was an experience for me not unlike that of the military school: for just as then a great fearful astonishment had seized me, so now I was gripped by terror at everything that, as if in some unspeakable confu-sion, is called life. . . . The carriages drove straight through me, and those in a rush made no detour around me and ran over me full of disdain, as over a bad place in which stale water has collected.[18]

The letter continues with observations about Paris that will reappear almost verbatim in the novel. But the experience of Paris is intimately connected to Baudelaire when he wrote:

> And at night I got up and looked for my favorite volume of Baude-laire, the *petits poèmes en prose*, and read aloud the most beau-tiful poem, the one titled *A une heure du matin*.[19]

Baudelaire's poem "Une Charogne" ("A Carcass") appears in the novel at a crucial juncture when Malte reflects on the abject in metropol-itan life.[20] Rilke was the first writer in German to try something sim-ilarly ambitious on the threshold between poetry, prose, and the me-tropolis as Baudelaire did several decades earlier, yet with a very different goal and outcome.

Just as Baudelaire's poetry, critical writings, and prose poems marked a major new departure in literary culture in mid-nineteenth-century France, Rilke's *Notebooks of Malte Laurids Brigge* have increas-ingly come to stand as a seminal text in the genealogy of German language modernism; at least as incisive, I would argue, as Hof-mannsthal's 1902 Chandos letter, which is often given pride of place in that genealogy. Hofmannsthal articulated the modernist language crisis in all-too-elegant and linguistically subtle ways, giving it an almost classically sublime form. He tried to overcome the crisis of language and vision by creating a historicizing Renaissance setting.[21] In a fictive letter, Lord Chandos describes the breakdown of his ability to communicate to his mentor, Francis Bacon. But he does so in safe retrospective after having recuperated his ability to express himself. In the *Notebooks*, there is no such classicizing retrospective on language loss and recuperation, a problematic Rilke/Malte shares with Hofmannsthal. Instead, Rilke inscribed the inability to narrate as an effect of modern urban life in the very form of his text, both in Malte's struggles to narrate his experiences and in the very disjointed form of his novel. It is precisely as a novel that Rilke's *Notebooks of Malte Laurids Brigge* marked a new departure in German narrative literature. As a writer of miniatures within the novel form, he first used the miniature to give voice to a dystopian urban imaginary widespread in the literature and visual arts of the expressionist and postexpressionist periods.

We must note here that both Rilke and Baudelaire came from poetry to prose: Rilke from the *Neue Gedichte*, which first attempted to come to terms with metropolitan experience, to *Malte Laurids Brigge*, Baudelaire from *Les Fleurs du Mal* to *Le Spleen de Paris*.[22] This distinguishes them from Kafka and Kracauer as much as from Benjamin, Jünger, or Musil. There is no question in my mind that the hidden *point de départ* for the short prose segments that initiate Malte's descent into Paris was Baudelaire's *Spleen de Paris*. Their Paris, however, is not the same Paris. The Paris of the Second Empire, Haussmann, and Manet is the backdrop of Baudelaire's work, while Rilke's Paris is the Paris of the Troisième République, the Dreyfus affair, and Rodin. But such political and cultural realities of Paris remain veiled in both authors, and concrete urban spaces are barely conjured up, let alone described in detail. It is no surprise, then, that despite the chronological and historical difference, there are remarkable affinities in tone, themes, and reactions to urban social space. To be sure, Rilke differs from Baudelaire in that his miniatures still feature a main character and a (however diminished) plot revolving around the protagonist's learning how to see and attempting to write. The novel as the main genre to render the prose of modern urban life is not challenged here as explicitly as it is in Baudelaire, who, in the dedication to his publisher, advertised his texts as not binding the reader's "recalcitrant will to the endless thread of a superfluous plot" (129). At the same time, Malte's learning how to see is not coded as a trajectory of *Bildung* via ekphrasis in the mode of the Bildungs-roman. At stake is rather the search for an alternative structure of subjectivity necessitated by urban life, a subjectivity that goes beyond the classical distinctions of mind and body, inside and outside, subject and object.

Given the arrangement of the text into seventy-one separate fragments, I want to argue that especially the twenty-six short prose pieces that make up the beginning of the *Notebooks* can be read as urban miniatures. Indeed, the notebook as a medium of writing does have a similarly transitory and fragmented quality as Baudelaire's "little work," which, as the Preface stated, could be chopped up into many fragments. But in contrast to Baudelaire's texts, the miniatures that lead us into the experiences of Rilke's fictional hero Malte cannot exist separately by themselves; they are bound together by the logic of the narrative featuring this 28-year-old Dane's descent into the double abyss of Paris experiences and his childhood memories before he reemerges only partly redeemed in the allegory of the prodigal son at the end of the novel. However minimal and inconclusive, there still is plot in the miniatures of the *Notebooks* that distinguishes them from the kaleidoscopic structure of feuilleton montage.

One often-remarked affinity between Rilke and Baudelaire lies in their intense visual sensibility. It is well known how Baudelaire's urban imagination was closely tied to the caricatures and sketches of Daumier, Meryon, and Grandville, not to mention Constantin Guys, the subject of his key programmatic essay "Le Peintre de la vie moderne." A similarly close relation to the visual in Rilke is indicated not just in Malte's desire of learning how to see but also in the impact Rodin and Cézanne as admired artists had on Rilke, who served for some time as Rodin's secretary. The visual is also present in the very title of the novel. The translation of *"Aufzeichnungen"* as "Notebooks" loses the German term's visual connotation as drawing (*Zeichnung*) or sketch. The sketch, after all, was what Constantin Guys excelled in. But the affinities reach much deeper yet.

Some immediately visible affinities are found on a structural and a thematic level. In neither author does the city appear in extensive empirical description. Concretely identified Parisian urban or social sites, as are characteristic of the earlier *tableau de Paris*, are few and

far between, though perhaps more frequent in Rilke than in Baudelaire. Baudelaire mentions a tobacco store, a public garden, the cem-
etery, a café on the boulevard, the faubourg, but names are never
given. Rilke, on the other hand, mentions the Hôtel Dieu and the
Salpétrière, the Pont Neuf and the rue Notre Dame des Champs,
but his purpose is never descriptive. Both authors thus practice a kind
of reduction or abstraction of urban space, as Baudelaire suggested
in his 1862 dedication (that treasure trove of pithy formulations)
where, in reference to Aloysius Bertrand, that mediocre writer of
urban prose, he suggested his texts offer "one modern and more abstract life" (129). True, Rilke's novel begins with a spatial and temporal marker—Sept 11, rue Toullier—but then spatial and temporal
references typical of a diary or notebook disappear immediately. The
short prose segments at the beginning of the novel could be diary
entries, but lacking place and date, they are never marked as such.
At the thematic level, the narrator's interest in the widows, the old
acrobat, the old woman's despair, and various paupers and prostitutes
in Baudelaire are matched by Malte's encounters with the *Fortgeworfenen*, the disenfranchised and abject characters he encounters on the
Parisian boulevards. The Haussmannian boulevard itself, sight of the
mingling of crowds and the homelessness of the individual, was a site
of abstraction. In his book about Offenbach and his time, Kracauer
described the boulevard as "a space removed from the structures
of social reality. A neutral meeting place. An unreal terrain."[23] It
was an alienating and alienated, almost extraterritorial space that
produced the strange and estranging encounters typical of these
miniatures in both Baudelaire and Rilke. A major difference, however,
is that Malte lacks the ecstatic experiences, the epiphanies of the Idol,
the getting high of Baudelaire's narrator. The sheer negativity of the
urban experience is overwhelming in Rilke. What he does have in
common with Baudelaire is the breakdown of boundaries between
inside and outside space. In Baudelaire it is the experience of a merger
with the crowds that is coded both as an active willful entering into
the crowd by way of embrace and active penetration in an erotic sense
and as a passive "holy prostitution of the soul which gives itself
totally . . . to the unexpected" (21). In Rilke only the passive dimension remains, the invasion of a threatening outside into the inner re-
cesses of the self that is no longer a self. Baudelaire's famous fencing

duel with the shocks of the city "in which the artist shrieks with fright before being defeated" (4) has no equivalent in Malte's experiences. Malte does not fight the shocks of the city; he succumbs to them.

This inability to fend off the shocks of the city is captured well by Rilke in a telling metaphor two years after the publication of his novel. In a letter to Lou Andreas-Salomé of October 21, 1913, we read:

> This time, Paris was just what I had expected: difficult. And I feel like a photographic plate that has been exposed too long, in that I remain forsaken to this powerful influence. . . . Out of fright I went right off Sunday to Rouen. An entire cathedral is necessary to drown me out. [24]

Of course, overexposure will eventually blot out anything to be seen. But as Stefanie Harris has persuasively argued, Malte can be said to function like a photographic plate on which images are recorded. The camera eye is passive, always open, subject to the recording process, which is then transformed into the writing of the miniatures. Malte has become a recording device, or the book "is like the photographic plate that continues to inscribe images."[25] Malte himself is like a camera whose shutter never closes. The German word *Aufzeichnung* after all also translates as "recording." The city is recorded in and on Malte's body as if on a photographic plate. His project of learning how to see also opens up that other uncanny dimension that always accompanies seeing: being seen. Indeed, being seen is the inherent structure of being photographed. Being seen immediately makes us think of Malte's social paranoia about the *Fortgeworfenen*, and ultimately it shapes the culminating mirror scene in which he sees himself seeing an alienated self.

In another letter to Andreas-Salomé, he lamented:

> I am clumsy . . . about events that come and go, without the gift of selection, without the calmness of reception, a mirror turned this way and that, out of which all images fall.[26]

Photographic plate or mirror, then: ultimately Malte's psychic condition, his inability to fend off the stimuli raining down on him in street encounters, is implicitly compared to a technological device, one that makes seeing itself into an alienated, threatening, objectifying thing linking it to being seen either by the camera eye or the mirror.[27]

On another topic, the affinities between Baudelaire and Rilke are stronger than the differences. The solitude, reverie, and spleen of the artist are equally pronounced in both works. In his incisive and monumental study of the myth of Paris from Mercier via Balzac and Hugo to Baudelaire, Karl Heinz Stierle has pointed to the Rousseauean beginning of the prose poems.[28] Indeed, the succinct short dialogue of "The Stranger" can be read as an homage to the Rousseau of the *Rêveries du promeneur solitaire*. The notion of *rêverie* as dialogue of a solitary man with himself—one of the titles Baudelaire considered for the collection was *Le promeneur solitaire*—captures Malte's fleeting thoughts and reflections as much as it does Baudelaire's. Rousseau's text begins:

> Here I am, then, alone on the earth, having neither brother, neighbor, friend, or society but myself.[29]

Baudelaire's stranger says:

> I have neither father, nor mother, nor sister, nor brother. (1)

And he goes on to confess to a lack of friends and fatherland. His only love is for the drifting clouds. Rilke's Malte writes in an equally lonely but less accepting mood:

> How ridiculous. I sit here in my little room, I, Brigge, who am twenty-eight years old and completely unknown. I sit here and am nothing. (12)

What Lukács described as the transcendental homelessness of the modern novel may have found its first embodiment in Rousseau's autobiography, only to reappear in exacerbated form in the city texts of these later writers.

Many of Malte's notations are indeed *rêveries*, especially when he is carried back into his childhood memories. But completely missing in Rilke are the aggressive and cynical states of mind that are so prevalent in many of Baudelaire's miniatures, countering the poetic ecstasies in some and mellow reveries in others. Some critics have seen empathy with social outsiders as key to Baudelaire's collection, but this misses the multiplicity of radically opposed moods and voices in Baudelaire's narrators.[30] If at all, empathy and identification coupled with paranoia seem to be more adequate to Malte's encounter with the *Fortgeworfenen*, the outcasts, but even here it would be important to point out that these encounters are not really about empathy as a social or even philanthropic affect; empathy rather points to Malte's always fearful need to identify with the abject, to read the *Fortgeworfenen* as figures of voiding and precondition for some new subjectivity. For at the same time, this closeness to the outcasts of the city heightens his anxiety about his own fate. The *Fortgeworfenen* always appear at salient moments to highlight Malte's own precarious state of mind and body in the urban world. In contrast to Rilke, who has often been accused of aestheticizing poverty, in Baudelaire abject poverty always suggests at least implicitly a social and political threat to the *juste milieu* ("Assommons les pauvres"; "Le joujou du pauvre").[31] At the same time, he remained as distant to progressivist left politics as he was contemptuous of the despised *juste milieu* itself. However one reads Baudelaire's politics—with Benjamin, as secretly subversive of his own class or even as compatible with Marxism[32]—even such rather implicit and anarchic politics are absent from Rilke's treatment of the disenfranchised of the city, just as Rilke's text lacks the ironic and satirical dimension of the *Spleen de Paris*.

The social interest of Baudelaire's narrator is also evident in that he focuses on certain urban types such as widows, aging artists, beggars, children at play. And yet there is no sociological characterization as E. A. Poe attempted in his "Man of the Crowd," a text Baudelaire first translated into French. Individuals do not appear as such but are rather embedded in allegorical reflection. Rilke, on the other hand, is drawn to the exceptional, the existential, the surreal, as in Malte's encounter with the epileptic on the Pont Neuf, the terrorizing vision of the man in the *crèmerie*, or the hallucinatory encounter with the woman whose face comes off her head like a mask, revealing

its horrific inside. The distance Baudelaire's narrator establishes from
the objects of his observations is cashed in in Malte, who flees in terror
from these appearances, all of which represent an existential threat
to his innermost being.

Encounters with the disenfranchised thus function in quite opposite ways in Baudelaire and in Rilke. At stake are differently structured observing subjectivities. The difference emerges clearly as one
compares Baudelaire's "Widows" with Malte's encounter with the old
woman in the street. Baudelaire's narrator is fascinated by the loneliness and despair of those widows, some of whom he follows for
hours walking through Paris, a narrative moment he appropriates
from E. A. Poe's "Man of the Crowd." As in Poe, the secret observer
shares his observations with the reader, but he always maintains a
distance from the scene observed. The encounter is anything but immediate, eruptive, horrifying as it is in Rilke, who observes a women
in the street who had "completely fallen into herself, forward into her
hands":

> The woman sat up, frightened, she pulled out of herself, too
> quickly, too violently, so that her face was left in her two hands.
> I could see it lying there: its hollow form. It cost me an inde-
> scribable effort to stay with those two hands, not to look at what
> had been torn out of them. I shuddered to see a face from the
> inside, but I was much more afraid of that bare flayed head
> waiting there, faceless. (7)

Baudelaire's miniature instead begins with a learned reference to Vau-
venargues' comments on public gardens as "meeting places for those
maimed by life" (23). He goes on for over a page, describing the features and clothing of such widows in general before zeroing in on
two specific cases. Such self-conscious reflective framings are rather
absent in Malte's encounters with social outsiders. It is as if the *Fortgeworfenen* erupt directly into Malte's subjectivity. There is no distinction between outside and inside. Malte's structure of subjectivity
is fundamentally different from that of Baudelaire's narrators, for
whom the merger of outside and inside is rather a positive, even epiphanic experience ("The Artist's Confiteor"; "The Crowds"). If one had

to put not too fine a point on it: in Baudelaire, subjectivity is still understood primarily as a state of consciousness, oscillating, often violently, between what Baudelaire described as the double tendency toward "the vaporization and the centralization of the self."[33] In Rilke, by, contrast the subject is fundamentally defined by his bodily reactions and a *Leiblichkeit* or corporeality that is no longer able to secure the boundary between self and environment. One cannot even say that there is vaporization, because there is no stable, centralized identity that could be vaporized in the first place, as Malte's childhood memories reveal. Baudelaire, in Benjamin's felicitous formulation, parries the shocks of urban modernity and translates them into verse, whereas Malte remains fundamentally permeable and defenseless as the shocks of urban encounters penetrate down to the deepest layers of unconscious memory traces, hurling themselves, as it were, into the quarry of his repressed childhood memories, breaking loose large image chunks that then float up to the surface and merge grotesquely with his ultimately anti-urban anxieties about metropolitan life.[34]

Loss of self also appears in Baudelaire. But it is always paired with its binary other: the active parrying of the shocks of urban life, as for instance in the poem "Le Soleil." Loss of self appears in the third miniature of the collection, "The Artist's Confiteor":

How penetrating are the ends of autumn days! Ah! Penetrating to the verge of pain!" (4)

Conjuring up a poetic scene of solitude, silence and the sea, the narrator continues:

—all these things think through me, or I think through them (for in the grandeur of reverie, the *self* is quickly lost!). (4)

But the interpenetration of subject and object cannot last. The second part of the miniature brings the radical reversal:

However, these thoughts, whether they emerge from me or spring from things, soon grow too intense. The force of voluptuous pleasure creates uneasiness and concrete suffering. Then my excessively taut nerves produce nothing but shrill and painful vibrations." (4)

And the miniature ends with an even broader reflection:

Studying the beautiful is a duel in which the artist shrieks with fright before being defeated." (4)

Loss of boundaries and spleen, vaporization and centralization go together, or rather oscillate from one to the other.

In another miniature—one of the few instances where urban crowds actually appear in Baudelaire's texts—there is the merger of the flâneur with the crowds, another vaporization, it seems:

The solitary and thoughtful stroller draws a unique intoxication from this universal communion." ("The Crowds," 21)

And then he goes on to speak of that

ineffable orgy, that holy prostitution of the soul which gives itself totally, poetry and charity, to the unexpected which appears, to the unknown which passes by." (21)

The comparison with Rilke/Malte's urban experiences makes us aware that there is still an active subject in Baudelaire that gives itself to the unexpected. Baudelaire's relation to the city is much less traumatic than some recent readings have suggested.[35] In "The Painter of Modern Life" he even speaks of the flâneur who merges sexually with the crowd, generating a standard gendered metaphor in which city and crowd are feminized as the other of the penetrating male subject.[36] So a flowing merger of subject and crowd there is, but its direction proceeds from subject to object. In Rilke it is rather the reverse. The crisis of boundaries between self and world is already present in the second miniature of the *Notebooks*. Malte describes his sensations while lying in bed with the windows open:

Electric trolleys speed clattering through my room. Cars drive over me. A door slams. Somewhere a window pane shatters on the pavement: I can hear its large fragments laugh and its small ones giggle. (4)

Here the breakdown between inside and outside refers to auditory perception, which is indeed even more inescapable in urban environments than the city's visual shocks. After all, one can close one's eyes, but not one's ears. The visual dimension of this breakdown appears in another passage in which Malte describes the horrifying, almost hallucinatory recognition of the residual inside wall of a demolished house as the outside wall of the adjacent building, revealing an inside that is no longer there. The wall of the apartment thus exposed is described in a language that actually conjures up organs of the human body, just as throughout the novel the dissolution of boundaries affects the boundary between body and things, the animate and the inanimate:

It was, so to speak, not the first wall of the existing houses . . . but the last of the ones that were no longer there. You could see its inside. You could see, at its various stories, bedroom walls with wallpaper still sticking to them; and here and there a piece of floor or ceiling. Near these bedroom walls there remained, along the entire length of the outer wall, a dirty-white space through which, in unspeakably nauseating, worm-soft digestive movements, the open, rust-spotted channel of the toilet pipe crawled. (46)

The passage ends with Malte's terror:

I swear I began to run as soon as I recognized this wall. For that's what is horrible—that I did recognize it. I recognize everything here, and that's why it passes right into me: it is at home inside me. (48)

Baudelaire fences with the shocks of urban life, succeeding in fighting them off or falling victim to them in the state of ennui. He is either victim or perpetrator. Malte's case is different: the urban terror goes right into him. He is always its victim. This total inter-penetration or *Durchdringung*, of outside and inside, in Malte's psy-chic structure is quite different from the oscillating psyches of Baude-laire's narrators.

Just as the erasure of boundaries between inside and outside in Rilke even pertains to urban sites such as buildings (the missing house) and to Malte's relationship with other inanimate things, Malte's past and present also intermingle to the extent that temporal boundaries separating his childhood past from his adult urban present disappear. Images of past and present intermingle as if Malte himself were a photo album in which the images had all gotten jumbled. The nar-rator in Baudelaire's miniatures, on the other hand, lacks a specific past—due to the fact of course that he is not given an individual his-tory, whereas Malte, as a fictional figure telling his own story in an almost confessional way, remains haunted by his past.

Ultimately, however, the major difference between Baudelaire and Rilke lies in the fact that for Rilke the writing of prose was but a way station toward a renewal of his poetic imagination that led him eventually to the *Sonette an Orpheus* and the *Duineser Elegien*. In Baudelaire, the break with the model of the carefully constructed cycle of poems as embodied in *Les Fleurs du mal* was much more rad-ical. It was not a crisis that could be overcome through introspec-tion and a largely autobiographically tinged prose, as in Rilke's case. Baudelaire's was indeed a rupture with a whole poetic past, including his own. It was his very consciousness of the challenges modern urban life posed to a poetic post-romantic imagination and to the medium of poetry itself that made him experiment with a new kind of prose writing. It was the insight into the multiperspectivalism of the me-tropolis that made him critical as well of omniscient narrators, or-ganized plot, and the unity of the subject. It was in Baudelaire, more so than in Rilke, that the modernist urban miniature emerged as gen-uine novelty in writing the city. It is hard to imagine that Baudelaire could have gone back to writing poems after publishing *Le Spleen de Paris*. Too scathing was his critique of the society and bourgeois read-ership of the Second Empire, a political dimension of his writing that is clearly lacking in Rilke, the writer from abroad who had settled in

Paris and created a fictional figure whose troubles emerge as much from the metropolis as from the traces of nightmarish childhood memories that are reactivated by the terror of the city.

In Rilke's life, Paris produced a crisis that the poet tried to overcome in the long years he was working on the *Notebooks* (1903–1910). Rilke's narrator, Malte Laurids Brigge, however fragmented, dismembered, and schizophrenic his imaginary of Paris may appear at times, is still very much a romantic subject, an aspiring poet suffering from the alienation of modern life. Memories of childhood, hauntingly surreal and mostly related to death, erupt, often violently, in his present. His turn toward childhood, triggered in complex ways by the metropolitan experiences in Paris, link Rilke to Wordsworthian melancholy looking back on another time and space. While Malte's childhood memories are shot through with anxieties, even terror, they also display a nostalgic longing for his mother, analogous to Proust's *Recherche* or to Benjamin's *Berlin Childhood* miniatures. There is not even an inkling of such temporal and familial nostalgia in Baudelaire. The urban spleen seems to have swallowed up any past of narrator and author alike. Baudelaire's desire is spatial rather than temporal: it imagines exotic lands, looks to the sea, the clouds, and the azure of the sky to trigger the reverie. Rilke's narrator never had a stable and firm sense of identity to begin with, but he has a name and is a character in the novel. Baudelaire's impersonal narrator rather seems to be a projection surface for the varying moods and radically changing affects the city with its incessant stimuli and mental shocks produces in human subjects. In "Crowds" we read:

> The poet enjoys the incomparable privilege of being able, at will, to be himself and an other. Like those wandering souls seeking a body, he enters, when he wants, into everyone's character. For him alone, everything is empty. (21)

The emptiness outside corresponds to and even requires a certain inner emptiness as a space for projections. In the radical shifts and changes in his moods, the narrator lacks the psychic unity of the bourgeois subject that is radically deconstructed and challenged in these texts. But there always is a subject, a male subject with his will, his misogyny, and his Catholic phantasms of the satanic—a subject who never escapes the spleen. By contrast, Rilke's Malte lacks the will to be himself and an other. After his terrorizing experience with the epileptic man on the Pont Neuf, he writes:

> What sense would there have been in going anywhere now; I was empty. Like a blank piece of paper, I drifted along past the houses, up the boulevard again. (71)

For Baudelaire, the emptiness is in the world for him to enter it. In Rilke, it is the self that is void. And this accounts for two very different notions of authorship: Baudelaire's energetic will to shape and form, whether in poetry or prose, stands against Malte's passive waiting to be written and the hope for the emergence of that other language he dreams of:

> But the day will come when my hand will be distant, and if I tell it to write, it will write words that are not mine. The time of that other interpretation will dawn, when there shall not be left one word upon another, and every meaning will dissolve like a cloud and fall down like rain. . . . This time, I will be written. I am the impression that will transform itself. (52-53)

This of course would be the moment of the high modernist epiphany beyond any spleen, the transcendence into a realm of writing that would leave all contingency behind and achieve some ultimate truth and coherence. However, Malte recognizes that he cannot take the step

> to understand all this and assent to it [because] I have fallen and I can't pick myself up because I am shattered to pieces. (53, translation modified)

Prerequisite for taking that step, for turning misery into bliss, as Malte puts it, seems to be some notion of a self that remains outside of Malte's reach, a nonshattered, even nondifferentiated self that would be symbiotically all-encompassing and whose writing would achieve transcendence in that other "glorious language" (257). What

Malte expresses here is the intense high modernist longing for another kind of language that would, in psychoanalytic or ontogenetic terms, correspond to a prelapsarian phase preceding the development of language itself, which is after all constituted quintessentially as differentiation. But the desire for such a fluid language before differentiation is accompanied by Malte's equally strong acknowledgment that such a language cannot be attained, that the desire for it is an impossible, even dangerous desire. Consequently he turns back to writing the language of others, not the other language. He copies others' texts into his novel, texts that serve him as prayers. A Baudelairean poem and a passage from the Bible are collaged into the narrative, proving how distant Malte is from the "time of that other interpretation." Malte's discourse, indeed, is not the desired authentic, transcendent discourse of modernism that might provide some unlimited plenitude of meaning; his discourse remains rather the discourse of various others: that of Baudelaire and the Bible as well as that of Rilke's own letters, often quoted verbatim, and a variety of other historical texts that proliferate in the second part of the novel. I am tempted to say that it is Rilke who is being written already while Malte is still waiting for this to happen, but if that is so, then it must also be said that Rilke's being written is an entirely different kind from the one Malte imagines and prophesies. He finds himself in the midst of Baudelairean spleen but does not realize it.

In the end, one could say that it was the project of Rilke's *Notebooks* to lead Malte to some realm beyond urban alienation and his haunting childhood memories in order to reconstruct a poetic subjectivity at a higher level. Rilke wants transcendence and redemption, ascending from misery to bliss. In Baudelaire, the trajectory is usually the reverse ("The Double Room"; "The Artist's Confiteor"; "The Soup and the Clouds"; "Twilight"). Baudelaire ends up staring into the abyss of urban life, *le gouffre*, acknowledging how the city tears up subjectivities and any stable fabric of life. It thus does not make much sense to accuse Baudelaire's texts of unresolved contradictions resulting from the author's syphilis.[37] It is the real contradictions themselves that make the text modernist and urban, whereas the shocks and terrorized states of mind pervading the miniatures at the beginning of Rilke's novel slowly but surely make way for a newfound coherence of thought and mind culminating in the parable of the prodigal son's return at the very end of the *Notebooks*. Only in the first part of the *Notebooks* do we hear Malte's authorial voice, haunted and threatened by his urban experiences. If the threat of photography looms inside Malte's project of learning how to see, it pertains only to that first part of the novel. This voice eventually disappears, yielding to more objectifying reflections about reading experiences, historical events, and the nature of love. There is discontinuity here as well, and the text ends with the parable of the prodigal son without telling the reader about the ultimate fate of Malte. It simply breaks off with the laconic note (not included in the English translation by Stephen Mitchell): "End of the notebooks." It is as if they were given to us by some anonymous editor. The traditional Bildungsroman had a telos. The *Notebooks* do not.

Baudelaire ends his collection of miniatures on a very different note. In "The Good Dogs," a text Baudelaire himself planned as a conclusion to his collection of miniatures and in which he turns to an animal allegory,

> I sing of catastrophic dogs, of those who wander, alone, in the sinuous ravines of huge cities, and of those who tell abandoned people, with winks and witty eyes, "Take me along, and out of our two miseries perhaps we'll create a kind of happiness!" (126)

And then, remembering an "immortal feuilleton" question "Where do dogs go?" posed by a Nestor Roqueplan, he continues:

> They go about their business.
> Business meetings, love meetings. Through fog, through snow, through mud, during biting dog-days, in streaming rain, they go, they come, they trot, they slip under carriages, urged on by fleas, passion, need, or duty. Like us, they got up early in the morning, and they seek their livelihood or pursue their pleasures. (126)

It is the street and the feuilleton, rather than the dream of some new poetic creation as in Rilke, that concludes *Le Spleen de Paris*, and the urban condition is allegorized in the image of the muddied dog, the poor dog, the homeless dog, the stroller dog, the acrobat dog, the dog whose instinct, like that of the poor, of gypsies and actors, is marvelously goaded by necessity, such a good mother, true patroness of minds! (126)

Just as he took *la petite presse* and its reporting of everyday life as the model for his miniatures, Baudelaire ends with an ultimate mockery of stray dogs as "four-footed philosophers" (127) and with the banality of necessity as key ingredients of his metropolitan imaginary.

2

Kafka's *Betrachtung* in the Force Field of Photography and Film

Zeno, pressed as to whether anything is at rest, replied: yes, the flying arrow rests.

—*Diaries*, December 17, 1910

WITH KAFKA'S EARLY miniatures collected in the volume *Betrachtung* (*Meditation*), the miniature form both expands in its relation to photography and film and contracts beyond the post-romantic model of aesthetic consciousness offered by Baudelaire and Rilke. It is particularly in its coding of subjectivity and identity that Kafka's texts perform an intervention significantly different from that of his predecessors. With Kafka, the miniature enters the twentieth century.

Consensus has it that the city of Prague is central to Kafka's writing. At the same time it has been noted that with the exception of a few early texts and certain diary passages, recognizable urban sites from Prague are absent from his work as a whole. This absence points to a conscious technique of omission that moves many of Kafka's urban scenes from mimetic realism into an indeterminate space, or even into the realm of dreams. When cities such as Berlin or New York appear in the *Diaries*, they often appear in accounts of dreams.[1] Dream and urban space enter into a symptomatic relationship that we also find later in Benn and Kracauer, Benjamin and Jünger. But even as the specific locations of the urban are avoided in most of Kafka's literary texts, critics seem to agree that Prague, this *"Mütterchen mit Krallen"* (old crone with claws), is implicitly present in the stories, parables, novels, diaries, and letters, all of which are integral parts of Kafka's writing project.[2] The city in Kafka, however, does not, as has often been claimed, refer only to the imaginary of the dark and ominous old Prague, isolated from modernity and mythologized by the Prague Circle and later critics. Equally one-sided is Pavel Eisner's influential theory of Prague's triple ghetto that presumably determined Kafka's work.[3] Kafka's Prague is rather a typically modernizing city with its lights and shadows; its bustling street traffic and modern bureaucracies; its loneliness, coldness, and alienation; its ecstasies and terror. At the same time, metropolitan dynamism appears more muted in Kafka than, say, in Kracauer, Döblin, or Keun, not to speak of the Italian futurists who developed their urban imaginary in words and images simultaneously with Kafka. Invariably, street scenes quickly give way to internal spaces—rooms in apartments, sparely lit corridors, dusty attics, and other enclosures that trigger the haunting and ghostly effects of Kafka's writing. Though smaller and more provincial than the typical European metropolis, Kafka's Prague must nevertheless not be seen as the radical other of Vienna, Berlin, or Paris but as a modern city in its own right that radiated deeply into urban developments in Central Europe.

It is precisely the omission of local markers that makes Kafka's urban imaginary comparable to that generated by the modernist metropolis in the other writers of urban miniatures. This structure of an absent presence in the literary articulation of metropolitan life is a common feature in early modernism that tried to uncouple itself from the mimetic prerogatives of the various nineteenth-century realist and naturalist aesthetics. It also stayed clear of the kind of aestheticist prose à la Joris-Karl Huysmans or Octave Mirbeau that created artificial paradises as a protective shield against urban chaos and tumult.[4] Just as in Benjamin's account the urban masses of Haussmannian Paris functioned as "an agitated veil" through which Baudelaire saw the metropolis, with the "amorphous crowd" a "hidden figure" imprinted on Baudelaire's creativity, Kafka looked at Prague through an equally invisible technological veil of photography and film that allowed him to create a highly mediated imaginary of modern city life and experience without providing mimetic descriptions of his native city itself.[5] Comparing Kafka's urban imaginary to Baudelaire and Benjamin, one can perhaps say that if the geometric figure central to Baudelaire's Paris was the straight line of the Haussmannian boulevard and the labyrinth was Benjamin's central metaphor, Kafka's Prague in a literal and metaphorical sense is represented by an enclosing circle, the old ring around the center of Prague where Kafka spent most of his life. Enclosure, even claustrophobia, is more characteristic of Kafka's urban spaces than any celebration of movement and dynamism of street life. His Hebrew teacher Friedrich Thieberger reports a conversation in which Kafka said, referring to the Altstädter Ring, "In this small circle my whole life is enclosed."[6] The enclosing circle with its center and periphery can indeed serve as a metaphor for Kafka's life and work, but the metaphor loses its comforting allure in a late entry of January 23, 1922, in the *Diaries:*

> A feeling of fretfulness again. From what did it arise? . . . It was as if I, like everyone else, had been given a point from which to prolong the radius of a circle, and had then, like everyone else, to describe my perfect circle around this point. Instead, I was forever starting my radius only constantly to be forced at once to break it off. (Examples: piano, violin, languages, Germanics, anti-Zionism, Zionism, Hebrew, gardening, carpentering, writing, marriage attempts, an apartment of my own.) The center of my imaginary circle bristles with the beginnings of radii, there is no room left for a new attempt; no room means old age and weak nerves, and never to make another attempt means the end.[7]

Given the permanent "fretfulness" (*Unruhe*) of modern life, there is no comforting completion of the beautiful circle. Certainly the level of abstraction from recognizable urban sites in Prague and from singular narratively defined urban scenes is more pronounced in Kafka than in Baudelaire's or even Rilke's Paris texts. As a result, only very few critics have focused on the nature of Kafka's urban imaginary in any significant detail.[8] And when they have, they have focused thematically on appearances of urban space such as the tenements, the courts, suffocating corridors, and the cathedral in works such as *The Trial* or they discussed *America/Der Verschollene*, Kafka's first novel, which imagines New York via a popular travel book by Arthur Holitscher and distorts the few recognizable sites it mentions beyond recognition: the statue of Liberty holding up a sword, the Brooklyn bridge connecting New York with Boston. By contrast, in my reading of Kafka's very first book publication, *Betrachtung* (1912/1913), I will not explore which urban and social spaces he sees and renders in his writing but how he sees them and how perception itself is coded in terms of the relationship to photography and film.

Early on, it was Brecht, author of a magnificent *Lesebuch für Städtebewohner* and of one of the best ever city plays, *In the Jungle of Cities*, who despite his critical, sometimes scathing views of Kafka succinctly pointed to the nature of Kafka's urban imaginary. In Walter Benjamin's diary entries from the summer of 1934 (August 31) we read:

> What it [*The Trial*] conveys above all else, he [Brecht] thinks, is a dread of the unending and irresistible growth of great cities. . . . Such cities are an expression of the boundless maze of indirect relationships, complex mutual dependencies and compartmentations [*sic*] into which human beings are forced by modern forms of living.[9]

Visible urban space becomes social space in which the maze of indirect and shifting relationships and complex dependencies inevitably creates blurred vision, blind spots, and invisibilities. This surely is a perceptive take on Kafka, clearly preferable to the later, often vague and mystifying consensus that the city of Prague with its ghetto is central to Kafka's writing.[10] Only in his very first text, "Description of a Struggle," does a plethora of recognizable sites from Prague appear, such as the Karlsbrücke across the Moldau, the Laurenziberg, the Ferdinandstrasse, the Franzensquai, the Schützeninsel, the Mühlenturm, the Karlsbrücke, the Karlsgasse, the Kreuzherrenplatz, and the Seminarkirche. Already in the miniatures of *Betrachtung* (1912/13), however, all such concrete references are retracted. Instead, *Betrachtung* focuses on urban life as the space of indirect relationships and mutual dependencies in which people and spaces remain anonymous, and it does so from several shifting angles of vision. In contrast to Baudelaire, whose miniatures conjure up singular events in city life observed by an always highly self-conscious narrator, Kafka's miniatures are characterized by an iterative structure of repetitive actions and encounters marked by a depersonalized form of narration. The individual observed instance is crossed by the statistical average.[11] The miniatures making up *Betrachtung* are key texts for any discussion of the changing place of the individual in city life in Kafka's early work. Reading them closely permits me to read Kafka's urban imagination as pivotal to that broader context of the urban miniature that reaches from Baudelaire via Hofmannsthal and Rilke to Kracauer, Benjamin, Jünger, and Musil. At the same time, it will also mark the distance that separates Kafka from the urban imaginaries generated by Paris, Berlin, and Vienna.

Like Baudelaire's *Spleen de Paris* and those later miniature collections, *Betrachtung*, too, has a journalistic prequel, even though Kafka's short texts were not written or intended explicitly for the feuilleton, as Baudelaire's, Musil's or Kracauer's were. Eight pieces of this collection of eighteen miniatures were first published in the ambitious, though short-lived, literary magazine *Hyperion* in 1908, and another grouping of five was published in the Prague paper *Bohemia* in 1910.[12] Later supplemented, partially retitled, and carefully arranged, these texts made it into Kafka's first reluctantly published book, which appeared with Rowohlt in late 1912 with an imprint date of 1913. This collection of miniatures has often been dismissed by scholars as an unsatisfactory and artistically irrelevant forerunner to the later "mature" works that began to emerge only with the legendary breakthrough of "The Judgment" in 1912. This negative view has been slow to change in recent decades, and close readings of *Betrachtung* are still few and far between.[13] As Kafka research follows predominantly the one-author approach, there have been no attempts to read *Betrachtung* as part of a broader development of metropolitan literature.[14]

In my observations on this early text, I will side with Robert Musil, who, despite offering some criticism, carefully praised the work in a

1914 review and attested to the author's "great artistic self-control."[15] As other critics did at the time, he compared Kafka's texts to Robert Walser's urban feuilleton pieces. For me, however, Walser's miniatures are really closer to that other tradition of the urban sketch or tableau—more descriptive, impressionist, ekphrastic than Kafka's. I read *Betrachtung* as a pivotal contribution to the trajectory of the metropolitan miniature—an experiment in urban writing that is conceptually ambitious and literarily daring in ways that transcend those more mimetic sketches of urban scenes as they were also prevalent in Austria in Peter Altenberg's feuilleton pieces.[16] With his parables and aphorisms, Kafka is of course known as a major practitioner of the small form, and the texts collected in *Betrachtung*, opaque as they seem at first sight, demonstrate Kafka's willed and self-conscious departure from the longer realist narrative of story, novella, and novel and from the impressionist urban feuilleton sketch. This departure appears here, as it were, *in statu nascendi*, at a time when he was experimenting in vain with several potential novel beginnings. It is a departure always plagued by self-doubt but inevitably triggered by the transformations of urban life, the metamorphosis of subjectivity, and the battle of literature with new media of communication.[17] And here it is especially the highly mediated relation of writing to the visual media, photography, and silent film that links these texts with the later development of the urban miniature in Kracauer, Benjamin, and Musil.[18]

We know from recent research that Kafka was obsessed with both cinema and photography throughout his life. Yet just as the city appears only indirectly via the narrator's perception of impersonal urban social relations in *Betrachtung*, photography and film are never explicitly mentioned in these early texts. It is a second significant structure of absence we need to acknowledge as we consider how precisely these visual media impacted Kafka's early writing.[19] Photographs will play a significant narrative role only in later texts by Kafka, for example in *America*, *The Metamorphosis*, and *The Castle*, but here it is the structure of photographic and cinematic seeing that implicitly shapes the texts collected in *Betrachtung*.[20]

What interested him was not so much the content of these new media but the ways they changed modes of perceiving and looking at the world as image.[21] It is striking that the themes of motion and its cessation, standstill and its sudden disruption are paramount in these miniatures. And it doesn't take much to relate those structuring devices to the two visual media shaping new modes of perception Kafka attempted to mediate literarily: motion corresponds to film and standstill to photography. Urban life obviously contains both. Photography in its early days focused necessarily on portraiture and other still subjects. By 1900, however, it had become, together with silent film, a major public medium exploring the city and creating new urban imaginaries of local and faraway places. We know that Kafka saw many of these early short silent films, which typically captured salient urban scenes. It is the very structure of seeing and looking in the city embodied in film and photography, respectively, that Kafka translated directly into his urban miniatures. As with the other writers discussed in this book, Kafka's writing of miniatures must therefore be read as a response to the challenge the new visual media and new urban realities posed to literary representation.[22] But since direct references to either medium remain invisible in *Betrachtung*, I will first draw on some more explicit passages on film and photography in Kafka's autobiographic writings, his letters and diaries, the correspondence, and in some uncompleted fragments that, here as elsewhere, functioned as Kafka's writing laboratory. I will also draw on accounts of his views by some of his contemporaries and on pertinent observations by Frankfurt School theorists who wrote miniatures themselves. I hope that this somewhat circuitous route will make visible the technological veil through which Kafka saw metropolitan life and translated it in the miniatures of *Betrachtung*.

Kafka on Film and Photography

For a long time, there has been talk about images in Kafka, but the amorphous metaphoricity of this discourse rarely helped elucidate the specific interaction between writing and visual media in Kafka's texts. For the trajectory of the metropolitan miniature after Kafka it is highly significant that three of its later practitioners, Kracauer, Benjamin, and Adorno, all acknowledged the media dimension of Kafka's writing, which has only recently become a center of scholarly attention.[23] Kracauer concluded his seminal essay on photography with a reference to the structural affinity of film and Kafka's writing. Like Kafka, he took film and photography to be closely related rather than simply successive stages of technological developments. Benjamin, in turn, saw Chaplin and silent film as key to the interpretation of Kafka, and in his Kafka essay he identified motion pictures and the phonograph as sources of urban alienation from others and from the self:

> The invention of motion pictures and the phonograph came in an age of maximum alienation of men from one another, of unpredictably intervening relationships which have become their only ones. Experiments have proved that a man does not recognize his own gait on film or his own voice on the phonograph. The situation of the subject in such experiments is Kafka's situation.[24]

Benjamin also made a photograph of the young Kafka a central topic not only in his Kafka essay, but in the "Little History of Photography."[25] Finally Adorno, in a 1934 letter to Benjamin, described Kafka's novels as "the last and disappearing texts connecting us to silent film," while at the same time suggesting that Kafka

> represents a photograph of our earthly life from the perspective of a redeemed life, one which merely reveals the latter as an edge of black cloth, whereas the terrifyingly distanced optics of the photographic image is none other than that of the obliquely angled camera itself.[26]

Here, as elsewhere, Adorno, too, links Kafka's texts substantively to film and photography. Even more important, however, Kafka as writer shared the same kind of complex stance toward the new media that was later articulated in more systematic and theoretical fashion by the three critical theorists, especially Kracauer and Benjamin: the mix of fascination and critique of the visual technologies, their political promise and simultaneous threat to memory, the pressures and challenges they represented to writing and to conceptual thought. Kafka was never a theorist of the media, but he acknowledged in his writing that literature had to respond to changing patterns of perception and subjectivity in new urban and technological contexts if writing was to maintain its pertinence to modern life. This insight into the historically changing relationship between script and image, writing and visual representation, words and pictures of course was an insight that not only came to be a central tenet of the modernist arts in general but also shaped much of Critical Theory in the interwar years and beyond. If Proust was one of the literary touchstones of Critical Theory's modernism, Kafka most certainly was the other one.

While it is commonly acknowledged that descriptions of perception in Kafka oscillate between the extremes of fast motion and standstill, the inherent link to film and photography has not been sufficiently explored. The cessation of motion is typically associated in his texts with fatigue and distraction of the human subject, while acceleration and ceaseless motion appear prominently in Kafka's repeated focus on traffic (*Verkehr*) in great cities, which, in its urban, social, economic, and sexual connotations plays such a central role in *America* and in "The Judgment."[27] Motion and its sudden arrest, however, are already central aspects of the texts of *Betrachtung* and are generally pervasive in early Kafka. Paradigmatic for this constellation of extreme movement and its cessation is the first sentence of the *Diaries*: "The spectators go rigid when the train goes past."[28] This is clearly a reference to the apocryphal story that the first audience of the Lumière Brothers' silent film *L'Arrivée d'un train à la gare de La Ciotat* jumped from their seats and fled the train rushing toward them on the screen.[29] Whether or not Kafka actually saw the Lumière Brothers' film version—and there were many other similar ones he might have seen at the time—is irrelevant for my argument. More important is the fact that Kafka reverses the fabled storyline: his spectators do not jump up from their seats to rush away in fear; instead they freeze. The reaction to the frontally approaching train on the screen is a body in deadlock. Whether the spectator flees or freezes, somatic tactility and shock as effects of the illusion on the screen is present in both reactions, which together testify to the power of the moving image in its early years. The effect of tactility and embodied vision is key to Kafka's writing and his understanding of the new media.

Film and city traffic are coupled with sexuality in another telling passage in "Die erste lange Eisenbahnfahrt (Prag-Zürich)" [The First Long Railroad Journey (Prague-Zurich)], from 1911, part of a narrative co-production with Max Brod to be entitled *Richard and Samuel* that has remained fragmentary.[30] The account of the train ride revolves around the relation of two male friends to a young woman in their compartment, and it is full of erotic allusions. During a prolonged stop in Munich, the two men take the reluctant young woman on an erotically suggestive nighttime taxi ride. While Samuel clearly has sexual intentions, the other one, Richard (presumably Kafka) is uncomfortable with his friend's behavior, feeling reminded of a film, *Die weisse Sklavin* (The white slave), in which a woman arriving at a train station is kidnapped and shoved into an automobile in an apparent sex trade operation.[31] It is especially the sound of the tires that reminds him of the film: "*Die Pneumatics rauschen auf dem nassen Asphalt wie der Apparat im Kinematographen. Wieder diese 'weisse Sklavin'*" (The whoosh of the tires on the wet asphalt sounds like the apparatus in the cinema. Again this "white slave").[32] Richard, the narrator, feels estranged from reality, as if he were in a film. Since nothing even close to a sexual enslavement happens—the young woman simply continues her travels alone—the intrusion of the film memory serves to mark the distance between imagination and reality. Film to Kafka is anything but a gauge of real life. It rather distorts reality, given the unnatural absence of sound and the effect of the sped-up motion of gestures and human bodies in the projection of early silent film. But it is precisely such distortion that is of interest to Kafka, since it breaks through customary perception and unmoors a presumably natural vision. There are no further reflections on film in this fragment, but railroad travel, city traffic, sexuality, and film form a dense cluster of associations and images that here, as elsewhere in Kafka, mark the tensions and overdeterminations of urban life.

Many of Kafka's critical thoughts about visual technologies are reported in Janouch's *Conversations with Kafka*, a text based on conversations late in Kafka's life that is not considered by scholars as all too reliable. And yet Janouch's account accords with the recent research on Kafka's relationship to visual media. According to Janouch, Kafka said that the characters in "The Stoker" are "images, only images," rather than, as Janouch had suggested, "full of life."[33] At the same time Kafka distanced himself from the mimetic and visible dimension of photography when compared to literature:

> One photographs things in order to get them out of one's mind. My stories are a kind of closing one's eyes. (31)

And the cinema seems to fare even worse. He called it a marvelous toy, and then continued:

> But I cannot bear it, because perhaps I'm too "optical" by nature. I am an Eye-man. But the cinema disturbs one's vision. The speed of the movements and the rapid change of images force men to look continually from one to another. Sight does not master the pictures, it is the pictures which master one's sight. They flood one's consciousness. The cinema involves putting the eye into uniform, when before it was naked. . . . Films are iron shutters. (160)

This statement recalls Kracauer's comment in his photography essay that the flood of photographic images in the media sweeps away the dams of memory. Kracauer, too, emphasized the homogenizing and disciplining dimension of cinema in the silent age that subsequent film critics saw as even more pronounced in Hollywood film narrative after the invention of sound. Kafka's image also evokes Adorno's attitude toward the movies that Alexander Kluge once summed up with the sentence: "I love to go to the cinema; the only thing that bothers me is the image on the screen."[34]

But then Kafka's seemingly contradictory statements privileging vision and the eye and yet criticizing photography and film are made of the same cloth. When Janouch discovered Kafka's drawings and showed interest in them, Kafka dismissed them as mere doodles but then talked about his passion for drawing:

> I always wanted to be able to draw. I wanted to see, and to hold fast what was seen. That was my passion. . . . My drawings are not pictures, but private ideograms. (35)

As in Rilke, there is an intense focus on learning how to see. Holding fast what is seen is the project of Kafka's early texts. But it is a holding fast in writing, not in drawing or any other visual medium. At stake is the difference between writing and image making. The *Bildlichkeit* (pictureness) of Kafka's miniatures and stories is a different one than that of either film or photography. But it recognizes that *"Bild"* as both image and picture can simply no longer be grasped by reference to metaphor, drawing, or painting alone.

Yet another visual technology of the nineteenth century, already obsolete in Kafka's time, comes into play in a diary entry from 1911 in which Kafka discusses the visual entertainment of the stereoscopic Kaiserpanorama and its relationship to the cinema:

> The pictures are more alive than in the cinema because they offer the eye all the repose of reality. The cinema communicates the restlessness of its motion to the things pictured in it; the repose of the gaze would seem to be more important. . . . Why can't they combine the cinema and stereoscope in this way?[35]

It is the dialectic of repose and restlessness (*Ruhe* and *Unruhe*) that can be had neither by film nor by photography alone. No seeing of a film is ever without the restlessness of the moving frames; repose of the gaze is guaranteed only in the confrontation with a photograph. But what about writing? Perhaps it can combine both repose and restlessness in the act of reading that is propelled along the axis of the text but can pause and rest or get stalled at any moment, zeroing in on a sentence, a motif, a word, precisely the kind of reading Kafka's texts demand and that film and even the Kaiserpanorama prevent. In contrast to the viewer of the film, here the reader seems to be in control, but then the nature of Kafka's texts challenges that illusion of control. Adorno had it right when he said:

> Each sentence is literal and each signifies. The two moments are not merged, as the symbol would have it, but yawn apart and out of the abyss between them blinds the glaring ray of fascination.[36]

I read the abyss as that which separates the repose of literal fixation
from the restlessness of the always frustrated attempts to interpret.
Kafka's texts, Adorno argues, thoroughly disturb the relationship between text and reader:

> His texts are designed not to sustain a constant distance between
> themselves and their victim but rather to agitate his feelings to
> a point where he fears that the narrative will shoot towards him
> like a locomotive in a three-dimensional film.[37]

Here the texts themselves are likened to the shock effect of the on-
coming train of early cinema. Adorno erases the temporal difference
between that legendary early film practice and the more recent 3D
technique, but it is significant to the extent that 3D film implies genuine stereoscopic vision that was technically available to early cinema
around 1900 but for economic reasons was not commercially exploited
at that time. The problem with two-dimensional film in general is
not just the restlessness of its motion but the lack of the kind of real
depth perspective and of the visceral illusion of tactility that the stereoscope offers in addition to the repose of the gaze. The screen in
the cinema is as flat as the photograph; both lack a key dimension of
the real, always embodied gaze in urban space that is physiologically
three dimensional and never separate from tactility, or, for that matter,
from smell and hearing. Indeed, the juxtaposition of motion and motionless depth-perspectival vision may not be a bad way to describe
Kafka's goal in his early texts. After all, only stereoscopic vision maintains the tactility and bodily affect that any vision is confronted with
in urban space. But it is a tactility mediated through the apparatus
of the stereoscope that remaps the tactile within the optical and thus
is anything but natural. Kafka's question is: How can literature achieve
a similar effect? The Kaiserpanorama offers stereoscopic effects in
arrest, in standstill followed by shocklike jerky motion from one
image to the next, as Benjamin has described it in *Berlin Childhood
around 1900*. Thus, the look at two identical photographs through
the two apertures for the eyes at the Kaiserpanorama is not at all like
the natural look of a subject moving in urban space. In this stereoscopic vision, the viewer is in a still position and the urban scene or

the landscape appears as frozen, like a theater prop, but it offers a perspective of depth that accentuates the gap between proximity and distance. The absence of any natural peripheral vision combined with added coloring of the images makes the images of the Kaiserpanorama look uncanny and artificial. Against the restlessness of motion in film and city life, this kind of stereoscopic image satisfies the desire for a slowing down of the gaze that is itself produced by the multidimensional acceleration of modern city life. Speedup and slowing down, acceleration and the concomitant physiologically inevitable deceleration are the two sides of the same coin, and they can be linked to the late-nineteenth-century scientific obsession with distraction and attention.[38] Kafka reproduces either acceleration or deceleration in the very structure of sentences and their rhythmic sequencing, thus speeding up or slowing down the reader in the reception of the text.

Kafka's Looks

The very title *Betrachtung*, which can be translated as meditation or observation in the sense of looking attentively, points to the dimension of repose in these urban miniatures. Deceleration always seems more important in Kafka than acceleration. We know that Kafka was upset when the editor of the Prague paper *Bohemia* used the plural form of *Betrachtungen* as a headline for the five miniatures published there in 1910.[39] Indeed, it is key that the whole text is one meditation on urban life that is encapsulated in small bursts of text, that give us either stereoscopic stills or short silent films, as it were, but silent films in language, which render unconnected snippets of urban life not unlike the cinema of attractions in its early days.[40] The distortions of natural movement in silent film are matched by unexpected observations on abrupt movements in the texts or the manipulation of figure and ground, proximity and distance, through which Kafka creates his dreamlike images. An unreliable perspectival seeing is displayed in these miniatures, and "*Betrachtung*," translated as "meditation," points to the fact that its fragments reflect on the very nature of perspective. The verb "*betrachten*" also means to look at in a concentrated and attentive fashion, but only as one looks at a photograph, never at film. Film does not allow for the repose of "*Betrachtung*," so Kafka saw it pulling the spectator instead into the restlessness of motion and creating ultimately a feeling of numbing and emptiness. While distraction can be an alternate form of attentiveness produced by urban life, what is at stake for Kafka here is the utterly negative dimension of distraction in film viewing that he, in contrast to Kracauer or Benjamin, sees merely as deadening and destructive. A typical diary report on a visit to the cinema ends with the lament:

> Am entirely empty and insensible, the passing tram has more living feeling.[41]

What he perceived as a lack at the center of the experience of cinematic motion, I take it, made him desire that imagined combination of cinematic and stereoscopic vision that only later 3D film would provide and that his texts, if Adorno is right, mimic in the medium of language.

The link between *Betrachtung* and photography, on the other hand, becomes visible in yet another telling biographic detail. Carolin Duttlinger has succinctly analyzed the role of photographs as fetishes in the correspondence between Kafka and Felice Bauer. As he sent Felice photos of himself, time and again he emphasized the distortions of his gaze caused by the flash, and he deemed all photographic portraits deficient, if not uncanny. That more is at stake here than simple vanity becomes clear in the following passage from the letter that accompanied one such photo:

> Don't worry, dearest, I don't look like that, this picture doesn't count, it isn't one you should carry around with you, I'll send you a better one soon. In reality I'm at least twice as beautiful as in this picture. If that's not enough for you, dearest, then things are indeed serious. In that case, what am I to do? However, you do have a fairly true picture of me; *the way I look in the little book* [Meditation] *is how I really look*, at least that's how I looked a short while ago.[42]

The miniatures of *Betrachtung*, Kafka suggests, appear as a more adequate personal portrait than photography as a medium might be able to achieve. Just as photography with its repose of the gaze is privileged over film, writing here is privileged over photography, but the visual dimension of portraiture is nevertheless ascribed to writing. At the same time, the strong representational claim is shot through with temporal flux in the final comment "at least that's how I looked a short while ago"; that is, when he wrote the texts that make up the collection. The passage even suggests a thematic coherence of *Betrachtung* that the seemingly banal advertising copy on the cover referred to as theme of the book: "life and longing of a young man of our days."[43] Indeed, there still are traces of the nineteenth-century novel here, though in minimalized and residual form only. Thus, the overall movement of the text—and, though perhaps hard to detect, there is a narrative arc here, as in other miniature collections—leads from country to city, from childhood to adulthood, from an adventurous and agitated beginning in "Children on a Country Road" to the static and claustrophobic internal space of "Unhappiness" at the end. Only the first two and the last miniature are told in the epic past tense; all the others, including the pivotal narrative of the onerous and always worried life of "The Tradesman" as a paradigmatic urban subject, are told in the present tense. But how are we to read the separate pieces of *Betrachtung*, which give us a variety of urban scenes as a portrait of the artist as a young man, as the letter to Felice suggests? Kafka himself did not come from the country to the city, even if his ancestors did. He was never a tradesman like his father, who dealt in clothing accessories and fancy goods (*Galanteriewaren*). On the other hand, he led the unhappy life of a bachelor, as it is conjured up in "Bachelor's Ill Luck," and the conclusion with "Unhappiness" and the protagonist's frustrating encounter with his ghostly childhood *Doppelgänger* certainly maps on to Kafka's own tortured life. But perhaps the portrait is to be found less in the storyline suggested by these four more narrative-oriented pieces than in the other seemingly disjointed fragments that all stand on their own.

Actually the English translation of *"so sehe ich auch wirklich aus"* as "the way I look in the little book [*Meditation*] is how I really look" can give us a clue. In contrast to the German *"aussehen,"* the English verb "look" carries the second meaning of active looking. The

English translation thus makes something apparent that is only hinted at in the German original. The dimension of portraiture, self-portraiture, then would be contained in the way he looks at the world. Indeed, the act of looking, so central in the correspondence with Felice about photographs, is the key to reading those miniatures that give us scenes of looking at people or events in the city. Looking is the overriding theme of *Betrachtung*. But it is a kind of looking that has gone through the school of cinematic movement, as we know it from silent film, and the freezing of the frame in photography or the single frame of a film.

Lichtblicke

Kafka once described these texts as "glimpses into endless perplexities, and one has to come very close to see anything at all."[44] The German word *Lichtblicke* (glimpses), with its connotation of suddenness, phonetically suggests the photographic *Blitzlicht*, the flash that lights up and isolates a scene. One such *Lichtblick* from up close shapes the center paragraph of "On the Tram" ("Der Fahrgast"), the miniature that best embodies the static dimension of *Betrachtung*, significantly though in the context of a moving tram. Thus, we first get a reflection on the narrator's insecure, even unjustifiable position in the world as related to his position on the tram's end platform:

> I stand on the end platform of the tram and am completely unsure of my footing in this world, in this town, in my family.[45]

As the German title "Der Fahrgast" (the passenger) suggests, the narrator is merely a guest in this environment, if not in the world.[46] There is an insecurity in the relation between figure and ground reminiscent of the "seasickness on land" that had already appeared in "Description of a Struggle" (33). In the second of this three-paragraph miniature, however, the narrator offers us a detailed close-up, an intense erotically loaded look at a girl standing next to him on the tram's platform. It is an almost tactile, invasive gaze rather than a distanced description, and, significantly, any peripheral vision from the moving tram toward the cityscape is excluded:

She is as distinct to me as if I had run my hands over her. She is dressed in black, the pleats of her skirt hang almost still, her blouse is tight and has a collar of white fine-meshed lace, her left hand is braced flat against the side of the tram, the umbrella in her right hand rests on the second top step. She has a lot of brown hair and stray little tendrils on the right temple. Her small ear is close-set, but since I am near her I can see the whole ridge of the whorl of her right ear and the shadow at the root of it. (388-389)

It reads as if to confirm what Kracauer said later in another context: "It is the fashion details that hold the gaze tight."[47] But in this passage, fashion detail merges with detail of the girl's body. There is no eye contact between the narrator and the girl dressed all in black. His gaze, voyeuristic as it is, registers with stereoscopically tactile precision. The absence of peripheral vision, for example, the movement of the tram, marks the affinity to the stereoscope. In contrast to descriptive passages in the nineteenth-century novel, the gaze here is completely decontextualized. Since there is no other context given to this chance urban encounter (Is she in mourning? Is she perhaps even a young widow?), the extreme precision of perception produces a sense of unreality in the reader. In its extended, almost frozen temporality, it is very different from that sudden flash encounter of the Baudelairean flâneur with a woman on the boulevard in "A une passante," which Benjamin interpreted as love at last sight. If at first the girl in her firm contours and seemingly stable positioning on the platform seems to function like a counterimage to the insecure and destabilized narrator, the final paragraph pulls back from embodied look and its description, reflecting instead on the lack of self-conscious perception in the young woman herself:

At that point I asked myself: How is it that she is not amazed at herself, that she keeps her lips closed and makes no such remark? (389)

Presumably she makes no such remark because she is not afflicted by the narrator's insecurities of perception. She is presented as object, not subject, of vision. While the look at the girl is static, at best in slow motion, we must recall that it all happens on a moving tram approaching a stop where the girl will get off. Again stillness and movement are juxtaposed in an effect, Kafka would suggest, neither film nor photography (in contrast to literature) could ever achieve alone by themselves.

In what follows I will first discuss the few longer miniatures that contain elements of traditional narrative, anchoring the collection, and contrast them with the extremely short two parables located toward the collection's end. I will then analyze some of the other miniatures under the rubric of kaleidoscopic viewing before concluding with some reflections on social space and the voided subject.

Narrative Residues versus Parable Form

The extreme decontextualization of the look in "On the Tram" can be said to function as the narrative equivalent of stereoscopic vision in the Kaiserpanorama, but it is framed as taking place on an urban vehicle in motion, thus combining the photographic with the cinematic. There are, however, those few other miniatures that serve as support for the residual diegetic structure of the book, offering the reader some minimum of narrative orientation. But even here the storyline is heavily disturbed by an obsessive oscillation between restlessness and repose of vision. Narrative causality and development are ignored, space and time jumbled. In "Children on a Country Road," the lead text of *Betrachtung*, we first find the narrator in the evening sitting still on a swing in his parents' garden listening to the traffic of wagons and people moving past on the country road outside. As his gaze follows a swarm of birds that "flew up as if in showers" (379), he has a sensation of falling, and in an attack of weakness he begins to sway, holding on to the ropes of the swing. Relations of up and down are set in motion. As other children come to pick him up after his supper, he joins in their frenzied running along the country road and through the fields, but then, exhausted and fatigued, he is tempted to rest, even sleep, in the roadside ditch, only finally to join the race again that increasingly seems to overcome the laws of gravity:

We ran bunched more closely together, many of us linked hands, one's head could not be held high enough, for now the way was downhill. Someone whooped an Indian war cry, our legs galloped us as never before, the wind lifted our hips as we sprang. Nothing could have checked us; we were in such full stride that even in overtaking others we could fold our arms and look quietly around us. (381)

Restlessness and repose seem to be united in this phantasmagoria of acceleration that has its later companion piece in the phantasmagoric ride on horseback in "The Wish to Be a Red Indian." But even before the climax of this evening scene, the simultaneity of fatigue and rest in the roadside ditch in one moment and racing along with the children in another clearly has dreamlike qualities. It resembles a filmic montage of two separate scenes not linked by narrative continuity as we know it from early silent film. As the group of running children finally comes to a sudden arrest on the bridge over the brook, their gaze turns to the passing of a lit-up train in the distance and the children begin to sing a popular catch (*Gassenhauer*) that they sing "much faster than the train was going" (381). Again stoppage and movement are juxtaposed in closest proximity in this passage.

The overall movement of narrative voice in "Children on a Country Road" is highly unstable, as the shifting of pronouns indicates. The narrator's "I," first isolated in the garden, turns into the frenzy of a collective "*wir*" and an impersonal and sleepy "*man*," only to end in another separation from the group of country children as the narrator escapes from his village to the distant city in the south, where people are said never to sleep because they never get tired. And they never get tired, the text continues, because they are fools. What appears here as a bizarre country legend about city people who never sleep has of course become a standard trope of the modernist metropolis as the city that never sleeps! Sleep, of course, would be repose—hard to achieve in the traffic of urban life where we find the anonymous protagonist in the second miniature, threatened by the confidence trickster (*Bauernfänger*), eager to cheat the new arrival from the countryside.

In "The Tradesman," the third of those four longer and more narratively structured miniatures, the first person narrator is no longer
the child on the country road but is a small clothes retailer in the
city. Now told in present tense rather than in the epic past voice, the
narrator shares his worries about the future of his business with his
reader. The use of the present tense, while still focusing on a single
situation, also suggests something habitual, an average occurrence,
iterative and not unique as it would be were it to be told in the past
tense. The tradesman complains about the unreliability of seasonal
fashions and his dependence on strangers who owe him money, whose
affairs are a mystery to him, and who might draw him into their ill
luck (*Unglück*).[48] The opaqueness of urban business relations and the
instability of the money economy make his life miserable. As his business closes in the evening and he returns home, exhausted but worried about facing hours of inactivity and loneliness, he speaks of the
"never-ending demands" of his business (385), to which he is subject. It is as if his business were a person and he that person's ser-
vant. This first part of the miniature gives us the tradesman's pained
reflection on the insecurities and invisible dependencies of business
life in the city. By contrast, the second part gives us a rapid succes-
sion of his perceptions and visual phantasmagorias, as the text now
describes him alone, enclosed in the elevator of his apartment building,
another technical vehicle of then-recent vintage that carries him upward to his apartment. Movement upward counters movement downward, as in "Children on a Country Road." The natural image of the
birds flying upward there is translated here into the upward movement of the city lift, while "the staircase flows down past the opaque
glass panes like running water" (386). The transition from country
to city is again taken up here in the imagery. Instead of natural flight
we have enclosure in a technical urban contraption. Alone in the lift
and gazing at himself in a narrow mirror, he speaks to his image, suggesting that his thoughts should take imaginary flight toward the village in the countryside or even to a city such as Paris. In a splitting
of thought from vision, he then admonishes a plural "you" (his
thoughts? himself? his imaginary listeners?) to enjoy looking out of
the window and to observe several disconnected urban scenes he conjures up—imaginary scenes that appear as a series of silent cinematic

shorts in the head, projected phantasmatically as he looks at his reflection in the lift's mirror. Opaque as it is, in this passage the miniature moves from reflection—that is, thought—in its first part to what might be conceived as a liberation of thought toward vision. It all ends with an ominous reference to a man being robbed and the image of the police on horses, "riding away already in couples, slowly around the corners, at full speed across the squares" (386). Interpretation, as so often in Kafka, runs aground. But with the image of the police on horseback we again have a coupling of slowness and speed. Then the lift stops at his floor and the tradesman sends it back down, rings the doorbell, and greets the maid who is opening the door. The shift from imaginary and phantasmatic urban scenes to the banal reality of coming home couldn't be more sudden and deadpan, leaving the reader befuddled by the concrete literalness of the text and its refusal of any satisfactory interpretation.

In the final miniature, "Unhappiness," which closes the narrative frame of the collection, the aching worries of "The Tradesman" have led to a life that, already in the first sentence, is now said to be unbearable. We find the narrator frantically running along the narrow strip of carpet in his room "as on a racetrack," frightened at the sight of the lit-up alley outside his window and screaming aloud as in the depth of the room he suddenly detects his image in a mirror. It's as if the scream conjures up a ghostly child that "blew in from the pitch-dark corridor" (390–391). This visitor, a not-unexpected ghost of his former self, challenges the inquisitive narrator to calm down and be quiet. Motion is stilled to the point that a conversation can begin. This conversation is usually taken to be a soliloquy of the adult narrator with his former childlike self. A claustrophobic psychic space inside a dark city apartment has replaced the open natural space of the lead miniature on the country road. But the conversation soon reaches a dead end. As the child ghost asks "Do you know how I'll be later on?," the narrator answers in a mode of self-denial: "I don't know anything" (393), a statement that ends the encounter with the ghost of his former self. Like the narrator on the tram's platform, he is completely unsure of his footing in the world. As he then is about to go out, he gets entangled in a conversation about ghosts with a tenant from his floor. The real fear of ghosts, he suggests, is "a fear

of what caused the apparition. And that fear doesn't go away. I have
it fairly powerfully inside me now" (394). Remembrance of childhood,
it seems, only serves to emphasize present life as unbearable, as a dead
end. Not surprisingly, then, and unlike the narrator in "The Sudden
Walk," he does not go out for a walk but stays at home and goes to
bed. "Unhappiness" marks the end of a trajectory in loneliness and
alienation. As life has become unbearable and even the encounter with
his former child self gives no reprieve, the only thing he can do is
sleep. Clearly this is a serious failure in the city where people never
sleep because they never tire. But it is also a reprieve from the pressures of urban life that, as the villagers say, turns people into fools.

Narratologically speaking, these four longer narrative miniatures
are at one end of a spectrum of writing strategies whose other end is
found in two extremely short parables tellingly placed just before the
final miniature "Unhappiness." As if offering a summary of the main
theme of *Betrachtung* and highlighting its parabolic perceptual core,
extreme movement and complete stillness are opposed to each other
in these two juxtaposed famous parables. They are also the shortest
texts in the whole collection. The frantic motion of the illusory ride
on horseback in "The Wish to Be a Red Indian" (the title should read
"The Wish to Become a Red Indian") captures the reader in the accelerating rhythm of its breathless phrasing that follows upon the
beginning of the initial sentence: "If one were only an Indian." The
imaginary ride on horseback is ultimately as unreal as the total stillness and alleged immovability of "The Trees" lying in the snow, a
parable about the illusion of human life being "firmly wedded to the
ground" (382). Everything here is illusion or deception, unreality for
sure. The photolike stillness of the image is made to function as counterpoint to the frantic ride in "The Wish to Be a Red Indian," which
points to a boy's fantasy and to the western as a genre of early cinema
that Kafka surely experienced. The uncertainty and unsettledness
of any perception, still or moving, is the theme of both miniatures,
just before the reader moves to the final miniature to encounter the
ghostly appearance of the child. The creation of ghostly images itself, we should remember, was one of the many wonders of early
photography and film.[49] What one sees in either parable is illusory
and, like any object in film or photography, never physically present:

thus, the fleeting disappearances of something never there to begin with in the first parable and the multiple delusions of stability and rootedness in the second. Cinema and photography are unreliable desiring machines based on deception, and Kafka understood this perfectly well as he took up the new media's dual challenge in his writing, his very own desiring machine that was to guarantee the impossible coherence of his life, the elusive completion of the circle.

The Kaleidoscope of the Other Miniatures

Given the experimental and exploratory nature of Kafka's first book, there is a clear difference in writing strategy between the two very short parables and the few longer miniatures that frame the collection narratively. It is not just a question of length but of the difference between a residually narrative and a cryptic parabolic form. What both have in common, however, is their resistance to transparent meaning and interpretation. The twelve other miniatures are somewhere in between in length, but in them, too, Kafka stages a variety of perspectives in order to circumscribe each miniature's field of perception. There are texts that compel the reader's compassion and identification with the ill-luck of a bachelor ("Bachelor's Ill Luck"), similar perhaps to the effect of Baudelaire's old acrobat. There is a fictive dialogue between a narrator and a young woman ("Rejection"), the narrator's reflections on women's fashion ("Clothes") and on victory and defeat at the races ("Reflections for Gentlemen-Jockeys"), and always the alternation between reflection, on the one hand, and either sensual, concretely observed movement or the cessation of motion, on the other. If you add to that a phantasmatic dimension as it appears in "The Tradesman" and "Excursion to the Mountains," you have a spectrum of writing modes that cannot be put into any generic vise such as parable, aphorism, or prose poem. The multiplicity of perspectives and forms of attentiveness as manifested in differing writing modes is reminiscent of Baudelaire, except that in Kafka the status of the narrating and narrated subject has undergone a fundamental shift from an intensely performed individual role playing toward anonymity.

It is the uncertainty of perception that makes the use of different writing strategies necessary for Kafka. The ultimately frustrated

attempt to overcome perceptual instability, introduced into the world
by new visual technologies and the metropolitan condition, becomes
Kafka's literary obsession. This requires multiple experiments.
Minute descriptions of acts and modes of seeing in various urban
scenes and in decontextualizing close-up characterize many (if not
most) of the other short miniatures. The question then becomes how
these disconnected short texts relate to the four longer and more narrative miniatures that I have tentatively described as providing a weak
narrative anchor for the collection. There is no stable narrative or-
dering system that would govern the sequence of miniatures. While
the first and last miniature provide a loose frame, the texts in between seem more like the images of a kaleidoscope that gives us ever
new and unrelated views at every turn. Scenes observed are not di-
egetically linked with each other, but, in analogy to the colored fragments in the kaleidoscope, they have certain words, phrases, rhythms
in common that allow the reader to slide from one to the next. Examples would be the words *"Entschluss"* and *"entschliessen"* that link
"The Sudden Walk" with "Resolutions" or the word *"glatt"* which
links the ending of "The Wish to Be a Red Indian" with the second
sentence of "The Trees." Most of this subtle cross-referencing of
words is unfortunately lost in translation. The word *Gespenst*, "ghost,"
appears several times, marking phantasmagoric residue. Riders, red
Indians, and horses pop up in unrelated and very different contexts,
pointing to the western in early cinema. Rise and fall, movements
upward and movements downward are repeatedly related. And the
unstable play with personal pronouns"I" and"you" for the impersonal
German *"man"* and"we" runs through several of the miniatures. Pronouns and sentence structures such as "when" and "often when" are
used to typify observations. Such grammatical strategies take out the
particular and move toward the generic and the habitual, a process
that accompanies the voiding of individuality both on the side of the
observer and that of the observed. But despite such linkages and rep-
etitions, which themselves point to the nonparticularity or average-
ness of the particular that is characteristic of the anonymity of urban
life, each miniature claims a space of its own. Kafka's insistence on
a large typeface and wide margins in the 1912 Rowohlt publication
guaranteed that each text had lots of empty space around it, which

stretched what now fits on thirty-two pages in the current critical edition to ninety pages. The visual appearance of the text was indeed important to Kafka, though it should not lead one to see these miniatures as prose poems. As in the case of Baudelaire, there is very little in them that is lyrical in any sense of the word. At the same time, the layout in an unusually large typeface in that first edition seems to suggest that the text be read slowly and carefully. It is as if the reader were looking at the text in close-up and as if the close-up slowed down narrative progress itself.

As I have argued throughout, looking is the explicit theme of these miniatures. Spatial closeness of a kind different from "On the Tram" is at stake in "Absent-Minded Window-Gazing" ("distracted" would be a better translation for the German "*zerstreut*" in the title). Here an impersonal narrator (*"man"*) looks at an afternoon street scene from the firm position at a window. In contrast to "On the Tram," the subject of vision is on firm footing, though distracted at his window, while the observed street scene is in motion. The main theme is the light of the sinking sun on a spring day that had begun clouded and grey:

> The sun is already setting, but down below you see it lighting up the face of the little girl who strolls along looking about her, and at the same time you see her eclipsed by the shadow of the man behind overtaking her.
>
> And then the man has passed by and the little girl's face is quite bright. (387)

Neither the girl nor the man, who might appear threatening to the girl in some other context, are given any features. It's like a short silent film scene alternating between light and shadow on a human face. And given the distraction of the impersonal narrator, there is no final reflection on the observed scene, as there was in "On the Tram." At the same time, the focus on the girl's face moving from light to shadow and back to light seems to suggest a stereoscopic tactile dimension combined with motion. It's as if Kafka's idea of combining stereoscopic vision with cinematic motion were realized here in language. But in contrast to the numbing effects of film, which troubled Kafka, distraction here is just another form of attentiveness.

We find a similar fixed position of the narrator in "The Street Window." But here the act of looking out to the street leads to a different result. The narrator, who leads a solitary life, like the bachelor in "Bachelor's Ill Luck," is without much desire as he goes to his windowsill to look out, but once there he is not able to maintain his distanced and distracted position. Despite his

> not wanting to look out and having thrown his head up a little, even then the horses below will draw him down into their train of wagons and tumult, and so at last into the human harmony. (384)

He is ripped (the German verb here is the violent *"reissen"*) from the stillness of his windowsill into an urban tumult that is strangely seen as moving him toward human harmony. Harmony (*"Eintracht"*) and being ripped down into a tumult convey completely contradictory and irreconcilable affects, as only dream would do. With its lack of commentary or contextualization, this reference to harmony cannot be read simply as an ironic denial of any possibility of human community. It could also mean that urban tumult is now the only form of community there is, one that threatens the individual and his interior space. At any rate, the windowsill is no longer a safe place of observation, as it once was in E. T. A. Hoffmann's late story "Des Vetters Eckfenster" ("My Cousin's Corner Window") or, for that matter, in perspectival Renaissance painting. Similar to the coding of space in many of the miniatures treated in this book, Kafka consistently violates the boundary between inner and outer space. In all of his explorations of the act of seeing in an urban environment, there lurks danger, the uncanny, the surreal. Not what one sees, but how one sees is crucial: intensely tactile and concentrated in "On the Tram"; distracted and from a distance in "Absent-Minded Window-Gazing"; fatigued, but with a minimal desire for some attachment to others in "The Street Window"; and avoiding any such attachment in "Passers-By."

Social Space and the Voiding of the Subject

Intimately tied to these different modes of perception, attentiveness, and distraction is the emptying out of the bourgeois subject with its interiority and sense of agency. Urban space is seen primarily as social space in Kafka. The city destabilizes human relations and endangers the subject's sense of self, but the result in Kafka is neither a sense of loss, as in Rilke's *The Notebooks of Malte Laurids Brigge* nor the protective buildup of a blasé attitude, as in Simmel's analysis in "The Metropolis and Mental Life," let alone the defensive armoring of a threatened subjectivity in what Hal Foster has described as Ernst Jünger's "*armor fou.*"[50] Instead there is something deadpan and simultaneously haunting and uncanny in these highly unstable urban encounters rendered in *Betrachtung.* We realize that we are no longer reading about existential individuals and their stories in the traditional sense. Rather, we are facing figures of a statistical average, men and women of an urban crowd, voided and nameless subjects. Edgar Allan Poe's story "The Man of the Crowd" reminds us that in the early days of metropolitan massification, this new constitution of subjectivity had something frightful and spooky about it. Thus, it is not surprising that there always is something strange, haunted, or uncanny about Kafka's anonymous narrators, however voided their subjectivity may appear to be. This is clearly so in the more narrative miniatures "The Tradesman" and "Unhappiness," but it is also the case in the following two miniatures, which push urban anonymity to an extreme.

The voided subject and the fundamental lack of individualized particularity in the anonymity of the big city finds its most stunning rendition in the sentence structure of "The Sudden Walk" and its complementary miniature, "Resolutions." This is another pairing that moves from stagnation and lethargy to quick and decisive movement in the former and from energetic movement back to a state of making oneself "an inert mass" (398) in the latter.[51] In these two miniatures the grammatical denial of self in the use of the impersonal German "*man*" is coupled with the theme of total standstill. Stagnation becomes first restlessness and then sudden motion in "The Sudden Walk." Motion, in "Resolutions," reverts back to "*letzte grabmässige*

Ruhe," a "final grave-like repose."[52] "The Sudden Walk" is structured as a hypothetical and impersonal when-then sequence of sentences. The text begins with nine "when" clauses describing a generic subject at home in the evening, after dinner, ready to settle down and go to sleep but suddenly caught by a fit of restlessness and eager to go out for a walk despite the lateness of the hour and the bad weather outside. When all of this happens to "you" (*"man"*)

> then for that evening you have completely got away from your family, which fades into insubtantiality, while you yourself, a firm, boldly drawn black figure, slapping yourself on the thigh, grow to your true stature. (398)

As the multiple "when" clauses first give a sense of slowness, stagnation, repetitiveness, which actually corresponds to the content of the scene described, they begin to speed up with the mention of restlessness and then erupt in the one single "then" clause that seems to ascertain the autonomy of a self finally liberated into motion from the stagnation and repetitive routines of family life at home. Except that the image of liberation is comically distorted by the fact that the newly active self slaps himself on the thigh as if he were a horse or a figure in a slapstick film marking some triumph. The second and final *"man"* -sentence paragraph of the miniature, however, which refers to the late-night *Spaziergänger* going "to look up a friend to see how he is getting on," seems rather a deadpan banality after the preceding comment about the subject's "true stature." There certainly is no "heightening" effect, as the text proclaims, but a petering out after the climax of the one-and-a-half-page-long first paragraph.[53]

This ending almost anticipates the futility of resolutions, subject of the following miniature. In "Resolutions," the energetic and consciously willed lifting oneself "out of a miserable mood" fails, and movement is already pushed back into stagnation in the second of four brief paragraphs:

> Yet even if I manage that [lifting himself out of a miserable mood], one single slip, and a slip cannot be avoided, will stop the whole process, easy and painful alike, and I will have to shrink back into my own circle again. (398)

In contrast to "The Sudden Walk," the narrator here uses the first-person singular. At the end nothing remains of the Münchhausen-like resolution but a futile minimal gesture that seems to seal the fate of the subject in the move from"I" to the impersonal phrasing in the final sentence:

> A characteristic movement in such a condition is to run your
> little finger along your eyebrows. (398)

It is again a gesture of resignation, almost lethargy, with which this miniature, too, comes to its end.

The move from "*ich*" to "*man*," from subjective will to objective determinations and statistical anonymity, is also present in the focus on clothes in several other miniatures. Time and again in *Betrachtung*, the unreadability and anonymity of social relations in the city is linked to fashion and to clothes as the opaque surface of human bodies. The narrator in his key instantiation in "The Tradesman" is described as the owner of a small clothing retail store deeply troubled by the impenetrability of financial relations and the circulation of commodities. Close-ups of women's clothes appear in three miniatures grouped together: "On the Tram," "Clothes," and "Rejection." But none of those texts allows the reader to glean anything much about the young women wearing those clothes. They are presented as anything but individuals: respectively, "a girl," "girls," "a pretty girl." It is as if their individuality had disappeared behind the surface of their clothes, which are described in close-up. As clothes come to be "worn out, puffy, dusty," they become a metaphor for the faces of their wearers when they look at themselves in the mirror, having returned home exhausted from some party in the evening (383). The faces themselves, markers of individuality, are said with subtle double entendre to be "*kaum mehr tragbar*," "hardly wearable any longer" (383) or, in the second German meaning, hardly acceptable any longer. Clearly we are no longer in the Baudelairean world of celebrating the erotic dynamics of female fashion. Eros and fashion are tampered here by futility, the transitoriness of youth, even mortality. Mark Anderson has cogently described clothes as a haunting master trope in early Kafka. In contrast to realist or naturalist writing, clothes no longer serve as legible signs of a protagonist's social standing and historical background, but as an impenetrable, opaque, "unreadable" surface—as a visual stimulus for the observer's imagination, but one which is not grounded in an external, social reality.[54]

Certainly not grounded in the social reality of the earlier nineteenth-century novel, but grounded instead in the new reality of statistical averages, of the men and women in the mass. Here it appears as if capitalism itself, elsewhere bound to the frantic pace of always-changing fashions, has come to a dead end, as if what Benjamin called the "sexual appeal of the inorganic"—that is, fashion—has been deadened, "no longer wearable." The visible world locks its meaning behind surface appearances such as clothes, but they become worn out like the individual physiognomies of those who wear them. The organic merges with the inorganic in clear opposition to all the vitalist celebrations of life around 1900. The visible surface is all there is, and it is photography and film that reduce the modern urban dweller to two-dimensional surface appearance.

This historical shift in subjectivity, analyzed in different ways by sociologists such as Georg Simmel and Adolphe Quételet, is determined less by psychological reasons, as it was the case with Rilke's Malte, than by the overwhelmingly leveling experience of the big city and the disorientations of the sense of reality that entered the world with the new technological image media, Herman Hollerith's electrical tabulating machine, mechanically generated motion, and the labyrinth of bureaucratic structures in the Austrian Empire. It is almost as if the animation of things, so popular in the cinema of attractions, had carried over into the human world, which itself becomes thinglike and reified.[55] If the existential expression of subjectivity, overstimulated and already disoriented by the experience of metropolitan space and time, was central to the metropolitan miniature before Kafka, differently in Baudelaire and Rilke, its reduction and ultimately its retraction gives Kafka's miniatures a pivotal position in the trajectory of this mode of writing. There is no loss of self in reverie, nor is there its painful reassertion in the experience of the spleen. What Kafka does have in common with Baudelaire is the retraction of realistic urban detail, the replacement of individualizing narrative by a focus on perception and a deployment of differing visual perspectives. In a certain way, spleen as self-alienation has become total in Kafka, a condition of life in a world in which all perception is illusory and stability of self and world is no longer to be had. Indeed, it has become so total that it isn't even experienced as spleen any longer, since its counterpart, the Baudelairean ideal, is no longer to be found. All that is left is an uncanny threat that nestles in the abstractions and anonymity of metropolitan life.

If standstill and motion, the freeze frame and the "unending stream" not of *Verkehr* but of celluloid (to cite and distort the last sentence of "The Judgment") are the two modes of perception in the city mediated by photography and film, then prose is the medium that in turn mediates those two modes of perception in its slow motion forward, drawing both on moments of standstill and quickening motion in the miniature's very sentence structure. Without the reflection on photography and film, Kafka's writing of the city would not have been possible. Whereas Baudelaire and Rilke simply rejected photography, Kafka absorbed its very structures into the literary text. Ultimately *Betrachtung* is my first example in this book of what I call remediation in reverse: a literary project energized by the new image media—an old medium that remediates the new ones rather than the other way around, thus insisting on the *Eigensinn* of the literary in its imaginative absorption of photography and film rather than their mimetic imitation. It is this remediation in reverse that links Kafka's miniatures at the deepest level to those of the interwar writers who are treated in subsequent chapters of this book.

3

Benn in Occupied Brussels:
The Rönne Novellas

We come from the giant cities—in the metropolis,
only there, do the muses exult and lament.

   —Gottfried Benn, *Doppelleben*

WITH GOTTFRIED BENN, an expressionist poet who hit
the literary scene in 1912, we encounter a writing practice very different from the miniatures of Kafka or those written by poets such as Baudelaire and Rilke. His miniatures are fewer in number, and each one is longer than those by most other miniaturists. This may explain their traditional, though problematic, designation as novellas. They also do not share the focus on photography and film that is so central to most of the other miniaturists discussed in this book. But their imaginary is fundamentally visual, with prose exploding into new hallucinatory and delirious realms drawing on the language of medicine, physiological science, and the mortal, sexualized body in a hostile urban environment. Written during World War I, they share the formative experience of the Great War with later miniaturists such as Jünger and Musil.

In August 1914, German troops invaded and occupied Belgium at the start of a war many German intellectuals and writers welcomed with enthusiasm. Not so Gottfried Benn, a young medical doctor

trained at the Militärärztliche Akademie für Medizin in Berlin and
known at the time only as author of that slim but clinically shocking
collection of poetry entitled *Morgue* (1912). Benn came to be stationed
in Brussels as a medical officer in charge of the St. Gilles hospital
for prostitutes run by nuns. Venereal infection of German officers
and soldiers was a major concern for the German army at the time
of occupation, and thus sanitary controls of prostitution had become
mandatory. Military personnel newly arriving from Germany were
greeted by a large placard at the Brussels train station warning them
of the health risks of the metropolis.[1] No need to specify: the metropolis as site of sexualization, debauchery, and risky encounters was
a common trope in early twentieth-century anti-urban discourse,
even without war and occupation. Benn remained stationed behind
the front in Brussels for the next three years, charged with super-
vising the sexual hygiene of Belgian prostitutes. It was in Brussels
that the Berlin doctor wrote his Rönne novellas, some of the most
opaque and hermetic texts in the tradition of the modernist miniature and a unique achievement in Benn's oeuvre. Due to Benn's later
mystifying comments about their origins, these texts, with few exceptions, have often been misread, if they were read closely at all.[2]
Never translated in their entirety into English, they have certainly
never been placed in the context of the larger trajectory of the metropolitan miniature.

   In contrast to Ernst Jünger, who celebrated the new type of hardened front soldier in *Storm of Steel*, his famous diary of the technological trench warfare of World War I, Benn never saw much action,
except for the brief attack and quick conquest of Antwerp behind the
battlefront in early October of 1914, in which he participated as a
Sanitätsoffizier (medical officer) and was decorated with a second-class
Iron Cross. Several years later, he described his life in the *Etappe*,
the back area behind the battle front, in an epilogue to his *Gesammelte Schriften* of 1922:

   I was serving as the doctor of a hospital for prostitutes, an
   isolated job. I lived in a billeted house of eleven rooms alone
   except for my assistant, had little work to do, could go out on
   leave, wasn't tied to anything or anyone, barely understood the

language. I walked the streets, strange people; an odd spring,
three incomparable months—what was the battle of the Yser
that informed everyone's daily reality?—life went on in a sphere
of silence and disorientation, I was living on the periphery where
existence falls and the self begins. I often think back on those
weeks: they were life, they won't come back again, everything
else was bust. (*P&A*, 251)[3]

After rather unsatisfactory professional beginnings in Berlin's
Charité and the Charlottenburg-Westend Hospital and a failed attempt to escape deadening everyday routines by serving as a doctor
on an ocean liner on its way to New York—a city that did not leave
much of a trace either in his work or in his mind—Benn remembered
Brussels during wartime occupation as something like an internal
state of exception. The weeks of spring he mentions are those of 1916,
the time when he wrote several of the texts that became known as
the Rönne Novellen after the name of their protagonist, Dr. Werff
Rönne, a fictional figure shot through with autobiographic matter
of Benn's prewar and war experiences. What Benn describes here as
life clearly was life as literature, literature as life. The reality of occupied Brussels looked different, when Benn himself rendered it years
later in his clinically distanced description of the execution in October 1915 of Miss Edith Cavell as enemy spy, which he witnessed as
the doctor on duty. In this text of 1928, written for a Berlin newspaper to counter the melodramatic heroization of Edith Cavell in a
British film, Benn coldly justified the execution of this courageous
British resistance figure. In the course of his description, we get a
better sense of what things were really like in occupied Brussels, especially in the early months of the war:

> The situation of the German occupation army was extremely
> difficult during the first months. . . . The cannons thundered
> from the Flemish front, now closer, now further off. At any mo-
> ment the Allies could return, every hour on the edge of a
> razor. . . . A weak, passive German battalion held the capital, the
> beautiful, impulsive, turbulent and hate-filled capital; at its
> summit stood the mayor who operated brazenly against the or-

ders of the German commandant; the population was absolutely open in its enmity. . . . Ambushes at night, the streets dangerous, soldiers forbidden to go out alone, attacks on the railway, tunnels blown up, assaults on the troop transports; thus a precarious situation, the war undecided.[4]

He topped off this mise-en-scène by highlighting the role of women in the organization that smuggled Belgian men and displaced British and French soldiers across the Belgian-Dutch border so that they could join or rejoin the fighting troops: "The women were aflame; they were the heads of the organization."[5]

Even if one considers that Benn staged this account to justify the military execution of Edith Cavell, a cause célèbre both during and after the war that the Allies often cited as testimony to the brutality of the German occupation, the distance from the earlier, almost idyllic description of his life as a member of the occupying forces is amply clear. It is not a question of Benn contradicting himself: the two descriptions pertain not just to different moments in the course of the war but to different registers of experience—that of the poet in his isolation and loneliness writing his Rönne texts and that of the Prussian officer on duty. Benn never ceased to be both. After World War II and his notorious yet short-lived public approval of the new Nazi state in 1933 to 1934, he gave a name to it: *Doppelleben* (Double Life).[6]

Gottfried Benn is not known as a writer of urban literature per se. He has never written urban miniatures in the vein of Kracauer, Benjamin, or even Kafka. And yet his early poetry, especially the collection *Morgue*, with its hard-edged images of death, prostitution, and anatomic dismemberment and decay, all of it tinged with touches of melancholy, is undeniably marked by the experience of Berlin, where Benn worked as pathologist in a West End hospital in 1912–1913 and where he was to run his never-very-lucrative practice that treated dermatological conditions and venereal disease in later decades. Experience here refers simply to the live environment of the young pathologist and medical doctor in the urban morgue, the cancer ward, and the night cafés, all of which are transformed in powerful and disturbing poetic imagery, opening up a whole new sphere of language and experience to poetry. But it was in his prose miniatures, later called Rönne Novellen, written between 1914 and 1916 and first published separately during the war in 1916, that those typical phenomena of modern urban experience we associate with the turn of the century came to a head: neurasthenia and fatigue, the crisis of consciousness and of language, the attempt to protect the self against urban stimuli à la Simmel, the disintegration of reality accompanied by a dissociation of subjectivity, the sexualization of urban space, the collapse of the ego, and hallucinatory imaginaries as we know them from Rilke's *Malte Laurids Brigge* and untold other urban texts from the same period. Helmut Lethen has described the hothouse atmosphere of wartime Brussels as the "eye of the hurricane" and a "terminal moraine of nervosity."[7] Benn deployed the occupied city as a space for projections: projections of male sexual fantasies, regression to nature as artifice, encounters with social decay, flights of the imagination, and, strangely, Mediterranean orientalisms. Given Benn's obsession with what he later called *"das Südwort"* (the southern word), he saw Brussels and Paris as southern cities, realms of a non-Germanic alternative culture predicated on sensual form and poetic language. Urban sites conjured up in these texts include broad avenues and narrow alleys, the café, the officers' club, the brothel, the slaughterhouse, poor neighborhoods, a clinic for prostitutes, parks, a palm garden, the cinema, but as in Kafka, there is never any thick description of the urban environment. The *Morellenviertel*, Brussels' old Jewish quarter, is mentioned once, but this is the only naming of a recognizable space in Brussels. Rather than ekphrastic description, it is always the mise-en-scène of the protagonist's psychic state in relation to his bodily conditions that is at stake.

The Rönne miniatures, problematically called "novellas" by editors and critics, as if they belonged to that genre so dominant in nineteenth-century German, Austrian, and Swiss literatures, consist of five texts, each between five and ten pages long and held together by their common protagonist, Dr. Werff Rönne.[8] The first four, entitled *Gehirne* (Brains; written in 1914, first published in *Die weissen Blätter* 2, Heft 2, February 1915, an expressionist magazine edited by René Schickele), *Die Eroberung* (The conquest; first published in *Die weissen Blätter* 2, Heft 8, August 1915), *Die Reise* (The trip; first published in *Die weissen Blätter* 3, Heft 6, June 1916), *Der Geburtstag* (*The Birthday*; first published in *Gehirne. Novellen* [Leipzig: K. Wolff, 1916], 1917 in the colophon; the only one ever translated into English), can be taken as sequence of frames focusing on exemplary moments of Rönne's life, while the fifth *Die Insel* (The island; first published in *Die weissen Blätter* 3, Heft 12, Dec. 1916; republished in the 1916 collection entitled *Gehirne*) was excluded by Benn himself from the body of this work in subsequent editions.[9]

These four texts also stand out in that they are longer than other miniatures treated in this book, except for a few in Musil's *Posthumous Papers*. If the traditional novella was characterized by what Goethe called the *unerhörte Begebenheit* (an unheard-of event) that demanded the narrative *Wendepunkt* (peripeteia) of the action, then these texts would better be described as anti-novellas. Time and again the possibility of a peripeteia is frustrated. In all four texts, Rönne attempts to overcome his pervasive crisis of fatigue, his failures of communication, his nervous exhaustion, and his sexual desire by breaking out of his life's routines toward the unknown, but he fails in every single attempt. The narrator is not sparing in his sometimes subtle, sometimes strident and satirical critique of Rönne's failures. Rönne is not successful as a temporary replacement of a clinic's director in *Gehirne;* he fails in his attempt to conquer the occupied city and is instead himself conquered in sexual intercourse "by a foreign roundness" in *Die Eroberung;* he fails to undertake a planned trip to Antwerp in *Die Reise;* and he ends up with an orientalist sexual fantasy preceding anticipations of a potential new beginning, which can also be read as an anticipation of death, in *Der Geburtstag.* There is never a singular event (*Begebenheit*), but a sequence of states of mind and body characterized by repetition and frustration.[10] Every attempt at uplift is inevitably followed by a precipitous drop. One could call it Benn's version of the Baudelairean spleen, except that Rönne only aims at but never reaches the epiphany of the poetic ideal. If there is anything unheard of (*unerhört*), then it would be Benn's language, its metonymic procedure of heaping association upon association, of dissolving stable relationships of time and space, of creating word compounds from a web of motifs including the south, the azure, the sun, the sea, and the dissolution of rational common sense perception with phrases such as the forehead turning to dust or the temple's soaring flight (*Zerstäubungen der Stirne; Entschweifungen der Schläfe*). Perhaps it is the experience of dissolution of space, time, and ego itself that is the unheard-of event in Benn's expressionist modernism, but then this is rendered as a slow and drawn out, repetitive process rather than a single event, as the traditional novella would require. Here as in Baudelaire, the modernist miniature rewrites and transforms a traditional genre dominant in nineteenth-century realism. Only in that sense does the designation of these texts as novellas have any purchase.

All too often the figure of Rönne has been read as a stand-in for Benn himself. Benn actually nurtured that view when in his autobiographic text of 1934, *Lebensweg eines Intellektualisten* (Life of an intellectualist), he quoted extensively from the Rönne texts to conjure up that earlier phase of his life. Indeed, there can be no question that Rönne contains autobiographic elements, but these texts do not represent a kind of auto-psychotherapy of their author.[11] Apart from the fact that in light of Benn's later developments one would have to acknowledge therapeutic failure, such a reductive reading misses the consistent doubling of narrator and figure, manifest in the shifts from first- to third-person narration, from inner monologue to free indirect speech and to a distanced critique of Rönne's behavior and delusions. It also misses the objectifying satirical dimension that makes these texts a much broader clinical and social case study that, one might say, brings them into the vicinity of the novella's exemplarity after all, though in a different mode. Rönne, then, must be read not as Benn's self-portrait, but as an exemplary case for a certain kind of mind-body constellation in early twentieth-century modernity that also generated texts such as Rilke's *Notebooks of Malte Laurids Brigge* and Carl Einstein's *Bebuquin*. The question to what extent Benn himself might embody this constellation is certainly less interesting than an analysis of the ways this constellation is literarily articulated. If one wanted to put Benn himself back into the texts, as it were, one would have to say that his shadow falls on Rönne but even more so on the narrator who constructs the protagonist.

The focus of the narrative is not only Rönne but also the social and institutional framework of medical science in general in wartime conditions. It is no coincidence that Benn places Rönne among doctors, nurses, and psychiatrists who represent the norms of bourgeois society and the medical scientific establishment of his day. They are painted throughout with a satirical brush, if not always by Rönne himself then certainly by the narrator. Rönne may well be an imaginary projection of some dimensions of Benn's own makeup, but he is also a kind of historical and epistemological prototype that Benn would later call the phenotype. We must acknowledge the strong critique to which the Rönne figure is subjected by the narrator throughout. Both Rönne and his narrator must be read as fictional figures embodying a fundamental opposition not only to the chauvinist militarist bragging and posturing in the officers' mess but also to the whole of bourgeois progressivist and scientific culture of the nineteenth century. This social critique of the conjuncture of science, war, and bourgeois morality may be more radically articulated in some of Benn's dramatic sketches written at the same time ("Etappe" of 1915 is a stunning example of antiwar literature), but it also marks the horizon of the Rönne texts. It is this subtle political dimension inherent in these texts that separates this deliberately anti-political author from any *haut goût* of *l'art pour l'art* and brings him close to Baudelaire's *Spleen de Paris*. Not surprisingly, some critics have linked the Rönne prose to the tradition of French symbolist prose poetry. And yet Adorno was right to claim that Benn's early prose, "his wild and grand beginnings," has little to do with *poésie pure*.[12] Indeed, there is no record of a deeper engagement on Benn's part with the post-Baudelairean tradition of French poetry, as one can find it in the work of Stefan George or Rilke. What is true, however, is that Benn from early on posited the world of art and the language of poetry as a kind of counterworld confronting the world of history, politics, and progress that he saw, not unlike the late Benjamin, as a sequence of unmitigated debasement and decay, if not catastrophes. The difference between Benn and Benjamin, these two towering modernists, of course, lay in the way they conceptualized an alternative to a modernity gone awry.

It was not until the 1920s that Benn began to toy with the high modernist idea of a pure medium, which he fully embraced again later in the 1950s. In the late Weimar Republic and especially after his

deluded and short-lived affirmation of the Nazi state, Benn became
the whipping boy of the intellectual left whose privileging of committed political art he rejected publicly, just as Musil did at the 1935
Paris Congress on the Defense of Culture. Musil, of course, never
compromised with Nazi ideology and was forced to emigrate after
the *Anschluss*, while Benn emigrated, as he put it, into the German
army.[13] In the post-fascist 1950s, after he had emerged from his kind
of inner emigration, he became a key figure in West German poetry debates, where his embrace of the high modernist position served
as a useful strategy to make the public forget his entanglements with
the Nazis. It could gain traction at the time because it functioned
well as a weapon in the cultural cold war between modernism and
socialist realism. True to his Protestant Prussian upbringing, Benn
wrote in a brief autobiographic text of 1956: "In the beginning was
the word, not chatter. And in the end it will not be propaganda, but
again the word."[14] The Rönne texts are all about "the word," especially *"das Südwort,"* (the Southern word) and yet they are anything
but *pure:* they are contaminated through and through, contaminated
by urban experience, sexual fantasies, neurasthenia, and Rönne's
(though not Benn's) failure to break through to some other language,
as Rilke's Malte desired. It is Benn's poetic success predicated on
Rönne's failures that gives these texts their compelling power.

The urban crisis phenomena Rönne experiences are rather typical of what is usually described as the crisis of modernity in a key
period of metropolitan development in Europe. But identifying
Rönne's experiences does not really tell us much about these texts
themselves, their language, their emplotment, their structure. Crisis
discourse always seems to pertain within modernism, but the various crises of modernity produced arguably different texts in Baudelaire, Hofmannsthal, Rilke, Kafka, Benn, Aragon, Benjamin, and
Musil. If there is a loss of individuation, *Ich-Verfall* (decay of the ego)
and *Ent-Ichung* (deindividualization) in Rönne, then it does not come
couched in the anti-urban discourse of mourned ego loss, decadence,
and nostalgia, as it does in Hofmannsthal and even in Rilke. Instead
it comes in a cold analytical register that is closer to science than to
poetry. It is precisely this loss of individuation that generates new
possibilities for poetic language in Benn. To account for such literary

differences among the modernists, which is one of this book's goals, is more rewarding than repeating the mantras of crisis discourse.

First we should note that unlike Kafka, Musil, and Kracauer, Benn comes to the modernist miniature as a poet like Rilke and Baudelaire, with whom he shares, despite all other considerable differences, the focus on a poetic subjectivity that has become highly self-reflexive, suffers radical mood swings, lashes out satirically, and is in danger of imploding. As in Baudelaire, the city functions as a medium of excitement and sensual stimulation, present in its effects on poetic consciousness rather than becoming visible in concrete descriptions of built space or urban life. In both Benn and Baudelaire, the language shifts abruptly between the banal and the sublime, thus striking poetic sparks out of everyday life and often disorienting the reader. At the same time, Benn's reliance on scientific and medical discourses marks the distance of his poetry and prose from both Baudelaire and Rilke, even if death and disease, asylums and hospitals appear prominently in their texts as well, though never in the clinical perspective foregrounded in Benn.

Recent discourse archeology has shown that in Benn the crisis phenomena of urban modernity are coded very consciously on the basis of the associational psychology his teacher in medical school, Theodor Ziehen, was developing at the time.[15] Ziehen, a professor at Berlin's Charité, who, at an earlier time, had treated Nietzsche in Jena, was a leading representative of a philosophically tinged psychology of associations, a scientific trend in psychiatry at the time that believed in the empirical calculability and measurability of bodily and psychic interactions.[16] In his early years, Benn was very influenced by this trend, as is reflected in several of his medical writings.[17] But in his prose he increasingly distanced himself from the teachings of Ziehen, to the point where he satirized Ziehen's associationism. And yet it is Benn's closeness to the psychiatric discourse of his time that can help us find an answer to his Brussels friend Thea Sternheim's telling question: "What explains the blossoming of his vocabulary?"[18]

Marcus Hahn's work has toppled one of the standard tropes used to describe Benn's early work. The technique of verbal association and the creation of wildly disparate word clusters and imaginary compounds of nouns deployed in Benn's poetry and prose is not an eruption of the irrational, as has so often been claimed. Instead, it results from a poetic reworking of a new scientific rationality based on advances in psychophysics and the physiology of perception. Ziehen did not see mental processes of association as failures of reason and logic; instead, he acknowledged that they possessed a deeply embedded rationality of their own that was rooted in the body. The flights of associative imagery in the Rönne texts must therefore not be read as an outbreak of irrationality but as an attempt to find a mode of articulation beyond and outside the rationality of positivist science. Benn's poetological deployment of associationism is contained in what, in a letter to Dieter Wellershoff of November 22, 1950, he called *"das Südwort."*[19] Examples are *"Mittagssturz des Lichts"* (the noonday plunge of light), *"Entschweifungen der Schläfe"* (the temple's soaring flights), and *"das Anemonenschwert"* (the anemone sword), plus all the words related to the azure of the sky, the clouds, images of flying, verbs pointing to dissolution and flow such as *"wehen"* (to waft), *"blauen"* (a neologism; to become blue), and *"rinnen"* (to flow). These words and word combinations form a fairly consistent cluster that remained key to Benn's later poetry. This language is rarely attributed directly to Rönne himself, except at the end of *Gehirne*. At the same time, associative perception is ridiculed when its technique of metonymic accumulation borders on the very scientific positivism Benn and his narrator figure are bound to reject. A good example would be the military doctors' absurd luncheon discussion of how to spice and to eat a strange tropical fruit. But it is important to note that Rönne himself indulges in that very positivism of association in his failing attempt to find stable ground in *Die Eroberung* and *Die Reise:* his compulsion to associate about the slaughteryard, his ecstasy when he moves from a Maita cigarette ad to Malta, beaches, ports in *Der Geburtstag*. Rönne's failures are similarly described with the technique of associations when he collapses in the palm garden (*Die Eroberung*) or in a park (*Die Reise*). Association is driven to a hilarious, almost slapstick extreme in *Der Geburtstag:* "the olive happened to him, the sultan's bird." Thus, it is not surprising to see that another supplemental line of research indebted to intellectual history has persuasively

shown how the associational montage technique Benn and other
writers and visual artists of the time used to create often impenetrable or barely comprehensible texts is not radically new or emphatically avant-garde in the sense of a tabula rasa breakthrough but is
prefigured in the accumulation and juxtaposition of often disconnected data and facts in positivist historiography of the nineteenth
century.[20]

Association functions critically in Benn's texts, including the various levels of satire of associational psychology itself. I would suggest that Benn's transformation of the extrinsic discourse of science
is analogous to Baudelaire's transformative uses of the modes of
writing found in *la petite presse*. Both authors use their discursive
models—journalism and science, respectively—in order to subvert
them and push them toward other, literary goals. Both authors create
something new out of preexisting discourses. The modernist dream
of a pure language, as Rilke's Malte imagines it, is revealed as a delusion. There is no safe escape route either from existing social discourses or from the fundamental structures of metaphor or metonymy, as *Der Geburtstag* especially makes clear.[21] Such findings
force us to abandon a favorite reading of the Rönne texts or of the
Morgue poems as *creatio ex nihilo*, the unconditional and unconditioned
explosion of poetic genius in verse or in prose. Benn himself of course
advanced this faulty reading (and generations of critics have repeated
it) when he later wrote about *Morgue* in *Doppelleben:*

> It was a cycle of six poems, which all came to me in the same
> hour, flung themselves up from below, were there where previ-
> ously nothing had been. When my semi-conscious state ended,
> I was empty, hungry, dizzy and climbed with difficulty out of
> the great decay. (*P&A*, 376)

And right after this passage he remembers a similar experience in
the streets of Brussels that gave rise to one of his major poems of
those years, *Karyatide*, a poem quite close in spirit and letter to the
language ecstasies in the Rönne miniatures. The point is not to question the conviction of Benn's retrospective account, however much
it may also have been a clever self-serving mise-en-scène; the point

is rather to insist on the always extant split between an experiencing authorial subject and the discourse network in which that subjectivity, knowingly or not, is embedded. But even more important, the fictional dimension of the Rönne figure is always shadowed, sometimes ironized, sometimes embraced, by an observing narrator who is as much a fictional construction as Rönne himself is. It is the shadow play between protagonist and authorial narrator, the narrative oscillations between the two that are constitutive of these texts, undermining any sense of a fixed and stable subjectivity. Another way of putting it is that the dissociation of subjectivity is not simply a negative phenomenon of alienation and loss but rather a splitting of the subject that opens up new possibilities both in writing and in experience.

As in Baudelaire or Kafka, the city itself, whether Berlin in *Morgue* or Brussels in the Rönne texts, is an absent presence in these miniatures. Given Benn's professional and poetic obsessions with death, decay, sexuality, and disease, the other even more stunning absence is the war. But then the mass slaughter in the trenches of the Yser or the Somme was far enough away and the city was teeming with luxury, entertainment, and sexual license that created a sense of unreality, given the news from the front. Years later, in the autobiographic and highly stylized text *Lebensweg eines Intellektualisten* (1934), Benn himself highlighted the importance of Brussels in rational interpretive prose:

> In war and peace, on the front lines and behind them, as officer and as doctor, between scum and nobility, psychiatric and prison cells, beds and coffins, in triumph and decay, I never came out of the trance in which this reality didn't seem to exist. I generated a kind of inner concentration, activating hidden spheres; the realm of the individual was submerged and a primordial layer arose, intoxicated, rich and ecstatic with images. Strengthening itself periodically, the year 1915/16 in Brussels was huge. That was when Rönne was created, the doctor, the flagellant of single objects, the naked vacuum of facts; the one who couldn't stand any reality, couldn't register it either, who knew only the rhythmic opening and closing of the self and the personality, the contin-

uous breaking of his inner being and who, placed before the experience of the profound, boundless, and mythically ancient al-
terity between man and world, unconditionally put his faith in
myth and its images. (*P&A*, 314)

But even this explanatory passage speaks of hidden spheres, the emergence of some ecstatic primordial layer, thus carefully hiding the scientific discourse that lies at the core of the Rönne miniatures. Benn
adequately described Rönne's sense of unreality as an "as if" existence
à la Hans Vaihinger's *Philosophy of As If* (1911). But this "as if" was
massively overdetermined. It was the "as if" of an occupier, distanced
from the local population by his uniform, his language, his function.
In the wake of Benn's own limited and highly controlled use of the
"Alkaloide," it was the "as if" of cocaine use. And it was an effect of
Benn's disgust with the mindless and pompous bantering and brag-
gadocio of his fellow officers in the officers' club—the world of chit-
chat, military machismo, banalities, whorehouse anecdotes, and emp-
tied-out language in the face of the mass death in the trenches. And
yet he does not describe this sense of unreality as deficient, as a
threatening dissociation of subjectivity, but celebrates it in the most
triumphant of terms: "I often think back on those weeks; they were
life, they won't come back again, everything else was bust" (*P&A*,
251). If we ask now how this idealized life appears in the individual
novellas, a picture very different from that later characterization
will emerge.

Gehirne (Brains)

The setting of the first novella suggests that it was not only the war
and the occupation that produced the trance of unreality. Benn already brought that with him when he was first stationed in Brussels.
The first Rönne miniature, *Gehirne*, written perhaps as early as July
1914, sets the stage for the tribulations of Dr. Rönne. The brain held
special fascination for Rönne, as it did for Benn, in its ambivalence
of being both a bodily organ of nature and the site of intellect. Even
if it had been written somewhat later and thus during Benn's time in
Brussels—the sources are not entirely clear on this[22]—the content
of the miniature clearly precedes war and occupation, as it draws in

a displaced way on Benn's work as pathologist at a Berlin hospital in 1913.

The beginning is rather traditionally narrated, analogous perhaps to the seemingly realistic beginning of Kafka's first miniature in *Betrachtung:*

> Rönne, a young physician who previously had performed many dissections, traveled in the summer of the preceding year through southern Germany to the north. (*P&A*, 19)

But as in Kafka, this "realistic" beginning is misleading. It is soon enough denied by the movement of the text. Rönne, who has worked for two years as a pathologist handling some two thousand corpses *"ohne Besinnen"* (thoughtlessly), is traveling to a sanatorium in the north, where he is to substitute for the clinic's director for a few weeks. Standing in for someone else, as it were, already undermines his sense of self-determination and agency. On the other hand, this trip pulls him out of his routines as pathologist that had exhausted him "in a curious and unexplained manner" (*P&A*, 19). The word "unexplained" suggests that more is at stake here than simply alienated routine labor as Benn had experienced it in the pathology section of Berlin's West End hospital, work that had totally exhausted him physically and psychically.[23]

Already in the second paragraph, Rönne, traveling by train, opens up to the sensuality of poetic perceptions that in turn trigger his desire to write:

> Now he was sitting in the corner of the compartment and looked ahead, into the journey: the route goes through vineyards, he recited to himself, quite flat land past scarlet fields smoldering with poppies. It's not all that hot; a streak of blue flows through the sky, moist and billowing from the riverbanks; every house leans against roses, some are completely submerged. I need to buy a book and a pencil; I want to write down as much as I can so that everything doesn't just flow past. (*P&A*, 19)

He bespeaks himself as if he were a medium, separate from the self, at any rate. Visual perceptions are expanded or condensed, distorted by reversal of common sense: scarlet fields smolder or fume (*"rauchen"* also means to smoke) with poppies, the flower that produces forget-fulness when smoked as opium. Scarlet suggests disease; the blue flowing through the sky merges with the blue mirrored in the waters below, thus dissolving spatial distance just as temporal differentiation is dissolved in the later phrasing "the roses blossomed, sweetly decapitated" (*P&A*, 22)—two subsequent phases of a rose's life pulled into one simultaneous image. Another spatial disturbance of vision with special poetic effect obtains when, unrealistically, houses seem to lean against an exuberance of roses rather than vice versa. The metonymy of wine country, poppy fields, and the river actually conjures up the major south-north railroad line in Germany that hugs the Rhine River and traverses the wine country of Nord-hessen. But such specific geographic markers can only be inti-mated, since they are absent from the text. At the end of the para-graph, Rönne intends to buy a book and a pencil to write things down "so that everything doesn't just flow past" (*P&A*, 19). In a way, this whole paragraph is already such an exercise in writing, but it is a kind of writing that seems to flow poetically rather than stabilizing the gaze via realistic description. Unlike Rilke's Malte, however, Rönne is never actually shown in the act of writing. That remains safely in the hands of his narrator, who weaves in and out of Rönne's perspective.

"Illumined by his solitude" (*P&A*, 19), Rönne takes up his tem-porary job as the director's substitute at the sanatorium. This em-phatic designation, whether attributable to Rönne himself or to the narrator, contrasts curiously with the fact that he serves merely as a substitute doctor. The sanatorium is located in a mountainous and wooded area—it suggests nature as healing, an alternative to the urban condition. But Rönne's belief in medicine's ability to heal is badly shaken as he confronts terminally ill patients. Instead, he experiences increasing paralysis when dealing with patients and nurses:

Something from up above is weakening me, I no longer have any firm ground behind my eyes. Space heaves endlessly; once it flowed in one place. Rotten is the cortex [*die Rinde*] that car-ried me. (*P&A*, 21)

The *Rinde*, short here for *Grosshirnrinde* (the cortex), is a word that means bark of a tree, that which protects the tree on its outside. But Benn has the cerebral cortex in mind, considered by scientists at the time to be the seat of what used to be called the soul and certainly the guarantor of the rational bourgeois ego. Deindividualization is at stake here, the crumbling of the ego, the disintegration of his life's temporal coherence. The self is no longer being carried, supported. It is exposed, like a tree without bark. Then one day an animal is slaughtered at the sanatorium. Significantly, Rönne's reaction is conditioned by his work as pathologist. As he passes by just as the animal's skull is cracked open, he takes the animal's brain, as if by coincidence, in his palms and bends its two halves gently apart in an almost unconscious and automatic gesture, as if to find some deeper meaning. Of course, looking into the inside of a brain like that reveals nothing but a void. At the same time, however, he experiences another hallucinatory condensation of the nonhuman: animal life, flowers, plants, earth crowd in on him:

> Rönne however walked through the gardens. It was summer. Adder tongues rocked the sky's blue, the roses blossomed, sweetly decapitated. He felt the surge of the earth: all the way to his footsoles; he felt the swelling of powers: no longer through his blood. Primarily he chose paths that lay in the shade and those with numerous benches. Often he had to rest from the brashness of the light, and he felt exposed to the breathless sky. (*P&A*, 22)

Fatigue sets in, and he becomes unable to communicate with the hospital staff. He doesn't perform his duties and has a breakdown, lying paralyzed on his back on a long chair in his room, as if dead already. The cortex may have disintegrated, but the body is still there, reduced or metamorphosed into an animal body floating in cosmic space:

> Apart from a few birds, he was the highest animal. Thus the earth carried him quietly through the ether, without tremors, past all stars. (*P&A*, 23)

Unlike Musil, Benn was not concerned with the human relationship to animals per se; instead he simply pointed to the animal nature of the human. Fatigue, neurasthenia, paralysis—the disease of the epoch preceding the Great War, much diagnosed in scientific discourse across the disciplines—is what plagues Rönne. At the end of *Gehirne*, he imagines holding his own brain in his hands and imagines what might be possible with him. Clearly he has failed in his task as deputy for the head physician. But in the final passage he breaks through to some other reality: that of words, association clusters, dissolution of gray matter into poetry, the third and most intense verbal hallucination in this text:

> What is it then with brains? I always wanted to fly up from the ravine like a bird. Now I'm living outside in the crystal. But now please clear my path, I'm gliding again—I was so tired—this walking moves on wings—with my blue anemone sword—in the noon-day plunge of light—in the ruins of the south—in the dissolving clouds—the forehead turning to dust—the temple's soaring flight. (*P&A*, 23)

Here it seems Rönne has achieved transcendence, the other side of the rational ego, in still-rational associations linked by a series of tropes central to Benn over much of his life: the desire to fly, blue anemones, the Zarathustran light of midday, the ruins of the south, the crystal as ultimate transparence. Whether or not such poetic ecstasies are achieved with drugs, such sweeping dispersals of thought (the temple as seat of thought) and language are carefully constructed throughout by the author. But they are always only temporary, never permanent. Each of the miniatures contains similar passages. In fact, they all oscillate between an imposed scientific, medical and bourgeois normality and flights of the imaginary into other psychic states—"the temple's soaring flights." It remains unclear if we are to read them as successful outbursts of poetic language or merely as a further disintegration of the linguistic material, an early version of the semiotic anarchy practiced by the Dadaists a few years later.

Die Eroberung (The conquest)

If *Gehirne* sets the stage for Rönne's fatigue, paralysis, and isolation, the second miniature, entitled *Die Eroberung*, suggests an active, even violent overcoming of such paralysis:

> Out of the paralysis of long months and unceasing displacements: I want to occupy this country, thought Rönne, and his eyes yanked in the white shimmer of the street. (*P&A*, 25)

Given Benn's participation in the conquest of Antwerp in October 1914, we might think of Antwerp here, but no, it turns out to be Brussels. Antwerp will appear only in the third miniature, *Die Reise* (The trip), as the goal of a trip that is aborted and never takes place after Rönne's paralyzing scruples have returned.

Here, however, in *Die Eroberung*, we are clearly in the context of military victory and the occupation of the Belgian capital:

> The conquest is over, he told himself; it's on firm ground. They still wear their helplessness in the colors of their hats, in ribbons, red and yellow, and small flags on their jackets. But for now we won't be driven out. On the other hand, everything that takes place does so for the first time. A foreign language. Everything is full of hate and approaches hesitantly across an abyss. I want to proceed step by step. If anywhere, I will succeed here. He stepped out; already the city was blossoming around him. (*P&A*, 25)

As Rönne gains confidence walking the boulevards, the city text is increasingly sexualized:

> He felt strengthened. He swayed across the boulevards; waves went back and forth. His step was lively, he carried the women in his folds like dust; they had lost their thrones; what was left? Small crevices and tufts of earth in the armpits. A blond woman's breathing heaved a rose back and forth. Together with the blood of her breast its scent wafted its way toward some man. (*P&A*, 25-26)

As evening falls, prostitution enters the scene:

> Lust stood openly between the soldiers and the women.
> (*P&A*, 26)

He longs for community:

> Dear city, let yourself be occupied. Give me a home. Take me
> into your community. (*P&A*, 25)

Then he drifts into a café, where he observes disassociated customers
but attributes community to them. Increasingly, the narrator's voice
is separate from Rönne's as he describes Rönne's longing to belong
as delusionary, only then to shift back into Rönne's own romanti-
cizing perspective:

> Sky around his head, he bloomed through the quiet play of the
> night. His were the small streets, for his passage, and he heard
> the echo of his steps without humiliation. He felt something un-
> locking, he rose up. (*P&A*, 27)

Then irony and banality intervene again. Rönne remembers his need
for a barber and goes to have his hair cut at a barber shop. Watching
how another customer's hair is being powdered while his own isn't,
he reflects on the different needs of dark and blond hair (his own),
giving a pretentiously inappropriate scientific explanation: light
reflex, coefficient of refraction. He goes on to pronounce on the
workings of reason:

> One must be able to relate everything that one sees to some-
> thing else, to bring it in accord with earlier experiences and
> place it in general categories—that is the way reason functions.
> (*P&A*, 28)

Increasingly, he practices Theodor Ziehen's associationism in an attempt to find rational grounds for his conquest of the city. But this
is precisely where the practice of association, which is central to the
writing of the Rönne miniatures, especially their poetic passages,

goes into a positivist overdrive and is subjected to the narrator's critique. Lest the reader be taken in by this fake rationalism of association, Rönne, seeing a sign in the streets for the slaughterhouse, immediately yields to the compulsion to comment in detail about slaughterhouses in general. From slaughter his associational train of thought then leaps to the figure of the hunter, "a strong compact figure" (P&A, 29). Imagining himself as hunter increases his self-confidence. With this potent male figure, "weathered hard and tan," we have a version of what critics have described as the armored body of a male imagination that is best represented in Weimar culture by Ernst Jünger.[24] Is it a coincidence that just as he gets caught up in pseudoscientific verbiage, he imagines such a figure? And is it a coincidence that Benn zeroes in on "slaughterhouse" with the very real slaughter going on in the trench warfare at the nearby front? Couldn't one further relate the figure of the hunter to the ways Ernst Jünger time and again described battles in the trenches as hunting down Englishmen like rabbits in the field? To ask such questions is of course itself a kind of associational reading, but both the historical context of the typical discourse in the officers' club and Benn's appropriation of an associational psychology makes it plausible. Here, as elsewhere in these miniatures, there is a logic to the associations, however disconnected they may first appear to be. In the end, not surprisingly, Rönne's attempt to subject these associations to general categories fails. In contrast to Jünger, the decorated warrior-hunter who sustained the imaginary armored body until the end of his life, Rönne's defensive armor breaks down. In an unmediated leap of narration, we hear of his child falling sick and presumably dying:

> The mythic loomed large in his life, the good and evil things, tears and blood. (P&A, 29)

This is the moment when the fantasy of conquest collapses. His human identity dissolves into a hallucination of nature, he becomes flower, "the coitus of animals." Urban space is replaced by forest, animals, and village. Critics have read the multiple instances of a merger with nature in these texts as regression and failure, but Benn's language remains ambiguous.[25] If it is regression in one register, these fantasy mergers with nature and animal life might also open up another language and an alternative experience, as we have in Kafka's and Musil's animal stories. But Rönne doesn't live up to that potentiality. The only kind of conquest Rönne now fathoms is offered by a whorehouse. In a state of vertigo he enters, encounters a pregnant woman, "sagging, heavy flesh, oozing juices from breast and body," and grabs a prostitute in an act that resembles rape (or a rape fantasy) more than a brothel's business transaction:

> He leapt onto one, broke her open, bit into her bones which were like his, ripped screams from them that sounded like his own, and expired on a hip, conquered by a foreign roundness. (*P&A*, 30)

Ironically, he who set out to conquer is being conquered. If his goal was to break out of his isolation and find community, he fails yet again. Small wonder, one is tempted to say, given the aggressive and violent approach that only reproduces male fantasies instead of questioning them.

The morning after, he walks through seedy quarters of the city toward the "palm gardens at the edge of the city":

> He, the solitary one; blue sky, silent light. Above him the white cloud: the gently capped edges, the effortless passing away. (*P&A*, 30)

Finding community as an occupier has failed, but there may be compensation in the breakthrough to the modernist locus classicus of the *paradis artificiel*—the *Palmengarten*, hothouse for nonnative trees and plants:

> I wanted to conquer a city, now a palm frond flutters above me.
> He burrowed down into the moss: at the shaft, nourished with water, my forehead, as broad as my hand, and then it begins. (*P&A*, 30)

This is as explicit a rejection of war and conquest as it gets: Resigned downward movement toward the ground, under palm fronds, close to the phallic trunk, the forehead. But what is the it that begins? Is it poetic ecstasy in union with artificial nature? Is it analogous to the poetically ecstatic ending of *Gehirne?* Or is it just another failure, a kind of escapism? If only the text would end here. But the narrator intervenes with an ironic return to the real that gives an unambiguous answer:

> Soon afterwards a bell sounded. The gardeners returned to their work; he too walked to a watering can and strewed water over the ferns, which came out of a sun where much evaporated. (*P&A*, 31)

From hunter to gardener, from city conquest to a Voltairean "*il faut cultiver notre jardin,*" the narrator's irony about Rönne's illusory project couldn't be more cutting.

Die Reise (The trip)

Irony about Rönne also pervades the third miniature, *Die Reise,* written in late 1915 or early 1916. The theme of travel is taken up again from *Gehirne,* in which the train ride to the north first triggered Rönne's fatigue and paralysis. Now the planned trip to Antwerp never even happens:

> Rönne wanted to travel to Antwerp, but how without falling apart? (*P&A*, 33)

He imagines having to justify his trip to his fellow officers at lunch. Not just tourism, he would have to assure them, but that

> he for his part sought out connections to the city, the medieval period and the Scheldequays. (*P&A*, 33)

He is longing again to establish connections, this time to the very town Benn himself had been part of conquering militarily just over a year earlier. But just the thought of having to have a lunch conversation with his fellow military doctors leads to another paralysis:

> He felt defeated, cold sweats. . . . A downpour of inhibitions and weakness drenched him. For where were the assurances that he

would ever be able to relate something about the trip, bring something back from it, bring it to life, so that something would enter into him recalling the experience? (*P&A*, 33)

Indeed, Benn himself never wrote in any detail about his role in the siege and conquest of Antwerp, not in the Rönne miniatures or elsewhere. Is this a significant omission, and if so, how does it relate to Rönne's inability to undertake the trip? For instead of traveling to Antwerp, Rönne gives up and joins his colleagues for lunch. He becomes witness and participant in a grotesque conversation about the nature of some unspecified tropical fruit that seems to be an avocado since it contains an egg-sized pit. As these doctors and officers discuss whether or not to eat it with salt and pepper like a boiled egg, worry about its effects on health, and brag about their experiences in exotic lands, Rönne triumphs with a skeptical question undermining all the professed certainties pronounced by the other gentlemen. It is again satire of the pretenses of rational scientific discourse, but Rönne's attitude itself does not escape the irony of the narrator, who sees Rönne deluding himself about being accepted by his colleagues:

Cheering broke out. Victory songs. Now the answer resounded with tenacity to the doubters, and that meant him. Time to close ranks, be judged; he ate meat, a well-known dish. (*P&A*, 35)

On the pages that follow we encounter Rönne briefly in his hospital before he drifts through light-flooded avenues in the outer boroughs, again feeling increasingly alienated and threatened. His ability to name the objects around him fails: "Individual objects remained untouchable" (*P&A*, 37). And as he reaches the periphery of the city, fear of having gone too far overcomes him:

Oh, he must have already gone too far! The field already swayed before the street, beneath yellow storms of speckled skies, and a car stopped at the hem of the city. Go back! something said, for waves of formlessness were already approaching, and the bottomless abyss lay in wait. (*P&A*, 37)

On the way back into the city, his erotic sense is triggered by a passing woman before he enters into the dark of a cinema, the next-to-final station of his trip that ends up being a trip into the imaginary only, the imaginary of the moving pictures. The silent film is conjured up with a few satirical comments that leave no doubt that the film offers nothing but clichéd and sexualized romantic kitsch. But Rönne reacts as if it offered a solution to his queries:

> Rönne was hardly breathing, careful not to rupture it. For it was finished, it had been done. (*P&A*, 39)

The biblical trope is then rearticulated in the narrator's secular language:

> Over the ruins of a diseased age had gathered the movement and the spirit, without any intermediary step. (*P&A*, 39)

Without any intermediary step: that is, without the mediation of language. It is still the age of silent film, after all. Rönne himself, however, is language, a form (*Gebilde*) disintegrating and atomized:

> Rönne, a form, a bright stepping together, disintegrating, nipped at by blue bays, the light giggling on his eyelids. (*P&A*, 40)

He steps out of the cinema and into an avenue, only to end again in a park:

> Expired negatively, justified only as the point of intersection. But he was still walking through the spring, and he invented himself along the bright anemones on the lawn and leaned against a herm, dead white, eternally marble, fallen here from quarries that never saw the southern sea die away. (*P&A*, 40)

This is a highly ambiguous ending that resonates more with the ruins of a sick epoch than with the idea that Rönne breaks through here to classical forms suggested by the image of the herm, as some critics, thinking of Benn's celebration of form in his later poetry, have suggested. Decay and ruin rule in the Rönne texts.

Der Geburtstag (The Birthday)

If Rönne has not been able to overcome his professional and personal crisis so far, the fourth and final miniature suggests overcoming with its title *Der Geburtstag*. According to Benn, it was written at the end of April and beginning of May 1916.[26] It is Rönne's thirtieth, which coincides with Benn's thirtieth in 1916. The miniature begins with a retrospective and expository taking stock. At the same time, he seems to be unsure of his identity. Life to him has become questionable:

> But hovering above it all was a faint, doubting As if: as if you were real, space and stars.[27]

As with Nietzsche's Zarathustra, Kafka's Josef K., Musil's Ulrich, Hesse's Steppenwolf Harry Haller, the thirtieth birthday of the protagonist points to a critical juncture. In almost eschatological terms, a kind of rebirth is suggested:

> Now, he said to himself, it is time to begin. In the distance roars a thunderstorm, but I happen. Clouds burst into May woods, but *my* night. . . . Then he searched for something metaphoric to tell himself and failed, but this he found significant and portentous: perhaps imagery itself was already escapism, a kind of illusion and a lack of fidelity. (*PV*, 4)

In the wake of Nietzsche, the critique of metaphor was a common trope in literary discussions at the time. Thus, in the second part of this four-part miniature, Rönne turns to free association, triggered by a cigarette ad:

> Still yielding to the delight of such extensive association, he noticed a glass sign with the inscription "Maita Cigarettes" illuminated by a sun ray. And now—via Maita—Malta—beaches—shiny—ferry—port—mussel-eating—corruptions—there

ensued a bright, ringing, gently splintering sound, and Rönne swayed with happiness. (*PV*, 4–5.)

Metonymy rather than metaphor is the principle of this flow of associations, but the narrator's irony about Rönne is unmistakable. Entering his hospital, Rönne's bliss gives rise to an unshakeable will:

> To connect today's sensations and feelings with his existing stock, omitting none, linking every one. He envisioned a secret construction suggestive of armor and the flight of eagles, a kind of Napoleonic fancy, such as conquering the hedge he lay behind. Werff Rönne, thirty years old, established, a physician. (*PV*, 5)

Here the physiology of association is not in the service of some new perception of a world in flux but functions as a pseudoscientific strategy to reassert the armored self.

The third segment of the text begins with an inner monologue while Rönne is conducting gynecological checkups of prostitutes. He describes a fine blue vein leading from a prostitute's hip toward her pubic hair, a satirical swipe at Thomas Mann, whose blue veins at the temple are a leitmotif of decadence in his early novellas, especially in *Tristan*. Rönne is in his element speaking the language of the gentlemen, just as in the officers' club in *Die Reise:*

> At the temples?? Ah, gentlemen!! I have seen them on other organs, too, thinly winding, like a sprig of violet blood. (*PV*, 5)

No self-doubt here, no paralysis. And then he addresses the prostitutes, collectively, as it were:

> And you, ladies, we know each other, don't we? Permit me to create you, to drape you in your essentialities, your impressions within myself. (*PV*, 5)

With his "lead organ" (*PV*, 5), which here may be brain or phallus or both, he conjures up orientalist sexual phantasies about Arabia and

Africa, female intercourse with "the white rat of Egypt," a brothel in Aden between the desert and the Red Sea, all of which generates real sexual desire in which the brain itself becomes the phallus:

Strong life pulsed through his head. (*PV*, 6)

And:

Now he wanted to love one.

He looked down the corridor and there she stood. She had a birthmark, strawberry-colored, running from her neck over one shoulder and down to the hip, and in her eyes, flowerlike, a purity without end, and about the lids an anemone, still and happy in the light. (*PV*, 6)

But instead of engaging the prostitute he sees in the hospital's corridor, he projects a fantasy image of this woman:

What would her name be? Edmée, that was enchanting. What else? Edmée Denso, that was supernatural; that was like the call of the coming new woman, the imminent, longed-for creature that man was about to create for himself: blonde, and with the lust and skepticism of sobered brains. (*PV*, 6)

All of this of course expresses deep irony about Rönne, including and up to the image of the New Woman that was popular among male expressionists. He indulges further fantasies of Egypt, villages on the Nile, orange gardens. Instead of approaching the woman who triggered these fantasies, he leaves the hospital and once again ends up in the park, where he imagines sexual intercourse with Edmée. Mixture, merger, amalgamation are both sexual and poetically expressed in synaesthetic perceptions that then vanish into the *informe* of ejaculation and self-abandonment:

In the garden mingling ensued. No longer did the flower bed riot with colors; the humming of bees no longer ochred the hedge. Extinct were direction and cadence: a drifting blossom

halted and stood in the blue, like the hinge of the world. Tree-
tops gently dissolved, chalices shrunk, the park submerged in
the blood of the disembodied one. Edmée sprawled on the
ground. Her shoulders smoothed, two warm ponds. Now, slowly,
she closed her hand about a shaft, the ripe abundance, brown-
ishly mown, on her fingers, under great sheaves of transfigured
lust—

There was a swell in him now; now a tepid escape. And then
the structure became confused as his carnal ego melted away—
(*PV*, 8)

Obviously the hand around the shaft can only be Rönne's own since
there never was a real woman with him. One might ask here whether
in these highly sexualized Edmée passages Benn succumbs to a form
of "Edelporn," a kind of high-culture pornography. But this would
underestimate the author. Even if the narrator's voice seems to merge
here with Rönne's, Benn is completely lucid in presenting the reader
with masculinist sexual fantasies that take place entirely in the imaginary. However much his investment in poetic eros may indicate that
he participates in such male fantasies, he also presents them as such,
as fantasies. And the Edmée passage ultimately leads to an even more
imaginary and abstract sexual act at the end of this third part of the
miniature, that of the strong sunlight streaming into his brain, as
he again questions reality:

But after all, it had remained play in the end, for nothing had
reality. Did he have reality? No; all he had was every possibility.
He bedded his neck deeper into the may-weed that smelled of
thyrsi and Walpurgis. Melting through the noon-day, his head
pebbled, brooklike.

He offered it to the light; irresistibly the strong sun trickled
into the brain. There it lay: scarcely a molehill, brittle, the animal scratching inside. (*PV*, 9)

Here we return to the image of the unfolding, the opening up of
the two halves of the brain. Rönne offers his to the sun; it is like an
impregnation by the sun, Danae and Zeus's rain of gold; the brain

as a female genital organ in the male body. These passages, in which Rönne embodies female passivity and abandonment, parallel the end of *Die Eroberung*, when he is being conquered rather than conquering himself.

As always the upsurge is followed by a descent. A new wave of despair overcomes him as he descends into the city—the *Morellenviertel*, Brussels' old Jewish and lower-class neighborhood. Street scenes with fortune tellers, gypsies, street vendors, urinating children challenge Rönne. His southern fantasies all gone, he takes refuge in a lowlife dive:

> And he? What was he? There he sat among his sensations; the rabble was what happened to him. His noon was mockery. (*PV*, 10)

Clearly this is not the Zarathustran high noon. Confronted with all these urban stimuli and the rabble of the dive, midday on his thirtieth birthday, he again questions his identity, the contingency of his birth:

> Once more his brain welled up, the dull course of the first day. Still between his mother's thighs—thus he happened. As the father pushed, he rolled down. The alley had broken him. Back: the whore screamed. (*PV*, 10)

Inevitable regression rather than rebirth. But the novella does not end here. Instead, a kind of miracle happens, almost a kind of rebirth out of the spirit of music:

> He was about to go, when a sound happened. A flute chimed in the gray alley, a song, a blue between the shacks. A man must be walking there, blowing it. (*PV*, 10–11)

A flute, blue skies, midday light, a Mediterranean harbor scene emerges in his imagination, only to be disrupted again by two surreal images with which the narrator marks his distance from Rönne in an almost slapstick-like way:

Europe, Asia, Africa: bites, deadly consequences, horned vipers, and the whorehouse on the quay meet the arrival: silently in the desert stands the Sultana-bird.—It still stood silently, when the *olive* happened to him. (*PV,* 11)

The rabble happened to him; a sound "happened"; the olive happened to him. The Agave, the Ligurian Sea, and Venice complete the set of associations. It is as if he were reborn into a Mediterranean existence. But is he reborn as a poet, as some critics have claimed? Clearly the "as if" is key, and yet there is some form of transcendence as we read about his path leading into silence:

There, he felt deeply, his way would now lead forever. A yielding came over him, a surrender of final rights. Mutely he tendered his brow, loudly its blood gaped. (*PV,* 12)

Again he offers his forehead, place of his brain, bleeding, thus wounded. A last sound of the flute hovers over the Morel quarter. Fulfillment, harvest, and anticipations of death mark the final paragraph in a language that returns from the urban to the rural:

A man decamped. A man hurled himself into his harvest, to be bound by reapers offering wreaths and verse. A man drifted out of his fields, aglow under crown and plumage, immeasurable: he, Rönne. (*PV,* 12)

One last time the narrator tries to fix Rönne with the final two words, personal pronoun and name, but what precedes has the same delirious quality as the last lines of *Gehirne* and *Die Reise.* Rönne vanishes, remains unforeseeable, immeasurable, incalculable. But perhaps it is only the old Rönne who dies and the thirtieth birthday is indeed a new departure. Whatever the case may be, this ending can be read as Benn's final verdict about the belief that the relations between psychic and bodily processes could be scientifically measured and calculated. The associational psychology that informed Benn's thinking at an earlier time implodes in these pages as a scientific venue toward some anthropological truth. What remains instead is a poetic prose, compelling in its hermetic beauty and satirical ethos.

Die Insel (The island)

In the 1916 book version of the Rönne Novellen, this fifth novella occupied the penultimate place. I will not offer a reading here, except to ask why Benn may have eliminated it from later editions. We know he didn't think much of this text because he wrote in a letter to his friend Oelze:

I always found the "Island" one of the weakest things I ever published.[28]

In this case, Benn's judgment makes perfect sense. The tone and execution of Die Insel make it look like a foreign body among the other miniatures. The text actually contains Benn's all-too-direct debate with Theodor Ziehen, the author of a cited review of a book by that "unknown Jewish doctor from Danzig," who, we know, is Semi Meyer, another lesser-known contributor to the scientific debates about stimuli, feelings, sensations that occupied the psychiatry of those days.[29] Ziehen, though not named and only described as author of that review in the text, is explicitly identified as Rönne's teacher. While Benn's writerly negotiation of Ziehen's psychology of associations remains properly couched in poetic and diegetic context in the other four miniatures, here it comes to the fore in a rather unmediated and crude way and in fairly traditional scientific discourse. It is as if Benn lets the cat out of the bag. Eliminating this miniature from later editions could then be seen as a kind of covering up his scientific tracks. And that may well have been one of Benn's motives when in later years he tended to mystify his early beginnings. But there is also a good literary reason why this novella simply doesn't fit the others. Rönne appears far too much as the rational scientist in control. He is almost "out of character" as someone who explicitly claims that he wants to create a new syntax eliminating what he calls the "second-person-singular structure of grammar" (P&A, 56). Whatever that might mean, and the text is not very illuminating on this issue, Rönne here says what he wants to do as a writer, while in the other miniatures he, or rather Benn, actually does it. While the Rönne of Die Insel is also threatened by a woman, he ends up unambiguously with the kind of armored ego and scientifically fortified self that is ultimately inaccessible to the Rönne of the other four novellas.

Conclusion

Overall, the Rönne figure displays certain symptoms of what Werner Rübe, editor of Benn's medical writings and himself a doctor, has described as a borderline schizoid personality that Benn actually diagnosed in himself as a symptom of his post-Nietzschean times. Benn made this condition productive in his ability to operate in two completely different and conflicting registers of writing. But his two clashing modes of language—the poetic and the diagnostic, the delirious and the cool—don't occupy opposite ends of a spectrum; they are mediated through and through. On the one hand, and far beyond the usual expressionist fare, there is the power of delirious poetic language, which Carl Sternheim, the expressionist playwright whom Benn knew in Brussels, described succinctly:

> Benn is the true rebel. He revolts from the depths of the atom, not from the surface; he shatters concepts from the inside so that language itself begins to stagger and philistines find themselves sprawled on their stomachs and noses.[30]

But it is not only language that is shaken. For on the other hand, there is an equally powerful revolt against the certainties of a scientific age, a despair about the limits of medicine's healing power, and a deeply pessimistic philosophy of history as a sequence of catastrophes, enlightenment having become myth, as Adorno and Horkheimer would argue in their later critique of the dark side of modernity.

That very ability to operate simultaneously in contradictory registers and to sustain their dialectic resulted from the psychic condition Benn described, again very rationally, in "Epilog und lyrisches Ich" (Epilogue and Lyrical I; 1927):

> I attempted to gain clarity about the source of my suffering. . . . I immersed myself in descriptions of the condition that is characterized as a depersonalization or alienation of the world of perception. I began to recognize the self as a construct which

strove, with a force compared to which gravity is like the breath of a snowflake, toward a condition in which nothing that modern culture designates as the gift of intellect has a role to play, but rather in which everything, which civilization under the tutelage of academic medicine had given a bad name by labeling it nervous disorder, neurasthenia, psychasthenia, acknowledged the unbounded, mythic foreignness between Man and World.[31]

Benn fought against this state all his life, and he fought it with a poetic writing aimed at what he called *Ausdruckswelt*, a counterworld of artistic expression. This world of art is not created in ecstasy or drug-induced states of mind. It is not subjectivist, as Lukács would argue in his famous 1930s attack on expressionism as the prequel to fascism. It is rather the result of sober work and controlled construction, of craft, as Rodin once put it in a saying both Benn and Rilke cherished.[32] Of course the early Benn was part of expressionism. Eight of his poems were included in Kurt Pinthus's seminal collection of expressionist poetry, *Menschheitsdämmerung* (1919), but among expressionists he was an outsider in his emphasis on what Adorno in a different context characterized as "objective expression," that dimension of the art work that transcended subjective states of being as much as it could not be reduced to political engagement and utopian longings. In his psychic and intellectual makeup, Benn was the phenotype of a metropolitan modernity at the turn of the century that found its aesthetic form in the miniature. Here we see something in Benn's aesthetic that was to resurface in equally anti-subjective writings in Kracauer and Benjamin and differently again in Musil. Like Kafka, Benn occupies a pivotal place of transition between the nineteenth- and twentieth-century miniatures. And yet, his Rönne texts, focused as they are on one fictional figure, still partake in the earlier attempts to articulate a subjective consciousness, however rationally controlled, that we have also seen operating in the metropolitan miniatures of Baudelaire and Rilke.

4

~~~

Photography and Emblem in Kracauer and Benjamin's Street Texts

Immense nausea of posters.

—Baudelaire, *My Heart Laid Bare*

KRACAUER AND BENJAMIN, together with Adorno, are key figures in creating a multilayered critical theory of metropolitan modernism. It is a theory of modernism from the inside, as it were, and thus modernist through and through in all its contradictions, fissures, and complications. It encompasses capital and culture, high and low; verbal and visual media; architecture and the impact of modern technologies; changing structures of perception and subjectivity; and reflections on shifting patterns of spatial and temporal experience. In unique and influential ways it offers cultural analysis within the social and political textures of the historical world of a now-classical modernism. The metropolis as formative dimension of their thought becomes most visible in their literary experiments with the short form, not just the essay but the miniature itself. In Kracauer and Benjamin's urban miniatures and street texts we find the glowing core of their theories of the metropolitan condition. While critics have recognized the importance of collections such as Benjamin's *One-Way Street, Berlin Childhood around 1900, Central Park, Thought Images,* and the *Moscow Diary* and Kracauer's *Strassen in Berlin und anderswo* and his multiple urban feuilleton pieces scattered in his collected works, these texts have not been read closely enough and their historical frames and conceptual ambitions have been neglected. Comparisons between them are few and far between. Only a comparative analysis, however, can reveal both affinities and fundamental differences that become most evident as one reads Kracauer's street texts of the 1920s and early 1930s in relation to Benjamin's *One-Way Street*.

1.

In the wake of Adorno's review of Benjamin's *One-Way Street*, Kracauer's urban miniatures and street texts have often been labeled thought images (*Denkbilder*), suggesting close proximity to, if not identity with Benjamin's writing about the urban experience. Such claims of proximity are highly exaggerated, if not false. Close reading reveals fundamental differences in form, content, and authorial gestus between Benjamin and Kracauer's urban miniatures. Similarly problematic is the scholarly tendency to relate Kracauer's miniatures too exclusively to film and flânerie, the moving pictures and the urban subject in motion, thereby neglecting their equally important relation to photography, manifest in a certain stasis of a cold allegorical gaze in and at urban spaces.[1] A close reading of Benjamin's *One-Way Street* (1928) together with Kracauer's urban miniatures of the 1920s and early 1930s, first published in the *Frankfurter Zeitung* and partially collected only much later by Kracauer himself in *Strassen in Berlin und anderswo* (1964), may help us make clearer distinctions between Kracauer and Benjamin's writing practices and their different approaches to urban perception in the context of the European avant-gardes of the 1920s.

It should give us pause that Benjamin himself did not speak of thought images until years later, when he published another collection of urban prose pieces under the title *Denkbilder* (Thought Images), texts that differ significantly from *One-Way Street* in their strongly ekphrastic dimension. In the 1920s, however, Benjamin kept calling his short prose texts aphorisms, though clearly at times with significant hesitation.[2] While several of the miniatures fit this genre description well and remind us of the aphoristic tradition reaching from the French moralists to the Jena romantics all the way to Nietz-sche, many others are far too narrative or essayistic to be considered as aphorisms. The texts of *One-Way Street* are thought images only in the sense that *Denkbild* is the German term for emblem, and, as I will show, they are emblems in a very specific sense related to the *pictura* dimension of the emblem. It was this aspect of the emblem, however, that Adorno ignored when he declared apodictically and influentially:

> Walter Benjamin's *Einbahnstrasse*, first published in 1928, is not, as one might at first think, a book of aphorisms but rather a collection of *Denkbilder*.[3]

Adorno put too much emphasis on conceptual thought and not enough emphasis on *Bild* (picture or image), a rather common professional blind spot with philosophers and literary critics. Even so, Adorno's further description is extremely perceptive:

> They [the pieces of *One-Way Street*] are scribbled picture puzzles, parabolic evocations of something that cannot be said in words. They do not want to stop conceptual thought so much as to shock through their enigmatic form and thereby get thought moving, because thought in its traditional conceptual form seems rigid, conventional, and outmoded.[4]

"Scribbled picture puzzles" is a wonderfully suggestive formulation, but it fails to define precisely what the pictorial dimension, which is central to the tradition of the emblem, might be in *One-Way Street*. The emphasis is on the effect of Benjamin's texts on conceptual thought, and this is, as so often in their exchanges, pure Adorno. As he goes on to mention dream as the stratum that connects spirit, image, and language, he has nothing more to say about the dimension of the very specific street imagery that gave rise to the miniatures in the first place.

If thought image in Adorno's sense may not be the most appropriate term to define Benjamin's short prose in *One-Way Street*, Kracauer never even called any of his texts thought images. Quite appropriately he spoke of *Raumbilder* (space images), a term that postulated a close relationship between built urban space, its varied social uses, and the human imaginary.[5] The miniatures of *One-Way Street* are precisely not space images à la Kracauer. To the extent that they offer imagery, or *Bildlichkeit*, drawn from urban space at all, they are primarily *Schrift-Bilder* (script images).[6] Indeed, one of the main themes of *One-Way Street* is script—script in urban space but also forms and genres of writing, practices of reading. It is in this distinction between *Schrift-Bild* and *Raum-Bild* and their different media dimensions that Kracauer and Benjamin part ways in their literary reactions to the city. What they do have in common, however, is the absence of real pictures from their texts.

Of course, both authors partake consciously in the writing of that very specific form of short prose, the literary genealogy of which goes back to Baudelaire's *Petits poèmes en prose*, itself a significant transformation of an even older type of urban sketch that had flourished in the newspapers of European cities since the eighteenth century. Given Benjamin's literary philological and Kracauer's architectural sociological imagination, the link to Baudelaire is clearly much more direct in Benjamin than in Kracauer, but there was a strong biographical and intellectual closeness between these two German-Jewish authors ever since the early 1920s. They spent time together in Marseille and by and large wrote about the same cities (Marseille, Paris, and Berlin). They also read and commented on each other's prose as it was first published in the feuilleton of the *Frankfurter Zeitung*, where Kracauer as editor for film and literature also published one of the very first incisive and not uncritical reviews of *One-Way Street* in its proximity to *Origins of Tragic German Drama*, Benjamin's failed *Habilitation* published in that same year of 1928.[7] Clearly, there was close intellectual affinity, for when Kracauer commented on Benjamin's study of baroque drama, he might just as well have been describing a key aspect of his own project:

> The difference between traditional abstract thinking and Benjamin's manner of thinking is thus as follows: whereas the former drains objects of their concrete plenitude, the latter burrows into

the material thicket in order to unfold the dialectic of the essentialities.[8]

While they do indeed share an affinity by burrowing into "the material thicket" and by thinking in images, a practice that was foreign to most contemporary philosophical thought, their understanding of the "material thicket" itself is significantly different. Kracauer's brief critique of *One-Way Street* is telling here:

> Yet Benjamin hardly takes into account the very life he intends to stir up. . . . He turns away from immediacy to such an extent that he does not even really come to terms with it.[9]

This critique, which seems to contradict the claim about burrowing into the material thicket, can guide us in coming to terms with the differences that separate Kracauer's urban miniatures from Benjamin's. What Kracauer criticizes as a deficiency may ultimately be one of the most interesting aspects of Benjamin's texts.

2.

So how did the *Frankfurter Zeitung* envision the function of the urban miniature? Clearly the primary dimension of the miniature in a newspaper's feuilleton would be reportage. Specific editorial comments are hard to come by, but the following 1929 gloss by Benno Reifenberg, editor in chief of the *Frankfurter Zeitung*'s feuilleton and close ally of Kracauer in the internal political disputes at the paper, articulated his and Kracauer's new understanding of the feuilleton:

> [The feuilleton] brings to general consciousness how the substances of our present era are layered and according to which purposes they change. Reportage points to the space in which politics can be generated.[10]

In his foreword to *Der rasende Reporter* (1924) Egon Erwin Kisch had described reportage as unretouched *Zeitaufnahme* (a photograph of a moment of time and/or of time itself). In the first of a series of feuilleton articles, later published as *The Salaried Masses*, a book dedicated to Benno Reifenberg, Kracauer picked up on the idea, suggesting that reportage corresponds to photography, thus assuming a correspondence between the visual and the verbal. Reality, however, is never contained in a single reportage but is a construction consisting of a mosaic of reportages . His definition of the single reportage is identical to Brecht's well known critique of photography:

> A hundred reports from a factory do not add up to the reality of the factory, but remain for all eternity a hundred views of the factory. Reality is a construction. Certainly life must be observed for it to appear. Yet it is by no means contained in the more or less random observational results of reportage; rather, it is to be found solely in the mosaic that is assembled from single observations on the basis of comprehension of their meaning. Reportage photographs life; such a mosaic would be its image.[11]

The critique of the single reportage corresponds to the critique of the single photograph: the mosaic as emphatic image here resonates with the idea of the archive of photographs at the end of his photography essay, where Kracauer tried to locate a politically progressive potential in photography as a medium while simultaneously criticizing its usage in the illustrated papers of his day. The idea of the mosaic is also pertinent to the construction of a mosaic of miniatures in *Strassen in Berlin und anderswo*.

While in his definition of the feuilleton, which at the time was not relegated to a special section of the paper but occupied the lower third of the newspaper's pages, Reifenberg spoke about *Berichte*, reportage, and his comment does indeed map onto the urban miniature, even if in a more mediated way. Certainly his conclusion would have been embraced by both Kracauer and Benjamin: "The feuilleton is the ongoing commentary about politics."[12] Joseph Roth, another important contributor to the urban sketch in major metropolitan papers of the times and defender of the feuilleton against Karl Kraus, called it the task of the feuilletonist "to say valid things in half a page." And in a 1925 letter to the *Frankfurter Zeitung*, where he felt underappreciated by Reifenberg, Roth articulated ambitions for the feuilleton which clearly go beyond simply reporting on cultural events:

> For the newspaper, the feuilleton is as important as politics, and
> even more important for the reader. The modern newspaper will
> be shaped by anything but politics. The modern newspaper has
> more need for the reporter than for the op ed writer. I'm nei-
> ther the supplement nor the dessert, but the main meal. It is *me*
> who is read with interest, *not* the reports from parliament, *not*
> the telegrams. I don't write witty glosses. *I draw the face of the
> times.* That is the task of a great paper.[13]

Indeed, Kracauer's urban miniatures give us the physiognomy of
urban space as the face of the times. Explicit proximity to social and
urban reportage is precisely what distinguishes Kracauer's space images such as "The Unemployment Office," "Homeless Shelters," "The
Underpass," and "Farewell to the Linden Arcade" from the texts of
Benjamin's *One-Way Street* such as "Filling Station," "Stamp Shop,"
or "Imperial Panorama."[14] Reading the titles only, one might be lulled
into that false sense of similarity. But certain key physiognomic dimensions of urban space and life that are very much foregrounded
in Kracauer are almost entirely lacking in Benjamin, however much
he may have theorized later about the experience of shock in city
streets. While both Kracauer and Benjamin's texts embody a kind
of hybrid urban writing, crossing the boundaries between the written,
the seen, and the sociopolitical realm, they do so in significantly different ways.

Since Kracauer was trained as an architect and had studied with
the author of the *Sociology of Space*, Georg Simmel, he had a very astute sense of urban space. Space in Kracauer's miniatures is typically
triangulated. There is the concretely described architectural and
urban locale such as the hotel lobby, the renovated arcade, a street
in a Paris neighborhood, the Kudamm in Berlin, the roller coaster,
the unemployment office. Urban space is coded here, long before
Henri Lefebvre's seminal work, as social space, which is then textually transfigured into a spatial imaginary or even into dream space.
In the miniature on the unemployment office we read: "The images
of space are the dreams of society."[15] Deeply influenced by Lukács's
notion of the transcendental homelessness of the modern subject,
Kracauer deployed this triangulation to allegorize the fallen state of

the world, at first in rather metaphysical, and later, from the mid-1920s on, in sociological and Marxist ways.[16] In an-as-yet-unpublished piece that is archived in his literary estate in Marbach, Kracauer spoke of "*das neue Raumgefühl*," the new feeling for space produced by the development of building technology that was "so far hardly understood."[17] This new feeling for space energized his urban miniatures as an interweaving of objective and subjective culture (Simmel), with built urban space generating psychic and bodily reactions that are not simply private and internal to the subject but enunciated and performed, as it were, in and by urban space itself. The new feeling for space, however, becomes conscious only when it is captured in photography or film. Like film, photography too has the ability to bring the optical unconscious (Walter Benjamin) to the surface of consciousness. In his essay on photography, Kracauer argued that the confrontation of human consciousness with what he called the "central archive," a kind of utopian archive of the whole world that is fragmented but present in the mass of photographic representations, may "awaken an inkling of the right order of the inventory of nature" itself and thus help usher humankind into an alternative social order.[18] As Kracauer was writing for a liberal bourgeois paper, his leftist politics remained partly hidden in this highly speculative language tinged with secularized theology, but the critical status of photography in his speculation was unambiguous when he wrote: "The turn to photography is the go-for-broke game of history."[19] This is of course a complete reversal of the negative take on photography in its relation to the privileged memory image with which Kracauer began his reflections in the photography essay. My hypothesis is that Kracauer's urban miniatures, most of which still await translation into English, were part of this gamble because as literary texts they could counteract the inherent deficiencies of photography as being too tied to the indexical and to commercial mass media circulation. The literary miniature could achieve in the medium of slow-moving language what film achieved by adding movement and montage to the still image. But if the motion picture caught the spectator in its inexorable speed of indexical images, the literary miniature allowed for a slowing down in the mix of description and reflection. It is no coincidence after all that when the photography essay turns from photography to the promises of film on its last page, Kafka's writing provides a mediating hinge between the two and thus an alternative to either film or photography. The turn to the urban miniature since Baudelaire was the literary response to an age when the literary imagination was increasingly challenged, if not threatened by new visual media. The feuilleton miniature faced this situation squarely and creatively.[20]

But how legitimate can it be to approximate a literary text to a photograph, whether snapshot or film still? "Snapshot" at first sight suggests superficiality, reification of time, arbitrariness of the image. After all, photography inevitably records the essential together with the insignificant in a field of vision without discrimination as early theorists of photography had already pointed out.[21] The literary miniature by contrast condenses, sharpens the focus, and avoids arbitrariness. "Snapshot" may also seem poorly chosen as a guiding concept to discuss the new modernist regime of space with its disturbances of vision. Photography, after all, remains tied to the very perspectival organization of space challenged and transformed in the urban miniature, just as it is in modernist painting, paradigmatically in cubism and constructivism, or in photomontage. But it is the temporal rather than spatial dimension of the snapshot that justifies its usage here. Snapshots can be fundamentally opaque and resist rendering a mystery they harbor. Any snapshot, as Roland Barthes has taught us, may have its *punctum*, the dimension of the photograph that eludes transparence, "that accident which pricks me (but also bruises me, is poignant to me)."[22] The easy legibility of the snapshot clearly is a myth, especially when a great temporal distance separates the time of the snapshot from the time it is being looked at. Both Barthes and Kracauer were very aware of this fact. Similarly, the modernist miniature seems easily legible at first sight, but more often than not it resists facile understanding. Snapshots also require that they be carefully read because, as Merleau-Ponty has argued, any photograph holds open a specific moment that the rush of lived time would otherwise have immediately closed.[23] In other words: it resists quick forgetting, and as such serves as an entry point for memory, even if memory may appear ghostly and uncanny, as Kracauer points out in his discussion of the grandmother's photo as a young girl. The snapshot marks the space where a present moment turns into memory, but simultaneously it preserves the appearance of a presence. What interests me in the miniature is precisely this unexpected eruption onto the scene of vision that Barthes called the *punctum* and Merleau-Ponty described in its temporal dimension as the "holding open" of the moment in space toward its present, its past, and its future. When transposed into writing, this holding open, as it were, allows for a palimpsestic writing of space, one that transcends the seen/scene and acknowledges the present and past imaginary any snapshot of space carries with it. Deciphering the *punctum* in Barthes perhaps corresponds to what Kracauer had in mind when he spoke of "deciphering the dreamlike spoken images of cities."[24] Any deeper knowledge of cities for him depended on making visible such unconscious images, "creatures of contingency" that were not subject to rational urban planning.[25] This job of deciphering cannot be done by urban photography alone; it needs the literary articulation in the miniature that supplements and transcends the mere photographic representation of the seen urban space. Kracauer's street texts must thus be read in conjunction with his theoretical reflections on the promises and deficiencies of photography. Even though Kracauer did not explicitly say so, the literary miniatures became part of his famous "go-for-broke game of history."[26] The photography essay suggests that photography permitted all urban configurations to be incorporated in that imagined "central archive," thus liberating urban space from its somnolent stage by distanciation and prefiguring a higher stage of human consciousness.[27] But it was the construction of the photographic archive or the collection of miniatures that created the "mosaic" as an image of life. Analogous to Benjamin, and similarly critical of the indexical dimension of the new visual media, Kracauer ascribed the potential of a political awakening to new media such as photography and film, a plausible idea in the context of the Soviet and Weimar avant-gardes of the 1920s and their utopian anticipations. Literary miniatures thus supplemented but did not replace photography, in the sense that they foregrounded that temporal dimension that is only implicit in photography itself. It was the miniature that made the urban *Raumbild* legible. In their literary form, which was never accompanied by real pictures either in the *Frankfurter*

Zeitung or in the later carefully constructed collection, Kracauer's miniatures thus articulated and unfolded literarily what single photographs or film were not able to fully capture by themselves.

As literary snapshots of space that had opened up to the passing of time, urban miniatures rendered that new dynamic experience of space that Sigfried Giedion described positively as *Durchdringung* (interpenetration, overlapping of spaces) in his 1928 book *Bauen in Frankreich, Eisen, Eisenbeton,* a programmatic statement about the promises of modern architecture and new forms of seeing space.[28] Kracauer knew the book well and Benjamin excerpted it extensively in the notes for the *Arcades Project. Durchdringung,* as architectural historian Hilde Heynen has defined it, "stands for the weakening of hierarchical models on all levels—social as well as architectural."[29] Giedion himself described *Durchdringung* in exclusively positive and liberatory terms in relation to a traditional notion of architecture:

> It seems doubtful whether the limited concept of "architecture" will indeed endure.
>
> We can hardly answer the question: What belongs to architecture? Where does it begin, where does it end?
>
> Fields overlap: walls no longer rigidly define streets. The street has been transformed into a stream of movement. Rail lines and trains, together with the railroad station, form a single whole.[30]

Kracauer's street texts not only complicated the common sense understanding of the snapshot, they also revealed the threatening aspect of the new experience of space, which is absent in Giedion's rather utopian account of building in glass, iron, and ferroconcrete. They articulated a negative side of *Durchdringung,* its threatening, even horrifying dimension as experienced by the subject lost in urban space, paradigmatically in miniatures such as "The Quadrangle," "Screams in the Street," or "The Underpass." This fundamental difference between Kracauer and Giedion in assessing the phenomenon of *Durchdringung* as central to the experience of urban space could be further explored, but it is no coincidence that it was in Kracauer's writing that the two opposing utopian and dystopian senses of the concept meshed most compellingly.[31]

3.

In "Aus dem Fenster gesehen" (Seen from the window, 1931), Kracauer wrote: "Outside my window, the city condenses itself into an image, which is as glorious as a natural spectacle."[32] It is one image rather than a sequence of moving images he had in mind here. But this metropolitan image, which arises without design and independent of urban planning, does contain movement after all: the trains on bundled railroad tracks above and the perpendicular car traffic below in the streets. It is as if movement and repose were combined in this one image, the natural spectacle that is anything but natural.

The difference between movement and stillness is again the very topic of "Lokomotive über der Friedrichstrasse" (Locomotive above Friedrichstrasse, 1933). After first sighting the express train locomotive standing still on the overpass at Bahnhof Friedrichstrasse, the narrator imagines the train engineer's previous visual experience while speeding through the dark, with cities and stations as brief interruptions, villages fleeing by as dispersed groupings in the landscape, signals, lights, and tracks racing toward him and vanishing instantly. Here Kracauer rewrote one of the initial sequences in Walther Ruttmann's film *Berlin Symphony of a City*—the express train coming out of the night and the open landscape and entering into the city. In Ruttmann it is dawn, in Kracauer still night. The only thing of permanence in the engineer's visual field are "the railroad track's banks and the telegraph poles, the surface patterns and infinite spaces."[33] But now, at Bahnhof Friedrichstrasse, all motion has ceased. It's like a still isolated from cinematic movement. The locomotive has come to a halt right on the railroad overpass above Friedrichstrasse, that major commercial artery of Berlin's east that extends straight and seemingly infinitely in both directions perpendicular to the railroad tracks. With its bustling life and traffic, Friedrichstrasse must appear to the locomotive engineer as the world's axis, Kracauer wrote, as the center of life rather than as another transit station:

As an alien guest the man up above looks into the street as if through a narrow crevice. Though his eyes, still used to darkness, are unable to distinguish details, he recognizes the frenzied activity that bursts open the narrow canyon of houses; he takes in the glamor which is of a deeper red than the wheels of his machine. (34)

It is as if the street had sucked him into its debauchery:

It emerges from the background, embraces the poor and the rich, street walkers and cavaliers, and it moves, like a glowing frenzy of letters, along the façades all the way up to the roofs. The man feels as if he were wearing a magic hood and the street of streets had surged over him. (34)

As the train finally moves on into the dark night, Friedrichstrasse remains impressed on the engineer's brain as a "blazing line" transcending space and time and becoming a parable of "reddish life" (34). Friedrichstrasse in the 1920s, after all, was a prime artery for street-walkers and late-night entertainment. Urban life is condensed here into one single erotically loaded image for the man on the locomotive, while none of the pedestrians on bustling Friedrichstrasse have even noticed the locomotive above.

As this example demonstrates, the job of deciphering "the dreamlike spoken images of cities" cannot be done by urban photography alone. No photograph could possibly condense the visual experience of the engineer on the locomotive into a single image. It needs the literary articulation in the miniature, which supplements the central image of a specific urban space with its before and after, thus merging the achievements of the photographic still with the moving image.

Temporality plays out differently in "The Bay," the first of two pieces juxtaposed under the umbrella title "Two Planes," first published on September 26, 1926, in the feuilleton of the *Frankfurter Zeitung* and republished in *Das Ornament der Masse* in 1963 in the introductory section entitled "Natural Geometry."[34] Here Kracauer gives us a snapshot of the old harbor of Marseille from a bird's-eye view, with the city of Marseille rising like a "dazzling amphitheater" around the rectangle of the now largely abandoned and empty old harbor, "a square paved with sea" (37). It's like a mix of a Google Earth map with architectural and social detail, but the language immediately introduces a temporal dimension:

> During the sail-fishing era, the harbor used to be a kaleidoscope dispatching moving patterns across the quays. (37)

But now

> The splendor has lost its luster, and the bay has degenerated from the street of all streets into a rectangle. (37)

The harbor has become "desolate," an "emptiness," a "cavity" (37). Kracauer was one of the first critics to draw on photography's constitutive relationship to transitoriness and lost temporalities in order to give it a place in the trajectory of capitalist culture. But rather than reading a photograph only in terms of reification and forgetting, as Adorno would, he insisted on the dimension of a past presence, however specterlike and spooky it might appear to later generations. His example in the photography essay of photography's endangered sense of presence is the photo of the grandmother as young girl who appears as a specter to the later generations. In "The Bay," it is the miniature that is able, through its verbal strategies, to hold the snapshot of the old Marseille harbor open to its teeming past and thus perhaps to some as-yet-unimagined future, even when the pessimistic tones of *Kulturkritik* and a dystopian modernity prevail in the end of the text. If life has been drained from the old harbor, its memory still holds a residue of another life to be imagined and counterposed to a modernity that has become a void, an empty shell.

Quite a different view of the Marseille harbor was offered in a short film by Moholy-Nagy, made three years later in 1929 and entitled *Impressionen vom alten Marseiller Hafen* (Impressions of the old Marseille harbor). While Kracauer minimized empirical visual references, introducing instead interpretive tropes such as desolation and the void, Moholy-Nagy's camera reveled in the hustle and bustle of the harbor life that had not simply vanished as a result of the new modernized harbor built further out on the coast for ever-bigger ships. Read, however, with Kracauer, his film may strike us as subliminally nostalgic for that older form of harbor life that Kracauer already saw as disappearing or even vanished altogether.

But the film also demonstrates that the opposition of old and new harbor as we have it in "The Bay" cannot be so clearly upheld. The old harbor, after all, featured one of the major technological iron constructions that exemplified *Durchdringung* and industrial modernity for Giedion: *le pont transbordeur*, a giant movable crane structure arching over the whole of the old harbor. Built in 1905, this emblem of industrial modernity, however, is not part of Kracauer's image of the old harbor at all, while it is a central component in Moholy-Nagy's film. But even so, it seems to be in sync with the director's nostalgic take that this industrial contraption is never shown in real action in the film. Instead it is used only as the site of point-of-view shots of the harbor from above and as geometric abstract structure seen from below against the sky. It is highly likely that Moholy-Nagy knew Kracauer's text. After all, the film begins, like Kracauer's "The Bay," with a bird's-eye view, except that it is a view from above not of the harbor itself but of a map of Marseille. As the harbor area of the map is slowly cut out and lifted up, it opens a black empty space in which the moving images of the film then appear, a brilliant cinematic device to combine the abstraction of the map with the concretion of the filmed street scenes.[35]

One of the most stunning space images in Kracauer is "The Quadrangle," the second miniature of "Two Planes" in the section of *The Mass Ornament* entitled "Natural Geometry." Of course, there is absolutely nothing "natural" about this piece, except that its juxtaposition with "The Bay" suggests to the reader that its location is again the same Mediterranean city. From the Kracauer-Benjamin correspondence we also know that Kracauer named the quadrangle Place de l'Observance, that "uncanny square we encountered at night," as Benjamin, remembering his Marseille walks with Kracauer, wrote after receiving a copy of the miniature from Kracauer himself.[36] But the place name is estranged to the abstract "quadrangle," and the name of the city is never mentioned.

The very first sentence of the German text contains a *punctum:* "*Nicht gesucht hat den Platz, wen er findet.*"[37] It reads like a translation into urban space of Kafka's aphorism "Those who seek will not find, those who do not seek will be found."[38] The translation "Whoever the place finds did not seek it" does not quite capture the reversal of subject and object as succinctly as the German does.[39] The meaning, however, is clear enough: "He whom the place finds did not seek it." The uncanny reversal of human subject and urban space in the German sentence immediately disorients the reader. The human subject becomes grammatical object. The empirical object becomes grammatical subject. The following sentences then conjure up a chaotic urban landscape that is rife with putrefied smells, red lights suggesting brothels, signs in Arabic, and dreamlike contorted architectural space—the condensed imaginary of Marseille's infamous harbor quarter as sensuous and sleazy labyrinth:

> A backstairs quarter, it lacks the magnificent ascending entrances. Grayish-green smells of sea waste come smoldering out of open doors; little red lamps lead the way. In the spaces that afford a view, one finds improvised backdrops: rows of flying buttresses, Arabic signs, stair windings. (38)

Then the quadrangle, "which has been stamped into the urban tangle with a giant template" (39), finds the flâneur, who instantly becomes its prisoner. The dreamlike spatial imaginary of the first sentences, reminiscent of urban scenes in Hofmannsthal's *Märchen der 672. Nacht*, is replaced by a very different spatial regime:

> On the deserted square something happens: the force of the quadrilateral pushes the person who is trapped into its center. He is alone, and yet he isn't. Although no observers are visible, the rays of their gazes pierce through the shutters, through the walls. . . . Fear is stark naked, at their mercy. (39)

The further analogy to certain court scenes in Kafka's *Trial* are obvious: "On invisible seats around the quadrangle a tribunal is in session" (39). The whole setup is kind of a Foucauldian panopticon in reverse, but no less oppressive for that. The quadrangle with its military barracks, its "horizontal lines drawn with a ruler" (39), and the "canine obedience" (38) of the wall with its strangely nonvanishing

lines leading into the quadrangle represent the natural geometry of
Cartesian perspectival space. But instead of liberating the subject's
body and permitting visual control over the environment, this abstract perspectival space exudes invisible power and domination, discipline and surveillance. Kracauer's agoraphobia, which Anthony
Vidler has so brilliantly analyzed, is not just the fear of empty open
spaces that dwarf the subject and unmoor its perception.[40] It is also
linked to the recognition of the disciplining power of a rationalist
and abstract regime of visuality that denies agency to the human body
as the subject of sensual perception. It is in this second sense that
the quadrangle is turned into an allegory of the state of the world in
the concluding paragraph:

> In this tangle of pictorial alleys, no one seeks the quadrangle.
> After painstaking reflection, one would have to describe its size
> as moderate. But once its observers have settled into their chairs,
> it expands toward the four sides of the world, overpowering the
> pitiful, soft, private parts of the dream: it is a square without
> mercy. (39)

The translation of "Knäuel der Bildergänge" as "tangle of pictorial
alleys" inevitably loses the notion of the walking subject contained
in the neologism *Bildergänge* (image walks). Also note the move in
German from the concrete "*Karree*" to the abstract "*Quadrat.*" The
translation of *Quadrat ohne Erbarmen* as square without mercy does
not capture this move, since square in English signifies both the geometric figure and the urban square, while *Quadrat* only refers to the
geometric figure. On the one hand, then, this ending may strike the
reader as embarrassingly didactic. But its didacticism is thrown off
track, estranged by the comment about the observers settling into
their chairs. What observers? What chairs? Where are we? The
quadrangle is displaced and becomes a theatrical mise-en-scène in
which the observers take their position in a perspectivally organized
theatrical space. But is it the natural geometry of the *Guckkastenthe-
ater* or do these observers look inward from all four directions, as if
in a theater in the round, or, better, a theater in the square. The text
remains enigmatic on this score. But what it does suggest is that the

terror of the invisible gaze of these observers overpowers the subject in the center of the now-worldwide imaginary quadrangle, the *Quadrat ohne Erbarmen*, the "square without mercy." The cold geometry of invisible gazes overwhelms the "soft, private parts of the dream," just as the quadrangle wins out over the labyrinthine "tangle of alleys." The *ratio* of urban space invades body space just as the *ratio* of the assembly line in "The Mass Ornament" is embodied in the synchronized legs of the Tiller Girls.[41] The fate of the subject becomes identical to that of the city. The condensation of urban space into the allegorically read quadrangle comes with an imaginary expansion of the oppressive power of geometric space across the world: natural geometry without mercy. No need to point out how this text translates Max Weber's "iron cage," his critique of rationalization into concrete urban space and its imprisoning effect on the human subject. Indeed, "Das Karree" can be read as exemplifying the dystopian dimension of Kracauer's mass ornament itself.

A different form of spatial terror is described in "Erinnerung an eine Pariser Strasse" (Remembering a Parisian street).[42] The narrator in one of his flâneries and in a state of mind he calls *Strassenrausch* (street euphoria or intoxication) is lost in a side street unknown to him in the proletarian Quartier Grenelle.[43] Suddenly a nightmarish perception overcomes him:

> But now it happened: hardly had I come detached from the white, excessively high wall of the theater when I had trouble walking on, and I felt invisible nets holding me back. The street in which I found myself kept me captive. (8)

He then sees several hotel signs without names on derelict buildings that suggest prostitution. Stepping up to one of these hotels, the narrator suddenly becomes conscious of the fact

> that I had been observed. From the upper story windows of several houses, lads in shirtsleeves and slovenly clad women were looking down upon me. They didn't utter a word, they just kept looking at me. Their mere presence exuded a terrifying force, and I considered it almost a certainty that it was them who had

put me in fetters. As they were standing mute and motionless, they seemed to have been hatched out by the houses themselves. Any moment they could have stretched out their tentacles and pulled me into the rooms. (9)

Illicit sexuality and class anxiety combine in this surreal scene that I consider to be a rewrite of Freud's very similar experience described in *The Uncanny*, which is arguably a rewrite of another analogous scene in Hofmannsthal's *Märchen der 672. Nacht*.[44]

I read the spooky grammatical reversal at the beginning of "The Quadrangle" and the scenes described there and in "Remembering a Paris Street" as the literary equivalent of Moholy-Nagy's experiments with reverse perspective. With these experiments in some of his design and photographic work, Moholy-Nagy set out to undermine the certitudes of Renaissance perspectivalism. It was a technique that produced disturbances of vision and a fundamental insecurity in the position of the spectator. Kracauer mobilized such a disturbance of the subject in his miniatures by confronting a surreal dream space with the geometric rationality of that real urban space that pulls the subject in. The position of the spectator is destabilized by a gaze emanating from urban space itself.

A comparable spatial situation appears in a more purged, abstracted, and more violent form in Kafka's diaries, one of the rich sources of modernist miniatures:

To be pulled in through the ground-floor window of a house by a rope tied around one's neck and to be yanked up, bloody and ragged, through all the ceilings, furniture, walls, and attics, without consideration, as if by a person who is paying no attention, until up on the roof the empty noose appears, having lost hold of what remained of me only as it broke through the roof's tiles.[45]

Here the miniature is condensed into one breathless single sentence at the end of which the narrator's body has been thoroughly disappeared, leaving only the empty noose—a surreal vision of an urban hanging that destroys both human body and built space. The passive voice barely hides the absence of any executioner. Rather than provide protection and shelter, the building has become a tool, if not the agent, of the execution. Here, as in that first sentence of "The Quadrangle," it is urban space itself that finds, confines, and ultimately destroys the human subject.

The link of terror emanating from urban space and its dream-like contortion is something Kracauer indeed shared with Kafka, whose novels he was one of the very first to review for the *Frankfurter Zeitung* in the mid-1920s. At the same time, Kafka's *Angst-Räume* (spaces of anxiety) and *Angst-Träume* (anxiety dreams) lack the social and philosophical language that characterizes Kracauer's rendering of urban space, which, as a result, poses fewer riddles to the interpreter. And yet reading all these texts from Hofmannsthal to Freud to Kafka together makes it clear that we are not simply confronting a case of intertextual influence. These writers' approaches to urban space are grounded in the similar effects the modern city had on its most astute observers—a space of disorientation, social and sexual conflict, and disturbances of vision and perception.

4.

Kracauer's urban imaginary, however, is not limited to creating literary *Angst-Räume* and *Angst-Träume*, spaces of anxiety and nightmares. Critics have pulled Kracauer's city images too much into the orbit of his philosophy of history, which interprets the city exclusively as emblem of alienation, ego loss, reification, and anomie, as the catastrophic space of a modernity gone awry and overwhelmed by abstract forms of empty time and empty space. True, the notion of emptiness or void appears frequently in his miniatures, and it can be compared with Benjamin's notion of an empty homogeneous time or with Bloch's characterization of Weimar's *Neue Sachlichkeit* as "functions in the void."[46] But as the differentiation of spatial models in "The Quadrangle" has already suggested, urban space in Kracauer is not coded exclusively as homogeneous negativity. As Paris and Berlin provided the privileged spaces for his texts, one can certainly note how he differentiated between the two cities. The street in Paris still functions as site of memory and experience while streets in Berlin either scream with emptiness, as in "Screams in the Street," or

undergo such rapid architectural change that they no longer hold
any memory of the past, as in "Street without Memory."[47] Clearly
Berlin is seen as the decisive cauldron of modernity in political and
social crisis, while Paris is described as a city of the past. The modern
world seems to be absent in Paris in this perspective of the visitor
from Berlin. In "Pariser Beobachtungen" (Parisian observations;
1927) Kracauer writes with cutting irony about France:

> Society persists as if it had really won the war. One speaks about
> art and literature as in lost decades. Property and dowry exude
> an odor of holiness, and their generals are authentic generals.[48]

The visitor returns to Berlin "conscious here of breathing the air of
harsh reality, as they say."[49] This harsh reality, however, harbors a
politically promising contradiction that Kracauer has paradigmatically analyzed in the well-known essay on "The Mass Ornament."[50]
The tension he developed there between the dystopia and the utopia
of reason, as one might say, also emerges if we compare the several
miniatures that focus on advertising. In "Boredom" (1924), Kracauer analyzed the historical decline of *Langeweile* as a creative
mental state. Here is what he wrote about the flâneur walking the
street in the evening:

> Illuminated words glide by on the rooftops, and already one is
> banished from one's own emptiness into the alien *advertisement*.
> One's body takes root in the asphalt, and, together with the en-
> lightening revelations of the illuminations, one's spirit—which
> is no longer one's own—roams ceaselessly out of the night and
> into the night. If only it were allowed to disappear.[51]

This is still the subjective discourse of loss that is typical of an anti-
urban German *Kulturkritik* before Kracauer turned to more sociologically and politically inflected views. Very different, therefore, is
the description of "Lichtreklame" (Electric advertising) of 1927:

> Electric ads rise in the heavens that no longer harbor angels, but
> are not all commerce either. They exceed economics, and what
> is meant as advertising becomes illumination. Such things

happen when businessmen handle light effects. Light remains light, and when it shines in all its colors, it really breaks the bounds set by its contractors. . . . The drizzle of advertising poured forth by economic life is transformed into a constellation in an alien sky.[52]

Electric advertising as uncontrollable excess points to an alternative future to be read as a *Sternbild*, a constellation, in an alien sky. Even if overall the rhetoric is less apocalyptic than in the earlier text, the form of the miniature is pretty much the same. And it remains so until 1933, by which time, however, the dystopian vision has returned, supported now by Kracauer's concrete observations of social realities after the crash of 1929 and the political rise of National Socialism. In "The Underpass," a miniature about a passage under the railroad tracks at Bahnhof Charlottenburg that was always crowded with travelers, beggars, and hawkers, Kracauer made much of the opposition of the oppressive and unshakable iron and concrete low-ceiling construction and the human chaos of motion. Both, however, elude any kind of positive human rational *Durchdringung*:

Inhuman is not only the aimlessness [*Planlosigkeit*] with which people drift about, but also the planned construction of the passage. . . . It is a system just as opaque [*undurchdrungen*] and forsaken as the anarchic mix of passers-by and beggars.[53]

The utopian dimension of *Durchdringung*, which Giedion articulated before the 1929 crash, has thoroughly shipwrecked. One of Kracauer's last Berlin miniatures, published just a couple of days after its author left Berlin for good on February 28, 1933, to enter the extraterrioriality of exile, describes the silent crowds looking at the burned Reichstag the day after the fatal fire:

The gazes penetrate and go through [*durchdringen*] this symbol, and they dive down into the abyss opened up by its destruction.[54]

In certain ways, "Around the Reichstag" marks the logical, though not chronological, endpoint of the modernist miniature as a specific form of the urban feuilleton in pre-fascist Germany. If the main function of the form was to enable readers to see the dangers and pleasures of urban life in new ways, to open up the surfaces of urban space to the dangerous and exhilarating depths underlying them, that depth has now been transformed into an *Abgrund*, the abyss that six years later was to engulf the world.

5.

The miniatures of Benjamin's *One-Way Street* are not space images comparable to Kracauer's writing practice, nor are they, as Bernd Witte and, more recently, Gerhard Richter have claimed, snapshots in any rigorous intermedial sense.[55] Ernst Bloch got it right but failed to pursue his insight when he said that Benjamin perceived reality "as if the world were script . . . as if he were writing a book made up of emblems."[56] Emblems instead of snapshots, then: How can this be read, apart from the fact that the German term for emblem would indeed be *Denkbild*? Any number of critics, to be sure, have referred to the emblematic nature of *One-Way Street* that is nowadays read in close proximity rather than opposition to the earlier *The Origin of Tragic German Drama*. Both books, after all, were published in the same year, 1928. But critics have failed to pay attention to the media-specific nature of the emblem that, for Benjamin, is primarily the emblem of the baroque. My argument here is briefly this: what photography and the snapshot were for Kracauer's writing practice, the baroque emblem is for Benjamin.[57] Both the differences and the affinities of their writing practices and their conceptualization of the literary in relation to the visual result from these different intermedialities subtly inscribed into their texts.

   Now the art historical, literary, and philosophical debate about emblems can be as befuddling as that about allegory. I would start here with a simple observation. The baroque emblem, especially in the seventeenth century, was a multimedial mode of representing and interpreting a world out of joint. The coupling of words and pictures was of course not all that remarkable in a period that still upheld the Horatian view of *ut pictura poesis*. More important for my argument is the fact that the baroque emblem books were enormously popular; they were widely distributed all over Europe and used as educational and pedagogic tools in the period of the counterreformation. Most famous perhaps was the emblem book of 1531 by the Italian lawyer and humanist Andrea Alciati, which soon made it from its original Latin into vernacular languages in more than 150 editions. Images and words were combined in the emblem to re-create and secure or even enforce a kind of cosmic, religious, and secular harmony of the universe that had become historically elusive and threatened in an age of religious wars. Emblem books thus occupied a significant space in the epistemic shift Foucault has described as that from the pre-classical to the classical episteme. The critical view that the emblem articulates a fundamental crisis in the world was of course also Benjamin's own take when he wrote that "allegories are, in the realm of thoughts, what ruins are in the realm of things."[58] I suggest a para-phrase: Emblems are, in the realm of media, what ruins are in the realm of architecture. The notion of the emblem as ruin of course suggests a tension or conflict rather than harmony between its con-stitutive elements: words and pictures. This very tension, I would argue, is mobilized and translated in the miniatures of *One-Way Street*. Central to this translation of the baroque emblem smack into twentieth-century modernity, however, is a structure of absence: the absence of the emblematic picture in *One-Way Street*. This is a sig-nificant absence in the context of the historical avant-garde's, espe-cially the constructivists', privileged juxtaposition of word and image in the visual arts—developments for which Benjamin had great af-finity.[59] Nobody would have been surprised had he actually used im-ages together with the texts of *One-Way Street*.

When critics have read *One-Way Street* as emblematic prose they have not taken the specific media constellation of the emblem seri-ously enough. Time and again they have reduced the fundamental tripartite structure of the emblem to the binary of word and image, and image in this account has quickly lost its meaning as picture in the concrete sense and has been seen as literary or thought image. As literary-visual form, however, the emblem has not two, but three parts: the *inscriptio* (title), the *pictura* (the image as picture), and the *subscriptio* (the interpretation of or commentary on the image). In his influential reading of Benjamin's thought images, Karl Heinz Schlaffer spoke of bifurcations between report and reflection, experience and

knowledge and of the doubling of thought and intuition.[60] The notion of bifurcation is of course not incorrect as one approaches
One-Way Street superficially, but it is oblivious to the fact that the
visual, even as ekphrastic description in language (not to speak of real
pictures such as photos), is largely absent in *One-Way Street*, in contrast to Kracauer's *Strassen in Berlin und anderswo*, miniatures that
do use condensed description of urban spaces. The duality of report
and reflection pertains more accurately to the texts published under
the title *Denkbilder* in the *Gesammelte Schriften;* that is, to the texts
about Naples, Marseille, Moscow, and other concrete cities, texts
that indeed do mix astute ekphrastic description with reflection, a
mix that can properly be seen as the equivalent in language of the
alternation between *pictura* and *subscriptio* in the emblem. [61] Only these
city images contain extensive and lively descriptions of architectural
space and urban context. As urban sketches they are different from
the miniature. Neither *One-Way Street* nor *Denkbilder* includes pictures, but the linguistic dimension of *res picta* is overwhelmingly
present in the latter and largely absent from the former. It is thus
simply not adequate to short-circuit the later *Denkbilder* of the *Gesammelte Schriften* or even those few published in 1933 under the pseudonym Detlev Holz in the *Frankfurter Zeitung* with the texts of *One-
Way Street*. "Naples," for instance, written in 1924 together with the
same Asja Lacis to whom *One-Way Street* is dedicated, is thick with
urban description that *One-Way Street* lacks almost completely. The
same is true for Benjamin's astute observations on urban scenes in
Moscow that fly in the face of Third International politics but give
a very real sense of his idiosyncratic perceptions of Moscow's urban
environment.

My argument finds support in the so-called *Nachtragsliste*, a list of
short texts Benjamin presumably considered for an expanded second
edition of *One-Way Street*.[62] A number of these texts were actually
published separately or in series in newspapers and journals from 1928
to 1934, but the themes of the metropolis, technology, and the media
that are central to *One-Way Street* play no role in them, as their titles already indicate. They refer to superstition, pain, love, shame,
and other subjects of psychology, phenomenology, and anthropology.
Since *One-Way Street* followed the principle of naming an urban

"script-site" in every title, expanding this collection of miniatures with these additions would not have made much sense.

Once we note this difference from the *Denkbilder* collection and from the *Nachtragsliste, One-Way Street* appears as a very special case of urban writing. It does not, as is so often claimed, read the city in a broad metaphoric way—the city as a book, as it were, in Victor Hugo's sense, or the street as a text the way Franz Hessel proposed in his essay "The Art of Taking a Walk."[63] It rather reads script and only script in the city, the store signs, names of buildings, graffiti, advertisings, and public announcements. It focuses on where the city street is literally, not metaphorically, legible. As Bloch suggested, it is the city as script that triggers Benjamin's reflections. Urban script as a dimension of prose writing is also an element in Döblin's metamorphosis of the epic in *Berlin Alexanderplatz*, a novel that incorporates advertising copy, tram trajectories, public announcements, and other urban signage into its narrative. In Döblin, the city as script is interpenetrated (durchdrungen) with the city as sound-scape, construction site, and chaotic street scenes; in Benjamin it is the primary, if not only dimension that generates his wide-ranging reflections.

But then such textual images are not really being read in any deeper sense in *One-Way Street*. They are used in the titles only as triggers for reflections, dreams, literary allusions, aphorisms, and rather hermetic puns—anything but descriptions or negotiations of real urban space.[64] Benjamin's later work on Baudelaire and Paris as the capital of the nineteenth century is of course known for its compelling theory of urban shock and *Reizschutz*, the protection against stimuli as constitutive of the urban experience. But in contrast to Kracauer, who places such shock experiences in the center of his texts, Benjamin's early miniatures lack any sense of immediate experiential shock in the narrator's encounter with the urban environment.[65] It is as if the focus on writing and script-images itself provided a kind of *Reizschutz* against any real and disorienting experience of the city, that we find in so many other modernists. It is all quite far from Benjamin's Baudelairean fencer who screams out in fright in his encounter with the city. Actually, it bears out Kracauer's critical observation of *One-Way Street* that Benjamin "turns away from immediacy to such an extent that he doesn't even come to terms with it."[66] At the same time, it is this focus on writing that allows Benjamin to give us one of the most beautiful images for the miniature as text in "Antiques":

> The faculty of imagination is the gift of interpolating into the infinitely small, of inventing, for every intensity, an extensiveness to contain its new, compressed fullness—in short of receiving each image as if it were that of the folded fan, which only in spreading draws breadth and flourishes, in its new expanse, the beloved features within it.[67]

This image of the unfolding fan captures in a stunning spatial image what I had in mind when I described Kracauer's miniatures as compressed street images that open up to their temporal dimension in language. But it also describes in a different sense what happens when Benjamin encounters script in urban space.

The absence of any negotiation with the real street, with real urban space in *One-Way Street* is further reinforced by the fact that that the *pictura*, which is central to the baroque emblem, is missing. Only the *inscriptio* and the *subscriptio* are left, as title and text. The baroque emblem, signature of a ruinous world, has become ruin twice over. The only images conjured up in the head of the reader are the internal images generated by the miniatures' titles, all of which refer to something lettered and seen in urban space such as "Caution— Steps," "Nr. 13," and "Ministry of the Interior." I have already noted that most of the miniatures avoid any explicit ekphrastic or indexical dimension. So *pictura* is missing not only literally as real picture but even in its linguistic transformation—except, that is, in the titles. But then the titles are closer to naming than to any recognizable ekphrasis. Names of sites of course do conjure up images, but these images remain rather generic in the text just as the names themselves do. Here they refer to specific urban sites such as Filling Station, Imperial Panorama, and Construction Site or to specific stores such as Chinese Curios, Stationers, and Stamp Shop or to public buildings such as Mexican Embassy, Ministry of the Interior, and First Aid or to advertisements such as Germans, Drink German Beer, This Space for Rent, and so forth. The sequence of the miniatures, then, resembles a street of shops and public buildings, but only insofar as they are visibly named in letters in their urban environment.

By foregoing the emblematic picture in the text, Benjamin marks his position vis-à-vis the avant-gardist montage experiments with word/image constellations, practices toward which he felt drawn theoretically and philosophically. In this context it remains puzzling that Benjamin, who did so much, together with Kracauer, to validate the new media of technical reproducibility, never used images in his own literary experiments.[68] Benjamin does not defend *Schrifttum* (print culture) in a traditional sense, as Hofmannsthal and others who were fearful of the new media would have done at that time. But he does go all out for script in his focus on the radical change of literary culture that he calls for in the first miniature, "Filling Station." Phrases there such as "The construction of life" or the "the power of facts" and the privileging of "leaflets, brochures, articles, and placards" come directly out of constructivist manifestos and the magazines of the early 1920s, to which he himself contributed occasionally.[69]

The key programmatic text here is "Attested Auditor of Books," with its claim that "that the book in this traditional form is nearing its end."[70] It elaborates the theme already struck in the very first miniature, "Filling Station," which argues that "true literary activity cannot aspire to take place within a literary framework."[71] "Attested Auditor of Books" provides the rationale. After a reference to Mallarmé, the Dadaists, and new typographic experiments, the text continues:

Script—having found, in the book, a refuge in which it can lead an autonomous existence—is pitilessly dragged out into the street by advertisements and subjected to the brutal heteronomies of economic chaos. This is the hard schooling of its new form. If centuries ago it began gradually to lie down, passing from the upright inscription to the manuscript resting on sloping desks before finally taking itself to bed in the printed book, it now begins just as slowly to rise again from the ground. The newspaper is read more in the vertical than in the horizontal plane, while film and advertisement force the printed word entirely into the dictatorial perpendicular. And before a contemporary finds his way clear to opening a book, his eyes have been exposed to such a blizzard [*dichtes Gestöber*] of changing, colorful, conflicting letters that the chances of his penetrating the archaic stillness of the book are slight. Locust swarms of print [*Heuschreckenschwärme von Schrift*], which already eclipse the sun of what city dwellers take for intellect, will grow thicker with each succeeding year.[72]

What Benjamin described here as new forms of script creating both an urban imaginary and a new form of mediated subjectivity is noticeably close in language to how Kracauer, in his 1927 essay "Photography," wrote of the "*Schneegestöber der Photographien*" (blizzard of photographs). Kracauer's own writing of urban miniatures is indeed as suggestive of the photograph as Benjamin's is close to the emblem. But photography as (arguably) the modern media equivalent of the baroque emblem's etching is precisely denied in *One-Way Street* and replaced by the focus on script in its new urban transformation. Indeed, even when writing about photography, Benjamin saw script as indispensable. Thus, in his essay on photography, he referred to Moholy-Nagy's famous statement that "the illiteracy of the future will be ignorance not of reading and writing, but of photography." But then he followed up with a rather rhetorical question:

> But shouldn't a photographer who cannot read his own pictures be no less accounted an illiterate? Won't inscription become the most important part of the photograph?[73]

And five years later in his "Letter from Paris (2)"on painting and photography, he criticized the surrealists' failure

> to recognize the social impact of photography, and therefore the importance of inscription—the fuse guiding the critical spark to the image mass (as is seen best in Heartfield).[74]

If in Kracauer the "image mass" or "blizzard of images" needed to be *umfunktioniert*, or refashioned by critical consciousness, that is, by philosophical and sociological intervention, in order to develop the medium's emancipatory potential, in Benjamin the same need for refashioning is ascribed to inscription—*Schrift*. Thus, Benjamin, in "Attested Auditor of Books," imagines a radically new "eccentric figurativeness," a kind of "picture writing" in which poets will be able to participate only by mastering fields of construction such as statistical and technical diagrams.[75] This, of course, is over the top. For the lover of letters such as Walter Benjamin, it is an almost masochistic embrace of constructivist Soviet-style factography and its entropic minimalism of both language and vision.

His insistence on critical captions for images—captions that are more than just explanatory—suggests that Benjamin shared a then-widespread view of photography as merely mimetic reproduction of the seen. Thus, adding photographs to the texts of *One-Way Street* might have completed the three-partite structure of the emblem, but at the price of sacrificing the truly allegorical nature of the baroque visual emblem—allegorical images that were not immediately accessible to understanding without the *subscriptio*. If the baroque emblem already was a sign of a ruinous world, the structure of absence in Benjamin's prose miniatures mutilated the emblem even further endowing the remaining script with the hope for some new awakening and for the imagined new social order toward which that one-way street was pointed. Throughout *One-Way Street* Benjamin imagined another *Schrifttum* destined to join the phantasm of an alternative technology that would reestablish a mythical union of man and nature, the world and the cosmos, as it is laid out in "To the Planetarium," the final text at the end of his textual one-way street.

To be sure, the degree of confronting language with the visual varies widely in these texts. Apart from the logic that links the two introductory miniatures with the last one as beginning and end points of the one-way street, the sequence of texts overall does not follow any detectable order. Nor are tone, style, affect, and length of the miniatures uniform throughout. The text includes rather forced puns such as *"Überzeugen ist unfruchtbar"* ("To convince is to conquer without conception"), a one-sentence aphorism entitled "For Men," the sign for a public pissoir.[76] The sentence's meaning reveals itself only if one first looks closely at the German word's stem, "zeugen," which means to procreate. To put it crudely, "zeugen" is fertile; and for Benjamin, "über-zeugen," to convince, is as infertile as pissing. The idea links up, however, with "Filling Station," which holds that the "construction of life" is and should be under the hold of facts rather than convictions ("*Überzeugungen*," translated as "opinions" in "Tankstelle").[77] A miniature such as this one pushes against the limits of translatability. In a very different mode, there are miniatures in which the visual vanishes and leaves only text, such as the three series of thirteen theses, each about the technique of writing, against snobs, and the technique of the critic. These theses are posted where the urban stroller sees the sign "Post No Bills." Of course, these postings do not reflect anything seen in the street. They are entirely constructed at the writing desk. Had these theses actually been posted, they could hardly be imagined to trigger a public reaction like the theses Luther nailed to the door of the Wittenberg church. Thus, the miniatures assembled in this book are quite heterogeneous, and not all are equally successful and incisive, which is why several critics have even spoken of a writerly failure in their assessment of the work.

I disagree with such a one-dimensional view. The absence of real pictures notwithstanding, Benjamin's text is chock-full of wonderful literary images and similes. It begins with the stunning dedication to his lover, Asja Lacis, who as an engineer cut the street through the author, that one-way street to a revolutionary future; it continues with the comparison in "Filling Station" of the new literary forms to the mere drops of oil being applied gingerly to the hidden spindles and joints of the machine of social life; the comparison in "Chinese Curios" with the archway over the gate on the way to the house of a lover compared to "an ear that had lost the power of hearing" after the beloved has parted; the comparison of copying a text to walking a street and reading a text to flying above it; the imaginatively wrought images of the historical trajectory of script and the book in "Attested Auditor of Books"; and finally the cosmic images of nature, technology, and war in the final text "To the Planetarium." As Benjamin summed it up in "Prayer Wheel," one of the aphorisms under the general title "Antiquities":

Only images in the mind vitalize the will. The mere word, by contrast, at most inflames it, to leave it smoldering, blasted. There is no intact will without exact pictorial imagination. No imagination without innervation.[78]

The privileging of the image in the mind of course implies the deprecation of the real emblematic picture, whose absence in the work is once again legitimized.

Let me conclude with some comments on another key text from *One-Way Street* that may stand as counterpoint to "Attested Auditor of Books" and with a reading of the only image that was part of the original 1928 edition, the photographic montage by Sasha Stone that covers both the back and the front of the book. The multiplied one-way street sign on the front cover suggests unidirectionality, linearity. But this model is denied by the text itself, which displays a rather elliptical structure with two focal points: the first being life, or rather script in the modern metropolis, the other, quite far apart from the first, the lead idea of the baroque emblem. I have argued that we need to read *One-Way Street* in terms of a structure of absence, the absence of the *pictura*. However, there is one miniature that focuses on an emblem-like phenomenon that includes the *pictura*. It is found in the discussion of stamps in "Stamp Shop," in which stamps on postcards or letter envelopes represent the very image/word combination of the baroque emblem in a later age.

"Stamp Shop," a text prefigured in a passage of Aragon's *Paysan de Paris*, which Benjamin translated and published in *Literarische Welt*, gives us the miniature of the miniature, the emblematic combination of image and print on the stamped stamp on a postcard or a letter envelope. Here is a piece of Benjamin's *subscriptio*:

> Stamps bristle with tiny numbers, minute letters, diminutive leaves and eyes. They are graphic cellular tissue. All this swarms about and, like lower animals, lives on even when mutilated. This is why such powerful pictures can be made of pieces of stamps stuck together. But in them, life always bears a hint of corruption to signify that it is composed of dead matter. Their portraits and obscene groups are littered with bones and riddled with worms.[79]

Numbers and letters here are residues of a live communication that has inevitably gone dead as soon as it was buried in script. This is the age-old Platonic trope of script as dead in comparison to the voice but with the added baroque imagery reveling in organic decay. Depicted territories and political figures in this stamp world of ruins are subject not just to the letters of inscription but also to numbers:

> On stamps, countries and oceans are merely the provinces and kings merely the hirelings of numbers that steep them in their colors at will.[80]

And yet these miniature emblems open up horizons in the imagination of a child:

> The child looks toward far-off Liberia through an inverted opera-glass: there it lies behind its little strip of sea with its palms, just as the stamps show it.[81]

"Stamp Shop" concludes with comparing stamp language to Morse code, another sample of Benjamin's privileging the technological dimension of transmission. And it ends with the anticipation that stamp language will not survive the twentieth century—a rather accurate prediction for the age of e-mail, iPhones, and FedEx. If "Stamp Shop" stands out among the miniatures in that it is triggered by reflections on the word/image/number constellations that broaden the horizon of the urban dweller toward other lands, other continents, and even the cosmos, it still does not offer any real images as it inscribes the tripartite structure of the emblem into this specific text.

The only real image of the original edition of *One-Way Street*, however, is Sasha Stone's image montage on both back and front cover that is rarely reproduced in toto. On the front cover we look straight into the depth of a street with storefronts and pedestrians on the sidewalk. Perpendicular to the direction of vanishing point is the multiple of the road sign "Einbahnstrasse" pointing out of the frame to the right. The direction indicated by the sign is reinforced by the direction of a public bus occupying most of the space on the back cover. The architecture of the storefronts on the front cover looks rather nineteenth century, while both the double-decker bus and the traffic sign are clear markers of 1920s Weimar that featured its very first one-way street in 1927. My point is that the text's one-way street

Sasha Stone, book cover for Walter Benjamin, *Einbahnstrasse*
(Berlin: Rowohlt, 1928).

is not the street you see on the front cover, but rather a street outside the frame and outside the image—invisible unless, of course, you
open the book and begin to read.

Critics have correctly linked the image of the shopping street on
the cover with its deep vanishing point to another image Benjamin
mentioned in direct relation to *One-Way Street*, an image that Sasha
Stone must have known about when he designed the book's cover.
In his letter to Scholem of September 18, 1926, Benjamin wrote: "It
has turned out to be a remarkable arrangement of construction of
some of my street that is meant to reveal a prospect of such precipitous depth—the word is not to be understood metaphorically!—like,
perhaps, Palladio's famous stage design in Vicenza, *The Street*."[82] The
"prospect of precipitous depth" of *One-Way Street* itself is not seen
on the cover, where the one-way street signs point in a direction perpendicular to the depth and vanishing point of the shopping street
that only at first sight suggests the visual parallel to Palladio's theater prop. The signs, however, point to the inner pages of the book.
The prospect of steeply plunging depth is, in other words, not what

Vicenza, Teatro Olimpico © Centro Internazionale di Studi di Architettura
A. Palladio

we see on the cover; instead it is the street of textual miniatures that
make up the book. The cover's traffic sign itself points to writing,
script, and letters in urban space. Here we have the ultimate overall
emblem. *Inscriptio* and *pictura* combine on the title page and back cover
in the conflictual constellation of two different urban temporalities—

nineteenth-century static architecture versus Berlin's motorized traffic of the 1920s—and the *subscriptio* would be that "prospect of precipitous depth" referring to the plunging depth of critical reflections in the series of purely textual miniatures.

6.

What, then, can we conclude from this comparison of Benjamin's and Kracauer's city images? Emblem and photograph are very different media of reproducibility. And yet both rely on a combination of the visual with the verbal in print, with *subscriptio* in the emblem corresponding to the caption of the photograph. Both are part of popular or mass culture. But this is as far as the affinity between Kracauer and Benjamin goes. For while Kracauer always conjured up the sheer visible materiality of built space and constructed it as social space, Benjamin focused on script and legibility only, leaving observed architectural and urban realities out of the picture. In addition, Kracauer always operated within the dialectic of photography and film, while, true to the nature of the traditional emblem, Benjamin's miniatures never conjured up moving images. If I am right in suggesting that Benjamin consciously tried to articulate a conflict between the visual and the verbal, emblemlike, in his texts, then the absence of images, except of course on the famous cover picture designed by Sasha Stone, is indeed stunning. What else could these images have been in the twentieth century but photographs of urban scenes about which Benjamin wrote eloquently in his comments on Atget? And yet Benjamin, who has done so much to validate image media such as photography and film, betrayed a deep mistrust of pictures alone, a mistrust he shared with Kracauer, Kafka, and Baudelaire. Thus, the absence of photographs in both authors' texts points to another affinity underlying very different writing practices. Reading Kracauer's street texts back from Benjamin, then, it becomes clear that Kracauer, too, could not have placed real snapshots of urban spaces into his texts. Any such illustration would have simply undone the complexity of *Durchdringung* he had achieved in the writing of his urban texts, the kind of literary maneuver I described as remediation in reverse in the introduction.

This brings up a final question: Which street texts are more successful in getting at urban imaginaries—*One-Way Street* or *Strassen*

in Berlin und anderswo? Benjamin's book has often been read as a literary failure. The rigor of his focus on the presence and legibility of
urban script has indeed limited the range of his insight into urban
space itself. But if it is a failure, it is a conceptually highly persuasive
one resulting from the need to rethink the relationship between the
visual and the verbal in urban modernity in novel ways. Yet it is un-
derstandable that critics have considered them a journalistic failure.
Joseph Roth, for instance, marked the difference between Kracauer
and Benjamin thus:

> Krac [*sic*] is clear, well-grounded in the facts, pungent, bitter.
> Krac picks abstractions out of the air and brings them to life.
> Krac is a philosophic poet and therefore should be valued as a
> journalist. Krac is a Siamese prince.[83]

I leave out what Roth had to say, unfairly, about Benjamin getting
lost in "*Luftgeschäfte*," being an airhead. Nevertheless, he was right
about one thing: for many readers, Kracauer's urban miniatures may
be a better read, since they are more saturated with concrete perceptions of urban life. But Benjamin's *One-Way Street* remains a
uniquely powerful and demanding work in its relentless focus on the
centrality of script, the written word in an urban world increasingly
described as overwhelmed by the visual.

5

———⌁———

Double Exposure Berlin: Photomontage and Narrative in Höch and Keun

WHEN Baudelaire, Rilke, and Kafka zeroed in on the deficiencies of photography, they all had the single-perspective, seamless photographic print in mind. In the artistic practices and the illustrated press during the Weimar Republic, however, the multiperspectival image took off, both in high culture and in mass culture. It was especially in the photomontage work of Hannah Höch and John Heartfield that the reciprocity between the visual and the verbal and the interpenetration of high culture and mass media culture found new experimental forms, but avant-garde cinema and the novel soon followed suit.[1] Since multiperspectivalism, montage structure, and a close relationship to the mass media were important parts of the metropolitan miniature starting with Baudelaire, photomontage must be considered as a visual/verbal form that has close affinities with the metropolitan miniature.[2] This is especially important for a reading of the interwar miniaturists such as Kracauer, Benjamin, and Musil, who were all theorists of the visual media of their time and developed their writing of miniatures in relation to them. In that same period, montage also invaded the city novel in the work of writers such as Alfred Döblin and Irmgard Keun. Photomontage, the modernist novel, and the miniature had entered into a new triangulated relationship that must be considered as important backdrop for the metropolitan miniature of the interwar years.

When Döblin mounted urban icons, publicly posted announcements, or trolley schedules with their respective stops in *Berlin
Alexanderplatz*, he adapted the techniques of photomontage to literary fiction. At the same time, he juxtaposed urban montage, as the
subtitle of the novel indicated, with the story of Franz Biberkopf.
This jarring juxtaposition—itself of course a daring montage—
undermined the traditional model of the narrated city as we know it
from the urban novel of the nineteenth century. In Döblin's modernist epic, political and economic affairs of the city became abstract
and increasingly spatialized in their representation. The text of the
city as a network of traffic, commerce, information, political slo-
gans, and flows of commodities created the sense in the reader that
the city narrated itself in these montages, which deny both the
protagonist-centered perspective and omniscient narration. The city
itself became the narrator in the chapter "Rosenthaler Square Is
Talking" or when the text assembled pieces of information, fragments of stories, and representations of capital via a listing of addresses of a corporation's Berlin factories and subsidiaries.[3] Döblin's
literary montage resonates with Brecht's critical observation about
single-shot photography "that less than ever does the mere reflection
of reality reveal anything about reality."[4] Photomontage and literary
montage, with their multiperspectivalism and pileup of images and
information are as metropolitan as the assemblage of miniatures, but
it was the literary miniature that first blazed the trail the novel could
follow and photomontage could expand on when the technical pre-
requisites of camera and reproduction technology were in place.
    Within the visual arts, photomontage emerged as a minor form
in conscious departure from easel painting. Like the literary miniature, it was deeply implicated in the mass media, which it cannibal-
ized for its images and into which it fed its montage work as political
satire or propaganda. A good example is Hannah Höch's *Cut with the
Kitchen Knife Dada through the Last Weimar Beer-Belly Cultural Epoch
of Germany*, a collage of pasted papers that offered a satirical narrative of 1919 Weimar through cutout images of major public figures
in politics and the arts combined with images of ball bearings, car
wheels, and other machine parts and fragmented typography from
newspaper headlines.

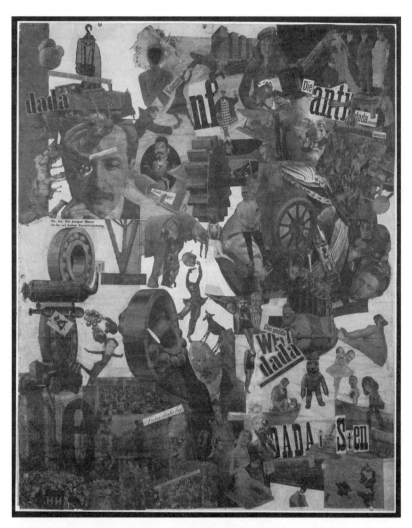

Hannah Höch, *Schnitt mit dem Küchenmesser durch die letzte Weimarer Bierbauchkulturepoche Deutschlands*, 1919, Nationalgalerie, Staatliche Museen zu Berlin, Germany. Photo: Jörg P. Anders. Art Resource, NY © 2014 Artists Rights Society (ARS), New York/VG Bild-Kunst, Bonn

John Heartfield's later anti-fascist photomontages published in the *Arbeiter Illustrierte Zeitung* similarly relied on media images, newspaper headlines, and quotations to reveal the link between big capital and the Nazi movement. The photomontage *Der Sinn des Hitlergrusses* (The meaning of the Hitler salute) combines the title

John Heartfield, *Der Sinn des Hitlergrusses: Kleiner Mann bittet um grosse Gaben. Motto: Millonen stehen hinter mir!*, 1932, Getty Research Institute, Los Angeles (87-S194) © 2014 Artists Rights Society (ARS), New York/VG Bild-Kunst, Bonn

with a Hitler quote as motto: "Millions stand behind me," and an emblem-like commentary as caption: "Little man asks for big gifts." "Millions" in this montage functions like the Wittgensteinian *Kippfigur*, that simple drawing that looks either like a duck or a rabbit, depending on how one looks at it. Its first meaning refers to National Socialism as a mass movement. But then Hitler's hand is bent backward to receive capital's donation of millions from a heavyset larger-than-life figure of an anonymous industrialist, seen in profile with only the lower part of his face visible. The photomontage takes

John Heartfield, book cover for Upton Sinclair, *Die Metropole* (The metropolis)
(Berlin: Malik, 1925), Getty Research Institute, Los Angeles (91-B35500)
© 2014 Artists Rights Society (ARS), New York/VG Bild-Kunst, Bonn

the linguistic image of the Hitler quote at its word and translates it
directly into visuality.[5]

As Benjamin once noted about Heartfield's montages, it was the
inscription that functioned as "the fuse guiding the critical spark to
the image mass."[6] In both Höch and Heartfield it was the combination of language and image that carried the political message. The
reciprocal translatability of the verbal and the visual was also evident in photomontage in the service of book publishing, another salient achievement by John Heartfield, who developed Weimar book
cover design in a stellar mix of typography and photography, especially in his covers for the Malik Verlag's translations of Sinclair Lew-
is's novels.

One of the most stunning book covers that extended front to
back and back to front is Sasha Stone's photomontage for Benjamin's
One-Way Street, the only image in an otherwise imageless book.[7]
While the literary miniature deliberately shunned pictures, photomonteurs such as Heartfield or Höch shared the miniaturists'
skepticism toward photography.[8] Photomontage arose not from

John Heartfield, book cover for Upton Sinclair, *Boston* (Berlin: Malik, 1929),
Getty Research Institute, Los Angeles (91-B10227). © 2014 Artists Rights
Society (ARS), New York/VG Bild-Kunst, Bonn

enthusiasm about photography but from disappointment with
a medium that had been very effectively abused by nationalist
Wilhelmine wartime propaganda.[9] Skepticism about mass media
photography, especially its claims of immediacy and authenticity,
also underlay the gender-critical photomontages of Hannah Höch.
In general, photomontage and large parts of the New Objectivity
(Neue Sachlichkeit) movement of the 1920s can be read as offering
"strategies devised by Germany's young artists to salvage, reclaim,
and reinvent a medium whose validity had been deeply impugned by
its heavy-handed use in war propaganda and its flaccid deployment
in the revolutionary movement that followed."[10] Heartfield and
Höch's critique of the mainstream media's use of images, focused as
it was on specific political and social realities in Weimar Germany,
parallels the theoretical critique of photography and film developed
by Kracauer and Benjamin at the time. And their project of reinventing a medium through photomontage runs parallel to the miniaturists' project of reinventing the medium of urban literature in
light of new forms of perception. Both photomonteurs and miniaturists could subscribe to Laszlo Moholy-Nagy's famous statement

in his programmatic 1925 Bauhaus book *Painting, Photography, Film* "that we see the world with entirely different eyes."[11]

This chapter touches upon those two cultural phenomena triangulated with the metropolitan miniature: photomontage on the side of the visual arts and montage in the novel on the side of a more traditional literary genre. Heartfield and Döblin have long been recognized as masters of metropolitan aesthetic practices that were new in the Weimar years. Focusing here on Höch and Keun as quasi-miniaturists in their own right has the advantage of opening up a gender dimension that has been largely lacking from the metropolitan miniature discussed so far in this book. Women's experience in the city of men and the ways women are seen and projected in urban context are central to both artists. Analogous to the miniature, their work is fundamentally grounded in photography and film, though at an explicit rather than implicit level. Höch deploys photomontage to transcend the limits of the photographic medium, while Keun incorporates cinematic vision into literary narrative.

Both Höch and Keun participate in fundamental ways in the problematic of metropolitan vision, of seeing the world with different eyes, Höch in her highly sophisticated ironization of male vision in her photomontages from the early 1920s, which achieve via montage what photography alone would not be able to render, and Keun in her equally complex fictionalization of what Doris, the protagonist of *The Artificial Silk Girl* (1932), calls cinematic writing. Their work lends itself well, both thematically and formally, to exploring the relationship between writing and visuality, script and image in both the visual arts and the fictional literature of the times. It is the reciprocal interweaving of script and image, narrative and visuality, that I would like to explore by reading a few of Höch's photomontages together with what I take to be the hidden montage aspect of Keun's deceptively simple novel.[12] My hypothesis is that double exposure as a montage strategy relying on metonymic assemblage is the key element that can ground the cross-media comparison of Höch's photomontage work with Keun's novel. In this context, double exposure not only points to the coupling of Höch and Keun in this chapter, nor is it simply meant to refer to the gendered doubling of vision in metropolitan experience. The term double exposure, which describes a common photographic technique, is used here to get at a principle of poetological construction that refuses the facile transparency of meaning and interpretation. This is an aspect their work shares with the metropolitan miniature, as it sits like a foreign body in the easily consumable feuilleton. At the same time there is no double exposure in the literary miniature, which instead is haunted by the deliberate absence of anything explicitly visual. Double exposure thus captures both Höch's and Keun's difference from and affinity to the literary miniature, and it points to these artists' stunning strategies of representation that are both photographic and verbal in Höch's urban photomontages and cinematic and narrative in the structure of Keun's novel.

At the same time, much seems to separate Höch's photomontages of the early 1920s from Keun's narrative from the early 1930s, a late-comer to the Neue Sachlichkeit. Höch's early work marked the beginnings of the Weimar Republic, with its revolutionary upheaval in politics and the arts. The idea of the New Woman was on the horizon, and Höch confronted it critically as a media projection at the time of its emergence. As a member of Berlin Dada, Höch belongs to the realm of avant-garde high art, whereas Keun's novels have often been read as belonging to mass cultural entertainment. Published in the early 1930s, they also marked the Republic's last phase after the receding of the avant-gardist energies of the 1920s, at a time when the ideal of the New Woman had shipwrecked on the economic and patriarchal realities of Weimar society. By the time Keun wrote, there was only one politically effective radicalism left—that of the Nazis. The Comintern, wed to Stalin's politics of "socialism in one country," had become delusional in its designation of social democracy as its main enemy, and this internecine battle split the Weimar left, including its major writers and artists. The issue of women's emancipation had faded into the background or was actively pushed back by economic realities after the 1929 crash. Keun narrated the radical disillusionment with the New Woman and *Girlkultur* that had set in long before the crash of 1929 produced its dismal effects on female employment, as analyzed by Alice Rühle-Gerstel in January 1933 in *Die literarische Welt*.[13] The difference in historical moments embodied in their work notwithstanding, both Höch and Keun drew explicitly and critically on the pleasures and promises of mass cul-

ture while developing complex visual and narrative strategies of representation. Both focused critically on gender, media, and vision in the
representation of women in Weimar culture. The political context
of Keun's critique was the social regression and political cul-de-sac
young lower-middle-class women of the late Weimar Republic faced,
while Höch's was the short-lived radical upsurge of the early republic.
Yet both indict patriarchal culture and its image media in remarkably
similar ways. Their feminist critique opens up another dimension
in the contemporary critical discussion of visual media central to
the emergence of the metropolitan miniature. Höch deployed photomontage as a critique of photography; Keun's novel revealed cinema
as a factory of illusions.

Hannah Höch

The genealogy of photomontage in popular culture is well known.
In Höch's recollection of 1966, Dada photomontage

> began with our seeing an amusing oleograph on the wall of our
> guest room in a fisherman's cottage on the Baltic sea. It depicted—
> fitted in among the pompous emblems of the empire—five
> standing soldiers in different uniforms—yet photographed only
> once—upon whom the head of the fisherman's son had five times
> been glued. This naively kitschy oleograph hung in many
> German rooms as a memento of the son's service as a soldier. It
> provided the occasion for Hausmann to expand upon the idea
> of working with photographs. Immediately after our return we
> began to do pictorial photomontage.[14]

It is easy to see how Höch's perhaps best-known political photomontage, *Cut with the Kitchen Knife Dada through the Last Weimar Beer-
Belly Cultural Epoch of Germany* (1919/20) (photomontage and collage
with water color, 114×90 cm), a work that was prominently displayed
at the famous Dada Fair of 1920, evolved from such popular representations in magazines, especially the *Berliner Illustrierte Zeitung*.
Cutouts from newspaper photos, advertisements, and newsprint in
fragments created a complex kaleidoscope of early Weimar political
and cultural realities.[15] But explicit political satire of the Kaiser, the
military, and the Weimar Sozialdemokratische Partei Deutschlands

(SPD) was only one aspect of Höch's early work. Already in *Cut with the Kitchen Knife*, she foregrounded the theme of gender and patriarchy, women's voting rights (the voting rights map of European countries at the bottom right) and women's art and performance practices (dancer Niddy Impekoven's body with Käthe Kollwitz's head in center). Höch's playfulness, irony, and love of ambivalence, even in her political montages, have often been contrasted with the revolutionary heavy hitting of her Dada comrades Grosz and Heartfield, who, despite their blatant misogyny, are usually considered the real radicals. But her use of irony and ambivalence never took away from her radical critique of the social and cultural status quo. In her work, ambivalence and irony are not necessarily incompatible with radicalism. As facilitating double entendre in the spectator, they can be seen as major effects of double exposure.

Two of Höch's works from 1919/20: *Da Dandy* (photomontage and collage, 30×23 cm) and *The Beautiful Girl* (photomontage and collage, 25×29 cm) can be profitably related to Keun's novel in terms of double exposure. Both photomontages focus on gender issues, fashion, the gaze, and women's position in a world in which mechanization has taken command, to use Siegfried Giedion's famous phrase. In contrast to *Cut with a Kitchen Knife*, a work that tried to encapsulate the early Weimar Republic in an almost totalizing montage, these two photomontages concentrate attention on one specific issue, fashion and the male gaze. Condensation and laserlike focus is what approximates them as visual collages to the literary miniature. *Da Dandy* highlights the fragmented head and torso shots of three elegantly and very similarly dressed fashionable women, set against a background of collaged papers in soft reds, yellows, and blues. In her pathbreaking study of Höch, Maud Lavin wrote:

> This is the twenties version of the female dandy, upscale and flamboyant, dressed in an elaborate hat, pearl earrings, a pearl necklace, bracelets and a velvet dress, with a beaded purse and heels.[16]

In two of the women, one eye has been noticeably enlarged, as if it held a monocle, a favorite attribute of the male Dada dandy. Höch

Hannah Höch, *Da-Dandy*, 1919, private collection.
Giraudon/Bridgeman Images © 2014 Artists Rights
Society (ARS), New York/VG Bild-Kunst, Bonn

once quipped that her partner, Raoul Hausmann, was probably born
wearing a monocle. Clearly the montage draws attention to the eye,
to vision and to fashion in general, as any discussion of dandyism
would. But whose vision is it? Is it the vision of those women who
look out seductively at the spectator and whose monocled eyes seem
to have appropriated the male dandy's power of the gaze? Here we
remember, of course, that the dandy, like the flâneur, had been centrally coded as male ever since Baudelaire's seminal work on urban
life.[17] And feminist critics such as Griselda Pollock or Janet Wolff
have argued that if one did not simply want to imagine the flaneuse
as street walker, one needed a closer examination of women's spaces

Hannah Höch, *Das schöne Mädchen*, 1920, private collection, Berlin. Art
Resource, NY © 2014 Artists Rights Society (ARS), New York/VG
Bild-Kunst, Bonn

and women's experience in the modern city.[18] Höch and Keun contributed in major ways to such an investigation.

But does *Da Dandy* represent the vision of the New Weimar Woman
claiming public freedom and the independence of the female look in
both senses?[19] Is this a collage about the female dandy as independent woman, as Maud Lavin suggests? It is a plausible reading at first
sight. But then we notice that the three collaged women occupy a

space that reveals the silhouette of a man's head and torso seen in profile, the outline of his head marked by a bit of red backing paper. The flamboyant New Woman is lodged in the male head, a product of his imagination as it is splattered across the world of popular media and illustrated papers from which these photos were taken in the first place. This is Höch's subtle critique of the representation of women in the fashionable media. The monocled eyes assume a different, less emancipatory connotation in this alternative reading. And then we see the fragments of a fourth and fifth head, one female on the left, eyes lowered and as if kissing the shoulders of the leftmost woman or those of the profiled man, the other on the right between nose and mouth of the silhouetted figure, possibly male with the monocle effect in the right rather than the left eye and looking in the direction in which the profiled male figure would be looking. The three women in the male's head are thus framed by the lowered submissive eyes of a woman and the determined look of a man. The female dandy is morphed back into the male dandy, and we are still dealing with traditional gender tropes.

I suggest that the work hovers between these two readings. Both make valid points, but they are juxtaposed here without one yielding entirely to the other. The reading of *Da Dandy* as emancipated woman may be superficially more evident, but as soon as one looks closer while at the same time maintaining critical distance, that other dimension reveals a significant frame not visible at first sight. Clearly it is not all just evident surface. There is a kind of double exposure here of the figure of the dandy in the Dada age that explicitly states the theme of the fashionable modern New Woman while sublimi- nally inscribing the male as controlling her space and her looks. The opposing readings, both of which are feminist, reveal the work to be something like a Wittgensteinian *Kippfigur*.

Double exposure of a different kind is at stake in *The Beautiful Girl*. It is well known that one of the main fantasies of Weimar culture was that of technological liberation, the machine cult, and the imag- ined promises of Taylorization for everyday life, as paradigmatically embodied in the streamlined Frankfurt kitchen.[20] Höch countered this technological fantasy much earlier than some of her male col- leagues by focusing on the effects of technological utopias on women, thus anticipating Kracauer's critique of the Tiller Girls as Taylorized ornament.[21] The beautiful girl in a bathing suit with parasol and a huge light bulb for a head sits atop a structure made up of a girder, an I-beam, and an oil barrel. Behind her looms a huge head with an ad for some technical machinery in lieu of a face. A woman's bobbed and puffed hairdo surrounds the poster and fills almost the whole upper part of the work. It is as if the woman in the bathing suit actually had two heads. The space of the beautiful girl is strictly confined, threatened on the right by a crankshaft, on the left by a tire through which a black boxer, an image of heavyweight American champion Jack Johnson, is about to land a blow on her body.[22] Multiply repeated and overlapping BMW logos give the whole work the air of an advertisement, for *Körperkultur* and machines, for modern hairdos and the sport of boxing. The combination of a woman's body with the insignia of the automobile points to the identification of woman with the automobile in advertising culture, itself a rewriting of the much older topos of woman as allegory of technology, either threatening or beneficial: beneficial as in the many allegorical representations of progress and technology in images created for the universal expositions of the nineteenth century; threatening, for instance, in the robot Maria in Fritz Lang's *Metropolis* or in the female mutant in Ridley Scott's *Blade Runner.*

But in this work, too, there is another submerged dimension. The beautiful girl has no eyes to see, although some have read the light bulb as a signifier of the enlightened Weimar woman. But such a reading misses the critical gaze from behind the scene. For the only eyes in the work are those of a female head on the top right, in black and white, in contrast to the brown tints and painted colors in the foreground. It is this woman behind the scenes, as it were, who reinforces the critical dimension of the image. With her left eye she peers over a BMW logo, while her right eye is replaced by an enlarged cat's eye staring at the spectator. The estrangement here is not achieved by the male monocle, although the device of enlarging the eye is the same. It is rather a cat's eye, and cats are usually connoted as feminine. What we have here, then, is a woman looking at the use of women in advertising, the beautiful girl not being a sample of celebrated Weimar *Girlkultur*, but the instrumentalized product of advertising. A fleshy male hand separates the woman behind the

scene from the foreground, and it lets dangle a watch as if to demonstrate who is in control of production time (Taylorism) and of the
space of advertising and the media itself.[23] It is the disciplining rationalization of self and life that stands in the way of emancipation,
preventing modernity's promises from being fulfilled. Höch articulates in ironic photomontages what Kracauer, without irony and in a
broader philosophical context, will argue a few years later in "The
Mass Ornament" and in his sociological study *The Salaried Masses*.
By comparison with *Cut with a Kitchen Knife*, which, in its overflowing
assemblage of images, offers an almost totalizing vista of the early
Weimar Republic, *Da Dandy* and *Beautiful Girl* resonate with the
miniature as form in that they focus intensely on just one aspect of
metropolitan life: the photographic transformation of women's images into fashionable commodity images as products of the male
imagination. The kind of affirmative sabotage Baudelaire practiced
on feuilleton modes of writing appears here as a double exposure of
fashion journals and advertising imaginaries.

Irmgard Keun

At first sight there seems to be an insuperable difference between
Höch's avant-gardist montage practice and the episodic but continuous narrative of Keun's novel, which tracks a definite arc from up-
beat beginning to downbeat ending. In its sustained focus on the girl
from the provinces as protagonist, the novel is clearly less experimental than Döblin's *Berlin Alexanderplatz*. But its apparent narrative simplicity is deceiving. Here, too, one has to take a second closer
look. There are several longer passages about metropolitan Berlin
in the novel that can be read as a literary equivalent of photomontage in motion, a key example of what is often discussed as cinematic
writing in the literature of the Weimar Republic. The affinity of these
passages to the metropolitan miniature lies in their reliance on modes
of seeing mediated through film and photography. At the same time
they are clearly different from the miniature in that they are part of
a plot and told in a first-person narrative voice, the voice of the artificial silk girl.

Keun has her protagonist Doris tell her story in the form of loosely
arranged notations from everyday life, superficially analogous to the
narrator protagonist in *The Notebooks of Malte Laurids Brigge*, whose

Paris project is to learn how to see. But Malte has the high artistic ambitions of his author; Doris does not. She is a young lower-middle-class woman from the provinces who gets fired from her secretarial job in Cologne, has a brief stint as an extra in the theater, breaks up with her lover, borrows money, steals a fancy fur coat, and takes the night train to Berlin, where she dreams of becoming *"ein Glanz,"* a glamour.[24] In Berlin she never secures a white collar job, nor does she want to. She does not become a member of Kracauer's salaried masses. Instead, she maintains herself with the help of women friends and in a series of fleeting relationships with men. At the same time she is quite aware of the risk of slipping into prostitution. In her love for the movies and popular culture, she at first might appear like one of Kracauer's little shop girls who go to the movies in order to day-dream and take flight from their humdrum everyday reality.[25] But what distinguishes her from Kracauer's little shop girls is her project of writing about her life, a writing in which she sees herself seeing and being seen:[26]

> And I think it will be a good thing if I write everything down, because I'm an unusual person. I don't mean a diary—that's ri-diculous for a trendy girl like me. But I want to write like a movie, because my life is like that and it's going to become even more so. And I look like Colleen Moore, if she had a perm and her nose were a little more fashionable, like pointing up. And when I read it later on, everything will be like at the movies—I'm looking at myself in pictures.[27]

Reading and seeing a movie are equated in this last sentence. Her life is like a movie, and any movie wants to be seen. This means that she defines herself by the way she is seen by the spectator, and that spectator is invariably male. But she does not just look at herself in relation to the male gaze in her writing, she also looks at the city "in pictures," as if Berlin were a movie. At one point she deftly says: "My life is Berlin, and I'm Berlin" (78). Self-image and Berlin as movie image merge. Clearly she is not interested in the diary as a confes-sional mode focused on interiority. At stake for Keun and her pro-tagonist is the metropolitan young woman and the metropolis itself

as image—media image, to be precise. It is all about reproducible surface. Doris's arrival at Bahnhof Friedrichstrasse reads like a montage
of found images from the start:

> I'm in Berlin. Since a few days ago. After an all-night train ride
> and with 90 marks left. That's what I have to live on until I come
> into some money. What I have since experienced is just incred-
> ible. Berlin descended on me like a comforter with a flaming
> floral design. The Westside is very elegant with bright lights—
> like fabulous stones, really expensive and in an ornate setting.
> We have enormous neon advertising around here. Sparkling
> lights surround me. And then there's me and my fur coat. And
> elegant men like white-slave traders, without exactly trafficking
> in women at the moment, those no longer exist—but they look
> like it, because they would be doing it if there was money in it.
> A lot of shining black hair and deep-set eyes. Exciting. There
> are many women on the *Kurfürstendamm*. They simply walk.
> They have the same faces and a lot of moleskin fur—not exactly
> first class, in other words, but still chic—with arrogant legs and
> a great waft of perfume about them. There is a subway; it's like
> an illuminated coffin on rails [translation corrected—AH]—
> under the ground and musty, and one is squashed. That is what
> I ride on. It's interesting and it travels fast. (55-56)

It may be an incredible experience for Doris, but we know these prefab
images from Kracauer's writings, from Kirchner's paintings, from
Weimar cabaret, and as readers we take pleasure in their effective
rearrangement.[28] Clichés, *idées reçues*, metropolitan topoi are strung
together metonymically in Doris's first-person account of her new
life in Berlin. It is a language of *images trouvés* in accelerated succes-
sion and staccato style. In this micropassage, metonymic assemblage,
strung together by an excited narrating subject, creates a structure
analogous to the assemblage of miniatures in the other texts discussed
in this book. Even if the effect on the reader may be different, the
structure of metonymy pertains in both.

Just as Doris is more complex a figure than Kracauer's condescendingly and self-consciously described naïve shop girls who simply get

caught up in the cinematic machine of illusions, a closer look at the structure of the novel indeed reveals that it is much less conventional and seamless than it first appears. The stereotypical dream of poor girl meets rich boy, so central to Weimar cinema in Kracauer's account, is mercilessly dismantled by Keun's double exposure technique. There are two voices present in Doris's first-person narrative: the experiencing voice of the naïve young woman seemingly caught in false consciousness on the one hand, and a narrating critical voice that seems to transcend the voice of Doris's immediate experience and analytic abilities. The consistent use of first-person narration, however, guarantees that these two voices overlap and appear as one. Some readers have even taken them to be identical, which in turn has given rise to reductive readings of Doris as subject and agent of her own emancipation. But as subject—and this is where Keun's critique emerges as similar to Höch's—Doris sees herself as a screen for male projections rather than as an agent, and all her reflections circle around maintaining those projections. In that sense she, too, is a voided subject, analogous to and yet different from the many male figures in the modernist canon who struggle with their loss of identity. Sociologically one can think here of the voiding of interiority and psychological cohesion that Kracauer described as *condition moderne* of the salaried masses of Weimar's white-collar employees, even though Doris never aspires to hold a job in Berlin.[29] But it is perhaps no coincidence that the term "*Glanz*" as glamour also appears in Kracauer's account. He says of the mass of salaried employees:

> Nothing is more characteristic of this life, which only in a restricted sense can be called a life, than its view of higher things. Not as substance, but as glamour. Yielded not through concentration, but in distraction.[30]

If indeed there is a lack of substance underlying Doris's dreams of glamour, that other reading becomes pertinent with the suggestion that there are actually two voices in Doris, rendered in her writing style. On the one hand, Doris writes in grammatically flawed and stereotypical language, which, despite her undeniable street smarts, demonstrates her lack of education and limited awareness of larger social and political issues she is simply not interested in. At the same time, the narrating voice also demonstrates a critical understanding of her economically precarious situation as subject of the male gaze and victim of bourgeois hypocrisy that would clearly elude a simply naïve figure. The danger of slipping into prostitution represented by the story of her friend Hulla is a constant threat. This double exposure, masterfully handled by Keun, makes Doris a radical *Kunstfigur* rather than a psychologically realistic character.

Examples are abundant. Doris's endearing naïveté and faux sentimentality opens the novel:

> It must have been twelve midnight last night that I felt something magnificent [translation modified—AH] happening inside of me. I was in bed—I had meant to wash my feet, but I was too tired after that hectic night the day before. . . . And as I was lying there and my whole body was asleep already, only my eyes were still open—and the white moonlight was shining on my head, and I was thinking how nice that goes with my black hair and what a shame Hubert can't see me like that, when he's the only one, after all, whom I've ever loved. And then I felt the aura of Hubert surrounding me, and the moon was shining and I could hear a gramophone playing next door, and then something magnificent happened inside of me—as had happened before, but never anything like this. I felt like writing a poem, but that might have had to rhyme and I was too tired for that. But I realized that there is something unusual about me. (1-2)

Already here, however, reality intrudes. She is too tired to try rhymes just as she is also too tired to wash her feet. The epiphany of magnificence is shot through with reality particles, a pattern deployed time and again throughout the novel.

But then there is that other voice, the voice of Doris as street-smart critic of male sexual hypocrisy. As she describes an encounter in a bar, she uses a highly ironic allegorical name for the man who comes after her for quick pleasure, an estranging device often repeated in the novel whenever Doris wants to establish ironic distance between her and the suitor at hand:

At the Jockey Bar, I met the Red Moon—his wife is on vacation, because times are bad and seaside resorts are cheaper in
October than in July. He just happened to be in the Jockey Bar
by coincidence, as he's traditional and he's disgusted by the new
times because of their lax morals and politics. He wants the
Kaiser back and is writing novels and is well-known from the
past. He also says that he has esprit [*Geist*]. And his principle is:
men can and women cannot. So I'm asking myself: How can men
do it without women? What an idiot. (67)

The doubling of the voice allows Keun to tell the story in such a
way that the reader sees through Doris's illusions long before she
herself does. Doris's syntax is colloquial, her grammar faulty, her
writing marred by constructions that reveal more about her than
she herself can possibly be aware of.[31] If she sees herself in images,
the text leaves no doubt that these images correspond to male fantasies and cinematic framing. As Doris moves from one relationship
to the next, she never really shares the ideal of the Weimar New
Woman as an independent working woman. By the early 1930s,
Keun seems to suggest, it is too late for that. The novel takes place
in 1931, at a time of growing mass unemployment and rising re-
sentment about women wage earners as "double dippers," *Doppel-
verdiener*.[32] She does not seek independence through professional
clerical work, the kind of job she had held in Cologne. She wants to
rise socially to be a glamour with the help of and for the benefit of
her male acquaintances, who are usually anything but glamorous.
Accordingly, it is the male look that constitutes her wish image of
herself. She certainly knows that she does not look like film star
Colleen Moore: she is fully aware that one of her legs is thicker
than the other and that she has other physical "imperfections"
such as thin lips and an anemic complexion. But then she enters
into a relationship with a con man and takes on airs of a high society lady:

I pick up the phone from my bed with its silk cover and dial a
number and say: "Alexi, my ruby-red morning sun, why don't
you bring me a pound of *Godiva*."

"Aye, aye, dollface," he says, and I stay in bed resting in my lace nightgown or negligé. . . .

Alex says: "Come on, dollface, let's have some champagne. My little Mickey Mouse, you're like a drop of dew."

He's a gentleman, even though he's short and fat. All his friends—all of them big industries [translation modified— AH]—say to him: "Old curmudgeon, where did you find that beautiful woman?" and kiss my hand. (108-109)

She knows throughout the novel that the pretense of being a glamour depends largely on the stolen fur coat that gives her an air of superiority, beauty, and elegance she otherwise lacks. The glamour she aspires to is like an escape into the fur, a reading Simone de Beauvoir suggested in *The Second Sex*.[33] But the fur with its warmth and tenderness does not keep awareness of her short-comings at bay for long. Gendered reality reasserts itself ever more strongly as the novel comes to its conclusion in the waiting room of a train station in midwinter. But what we get is not simply a kind of female *éducation sentimentale* as a Weimar lesson in downward social mobility. Instead, and right from the start, we get the piti-less deconstruction of a female dream world that founders on the persistence of patriarchal moral hypocrisy and bourgeois double standards. This deconstruction is narrated in a series of episodic passages, each of which illuminates a station in Doris's life that is determined by specific relationships with men from different walks of life. The text offers a series of clichés of male behavior, one that Keun has summarized in a spoofy essay addressed to women on how to capture men.[34] She ends up leaving any of these fleeting relationships with some new clothes and accessories, but she always loses:

Things are looking up. I have five undershirts made of Bem-berg silk with hand-sewn seams, a handbag made of cowhide with some crocodile appliqué, a small grey felt hat, and a pair of shoes with lizard toes. But then my red dress that I'm wearing day and night is starting to tear under the arms. Thus I have started to make contacts in a bar with a textile enterprise

which, however, isn't going so well at the moment" (66, translation modified)

Double exposure again: the relationship with yet another suitor
isn't going well, and neither is the textile business, a condensed superimposition of the man in the bar with the state of his business.

   Though presented as continuous narrative, the novel is thus much
more of a collage text than is usually acknowledged: collage of voices,
of sentimental naïveté and street smarts, of fascination with the glittering surfaces of metropolitan life and their simultaneous disman-
tling as false promises. Key is a much-commented-upon scene in the
novel that makes metropolitan vision itself the theme of narrative.
It is the only time where Doris can be an active subject of her own
vision, but it, too, ends in disappointment. It is the scene of Doris's
encounter with a blind World War I veteran, with whom she has the
most emotionally intense relationship in the novel. The premise is
simple:

> I collect images [*Sehen*] for him. I walk around the streets and
> the restaurants and among people and lanterns. And then I try
> to remember what I've seen and bring it to him. (83)

She can do this because in her relation to the blind Mr. Brenner she
doesn't have to worry about how she is being seen by him. And as
she says "My life is Berlin and I'm Berlin" (78), she gives herself to
the shy and unhappily married Mr. Brenner, who doesn't even dare
to kiss her. "I offer him Berlin which is resting in my lap" (87), she
says with obvious double entendre.

   What follows is a lengthy montage of street scenes Doris has observed on her way through the city and as we know them from Weimar
cinema. Her account is interrupted time and again by Brenner's question: "What else do you see? What else." The present tense empha-
sizes that Doris actually brings Berlin to him in a series of memo-
rized metonymically linked observations, images, experiences in
accelerated staccato style that try to make the blind man see anew:

> I saw men standing at corners selling perfume, without a coat
> and a pert face and a gray cap on—and posters with naked and

rosy girls on them and nobody looking at them—a restaurant
with more chrome than an operating room—they even have oys-
ters there—and famous photographers with photos in showcases
displaying enormous people without any beauty. And sometimes
with. (87)

And as Mr. Brenner keeps asking impatiently as if to accelerate the
speed "what else do you see, what else?" she continues:

I see—swirling lights with light bulbs right next to each other—
women without veils with hair blown into their faces. That's the
new hairstyle—it's called "windblown"—and the corners of their
mouths are like actresses before they take on a big role and black
furs and fancy gowns underneath—and shiny eyes—and they
are either a black drama or a blonde cinema. Cinemas are primarily blonde—I'm moving right along with them with my fur
that is so gray and soft—and my feet are racing, my skin is
turning pink, the air is chilly and the lights are hot—I'm looking,
I'm looking—my eyes are expecting the impossible. (88)

It is as if Doris showed him a film of Berlin, quite analogous to Höch's
montages that juxtapose aspects of modern life in a mix of irony, melancholy, and a kind of knowing playful distanciation from the world.
Both Höch's images and Keun's narrative are collected seeing, miniatures of the urban, never immediate but mediated through the world
of mass media reproductions in one case and the memory and fantasy world of a mass media consumer on the other. But in both cases
it is the hand of the artist who creates the effect of double exposure.
      Double exposure is also present in the following scenes with blind
Brenner, when disillusionment sets in. Eventually Doris tires of all
this seeing: "I unpack my eyes for him," she says reaching the end of
her rope. "What else did I see?" (92) and "but I keep staring—and
that's just the way I have to stare now, because I have to see so much"
(94). Another day when she takes Brenner on an exceptional outing
into the city, reality asserts itself. They crisscross Berlin in taxis and
buses, drink vodka in a Russian restaurant, beer at a restaurant at
Wittenbergplatz, wine at Haus Vaterland, but that is when, under
the influence of alcohol, everything turns sour:

All I want to do is cry. Let's go—everything looks different all of a sudden—in front of the Vaterland, someone is beating a poor girl—she's screaming—and a police officer arrives—a lot of people are standing around, not knowing where to go and there's no glamour and nobody there—only dead tombstones. (101-102)

Her only wish is that the blind man love her and her Berlin as she loves it. But the blind man sees something she doesn't want to see:

"The city isn't good and the city isn't happy and the city is sick," he says—"but you are good and I thank you for that." (103)

The Berlin dream has collapsed. Coldness and distance now envelop their relationship, just as he anticipates moving into a veterans' home because his wife can no longer care for him. It is the end of their relationship.

There is only one other scene that promises emotional fulfillment for Doris before her final descent into an unknown and insecure future. After yet another failed relationship, she is alone again:

My head felt like an empty swirling hole. I created a dream for myself and rode up and down the streets of Berlin for hours on end, all by myself.

And I did that because usually I get to take taxis only with men who want to smooch. . . . But today, I rode around in a taxi like rich people, leaning back in my seat and looking out the window—lots of cigar stores on the corners—and movie theaters—*The Congress Dances*—Lilian Harvey is blonde—bakeries—and lit-up street numbers on houses and some without—and tracks—yellow trams gliding past me and people inside could tell that I was a glamour [translation modified—AH]—I'm leaning way back in my cushions and I don't watch how the fare is adding up—I won't allow my ears to hear the click—blue lights, red lights, millions of lights—shop windows—dresses, but no models—sometimes other cars go faster—

bedding stores—a green bed that isn't really a bed, but more modern. It's flipping around itself, feathers whirling around in a large glass—people on foot—the modern bed turning.

I would so much love to be happy. (111-112)

If in the relation with Brenner she gives him a Berlin as an imagined movie, functioning like a camera eye, in this passage she is both camera eye and object of the spectators' gaze. She imagines the passengers on the tram imagining her as a movie star enveloped by glamour in the taxi. But the moment of glamour and imagined stardom is illusion, and she knows it.

Cliché as Critique

Höch takes her idiom from the banal images of the mass media (much of it from the *Berliner Illustrierte Zeitung*), but creates a syntax different from that of illustrated papers by deploying ironic and exuberant montage, metonymic *enchainement* of seemingly unrelated materials and thematic clusterings. Analogously, Keun draws on the linguistic and cinematic clichés of metropolitan life while her protagonist moves from one man to the next. She recycles men and clichés through lower-class nongrammatical language with faulty syntax, inverted word order, malapropisms, and seemingly uncontrolled random associations. All of it is as carefully constructed and shaped for poetic effect by the author as is the deliberate arrangement of cutouts in Höch's photomontages. The visual montage in Höch always tells some story about life in the metropolis, and the narrative unit in Keun always remains oriented toward the visual surfaces of urban life. Both artists focus intensely on gendered vision. In both, woman appropriates male vision but remains caught within it: Höch by outfitting her montaged women with oversized monocles like eyes, Keun by having Doris offer her collected seeing to her blind veteran neighbor. But in both cases, the attempt to claim an independent female identity mobilized by vision shipwrecks on the persistence of social structures that neither radical art nor radical politics have been able to change. Both artists make cutting critical use of the clichés provided by popular culture, but in the end it is the power of convention that prevails, outliving the challenge to patriarchal structures of Weimar society. With their pessimistic take on women's emancipation performed in a poetics of double exposure, Höch's and Keun's critiques of a photographic and cinematic imaginary joins the critique of media and the metropolis articulated in the literary miniature.

6

——⟋⟍⟋——

Benjamin and Aragon:
Le Paysan de Berlin

There are words that are mirrors, optical lakes towards which
hands stretch out in vain.

       —Aragon, *Paris Peasant*

BENJAMIN's *Berlin Childhood around 1900* is a collection
of miniatures that is fundamentally different in tone, sensibility, and
execution from *One-Way Street*. It is not focused on the present and
the future but on the past, including the future of that past, intimated
in retrospective thirty years later. The focus still is on images and
space, but not on urban *Schrift-Bilder* and street scripts enlarged by
commentary and reflection, as in that earlier collection of miniatures.
The collection evokes a bourgeois child's experiences of urban life,
reimagined and written with a sense of the irrecuperability of a past
submerged deep within, fragmented by temporal and spatial distance
across the political divide that was World War I, and haunted by a
life of homelessness and exile in flight from the Nazis. The writing
is saturated with sensual experiential material shaping a typical bourgeois childhood rather than indulging in existential lament about loss.
Especially the final version of *Berlin Childhood* thus partakes in the
kind of desubjectivized writing Kafka first introduced in the miniature. And yet it is a desubjectivized writing of a very different kind.

It is a memory text, after all, narrated by an unsentimental, doubly historicized *ich*, and as such quite different from Kafka's short prose in *Betrachtung*. Clearly the carefully constructed first-person narration can be read here as a strategy of self-protection from nostalgia, but if anything, it increases the emotive effect of loss and melancholy on the historically aware reader who sees a disappeared world reappear in ghostlike yet objectivized form. There is something surreal about the scenes and fragments conjured up in these miniatures. Rather than focus on personalized memories, Benjamin creates generic moments, drenched, like the images at the Imperial Panorama, in an aura of vanishing, repeatable in time and space though they may be. It is no coincidence that the miniatures focus on seasonal experiences, on festive days such as Christmas, walks to the market, visits to relatives or to the zoo. Darkness prevails throughout, multiple snowfalls and rainy days enticing dreamy states of mind. The telephone located in a dark corner of an apartment corridor is associated with nocturnal noises. There is the lighting of a fire in the coal stove on an early winter morning, the walk with his mother to the store through gaslit streets on a winter evening, the visit at Aunt Lehmann's apartment, dimly lit by gaslight, the twilight on the way home from the much-disliked public swimming pool, the black and impenetrable depths of the basin's waters from which the zoo's otter suddenly emerges in order to disappear just as quickly, and finally the danger of the apartment break-in at night and the child's gaze downward into the small skylights of subterranean basement apartments, from which reciprocal mysterious looks then haunt him in his dreams. Images of death are ever present: the death of Luise von Landau as a young girl, the grandmother's death, the father telling his son about a distant cousin's death from syphilis. Death is even present during summer vacation outside the city at Potsdam's Brauhausberg when the boy engages in a butterfly hunt, that childlike collecting activity that ends inevitably with the captured animal pierced by a needle. Time and again, the narrator conjures up heterotopic spaces in the labyrinth of the city, among which the Berlin zoo takes pride of place. A porousness between human and animal is subtly hinted at in several miniatures, a theme that was to become central to Musil's *Posthumous Papers of a Living Author*. Even language is haunted by the kind of indecipherability that twilight brings: the distortions and oscillations between written and spoken language in the child's mind, as in "Market Hall," "The Mummerehlen," and "Blumeshof." It may not be the kind of surrealism we know from the work of André Breton's prose, Paul Eluard's poetry, or Max Ernst's collages. But it is—this is my hypothesis—something akin to what Aragon, in the early phase of surrealism, called *le merveilleux quotidien* (the marvelous of the everyday), except that in Benjamin it appears in the guise of a child's experience reconstructed decades later by the adult author.[1]

Aragon's and surrealism's influence on the writing of *One-Way Street* and on the initial stages of the *Arcades Project* has been duly noted in the critical literature.[2] But there is also a consensus that Benjamin, in the wake of his turn toward Marxism, came to be increasingly critical of surrealism from the late 1920s onward, especially in his celebrated essay on surrealism and with a few scattered but often-quoted comments on Aragon in the *Arcades Project*. This assumption of Benjamin's rejection or overcoming of surrealism has by and large blocked from view what I take to be a continuing subterranean debt to Aragon, a debt that I propose to trace in *Berlin Childhood*, Benjamin's major literary work of the 1930s. In question here is the lingering impact of early Aragon texts such as *Une vague de rêves* (1924) and *Le Paysan de Paris* (1926), both of which Benjamin read shortly after they were published.

Le Paysan de Paris is of course not a text assembled from miniatures. As a city novel, it stands in a similarly oblique relationship to the urban miniature as Rilke's *The Notebooks of Malte Laurids Brigge*. Both authors greatly admired Baudelaire: Rilke at the level of poetic language and allegory, Aragon at the level of Baudelairean aesthetic categories he appropriated and transformed such as the ephemeral and the transitory, the bizarre, and *le beau banal* (the banal as beautiful). Both works elude any clear-cut classification as novels, marking key moments in the trajectory of modernist narratives. They are hybrid texts. The mixing of genres and styles, the inclusion of descriptions, anecdotes, theoretical reflections, and prose poems is common to both. Both foreground sensual perception in the metropolitan context, especially vision but also sound and tactility. Aragon, due no doubt to his closeness to the Dada experiments with word and image, actually montages visual materials into his text such as newspaper clips, ads, commercial signage, and bar menus, but in contrast to Breton never any photographs. Both Rilke and Aragon's narratives are autobiographically loaded in quite explicit ways. But where Paris generates fears, anxieties, paranoia, and a threat to any stable subjectivity in Malte, Aragon's narrator searches for ecstatic illuminations in an urban environment in which he privileges marginalized heterotopic spaces such as the old arcades and the Buttes-Chaumont Park in Paris's proletarian east. The strong link backward to Baudelaire's miniatures in Rilke corresponds to Benjamin's transformative use of an Aragonian inspiration in his urban miniatures of *Berlin Childhood around 1900*. My focus on Aragon and surrealism is meant to supplement rather than replace the standard account of Proust and Baudelaire's influence on what is arguably Benjamin's most captivating literary text.[3]

Textual History: The Versions of *Berlin Childhood around 1900*

Many of these memorable miniatures were written just before Hitler came to power and then reworked under precarious conditions of exile from 1933 to 1938. Twenty-six pieces were prepublished from 1933 to 1935 in the *Frankfurter Zeitung* and *Vossische Zeitung*, usually under a pseudonym due to Nazi censorship, but several of them appeared without any attribution at all. Seven more were published in Thomas Mann's exile journal *Mass und Wert* in 1938. A first book edition with thirty-seven miniatures was published by Adorno in 1950, a decade after Benjamin's tragic suicide in Port Bou at the French-Spanish border, but it was still based on a very unstable and incomplete print and manuscript situation.[4] The 1972 version in *Gesammelte Schriften* was based on Adorno's edition, but it now contained forty-one pieces. The manuscript of a heavily reworked and abridged final version that Benjamin himself assembled and provided a foreword for in 1938 was discovered by Giorgio Agamben in 1981 in the Bibliothèque Nationale in Paris and published in volume 7 of the *Gesammelte Schriften* in 1989, but even here there are legitimate doubts about how final that version really is.[5] Yet another early manuscript version of 1932 (thirty pieces like the 1938 manuscript but not yet containing some key pieces written after 1932) was discovered even later, in 1988. This so-called Giessen version was published separately by Suhrkamp in 2000.

This complex textual history of *Berlin Childhood*, which itself emerged from another set of more traditionally discursive urban tableaux entitled *Berlin Chronicle*, poses challenges for those who attempt to identify clear-cut Aragonian traces. Certain affinities, such as the foregrounding of an unveiled autobiographical narrative voice, as we have it in *Le Paysan*, are still visible in the earlier more expansive and anecdotal vignettes, but they have been eliminated in the highly condensed miniatures of 1938.[6] As early as 1932, Benjamin took an anti-autobiographical stance in *Berlin Chronicle*:

> Reminiscences, even extensive ones, do not always amount to an autobiography. And these quite certainly do not, even for the Berlin years that I am exclusively concerned with here. For autobiography has to do with time, with sequence and what makes up the continuous flow of life. Here, I am talking of space, of moments and discontinuities.[7]

The concern with space, moments, and discontinuities also characterizes Aragon's *Paysan* and Breton's *Nadja*, despite their autobiographical first-person narratives. In what follows I will focus on the 1938 version, the least autobiographically coded one, which is literarily the most accomplished though it also lacks some wonderful passages from earlier versions that I will draw on as appropriate.

Despite this complex genealogy of manuscripts of varying lengths and different treatments of language, narrator figure, imagery, and metaphors, the different versions have much in common. All memories are organized in spatial images, as if to remind us of the age-old insight that memory attaches first to space and only secondarily to time. Key urban spaces are the Tiergarten, historical monuments and statues such as the Victory Column and statues of royalty in the Tiergarten, the imperial panorama, and the Anhalter train station. Other sites include the vacation home at Potsdam's Brauhausberg, the apartments of an aunt and the maternal grandmother, stairways in the apartment houses of Berlin's West End, the market hall, a dark corner in the zoo with a mysterious otter, Peacock Island, winter mornings and evenings at home, being sick in bed, the larder, the school library, and, very prominently, the loggia of his home apartment with its caryatids. The spaces are socially very circumscribed by Berlin's upper-class West End, which offered Benjamin a protective bourgeois childhood. Other social realities of the metropolis remain on the margins in just a few miniatures about beggars, poor children, prostitutes, and a scary all-night robbery of his family's apartment. Key philosophical concerns worked in detail into the miniatures are reflections on remembrance itself with its dual temporality, the child's mimetic abilities and his attempts to decipher his world, distortions of language, perceptions of objects and their relation to signs, the proximity of things in relation to faraway other worlds, the thresholds between reality and fantasy, the presence of myth, the ultimate threat of forgetting that is embodied in the little hunchback in the final miniature. Absent, given the focus on early childhood perception, are architectural, media, and political considerations that make up so much of the work on the *Arcades Project* and the essays of the 1930s.[8] Cultural analysis and theoretical reflections of that kind would have interfered with the attempt to recreate the child's sense of wonder in his encounters with the urban world. Also absent for the same reason are the allusions to eroticism and sexuality that are so prominent in Aragon.[9]

Rereading Benjamin's Ambiguous Appropriation of Aragon

Any attempt to find Aragonian traces in *Berlin Childhood* must begin by acknowledging a certain cagy ambivalence in Benjamin's extant comments on the French author, an ambivalence that is no doubt shaped by the Weimar intellectual left's hostility toward "bourgeois" authors.[10] Given Benjamin's critique of Aragon and surrealism, the idea of reading *Berlin Childhood* along with Aragon does not seem to make much sense at first. Even if there also are positive remarks about *Le Paysan*, differences seem to be predominant. Benjamin's construction of the child's urban experience has something innocent, almost romantic about it, while Aragon's Paris experiences are highly self-conscious, eroticized, and full of social commentary about urban planning and the transformation of Paris during the last stage of Haussmann's project that lasted decades beyond the masterplanner's death. Benjamin's urban miniatures, which conjure up a pre–World War I childhood in Wilhelmine Berlin in a highly condensed anti-memoir mode, have always been read first in relation to Proust's exploration of childhood and memory and second, though less so, in relation to Baudelaire's urban imaginary.[11] My argument here is that Aragon's *Paysan* must be seen as an important third literary intertext, for any closer look will also reveal how fundamentally distinct Benjamin's writing of the past is from Proust's (e.g., no *mémoire involontaire* triggered by a madeleine in Benjamin) and how Baudelaire's miniature form leads to a very different writing strategy in *Berlin Childhood* (e.g., deindividualization of the first-person narrator). Thus, adding Aragon and surrealism to this literary constellation that shaped Benjamin's project may seem less frivolous, especially since Aragon's early work is emphatically connected with Baudelaire, the key figure in Benjamin's *Arcades Project*. Of course, any such reading will have to pay close attention to how Benjamin appropriated and transformed Aragon.

It remains puzzling to me that Benjamin never wrote a substantive essay on Aragon, one that could help us locate Aragonian traces in his writings. In contrast to Benjamin's extended critical reflections on Proust and Baudelaire, we have to rely on scattered references to Aragon that are often determined by larger contexts that may hide more than they reveal. As a writer, Aragon may not be in the same league as Baudelaire and Proust, but then Proust had not yet been canonized in the 1920s, and Benjamin never shied away from focusing his critical attention on less canonical writers. Nicolai Leskov in the essay "The Story-Teller" is a good example. And a certain type of alternative storytelling—the metropolitan miniature as a modernist transformation of the oral storytelling in an earlier age—is very much at stake in the miniatures of *Berlin Childhood around 1900*. The miniaturists in general tried to develop the anti-story just as Aragon's goal was to write an anti-novel, a goal he shared with Breton. Experience of the city and its critical articulation was central to both Aragon and Benjamin, even if they pursued this goal with different writing strategies.

We must remember that in the 1930s, when Benjamin began to write *Berlin Childhood*, his relationship to Aragon's early surrealism was already a relationship to the past. The political and social up-heavals in the Weimar Republic in the wake of the 1929 crash and the electoral successes of the Nazis put Benjamin's time in Paris in the mid-1920s into a deeper past than chronology alone might suggest, and by then Aragon himself had shed his earlier surrealism and turned toward communism. In "The Reading Box," one of the miniatures not included in the 1938 manuscript, Benjamin argued that any remembered past will remain impenetrable and an object of desire and longing:

> We can never entirely recover what has been forgotten. And this is perhaps a good thing. The shock of repossession would be so devastating that we would immediately cease to understand our longing. But we do understand it; and the more deeply what has been forgotten lies buried within us, the better we understand this longing.[12]

Nostalgic longing was thus a function of a forgetting that still preserves the forgotten, which nevertheless remains out of sight. After about three decades and across the unbridgeable abyss of World War I, the forgotten of his own childhood was indeed submerged and could only be understood through an act of will instead of being recuperated in its entirety. The necessary form of such partial recovery resulted from a calling up and arranging of fragments in their aura of submersion. But it was not just Benjamin's childhood that was submerged. His whole relationship to Aragon, so central for his life project, now seemed hidden behind a veil, ruptured only once in his letter to Adorno of May 31, 1935, when he tried to calm Adorno's worries that Brecht's Marxism might exert an undue influence on the development of the *Arcades Project*. Here Benjamin emphatically referred to the beginning of that project in the context of early surrealism—an art movement Brecht disliked intensely and that later Adorno himself also criticized from a post-Holocaust perspective.[13] In that 1935 letter to Adorno, Benjamin recalled the powerful impact Aragon's *Paysan* had on him when he read it in Paris in the mid-1920s:

It [the *Arcades Project*] opens with Aragon—the *paysan de Paris* [*sic*]. Evenings, lying in bed, I could never read more than two to three pages by him because my heart started to pound so hard that I had to put the book down. What a warning. What an indication of the years and years that had to be put between me and that kind of reading. And yet the first preliminary sketches for the Arcades originated at that time.[14]

Warning of what? Not, I would argue, of the insidious influence of an ideologically suspect author, but of the fear of being overwhelmed, a fear he expressed elsewhere about his relationship to Proust as well. Indeed, being all too fascinated and therefore having to put Aragon down, in the double sense of the word, proved to be symptomatic of Benjamin's long-term relation to the French surrealist author whom, as far as we know, he never even met in Paris at the time he came under his sway.[15]

Much has been made of the fact that soon after reading *Le Paysan* Benjamin put down the early Aragon fairly severely. In the surrealism essay of 1929, while not mentioning Aragon by name, Benjamin saw nothing but an "irremediable coupling of idealistic morality with political practice" in the left bourgeois position of the surrealists.[16] And in the *Arcades Project* we read at a salient point with direct reference to Aragon:

Delimitation of the tendency of this project with respect to Aragon: whereas Aragon persists within the realm of dream, here the concern is to find the constellation of awakening. While in Aragon there remains an impressionistic element, namely the "mythology" (and this impressionism must be held responsible for the many vague philosophemes in his book), here it is a question of the dissolution of "mythology" into the space of history. That of course can only happen through the awakening of a not-yet-conscious knowledge of what has been.[17]

This "awakening of a not-yet-conscious knowledge of what has been" refers to what Benjamin celebrated as the revolutionary power of the obsolete first discovered by the surrealists, among them Aragon in his poetic and sociological reflections on the Passage de l'Opéra. It

is clear that Aragon's reading of urban experience as modern mythology impressed Benjamin deeply when he first read *Paysan*. And
yet soon thereafter he reproached Aragon and surrealism for having
remained mired in myth and dreamworlds. My suspicion is that he
may have wrongly associated Aragon's notion of modern myth, dream,
and image with reactionary theosophists such as Steiner or even
Klages, from whom, however, he took other potentially reactionary
concepts such as the aura only in order to refunction them for purposes of left-wing cultural critique.[18] So why would he not give the
same benefit to Aragon? The politics of a new mythology in the 1920s
was a wartorn battlefield requiring complex and sometimes contradictory positionings. But whatever the reasons for his critique of the
surrealists may have been, there is a curious doubling here: the reproach to Aragon is actually quite close to the reproach Adorno lev-
eled against Benjamin's *Exposé* of the arcades project when in the famous Hornberg letter of August 2, 1935, he warned him of an
undialectical use of myth and dream in his reading of modernism
and modernity. And it is also close to Aragon's own political self-
critique after his turn toward communism, when in 1930, in a strangely
defensive move, he called his novel *"une jacquerie de l'individualisme"*
(a riot of individualism).[19]

But there is another curious parallelism: Adorno may have been
as wrong about Benjamin's understanding of myth and the archaic
as Benjamin was wrong about Aragon's *"mythologie moderne,"* which
far from being simply impressionist, was very much a socially critical project rather than a regressive romantic dream.[20] After all,
Aragon sought out a modern mythology not in in the glittering commercialized new arcades of the Champs Elysées or in the new technologies but in marginal urban spaces destined for destruction and
rife with political protest. A close reading of all of Aragon's *Paysan*
rather than just the oft-cited few passages referring to the Passage
de l'Opéra suggests that the real rub for Benjamin may have been in
what he legitimately called "vague philosophemes," which indeed im-
pair the literary quality of Aragon's novel. But these philosophemes
are largely limited to the anti-Cartesian philosophical reflections in
the introduction and the anti-Hegelianism of the conclusion, whereas
the dimensions of myth and dream, fantasy and sensual experience,

with their focus on concrete material aspects of everyday life and on marginal urban sites, as they characterize the two long middle parts of *Le Paysan*, remained central to Benjamin's own thinking and writing up to the end of his life. This, after all, must have been what kept him awake at night reading with a pounding heart. Indeed, Aragon's work, too, called for an awakening from nineteenth-century delusions of progress and from the philosophy of rational consciousness, both of which were bankrupted in the course of World War I. As such, Aragon's search for a modern mythology, combining rationality of mind, the fantasy of the senses, and bodily experience, centered on metropolitan life rather than on regressive individualist utopias and was close in intention to Benjamin in its desire to create a new metropolitan image space. The critique of Aragon's philosophical ramblings in *Le Paysan* is one thing; the appropriation of Aragon's literary and imaginary project is another.

It is significant that the separation from Aragon appears most explicitly in the context of the *Arcades Project*. Here, Aragon's novelistic and Benjamin's scholarly critical project do indeed diverge. Instead of focusing, like Aragon, on a transitory present (the Passage de l'Opéra just before its demolition, the Buttes-Chaumont Park at night) and on a celebration of the ephemeral in contemporary urban life, Benjamin's work in the *Arcades Project* is that of the dialectical historian bent on creating an awakening from a mythical nineteenth-century past and translating it into a twentieth-century radical politics. Benjamin operated within the frame of a philosophy of history and he pursued a critical historical study of the nineteenth century, both of which are at best implicit in Aragon. Like Benjamin, however, Aragon was interested in the trajectory of modernity since the nineteenth century that he, too, wanted to leave behind. His turn against Hegel in the last part of *Le Paysan* and against any idealist philosophy of history was not so far from Benjamin's materialist intentions when he called for the "dissolution of 'mythology' into the space of history." Benjamin pursued this project, researching and writing in the Bibliothèque Nationale in Paris, but his concerns with the philosophy of history pervaded even the writing of *Berlin Childhood*. And yet, in comparison with Aragon, who abandoned surrealism, joined the Communist Party, and took to writing socialist realist novels and working as a journalist and editor for communist publications, Benjamin ultimately remained truer to the legacies of surrealism than Aragon himself. The question of who was politically and intellectually more radical at the time—a question that agitated earlier critics—seems rather moot in today's retrospective.

Ultimately, the brief and rather undeveloped put-downs of Aragon do not surprise in the context of Benjamin's intense reception of Marxism and the proliferating and often narrow-minded left-wing attacks on left-liberal "bourgeois intellectuals" since the late 1920s. All the more important, however, is Benjamin's acknowledgment in 1935 that in that first encounter he had to put Aragon's novel down literally because reading it caused an overwhelming bodily reaction. For me, this is the tip of the iceberg. For it is highly telling that Benjamin would remember this at a time when he had presumably overcome the lure of surrealism and thus should have forgotten or repressed the effects of reading *Le Paysan de Paris* in the mid-1920s. An emphatic memory like this almost ten years after the experience suggests that Benjamin called up or even reclaimed something here that was still alive in him despite all the years that had passed and despite his critical distance from certain aspects of surrealism. It is this bodily memory of reading Aragon at night that makes me want to argue that there is a much stronger and long-lasting subterranean influence of the early surrealist Aragon on Benjamin than is usually acknowledged. Tracing it as a literary intertext in the miniatures that make up *Berlin Childhood*, a work that is rarely if ever mentioned in relationship to Benjamin's reception of *Le Paysan de Paris*, will make the point.[21]

There is other evidence that Benjamin's critique of surrealism has been overemphasized in the critical literature at the expense of surrealism's continuing impact on his thought and writing. We know that Benjamin first encountered Aragon when reading his 1924 essay "Une vague de rêves" (A Wave of Dreams), which he mentioned approvingly in his essay on "Dreamkitsch" (1926) and from which he transposed several key phrasings into his later surrealism essay. Most important, however, in his 1934 essay "The Present Social Situation of the French Writer," he attributed the inspiration of a new image space created by the surrealist circle primarily to Aragon, and the idea of *Bild-Raum* is central to the construction of *Berlin Childhood*. This 1934 comment can now be read together with the letter to Adorno to support the argument that Benjamin's Marxism of the 1930s fully recognized the continuing importance of surrealism, helped along at that time, no doubt, by the political turn of the movement. The passage must be quoted in full:

> *Surrealism* would have been spared many enemies (from which [*sic*], incidentally, it derived enormous benefit) had it originated unambiguously in politics. But this was far from the case. Surrealism came to maturity in the confined space of the literary circle around Apollinaire. Aragon showed, in his *Vague de rêves* [Wave of Dreams] of 1924, in what an unprepossessing, home-grown substance the dialectical nucleus of Surrealism was originally found. At that time, the movement broke over its founders in an inspirational dream wave. Life appeared worth living only where the threshold between sleeping and waking had been eroded, as if by the footsteps of images, ebbing and flowing by the thousand. Language was itself only where, with automatic exactitude, sound and image, image and sound, had merged with each other so utterly that there was no space left for "meaning," not even the smallest fissure. To enlist "the forces of intoxication for the revolution"—that was the real program. The dialectical development of the movement, however, was such that the image space which it had so boldly opened up for itself proved more and more to be identical with the image space of political praxis. It was within that space, at any rate, that the members of the group located the home of a classless society.[22]

As if not to minimize but to supplement the reference to Marxism, he went on to say that this development of the surrealists owed less to dialectical materialism than to

> an anthropological materialism derived from their own experiences and from the earlier experiences of Lautréamont and Rimbaud.[23]

My point here is not to defend Benjamin's idealization of the image space of Marxist political praxis, which, by 1934 in the Soviet Union, was anything but what he attributed to it in the cited passage. It is rather to draw attention to the fact that this evaluation indeed sounds very different from the critique of surrealism in the 1929 essay, different also from the later comment about the need to keep a safe distance from Aragon's understanding of dream and myth. The notion of image-space (*Bild-Raum*), after all, came to be a key theoretical concept for Benjamin, and the evocation of such image-spaces pervades the writing of *Berlin Childhood*.

Actually, strong literary afterimages of his experience of reading Aragon are visible in those very same years in the early drafts on the Paris Arcades of 1927 and 1929, in his translation of a passage from *Le Paysan* for the *Literarische Welt* (1928), and in the miniature "Stamp Shop" in *One-Way Street*, clearly inspired by Aragon's treatment of the same topic in *Paysan*. These texts, all more or less simultaneous with Benjamin's emerging critique of surrealism, testify that Aragon's real impact was literary rather than philosophical. It is this primarily literary rather than conceptual impact of Aragon and its importance for the creation of an image-space in the Berlin miniatures that interests me as I read *Berlin Childhood* as including a creative adaptation of motifs from Aragon's major work.

In light of the above and returning one more time to Benjamin's much-touted critique of surrealism in the essay of 1929, it may be telling that Aragon did not play a significant role in that essay.[24] Instead, the essay placed Breton's *Nadja* in its center, a shift in focus that can be explained only insufficiently by chronology. It is true that by the time Benjamin was writing his essay, *Nadja* (1928) was the more recent surrealist and urban novel on the literary market, coming two full seasons after Aragon's *Paysan*. But criticizing the French surrealist intelligentsia primarily via this much more individualist and mystifying novel had the side effect of saving Aragon from explicit critique. While Benjamin accused not only Breton's novel but also *Le Paysan* of showing "very disturbing symptoms of deficiency,"[25] he exemplified these deficiencies only with passages from *Nadja*. By contrast, the drafts for the essay contained an explicit, very positive reference to Aragon that never made it into the final version, possibly because it would have contradicted the express purpose of the essay's criticism of surrealism. In the drafts we read:

> But above all, time and again, the city of Paris itself. The re-
> volt pushes the surrealist face of a city to the surface. And no
> face is as surrealist as the true face of a city. Aragon has dem-
> onstrated it.[26]

Of course, the essay was not altogether negative about surrealism. Benjamin retained the discussion of revolt, acknowledging the rad-ical potential in surrealism's focus on the outmoded, something Aragon and Breton shared. And he acknowledged surrealism's insight into "profane illumination, a materialistic, anthropological inspira-tion."[27] But he did excise Aragon from his discussion of what he de-scribed critically and with disapproval as the post-heroic phase of sur-realism. The question of course is whether in Benjamin's mind, *Le Paysan* still belonged to that earlier heroic phase. The surrealism essay doesn't say, but I tend to place it there, and not just because of the deleted praise for *Le Paysan* in the quoted unpublished passage. After all, the main examples of the outmoded were first found in Aragon's description of the Passage de l'Opéra and only later in Breton's *Nadja* in the celebration of the flea market. Aragon's name may be sub-merged in the 1929 essay, but he is still very present in Benjamin's search for that image-space that is accessible by profane illumina-tion, a concept that translates Aragon's *merveilleux quotidien* into Ben-jaminian parlance.

Urban image space and what Benjamin called the surreal face of the city is much more present and pronounced in Aragon than in Breton. To be sure, the passages about the Place Maubert, the Porte St. Denis, and the Place Dauphine in *Nadja* conjure up insurrec-tionary and revolutionary episodes of Paris's history, but such refer-ences appear coldly in the narrator's rational discourse or they re-main implied only in Nadja's very brief hallucinatory comments that seem to be mediated by telepathy and ghostly imaginings.[28] One of Benjamin's telling reproaches to Breton was that his text featured a fortune teller by the name of Madame Sacco while ignoring the po-litical protests in Paris against the United States' treatment of Sacco and Vanzetti.[29] Madame Sacco as clairvoyant claims to know the future, whereas Nadja seems to have an uncanny relationship to Paris's insurrectionary past. But the insurrectionary protest in the present is left out. In Aragon, by contrast, urban spaces such as the Passage de l'Opéra and the Buttes-Chaumont Park are described in much more detail, and the politics and economics of Haussmannian urban destruction are present in a montage of data and public signs about the Haussmann Building Society, the expropriations, and the ruins of the boulevard Haussmann. Description and positivist facts are unchained in *Le Paysan* to the extent that they too assume an air of hallucination in the context of *le merveilleux quotidien*. Objectification and facticity are present in both *Paysan* and *Nadja*, but only Breton actually used photographs of urban spaces, all devoid of humans and banal in their representation. Benjamin did not have much to say about Breton's use of photographs montaged into his text. He found their insertion strange, but attributed a most pristine intensity to them in their relation to their fictional context.[30] As later critics did, he too recognized their banality. Indeed, these street photographs have nothing mysterious about them, in contrast to some of the photographs by Atget that Benjamin saw as anticipating surrealist photography.[31] Actually, Breton consciously inserted photographs in all their banality only to testify to the fact that his book was not fiction, not a novel. But the presence of photos in this urban text of 1928 is interesting in itself if we hold it against the absence of photos in Benjamin's *One-Way Street*, which was published the same year.[32]

A Web of Resonances: Baudelaire, Proust, Aragon

I should emphasize again that the purpose of my comparison is not to replace Baudelaire and Proust as major intertexts of *Berlin Childhood*. My point is rather that tracing affinities with Aragon allows us to see these miniatures not just as conjuring up the prewar period and the world of the nineteenth century but also to link them back to a critical moment of the 1920s, the decade when a new and precarious urban imaginary emerged in both France and Weimar Germany.[33] At the same time, in its mode of assembling and juxtaposing short prose texts, *Berlin Childhood* may remind us less of Aragon than of Benjamin's own *One-Way Street*.[34] But the fundamental difference of *Berlin Childhood* from both *Paysan* and *One-Way Street* is the inevitably double temporality of memory as present past, a key theme of the late Benjamin but clearly not yet central in those texts from the 1920s, which focus on the present in Paris and Berlin, respectively.

Actually, Aragon never had much use for the Proustian memory world. He disliked, even disdained the Proustian project of evoking recollections of pre–World War I French high society, which he considered only as long-winded snobbery.[35] Benjamin's reading and translating of two volumes of Proust's *A la recherche du temps perdu*, in contrast, stood behind all of his thinking about memory and remembrance in both his critical historiography and his literary practice. Adorno recalled how Benjamin worried at the time he was writing his Berlin miniatures that he might "stray into an addictive dependency" on reading Proust.[36] And indeed, in *Berlin Childhood* there is an unmistakable cluster of motifs we know from the *Recherche*, such as the central role of mother and grandmother, the evening party that deprives the child of the presence of his mother (eliminated from the 1938 version), the description of the father's authority, the invention of the telephone, the role of photography (also eliminated from the 1938 version), and so on.[37] Unlike *Recherche*, however, *Berlin Childhood* privileges spatial juxtapositions at the expense of temporal sequencing.[38] It also shuns the logic of narrative development that is present in Aragon's Paris text despite its focus on disconnected urban spaces. In Aragon, montage and fragmented, seemingly arbitrary urban data are embedded in the arc of an argument about modern mythology, and the flânerie through urban space is conceived as a "labyrinth without a Minotaur," filled with unrecognized sphinxes.[39] The labyrinth and unrecognized sphinxes also appear in *Berlin Childhood*, as both authors privileged heterotopic places in the city. But there is no lighthearted flânerie in Benjamin's remembered urban labyrinth, and the threat of the Minotaur is always present.

In relation to the surrealist poetics of narrative, Benjamin's text actually seems closer to Breton and his indictment in the *Surrealist Manifesto* of any and all narrative plot and description à la Balzac than to Aragon's writing practice in *Le Paysan*, which liberally deploys both, even if in a significantly different way than the tradition of realist fiction. However, in contrast to Breton, neither Aragon nor Benjamin ever embraced *écriture automatique*, the writing strategy some surrealists celebrated as emancipatory and properly avant-gardist.[40] It is well known that while he called for an "inevitable rigor" of style in surrealist works, as early as the late 1920s Aragon held *écriture automatique* in contempt:

> If you write deplorable twaddle using surrealist techniques it will still be deplorable twaddle.[41]

Decades later Aragon had this to say about *Le Paysan* in his memoir:

> I was seeking . . . to use the accepted novel-form as the basis for the production of a new kind of novel that would break all the traditional rules governing the writing of fiction, one that would be neither a narrative (a story) nor a character study (a portrait), a novel that the critics would be obliged to approach empty-handed . . . because in this instance the rules of the game would all have been swept aside. . . . I was writing this novel-that-was-not-a-novel—or at least I thought of myself as writing it.[42]

Writing a novel that was not a novel also describes what Rilke did in *Malte Laurids Brigge* and what Musil aimed at in the short form with his unstorylike stories. And yet despite his emphasis on a radical break with the novel form, Aragon seemed to backtrack when he spoke of *Le Paysan*'s story as that of the

> evolution of a mind, starting with a mythological conception of the world, and leading towards a materialism which is not achieved in the final pages of the book, but only *promised* within the terms of a proclamation of the failure of Hegelianism, the loftiest of all those conceptions which allowed man to advance along the path of idealism.[43]

Despite Aragon's explicit turn against Hegel and idealist philosophy, residues of a philosophy of history are present in his aesthetic turn from myth to materialism and toward *le merveilleux quotidien*, which was charged with initiating a new experience of metropolitan modernity. As in Benjamin, it is not a philosophy of linear progress but one of rupture and change and thus compatible with Benjamin's thought in the 1930s. In this aesthetic sense, then, *Le Paysan*, like *Malte*, is still a novel despite its microstructure of discontinuities. At the same time, it was this very structure that made prepublication in piecemeal form possible in the *Revue Européenne* in 1924 and 1925, before Gallimard published the full text in book form in 1926.

When it comes to structure, *Berlin Childhood* can at first sight more profitably be compared with Baudelaire's structuring principle as laid out in the preface to *Spleen de Paris*.[44] The differing arrangements of the sequence of miniatures in Benjamin's manuscripts and in the subsequent published editions of *Berlin Childhood* resonate with Baudelaire's ironic comment that his collection of miniatures has neither head nor tail, suggesting tongue in cheek that their sequence was rather arbitrary and that the reader could skip around at will. As one looks more closely, it becomes clear, however, that both Baudelaire's *Spleen de Paris* and Benjamin's *Berlin Childhood* do display a certain organizational logic when it comes to the leading and concluding miniatures or even as we consider sequencing and the juxtapositions, some of which function as a kind of prosaic enjambment. As a matter of fact, all of the miniature collections discussed in this book do have some narrative arc, even if the reader has a sense that the assemblage of miniatures could have been different without damaging the respective works as a whole. Both Baudelaire and Benjamin arranged their miniatures spatially rather than temporally. Even the different beginnings in Benjamin's 1932 and 1938 versions can be easily justified without having to claim that one is better than the other. "The Mummerehlen," the lead piece in the 1932 version, and "Loggias," which was not written until 1933 and was the lead piece in 1938, both mark elliptical centers of *Berlin Childhood* deserving of pride of place, and Adorno's choice to begin with "Tiergarten," a choice made at the time without knowledge of the 1932 and 1938 typescripts, makes good sense as well.[45] It is simply impossible to establish linear unity and coherence of the text either in terms of narrative development and sequencing or in terms of major themes, and this should not be seen as a deficiency but rather as an achievement that fully acknowledges

the spatially complex structure of a metropolitan imaginary.[46] Any
reading will have to treat the text as a kaleidoscope with changing
constellations in a carefully textured web of connecting images,
themes, metaphors, observations, and philosophical concerns. Because some fragments in a kaleidoscope loom larger than others, some
miniatures will legitimately attract more attention than others. Nevertheless, it can be said that the incompletion of the text itself translates into the incompleteability of its readings. The same goes for
Baudelaire, whose prose miniatures must be seen as a key formal reference point for *Berlin Childhood*, including the very circumstantial
sense that neither text was brought to book publication by the author himself.

Strangely though, given all his writing about Baudelaire, Benjamin
never commented in any detail about the prose pieces of the *Spleen
de Paris*, just as he never had anything to say about the second major
part of Aragon's *Paysan*, the account of the nocturnal visit of Aragon
and his Paris friends to the Buttes-Chaumont Park. The *Arcades
Project* contains any number of quotes from the *Spleen*, but does not
even offer the slightest interpretive aside. Benjamin's silence is, ironically enough, reproduced in the scholarship that acknowledges the
importance of Baudelaire's urban imaginary as articulated in *Les
Fleurs du mal* for Benjamin's critical essays and occasionally even for
Berlin Childhood but fails to recognize the *Spleen de Paris* as a key literary intertext for *Berlin Childhood*.

As with Aragon, however, differences with Baudelaire spring to
mind. Both Aragon and Baudelaire used first-person narrative,
whereas Benjamin's narrator, especially in the 1938 version, seems
much more generic and less explicitly personal or existential than either Baudelaire's artist ego in his shifting masks and disguises or Aragon's undisguised autobiographic flâneur.[47] Perhaps this was one of
the reasons why Benjamin never commented in detail on Baudelaire's
late prose work of *Spleen de Paris* and kept a certain distance from
the surrealist Aragon. Nevertheless, the form of his prose miniatures
and their potential assembly must be read as inspired by Baudelaire's
city prose, just as their themes of memory and childhood cannot be
understood without reference to Proust's *Recherche*. If Benjamin
created a form of urban miniature resonant with the Baudelairean

model, its memorial content marks the distance from Baudelaire, whose miniatures focused exclusively on the present. Memory and *recherche* of a lost time, in turn, mark the affinity to Proust, though Benjamin did not have much use for a Proustian *mémoire involontaire*. No peaceful madeleine to work its magic in a world of political emergency, crisis, and exile. Here Benjamin rather stayed with Baudelaire's notion that "Genius is nothing more nor less than childhood recovered at will," a key concept in Baudelaire's aesthetic.[48] In the foreword to the 1938 typescript, we read, in a formulation that clearly departs from Proust:

> I deliberately called to mind those images which, in exile, are most apt to waken homesickness: images of childhood. My assumption was that the feeling of longing would no more gain mastery over my spirit than a vaccine does over a healthy body.[49]

Memory, in other words, as inoculation designed to avoid descent into nostalgia. What emerges is a childhood that is lost, thoroughly lost, and reconstructed deliberately and at will in fragments only. A bourgeois child's urban imaginary is captured from a distance and through the fog of time, a distance the text itself reflects on:

> I hope they [the images of his metropolitan childhood] will at least suggest how thoroughly the person spoken of here would later dispense with the security allotted his childhood. (38)

To be sure, as in Proust there is a sense of desire and longing for the past, but then Benjamin also had this to say in the foreword:

> I sought to limit its [the feeling of longing, *Sehnsucht*] effect through insight into the irretrievability—not the contingent biographical but the necessary social irretrievability—of the past. (37)

Thus, in the abridged late version of 1938, explicit biographic traits relating to family members and childhood friends were eliminated in order to focus on socially determined spatial images:

I have made an effort to get hold of the *images* in which the experience of the big city is precipitated in a child of the middle
class. (38)

The phrasings about memory accessible to will in the foreword sound
almost too rational if one holds them against the very complex reflections on memory in the essay "On Some Motifs in Baudelaire,"
written more or less at the same time. There, to be sure, Benjamin
acknowledged the role of the unconscious in the constitution of
memory, arguing that only events not consciously experienced leave
memory traces behind. Such memory traces, one might suggest, were
then reconstructed deliberately in the writing of *Berlin Childhood*
rather than emerging as an effect of a cookie dipped in a cup of tea,
as in Proust.

The images he got hold of are precisely those images that could
not have been conscious in the child's mind at the time. So how did
Benjamin, decades later, "get hold" of images the city precipitated in
a middle-class child? The final miniature of *Berlin Childhood* provides
an answer. Here, in "the Little Hunchback," he recalls how his former
self's fascinated gaze into the souterrains of buildings returned in his
dreams in the form of threatening looks from below, "looks flung at
me by gnomes with pointed hats" (120). These gnomes then turn into
the *bucklicht Männlein*, the little hunchback in the cellar, as the child
encountered it in the children's verses that gave the miniature its title.
In one register, the *bucklicht Männlein* is a figure for the oppressed
underclasses, those who live in the souterrain of society into which
the child peers curiously at the beginning of the miniature. Such spatial imaging of class divisions was a common trope that had been well
known since H. G. Wells's *Time Machine* and Fritz Lang's *Metropolis*. The hunchback's hump can be read as allegorizing the distortion and mutilation of the laboring body, the burden carried by the
oppressed.[50] He comes from the lower depth and is part of that
Lumpengesindel, the "riffraff" that haunts the child in dreams. At the
same time, the little hunchback is also the child's double—always
present wherever the child is, invisible but with his gaze trained on
the child. His invisibility, critics have claimed, points to forgetting,
evasion, perhaps repression.[51] When Benjamin spoke of the irretriev-

ability of the past he acknowledged forgetting as the inevitable shadow of memory. He knew that the time of remembrance and the time of that which is remembered are always separated by a gulf of non-synchronicity (*Ungleichzeitigkeit*). He welcomed this gap in the 1938 foreword, where he described his conscious attempt to call up the images of his childhood as a kind of inoculation against homesickness that might otherwise overwhelm him in exile. Analogously, the little hunchback appears to be the inevitable double of the child, invisible during childhood, only recognized in retrospective. The image of the little hunchback from the children's song is thus heavily over-determined. In the longer earlier version of the miniature, he is even said to hold the images of the narrator as child, having seen him at all the places conjured up in the earlier segments of the text:

> The little man has the images of me, too. He saw me in my hiding place and facing the cage of the otter.[52]

Both versions emphasize that the child never saw the little hunchback:

> Only, I never saw him. It was he who always saw me. (122)

And when Benjamin wrote "He has long since abdicated" (122), it is almost as if he attributed the writing of *Berliner Kindheit* itself to the hunchback, another instance of doubling and quite plausibly so, as the hunchback is said to hold the images of the child. Clearly the little hunchback becomes a cipher for everything that remained mysterious, invisible, submerged in both the child's perceptions of class divisions and the adult's memory of an irretrievable past.

Instead of a former self being conjured up nostalgically, it is as if the child became the sediment or medium of a class-specific metropolitan experience as it flashed by in the fleeting process of remembrance itself. Benjamin was both historian and memorian in this process. His writing strategy resulted in a mysteriously cool and highly controlled, linguistically self-conscious text about pre–World War I Berlin that resonated with later historical and social experiences—the destruction of that sense of bourgeois security that was still tenuously experienced around 1900 but lost forever with World War I and exacerbated during exile. Inklings of class divisions—the little hunchback looking at the child—emerge in certain images of the underground, the souterrain, the municipal swimming pool, but the full knowledge of social structure is accessible only in retrospective. In *Berlin Childhood* the directionality of memory moves from present to past, whereas in Proust's involuntary memory it went from the past to the present. Benjamin's memorializing reflections were not triggered by social occasions and encounters, as they were in Proust, but rather by urban spaces themselves—both in and outside the bourgeois home and increasingly on the thresholds of the child's protective cocoon. The forebodings of loss and a dark future are already inscribed in what is being remembered in some of the miniatures, even though Adorno's overarching claim that "A deathly air that permeates the scenes poised to awaken in Benjamin's depiction"[53] may owe much to Adorno's post-Holocaust perspective in 1950 on German cities in ruins and to the memory of Benjamin's suicide. And yet, Adorno was right to suggest that there is something ominous in Benjamin's depiction. This ominous dimension resulted from the fact that like Aragon and unlike Proust, Benjamin privileged heterotopic places in the city, sites that often remained unseen or avoided. As a folkloric figure from a children's poem, the little hunchback was the allegorical embodiment of such sites. Ultimately it is the figure of the hunchback that inscribes a strong social and political dimension into *Berlin Childhood* in an almost fairy-tale-like way that is appropriate for a child's perspective. What the hunchback from the souterrain was to Benjamin, the Buttes-Chaumont Park was to Aragon—an allegory of heterotopia.

Le merveilleux quotidien

Modern urban myth remained central to the miniatures of *Berlin Childhood*, which are dotted with mythological references throughout. The city as labyrinth to be traversed with the help of Ariadne's thread is only the most obvious and determining one, which itself had its model in Aragon. But all such citations from mythology, far from being only ornamental or culturally regressive, are transformed into something new. Whereas according to Benjamin, Aragon persisted in the realm of dream and myth, he claimed that his own texts dissolved mythology into the historical space of Wilhelmine Berlin. But then, as I have argued, Aragon's practice is not simply ahistorical, although he might not have fully embraced a Benjaminian kind of a philosophy of history. Actually, Aragon's portrait of the face of the city was not located in some mythological dreamland, but very much in post–World War I Paris. As the references to the looming destruction of the Passage de l'Opéra in 1927 and the violent history of the Buttes-Chaumont Park prove, the sites of his surrealist explorations were always historically loaded. More important, what Aragon called *"mythologie moderne"* had little to do with an embrace of the archaic. It emerged with flânerie and the estranging experience of the everyday urban. He, too, dissolved myth into a specific urban space at a specific time, except that his time was the postwar present rather than the fin-de-siècle past. At the same time, lingering residues of the nineteenth-century city, such as the Passage de l'Opéra and the Buttes-Chaumont Park, with their ghostly histories, generated his modern mythology in the present through the charm and seduction of the obsolete. Aragon was reading the physiognomy of the city in its invariably social and political spaces. This idea remained central for Benjamin's surrealism essay and it shaped *Berlin Childhood*, even if the explicit social dimension, because the child's limited perspective, is more narrowly circumscribed than in Aragon's *Paysan*.

Yet it is here that we encounter the core of *Berlin Childhood*'s Aragonian dimension. The true surreal face of the city is revealed in its hidden, marginal, and often banal spaces, sites that were especially noticeable to the gaze of the child, who still perceived what the routine instrumental look of the adult would overlook. This is what Aragon called the *merveilleux quotidien*, the ground for his modern metropolitan mythology that contrasted the knowledge of the senses and bodily experiences with the knowledge derived from reason.[54] Here is the key passage right at the beginning of the "Passage de l'Opéra" section of *Le Paysan* that in its metaphors and language resonates with the first and final miniatures of the 1938 edition of *Berlin Childhood*:

Man no longer worships the gods on their heights. . . . The spirit
of religions, coming down to dwell in the dust, has abandoned
the sacred places. But there are *other places* which flourish among
mankind, places where men go calmly about their mysterious
lives and in which a profound relation is gradually taking shape.
These sites are not yet inhabited by a divinity. It is forming there,
a new godhead precipitating in these recreations of Ephesus like
acid-gnawing metal at the bottom of a glass. Life itself has sum-
moned into being this poetic deity which thousands will pass
blindly by, but which suddenly becomes palpable and terribly
haunting for those who have at least caught a *confused glimpse* of
it. It is you, *metaphysical entity of places, who lull children to sleep*, it
is you who people their dreams. These shores of the unknown,
sands shivering with anguish or anticipation, are fringed by the
very substance of our minds.[55]

In "Loggias," the space that lulls the child to sleep is the city of Berlin
itself as the mother who lays the child in his cradle. The "confused
glimpse" of the quote translates the French *"maladroitement perçue,"*
with *"maladroit"* suggesting awkward, clumsy, blundering. The
German translation of *Paysan* says *"ungeschickterweise wahrgenommen,"*
a phrasing that points to the standard phrase *"ungeschickt lässt grüssen"*
["Greetings from Mr. Clumsy"], an adult's admonishing saying
when a child unintentionally breaks something.[56] This is, not co-
incidentally, I would claim, the phrase with which Benjamin's
mother comments on the child's little accidents and the faux-pas
Benjamin attributes to the agonizing interventions of the little
hunchback in the final miniature. Whether or not Benjamin had
Aragon's *maladroitement perçue* consciously in mind when he linked
the child's clumsiness to the *bucklicht Männlein*'s influence is less
important to me than the mere fact of a stunning affinity across
languages.

Such rather inconspicuous and perhaps unconscious appropriation
of minor detail can lead to broader analogies with Aragon's text.
Aragon found *le merveilleux quotidien* primarily in the two spatial heterotopias of the arcade destined for destruction and the urban park

in the proletarian east of Paris, both of them threshold phenomena. The arcade erases the distinction between inside and outside, street and interior, protected and exposed urban space. The urban park challenges the border between nature and city, the organic and the artificial. Thresholds have been identified as central to Benjamin's thinking, but they were already prevalent in Aragon.[57] While nature in an urban context reappears in "Tiergarten," which resonates with Aragon's Buttes-Chaumont chapter, there is no arcade in *Berlin Childhood*, even though arcades did exist in Weimar Berlin in a similarly decaying and heterotopic sense as in Aragon's Paris. We know this from Kracauer's marvelous description of the old *Lindenpassage* between Friedrichstrasse and Unter den Linden before its renovation, another feuilleton miniature no doubt inspired by Aragon or Benjamin. It is easy enough, however, to read Benjamin's celebration of the loggia, so typical of Berlin's bourgeois apartments, as a spatial metamorphosis of Aragon's arcade. Like the arcade, the loggia is a space between inside and outside, in this case between the salon of the bourgeois apartment and the outside of the Berlin inner courtyards in back of the apartment. Like the arcade, it was a dumping ground for obsolete things and a space for reflection. Like the arcade, it generated imaginings and sensual perceptions of life, more precisely the life in the courtyards, even though that life remained at a safe distance on a threshold between a still-interior architectural space and the exterior public space of the street.

Spatial threshold phenomena are pervasive in *Berlin Childhood*. Quite appropriately for a text that renders a child's perceptions, the primary inside urban space is the *Berliner Wohnung* (the Berlin apartment), a space that time and again is violated by irruptions from the outside into the privacy of family life. The telephone, "an outcast settled carelessly between the dirty-linen hamper and the gasometer" (49) wreaked "devastation" in family circles with its strident sound and mechanical requirements, and "its ringing served to multiply the terrors of the Berlin household" (49). But the most violent disruption of home space is an all-night burglary at their summer home in Babelsberg during which the parents seek refuge in the child's

bedroom—an event that stands as an allegory of the dangerous social *Durchdringung* of private, public, and criminal space in urban
life (100–103). The celebrated intimate space of bourgeois family life
was already under siege, even if the child only intimated but did not
fully understand its social implications.

As in all urban texts discussed in this book, the separation of
inner and outer, private and public is subjected to that process of
Durchdringung and is thus revealed as a delusion. As in Adorno's
Minima Moralia, "*wohnen*," dwelling or being at home, is described
as increasingly precarious in urban modernity.[58] This is true even
for the well-protected bourgeois child, who feels totally secure
and safe only in his grandmother's apartment at Blumeshof 12, a
space significantly beyond paternal authority. It was his retrospective view that had Benjamin focus on the uninhabitability of
the loggia that gave solace "for one who himself no longer has a
proper abode" (42), a comment that collapses the temporal distance between the child's experience of the loggia and the exile's
experience of no longer having a home of his own.[59] And yet the
loggia, "shaded by awnings [translation modified—AH] in the
summer" is described as "the cradle in which the city laid its new
citizen" (38). Outside and inside merge in an auditory experience:
"The rhythm of the metropolitan railway and of carpet-beating
rocked me to sleep" (39). In another miniature, "Blumeshof 12,"
the loggia is described yet again as a marginal space in its effect
on the child:

> The most important of these secluded rooms was for me the
> loggia. This may have been because it was more modestly fur-
> nished and hence less appreciated by the adults, or because muted
> street noise would carry up there, or because it offered me a view
> of unknown courtyards with porters, children, and organ
> grinders. (89)

Of course, the loggia lacked the commercial traffic of the arcade. It
was not a space of commodity circulation or flânerie, not to mention the prostitution nestled in Aragon's arcade. But like the arcade
it was also a depository of antique and obsolete objects.

Now a hanging lamp, now a bronze, now a China vase would steal into its confines. And although these antiquities rarely did the place much honor, they suited its own antique character. (41)

As Benjamin then mentions the "Pompeian red that ran in a wide band along its wall" (41), a future of destruction is already implied that parallels the anticipated destruction of the Passage de l'Opéra in Aragon.

The analogies go even further. Aragon's sphinxes of the inner city and the imaginary sirens appearing in the arcade's shop windows in *Le Paysan* are transformed into the loggia's caryatids supporting the loggia of the apartment above and coming alive to sing a lullaby to the child in the cradle. Even the theme of death is present in both spaces, as Aragon describes the arcade as "a big glass coffin" (34) and Benjamin concludes "Loggias" with this:

The child . . . however, dwells in his loggia . . . as in a mausoleum long intended just for him. (42)

Thus, "Loggias" begins with the newborn in his cradle and it ends with the mausoleum, running the whole gamut from birth to death. The theme of death is equally present in the Buttes-Chaumont chapter of *Le Paysan* in its discussion of the notorious suicide bridge and the veiled reference to the military's slaughter of communards in the park in 1871, and it appears in the "Tiergarten" miniature in its reference to the death of Luise von Landau, an aristocratic child young Benjamin was infatuated with and whose early death taught him about the link between love and death.[60] Even if the end of "Tiergarten" evokes the garden of the Hesperides, the Greek version of paradise, it is clear that the urban park, whether Tiergarten or Buttes-Chaumont, is anything but paradise. Of course, such motifs common to both books are not simple intertextual citations; whatever Benjamin took up from Aragon's text is transformed in *Berlin Childhood*, and one doesn't even have to claim that each and every one of these motifs is based on consciously calculated appropriation. They rather point to elective affinities, lingering traces of Benjamin's intense reading experience of the mid-1920s. They can be

seen as the result of Benjamin's ability to practice mimesis, to acknowledge similitude, here in relation to words, images, and metaphors of a text he admired rather than to objects, but then Benjamin
always understood words and metaphors in their material reality, in
One-Way Street as much as in *Berlin Childhood around 1900.*

Mimetic appropriation and transformation continue in the way
Benjamin describes perception. Perception of the city via muted sound
is central in the experience of the loggia, just as perception of muted
light in Aragon's arcade parallels Benjamin's descriptions of ambiguous gaslight in "Tiergarten" and elsewhere.[61] Aragon describes the
"sunless corridors" of the arcades as "human aquariums" (14), pervaded by a "glaucous gleam, seemingly filtered through deep water"
(14).[62] The "greenish, almost submarine light" (22) is accompanied
by a sound resembling "the voice of the seashells" (22). In "Paris, Capital of the 19th Century" Benjamin called the Paris of Baudelaire's
poetry "a sunken city, more submarine than subterranean."[63] And in
the early version of "Imperial Panorama," Benjamin called the
nineteenth-century panoramas "aquaria of distance and of the past."[64]
A real aquarium finally appears in "The Otter"; the child seeks out
the otter's basin in a far corner of the Berlin zoo, another deserted
heterotopic space on the margin of the zoo itself. But the metaphor
of submarine life, so present in Aragon, reappears in a key place as
the sound of the seashell in "The Mummerehlen":

> I was distorted by similarity to all that surrounded me. Like a
> mollusk in its shell, I had made my abode in the 19th century,
> which now lies empty before me like an empty shell. I hold it to
> my ear. What do I hear? Not the noise of field artillery or dance
> music à la Offenbach, not even the stamping of horses on the
> cobblestones or fanfares announcing the changing of the guard.
> No, what I hear is the brief clatter of the anthracite as it falls from
> the coal scuttle into a cast-iron stove, the dull pop of the flame as
> it ignites in the gas mantle, and the clinking of the lampshade on
> its brass ring when a vehicle passes by on the street. (98)

It is not, in other words, the typical sounds of the public sphere that
are heard in the seashell of memory, but the microsounds of everyday

life in the home that constitute *le merveilleux quotidien* in Benjamin's memory of his childhood.

Paysan de Berlin

Benjamin even appropriated Aragon's title when in "Tiergarten" he referred to Franz Hessel, without naming him, as a Berlin peasant (55). In Kafka's *Betrachtung*, we had the country bumpkin entering the city and having to fend off a *Bauernfänger*, a confidence trickster who deceives the new arrival. *"Paysan"* in Aragon's title, however, does not refer to the nineteenth-century country-to-city motif, even though it plays with it. Like Hessel himself, *Le Paysan de Paris* is a thoroughly urban figure, one that comes through in the French more than in the German word "Bauer von Paris." The city is as known by Aragon's observant flâneur as the *pays* is known to the *paysan* as his material *terre* or *terroir.* The detailed descriptions of the Passage de l'Opéra and the various cafés, hangouts, brothels, and theaters prove that Aragon is both flaneur and archeologist of the city, just as the long passage mapping the Buttes-Chaumont Park does. Encounters with sexuality and urban prostitution are of course more prevalent in Aragon, but they haunt from the margins of the Berlin child's world as well, though explicit references, as in the miniature "Awakening of Sexuality" were deleted in the 1938 version. In "Tiergarten," Benjamin rewrote the French *"pays"* as forest and coupled it with his idea of the city as labyrinth:

> Not to find one's way around a city does not mean much. But to lose one's way in the city, as one loses one's way in a forest, re-quires some schooling. Street names must speak to the urban wanderer like the snapping of dry twigs, and little streets in the heart of the city must reflect the times of day, for him, as clearly as a mountain valley. This art I required later in life; it fulfilled a dream, of which the first traces were labyrinths on the blot-ting papers in my school notebooks. (53–54)

The city becomes landscape, a kind of second nature in the imagina-tion. Not surprisingly, Aragon's notion of *paysage* in its relation to the city leads back to Baudelaire, who wrote in "The Salon of 1859" of

a genre which I can only call the landscape of great cities, by
which I mean the collection of grandeurs and beauties which results from a powerful agglomeration of men and monuments—
the profound and complex charm of a capital city which has
grown old and aged in the glories and tribulations of life.[65]

Both Aragon and Benjamin saw the city as landscape and as labyrinth. The motif of consciously and deliberately losing one's way, "*sich
verirren*," in the city, recodes and concretizes Aragon's celebration
of error (*Irrtum*) as the royal road to truth:

This darkness, which he imagines he can dispense with in describing the light, is error with its unknown characteristics, error
which demands that a person contemplate it for its own sake before rewarding him with the evidence about fugitive reality that
it alone could give. (6-7)

While valuable as a correction of overconfidence in the logic and rationality of "*les lumières*," the idea that "error is the corollary of evidence" (7) remains perhaps too abstract to make much sense, not to
mention its paradoxical claim to evidence. It is stunning, then, to see
how Benjamin transformed this notion of error poetically and topo-
graphically. At the very material level it becomes losing one's way in
the city, thereby illuminating what Aragon calls the unknown characteristics of error. On the other hand, error operates creatively in
the child's misunderstandings of certain words: *Muhme Rehlen* (Aunt
or Cousin Rehlen) becomes *Mummerehlen*, *Kupferstich* (copper
etching) becomes *Kopf Verstich* (eliminated in the 1938 version),
Blumeshof 12, the address of his grandmother, becomes *Blume-zof*,
and *Markt Halle* (market hall) becomes *Mark Thalle*, a mysterious
place where the market women become "priestesses of a venal Ceres"
or "procuresses, unassailable wool-clad colossi" (70). The linguistic
distortions and displacements open up another imaginary reality:

"Listen to my tale of the mummerehlen." The line is
distorted—yet it contains the whole distorted world of childhood. (98)

Distortion (*Entstellung*) and disguise (*Verstellung*) produce *le merveil-leux quotidien* of childhood. Even the hunchback can be read as a distortion, in this case of the body. Distortion operates at different levels, mental or physiological or physical. "The Mummerehlen" gives us the philosophical key. As the child does not understand the ancient word *"Muhme,"* which means aunt or cousin, *"Mummerehlen"* becomes a friendly spirit of mimicry and disguise (*"vermummen"* means to disguise):

> Early on, I learned to disguise myself in words, which really were clouds. The gift of perceiving similarities is, in fact, nothing but a weak remnant of the old compulsion to become similar and to behave mimetically. In me, this compulsion acted through words. Not those that made me similar to well-behaved children, but those that made me similar to dwelling places, furniture, clothes. I was distorted by similarity to all that surrounded me. (97–98)

Benjamin's notion of bodily mimesis pertaining between subject and object is of course closely related to his language philosophy, which assumed identity of word and object in some prelapsarian state, no longer fully accessible in modernity but residually present in children's play. The child's ability to become similar, to overcome subject/object division with a technique of *Vermummung* as mimicry and disguise is key to Benjamin's theory of mimesis, which actually took shape in essays such as "The Mimetic Faculty" and "Doctrine of the Similar" at the same time that he wrote the early versions of *Berlin Childhood*.

Here again the Aragonian theme of privileging error as central to the *merveilleux quotidien* is mimetically transformed. Aragon sums up:

> There are strange flowers of reason to match each error of the senses. (10)

A strange flower of reason emerging from aural error is the literal flower in Blume-zof, itself a metaphor for the home of his grandmother, a place where "I was safer even than in my parents' house"

(86). He quickly identifies the *Blume*, or flower, of the mispronounced word:

> It was a giant bloom of plush that thus, removed from its crinkled wrapper, leapt to my eyes. (86)

Couldn't we take Aragon's statement about the "strange flowers of reason" as the perfect comment on what happens to the child in the miniatures of *Berlin Childhood* when he imagines the *Mummerehlen* as a spirit, the market women as priestesses and procuresses of the *Mark Thalle*, or, as in *Blumeshof 12*, the flower hidden in the address of his grandmother? Secularized myth emerges from error— error as a kind of *sich verirren*, not in the topography of the city, but in the sounds and spellings of language, another labyrinth that is hard for children to negotiate.

According to Benjamin, this ability to practice bodily and linguistic mimesis was still residually present in the child as an ontogenetic dimension of phylogenesis. It is a dimension not found in Aragon, who did not share this emphatic kind of a philosophy of history and for whom, after all, *le merveilleux quotidien* may have been more banal and trivial than it was for Benjamin. But for both writers *le merveilleux quotidien* was that space and experience in the city where the social contradictions of capitalist life revealed themselves. And it is telling that Aragon himself ascribed the ability to perceive *le merveilleux quotidien* to young age:

> A mythology ravels and unravels. It is a knowledge, a science of life open only to those who have no training in it. . . . I am already twenty-six years old, am I still privileged to take part in this miracle? How long shall I maintain this sense of the marvellous suffusing everyday existence [*le merveilleux quotidien*]? (10-11)

Those who lack life experiences are of course the children, and it may well have been Aragon's animus toward Proust that made him avoid a direct reference to childhood in this passage. But the reference to the marvelous of the everyday does resonate powerfully with another observation by Benjamin in the surrealism essay:

We penetrate the mystery only to the degree that we recognize it in the everyday world, by virtue of a dialectical optic that perceives the everyday as impenetrable, the impenetrable as everyday.[66]

While Benjamin, elsewhere in that same passage, accused the surrealists of a "fanatical stress on the mysterious side of the mysterious," this reproach simply does not touch Aragon's *Paysan*. The Aragonian leitmotif of thresholds, which Benjamin recoded and expanded, invalidates any such reproach. For time and again *Le Paysan* speaks of thresholds, ranging from the threshold between reason and fantasy, between the factual and the mysterious to that between arcade and brothel, city and nature, the conscious and the unconscious. Key to all is the threshold that underlies all the others:

How mankind loves to remain transfixed at the very threshold [translation modified—AH] of the imagination. (60)

It is precisely at that threshold, which Benjamin recoded as the threshold between sleeping and waking, that the new image-space explodes, that images and sounds (and there are several almost Dadaist image/sound experiments in *Le Paysan*) flow into each other in the way Benjamin described in his retrospective comments on surrealism in 1934, which I must quote again:

Life appeared worth living only where the threshold between sleeping and waking had been eroded, as if by the footsteps of images, ebbing and flowing by the thousand. Language was itself only where, with automatic exactitude, sound and image, image and sound, had merged with each other so utterly that there was no space left for "meaning," not even the smallest fissure.[67]

Even the metaphor of awakening is prefigured at the beginning of *Le Paysan*, where Aragon critiques the modern spirit of rational analysis and logic:

This spirit of analysis, this spirit and this need, have been trans-
mitted to me. And *like a man tearing himself away from sleep*, it
costs me a painful effort to tear myself away from this mental
habit, so as to think simply, naturally, in terms of what I see and
touch. (8–9; my italics)

Sensual experience led Aragon to the threshold of fantasy and dream,
and he found one of the most successful images for the resulting activity of writing, an image that reminds us of Lautréamont's famous
definition of montage as the meeting of an umbrella and a sewing
machine on an operating table:

And how easy it is, amid this enviable peace, to start daydreaming.
Reverie imposes its presence, unaided. Here surrealism resumes
all its rights. They give you a glass inkwell with a champagne
cork for a stopper, and you are away! Images flutter down like
confetti. Images, images everywhere. (81)

Surely Benjamin must have loved the idea of the glass inkwell with
a champagne cork for a stopper—intoxication plus writing producing
what he called profane illumination in the surrealism essay. And
images fluttering down like confetti resonates with the blizzard of
letters and the locust swarms of print in "Attested Auditor of Books"
in *One-Way Street*. The images that emerge in *Le Paysan* are not fantasy or dream images per se; they always refer to concretely observed
material realities in the arcade or the Buttes-Chaumont Park. If *Berlin
Childhood* still created profane illumination in a surrealist sense, by
1938 that illumination had lost the utopian dimension that still pervaded the surrealism essay and the final section of *One-Way Street*.
And yet Benjamin's images illuminate the emergence of a child's
imaginary in the retrospective consciousness of their adult author
and they are thoroughly profane, a never-ending stimulus to the reader's imagination.

In Conclusion

So much of Benjamin's thinking in the 1930s—by no means only the
miniatures of *Berlin Childhood*—went back to Aragon's notion of

image-space first developed in *Une vague de rêves* in 1924. In their writerly concern with images and their translation into literature, both Aragon and Benjamin shared in the obsessions of a period forced to reflect increasingly on images in the mass media, in photography, film, and illustrated papers. Their literary experiments stand out as some of the most ambitious to come to terms with the new image worlds of the twentieth century. In the end, however, one may acknowledge that the images Aragon spread throughout *Le Paysan* are rarely as condensed, thoughtful, and poetically successful as Benjamin's. But without Aragon's pushing the idea of image space, *Bild-Raum*, and without the model of *Le Paysan*, it is hard to imagine the images of *Berlin Childhood* coming into being. If the little hunchback, invisible like the unconscious, functioned as the keeper of images, Aragon provided the inspiration for Benjamin to foreground image-space and to try and unlock those images from their hiding places. *Berlin Childhood around 1900* is, as has often been claimed, a highly poetic text crafted in a beautiful German that makes words resonate with deep memory. It is only logical that its verbal images are as difficult to read as the images of childhood in the author's mind itself. There are lacunae, gaps in the fabric, allusions and adumbrations sometimes not fully accessible, giving rise to all kinds of speculation. I am not arguing that *Berlin Childhood around 1900* is a fully surrealist text. After all, there always were not just multiple surrealisms but also much porousness and reciprocity between surrealism and the realisms of the interwar period. But the link of the miniatures of *Berlin Childhood around 1900* to surrealism must be acknowledged if we want to admire more fully Benjamin's ability as a writer and critic who was eager to approximate mimetically the writing strategies of other writers: not just Aragon, of course, but also Baudelaire and Proust. It is in *Berlin Childhood* that the impact of French literature on this German author came to be most productive and creative.

7

~~~

War and Metropolis in Jünger

THE INCLUSION OF Jünger in a book about the metropolitan miniature may puzzle readers who know the author mainly
from his internationally famous World War I diary *Storm of Steel* and
from novels such as *On the Marble Cliffs* or *Glass Bees*. But Jünger did
contribute importantly to the literary miniature with *The Adventurous
Heart*, a collection of short prose pieces that I read in relation to
Jünger's formative experiences in the Great War, his anti-urban imaginary, and his radical right-wing journalism of the 1920s. The war,
after all, had also been central, though in significantly different ways,
to Gottfried Benn's experiments with short prose, and it underlay
key aspects of Musil's miniatures in his *Posthumous Papers of a Living
Author*. For political reasons, Jünger has always had his vocal detrac-
tors since the 1960s.[1] At the same time, he had faithful fans among
Germany's post–World War II authors such as Hans Magnus En-
zensberger and Alfred Andersch. But especially since the publication of Karl Heinz Bohrer's *Die Ästhetik des Schreckens* (1978), a
view of Jünger as a major modernist writer in the tradition of Poe
and Baudelaire has been broadly accepted in Germany. His celebration of stereoscopic vision and his interest in technological
media such as photography supported his canonization as a modernist at a time when literary study was increasingly turning to
the visual media.

In this book, however, Jünger's early writings serve me as a largely
negative foil by comparison with the great modernists of the interwar
period. Of course, the experience of a destructive modernity that in-
forms so much modernist work is thematically present in his writ-

ings. But what distinguishes his work from that of Kafka, Kracauer, Benjamin, and Musil, apart from its reductive anti-urbanism, is the fact that his miniatures are never even close to problematizing the relationship between visual media and literature, as one might have expected from his intense engagement with photography. There is no literary remediation in reverse. Photography remains subordinated to literature, and it is significant that his publication ventures with photo books in the early 1930s did not have any effect at all on the rewriting of *The Adventurous Heart* in the later 1930s. Even as I question his status as a major modernist, his collection of miniatures shows in symptomatic ways how modernity was appropriated by the German right and how the miniature as a literary form could be deployed for politically right-wing ideas.

Jünger had become well known in the 1920s as the author of books, essays, and stories dealing with his experiences in World War I. He joined the war at nineteen, fought to the war's end as a storm-troop officer despite being wounded multiple times, and finished up by receiving the award of the highest military order, the Pour le Mérite, just a week before the armistice was signed. Late in life, this recognition was repeated in the context of French-German reconciliation. After the conservative turn in West German politics in 1982, Chancellor Helmut Kohl invited Jünger in 1984 to stand with him and François Mitterand during the commemoration of the seventieth anniversary of the battle of Verdun. It demonstrated yet again how much Jünger was still seen, both in France and in Germany, as the writer who had given literary shape to the Great War.

His *Storm of Steel*, based on his extensive war diaries, was first published in 1920 and amended multiple times in later editions. It still is celebrated for its unflinching gaze at the horrors of mechanized warfare, but it also became a key text in the construction of what George Mosse has called the myth of the war experience in the spirit of 1914 and, as such, the main counterpoint to Erich Remarque's antiwar novel *All Quiet on the Western Front*.[2] Fourteen editions had been published by 1934 with approximately a quarter million copies sold. Jünger never duplicated the success of this book, but the war experience remained central to most of his writings during the 1920s and early 1930s. Among all of Jünger's writings in the interwar period,

The Adventurous Heart is literarily the most interesting one, far more so than his post–World War II novels and diaries.

Episodes from *Storm of Steel* were narratively elaborated and expanded in the 1920s into separately published books such as *Copse 125* (1924) and *Fire and Blood* (1926). A long essay about the war with the telling title *Combat as Inner Experience* (1922) articulated a way to compensate for the fact that the war had been lost. Tracts such as *Total Mobilization* (1930), *The Worker* (1932), and *On Pain* (1934) conjured up a world beyond liberal democracy and beyond the despised culture of bourgeois security. In these writings Jünger constructed an ontology of combat and war as models for a new hierarchically ordered state formation to be born out of conflict, war, and a permanent state of emergency. In all these texts it becomes clear that the obsessive rewriting of the war experience was due as much to the trauma of the war itself as to the trauma that Germany had lost the war. This loss was to be remedied militarily by an inevitable other war in which a new race of steel hardened soldiers would redeem the destiny of the nation. The cold expressionless face under the *Stahlhelm* became its emblem. In a bow to late-nineteenth-century *Lebensphilosophie*, violence as a higher form of life was sanctioned as the midwife of that imagined new world of technology and cold conduct.[3] In *The Worker*, Jünger's most controversial book, this new society allegedly emerging from the battlefields of the Great War was built around the metaphysically coded gestalt of the warrior-worker whose body is the ultimate armored fighting machine welded in storms of steel, a cold post-expressionist version of the "new man." It is a kind of techno-romanticism that fused the machine and the human body, the organic and the inorganic into a higher form of life resistant to pain, moral consideration, and bourgeois sentiment—part of a reactionary romanticism and its cult of technology, *armor fou*, as Hal Foster once called it with reference to the contemporary surrealist investment in technology.[4] It is important to note that this ideological gestalt of the warrior-worker was not yet present in the original diary of the war, whose full text has only recently been published for the first time as a word-for-word transcription of the original notebooks.[5] This type of the new man did not emerge in Jünger's writing until the later 1920s, first in the increasingly right-wing framework of small militarized circles and the conservative revolution, and then in the 1930s, in an ultimately unpersuasive attempt to keep Nazi ideology at bay by embracing allegedly postnationalist, almost planetary claims for this new radical stage of technological modernity.

All these texts, which were obsessively written, revised, and rewritten time and again, can be read as traumatic symptoms. They represent a retrospective attempt to make belated sense of a war experience that in the lives of so many who escaped the mass slaughter had resulted in the ultimate destruction of all meaning, especially in the countries that had lost the war. Yet the original rather laconic diary, together with its increasingly aestheticized rewritings in the multiple editions of *Storm of Steel*, stand as major representations of the experience of extreme destruction in the Great War, due primarily to their qualities of hard-nosed perception rather than depth of thought or avant-gardist literary experimentation. Together with the later propagandistic texts, which approach the kind of nationalist bolshevism typical of some of the conspiratorial right-wing circles of the 1920s, they form the backdrop of Jünger's most ambitious literary experiment of those years, *The Adventurous Heart*. This book of miniatures exists in two fundamentally different versions, marking the transition in Jünger's writing from war-related propagandistic texts to a more literary project. The first version was published in 1929, the year that ushered into the final crisis of the Weimar Republic, the second in 1938, the year of the *Kristallnacht* pogrom and the *Anschluss* of Austria. The 1929 version contains many celebratory references to the Great War, calling it an "incomparable school," and it still reflects Jünger's political thought of the late 1920s, though in a somewhat muted and less activist form.[6] Significantly, all such propagandistic references to the war are purged from the strongly revised 1938 edition, which only contains about a third of the earlier version and strains to appear apolitical and ahistorical. It is ultimately a quite different book, and it reflects Jünger's increasing distance from his political views of the 1920s and from the Nazi regime.[7] Similarly, only the early version contains key passages about the modern metropolis couched in a then-widespread romantic anti-capitalist, anti-urban, and anti-bourgeois discourse. References to city life, too, have been mostly purged from the 1938 edition, leaving the reader with a purer, more abstract version of what Karl Heinz Bohrer in his influential study has called the aesthetics of terror and violence that indeed pervaded much of modernism and avant-gardism in the interwar years in politically very divergent forms.[8]

The subtitle of the first version was *Notations by Day and by Night*, that of the second version *Figures and Capriccios*.[9] The miniatures of the second version were never published separately or in groupings in the feuilleton. But several pieces of the first version appeared in 1927 under the pseudonym Hans Sturm in the radical right-wing journal *Arminius: Kampfschrift für deutsche Nationalisten*. A year later, the whole text was prepublished in the Berlin daily *Der Tag* from October 19 to November 18, 1928, a paper that was part of the right-wing Hugenberg media conglomerate. Only the first version, literarily much less accomplished than the second, deals substantively with metropolitan space. But its metropolitan imaginary, which clearly reflects Jünger's years in Berlin in the 1920s, resonates strongly in several of the key miniatures of the 1938 version, even though specific description and localizable references are purged there. This is of course not enough of a reason to ignore the second version here, since, as in Kafka, Kracauer, Musil, and Adorno, the metropolitan experience, even when not described in realistic detail, forms the very ground of Jünger's radical critique of modern urban civilization, bourgeois society, and democratic liberalism. As Jünger's war-related journalistic writings from the 1920s show, his urban imaginary was fundamentally shaped by his experience of the Great War: the spaces of the city morphed into a displaced projection of warfare. Any reading of *The Adventurous Heart* that ignores this constitutive link between war, violence, and the city in Jünger will inevitably reduce the political dimension of this text.

The Metropolis and War

This discursive linkage of war and the metropolis was not unique to Jünger at that time. The motif had already appeared during the war in Gottfried Benn's prose and later in Döblin's *Berlin Alexanderplatz* and in the Weimar working-class novel, in which the war's trenches became the barricades of class struggle. It can also be found in painters such as Kirchner, Dix, Grosz, and Beckmann and all the way to the painters of the *Neue Sachlichkeit*. And yet there is a weighty reason why one might be skeptical about including Jünger in a book that deals centrally with the miniature as a key phenomenon of literary modernism. In Jünger's work, the linkage of war, technology, and the metropolis is predicated on a pre-modernist traditional "heroic world view" that romanticized the eclipse of bourgeois individuality as ground for a new emerging world, as if it hadn't been the Great War itself that had made any form of such heroism, individual or collective, obsolete.[10] Thus we read in *Combat as Inner Experience:*

> The glowing dusk of a sinking era is at the same time a dawn, by arming us for new harder fighting. . . . The war is not the end, but rather the emergence of violence. It is the forge in which the world will be hammered into new limits and new communities. New forms filled with blood and power will be packed with a hard fist. The war is a great school and the new man will be taken from our race.[11]

Five years later, in 1927, he again celebrated this merger of organic nature and the machine as "these steel translations of our blood and our brains."[12] No wonder Walter Benjamin, himself a theorist of destruction, war, and technology, had this to say in his 1930 review of *Krieg und Krieger,* a book of essays edited by Ernst Jünger:

> This arch-Germanic magical fate acquired a moldy luster when set against the stark background of military service in army barracks and impoverished families in civilian barracks.[13]

To Benjamin, the delusional attempt to win war back, as it were, after it had been "lost" was "nothing other than an uninhibited translation of the principles of *l'art pour l'art* to war itself."[14] Since fascism incorporated modernity into its cultural and political synthesis and cannot be dismissed as simply anti-modern, one might be tempted to speak of the fascist modernism of Jünger. But *The Adventurous Heart* complicates such a clear-cut understanding.

The Adventurous Heart in both versions is a collection of seemingly unrelated but subliminally connected short prose pieces that make it analogous to the miniatures of modernists such as Kafka, Benn, and Musil. At the same time this superficial affinity with the modernists is negated by Jünger's traditional authorial habitus, his old-fashioned, overly pretentious language burdened with undigested metaphysics, and the lack of modernist self-reflection of the medium of language and narration. It is particularly his derivative reliance on the imagery and thematics of nineteenth-century black romanticism and decadence that prevents his texts from achieving the modernist self-reflexiveness and narrative perspectivalism that characterizes the writings of the other authors treated in this book. The difficulty is to spell out the ways this text participates in modernist imaginaries and ambitions while never quite living up to the demands of complexity and insight into the modern world that characterizes the best of modernist writing. Only if we put *The Adventurous Heart* into the context of Jünger's war-related writings of the 1920s and early 1930s will the differences from and affinities with modernist writing become visible.[15]

The ontologized and increasingly reified experience of war, violence, and technology and the subsequent mythification of war as telos of modernity also overdetermined Jünger's understanding of metropolitan modernity in the 1920s. War and the city merged into one and the same imaginary, illuminating each other and dissolving the boundary between the civilian and the military, the technological and the social spheres. In his essays and magazine articles, Jünger articulated this merger with unmatched prophetic enthusiasm, however cold and detached his observations may appear. Thus in the 1926 essay "Gross-Stadt und Land" (Metropolis and countryside), we read:

> We must penetrate the forces of the metropolis, which are the real powers of our time: the machines, the masses, the worker. For here lies the potential energy from which will arise the new nation of tomorrow; and every European people is now at work trying to harness this potential. . . . *The Great War itself is a good example of the way that the essence of the city has begun to take possession of the whole range of modern life.* The generation of the trenches went forth expecting a joyous war in the old style, a field campaign. . . . But just as the landscape of this battlefield

proved to be no natural landscape but a technological landscape, *so was the spirit that animated it an urban spirit. Urban, too, was the "battle of materials" and still more the mechanized "battle of movement" that developed from it.* Today any kind of revolt that does not begin in the urban centers is doomed from the start to failure.[16]

A passage such as this one may resonate with Walter Benjamin's famous description of the technological battlefields of World War I in "The Storyteller" or with his critique of war technology in the service of imperialism in the last miniature of *One-Way Street*. But Benjamin critiqued what Jünger embraced. "To the Planetarium" ends with a call for an alternative nondestructive technology and a bizarre erotic and anarchic image of technology as an "ecstasy of procreation" that was to follow upon the "frenzy of destruction" of the Great War.[17] Jünger, on the other hand, celebrated destruction, and his erotic fantasies relied stably and unselfconsciously on the language of masculinist cliché. Thus, in *Feuer und Blut* we get the gendered relationship between war as manly and the city girdled like a woman to be conquered:

> The green at the edge of the forests appears dark as if tinged by velvety blood; from the fields sparkling in the sunshine there radiates that great manly serenity of battle; and the cities whose battlements and towers penetrate the sunset's glow morph into rich fortresses whose girdle is busted open by the conqueror's fist and whose names are linked with his fame until the remotest times.[18]

Who really is this "we" who penetrates the forces of the metropolis, the conqueror whose fist breaks the girdle of the urban fortress? It is not yet the organized brown storm troopers of the Nazi Party but the now-demilitarized former combatants who were gathering in small conspiratorial right-wing circles of the so-called conservative revolution in the 1920s and to whose magazines Jünger frequently contributed. In the 1929 version of *The Adventurous Heart* the narrator says:

I note with pleasure that the cities have begun to fill up with armed men and that even the most barren system, the most boring disposition cannot do without warlike representation.[19]

Just a few pages earlier, in a critique of metropolitan life as a "gassy mix of betrayal, suffocating air, and hackneyed irony that keeps the motor of corruption in motion" we read:

The power of small warrior communities lies in scrupulously guarded boundaries and armed expectation.[20]

The remilitarization of Germany after Versailles was to begin in the city. Combat was to be continued at a higher level in the metropolis that needs to be conquered and purged. This was Jünger's reactionary urbanism, which radicalized the anti-urban discourse of conservative German *Kulturkritik* of earlier years.

The metaphysics of combat is especially pronounced in *Combat as Inner Experience:*

What is important is not what we fight for, but how we fight.[21]

This "how we fight" points to combat as pure transcendent event, a transcendence that is emphatically gendered when combat is described as "the male form of procreation."[22] Penetrating the city, which, as in Carl Schmitt, is always the place of feminization, decadence, and democratic weakness, is thus the prerequisite for the reassertion of a masculinity badly damaged by the loss of the war. Thus, Jünger articulated a widespread reactionary view when he wrote in *Standarte*, one of the right-wing journals of the 1920s:

We asked for the meaning of our experience and were able to determine only one thing: this meaning had to be totally different from the one we attributed to events at that time. . . . We must believe in a higher meaning than the one we were able to give to events, and we must believe in a higher destiny within which that which we believe we determine is being fulfilled. . . . We *must* believe that everything is meaningfully ordered, otherwise we shipwreck with the masses of the inwardly oppressed, the disillusioned, or the do-gooders, or we live in suffering like animals from day to day.[23]

"Higher meaning" and "higher destiny" usually comes in the form of poor writing. No doubt the "We *must* believe" is heartfelt rather than propagandistic strategy aiming to get his right-wing readers' attention, and it is typical of Jünger's decisionist grandstanding that is nothing but a desperate attempt to hide the loss of any "higher meaning" Jünger acknowledged elsewhere.[24] A sense of passivity prevails, as he conjures a "higher destiny" within which something is "being fulfilled" instead of resulting from human agency. It is as if Jünger was being spoken, like a ventriloquist's dummy, when he wrote in 1927 in another programmatic essay entitled "Der Geist":

> The spirit's nature is masculine and gives direction, it does not want to dissolve itself into the world; it rather wants to gain control of it. It wants the world to be its world, to be like itself. . . . The spirit needs the blood because it is embedded into life, but it can do without consciousness. . . . Under the mechanism of surfaces it searches for deeper meaning. Rather than theorize it wants to create. Rather than decompose [*zersetzen*] it wants to generate.[25]

The fear of dissolving and decomposing, the privileging of the blood, and the critique of consciousness, theory, and surfaces—all of this is language that entered the broad cultural synthesis on which the Nazis eventually would build their mass appeal. Jünger embraced the inevitability of catastrophic destruction of the old bourgeois world as the precondition for an emerging fully technological age, with its joyously anticipated synthesis of spirit and blood, flesh and steel, brain and camera, body and machine. When Siegfried Kracauer reviewed Jünger's *The Worker*, he judged it "anything but a political construction." Regarding one of Jünger's several photo books of those years, entitled *The Transformed World*, Kracauer said that "this gestalt show opens up not so much a path into politics as a line of flight leading away from politics"—a line of flight, we might add with hindsight, that was part of Weimar's cyborg phantasms.[26] The pathology of the armored self revealed the whole machinery of combat, in Klaus

Theweleit's sense, as a compensatory male fantasy.[27] In that sense, Jünger's texts articulated and exacerbated a widespread masculine insecurity, the demasculization resulting from the lost war. Clearly this was one of the key psychosocial dispositions on which the Nazi ideological synthesis could build its electoral politics, with or without Jünger's contribution.

Jünger's call to arms is also present in some of the miniatures of *The Adventurous Heart*, but another, darker tone begins to prevail in his references to the metropolis. Here we indeed find certain parallels to Kracauer, Kafka, Benn, and Benjamin when Jünger speaks of the "convoluted dream state of modern civilization" or describes alienation, angst, and loneliness as key metropolitan experiences.[28] But in contrast to Kracauer's street scenes from Berlin, Kafka's micro-encounters in Prague, or Benn's daringly poetic flights through Brussels, Jünger creates descriptions of terror and angst in the mode of a derivative black romanticism in scenes mostly located far from urban spaces. Nightmarish miniatures such as "The Stranger Visits," "The Black Knight," and "The Cloister Church" (all of which are found in both versions), with their laconically cold but voyeuristic descriptions of horror and torture, are unthinkable in the work of these other writers.[29] What is important is not the literary tradition he uses but how he uses it. Comparisons to Poe, Baudelaire, or Flaubert may work at the level of content and themes, but they break down as one considers language, narrative, style, and authorial position.[30] Formal considerations rather approximate Jünger to the lesser literature of the late nineteenth century by writers such as Huysmans or Octave Mirbeau, whose torture gardens are explicitly cited in "Vicious Books," one of the miniatures of *The Adventurous Heart*.[31]

Another such B-literature influence was Alfred Kubin's 1909 fantastic novel *Die andere Seite*, a cliché-ridden work that is much less compelling than any of Kubin's horrifyingly powerful drawings and etchings. Thus, one of the first passages on the metropolis in the first version of *The Adventurous Heart* reads:

I think it was in Kubin's remarkable novel "Die andere Seite" [The other side] and its pervasive deep anxiety of dreams that I sensed for the first time that a metropolitan café might create a devilish impression. It is strange that this feeling seems to be so rarely perceived in places where technology appears in almost pure form. Neon advertising in its glowing red or icy blue glistening fascination, a modern bar, an American cinematic grotesque—these are details of a gigantic Luciferian revolt whose sight fills the loner simultaneously with raging lust and with oppressive angst.[32]

Dream, anxiety, and the red glow of sexual lust were also present in Kracauer's response to glowing red neon advertising. But Kracauer's street scenes were always more specific; they give a sense of localizable urban spaces with multiple concrete details, while the quote above lives off the flat stereotypical trope of the city as demonic. Here, as elsewhere, Jünger's bent toward editorializing got in the way of literary construction. A page later Jünger describes the metropolitan physiognomy in a way that might resonate with Kafka's emphasis on motion and standstill, anxiety and dream:

> One will notice that the face of modern metropolitan man bears a double seal: that of angst and that of dream; the first emerges primarily in motion, the second in repose. That is why street corners and bridges in the big city exhibit such a dreary and oppressive character.[33]

In contrast to Kafka, however, the focus is not on a concretely observed urban phenomenon, estranged in a micrological gaze, but on an abstractly postulated general physiognomy. Jünger goes on to lament the masklike appearances of modern man:

> the completely frozen, automatic and quasi-narcoticized comportment [*Haltung*] of modern man in a state of repose, for instance in a means of public transport in motion or also during a stay in one of the so-called sites of entertainment.[34]

And a few pages later, in his praise of stereoscopic vision, which he defines traditionally and rather metaphysically as the opposition between bodily and spiritual vision, he claims provocatively and approvingly that advanced civilization and barbarism are identical, another theme we know from Benjamin and Adorno. But the similarity is again only superficial, for Jünger embraces what the critical theorists see as the dismal result of an enlightened modernity:

> In the cities, man is beginning to become simpler, which, in that certain sense, means deeper. He becomes more civilized; that is, more barbaric.[35]

What, then, is Jünger's metropolitan barbarism like? "Genuine cruelty" and "triumphs of an absolute *Schadenfreude*" characterize the cinema, especially comedy; street noise and its roar of engines is said to represent some ultimate threat, and the colors of the metropolis shine with hellish poisonous lighting.[36] It is not difficult to read such comments as displacements of the war experiences as described in *Storm of Steel*. The link becomes even more explicit as he mentions numerous city dwellers, presumably demilitarized veterans, who resemble "burned-out craters."[37] And yet it is in the cities, those "sites of a most complex barbarism," that the new world emerges:[38]

> It will not remain hidden to the attentive eye that a massive instinct reveals itself behind the seemingly mechanical hustle and bustle of our cities, that the economy is something beyond the economy, politics something beyond politics, advertising something beyond advertising, technology something beyond technology—in short, that every one of our most familiar everyday phenomena can be grasped simultaneously as a symbol of a more essential life.[39]

This kind of purple prose and abstract gesturing toward instinct and the deep is hard to reconcile with the claims about Jünger's celebrated cold and precise stereoscopic vision, and it mars Jünger's writing throughout the miniatures of the first version of *The Adventurous Heart*. Passages such as these confirm that Adorno was right when in a letter of December 28, 1949, to Thomas Mann he called Jünger a "wretchedly bad, kitsch-prone writer."[40]

By contrast, some of the miniatures in the second version are sober and precise in their prose and reveal the ambivalent and threatening dimensions of the metropolis in powerful images. Symptomatic of such more successful miniatures is the intense focus on perception itself rather than the ekphrastic description of horror as in a slaughter scene with a decapitated bearded head floating in an oversize soup kettle ("The Beach Walk"). A good example is the miniature entitled "Terror" ("Das Entsetzen"), which is taken over almost verbatim from the early into the later version. I quote its first part from the 1938 version:

There is a type of thin, broad sheet metal that is often used in small theaters to simulate thunder. I imagine a great many of these metal sheets, yet still thinner and more capable of a racket, stacked up like the pages of a book, one on top of another at regular intervals, not pressed together but kept apart by some unwieldy mechanism.

I lift you up onto the topmost sheet of this mighty pack of cards, and as the weight of your body touches it, it rips with a crack in two. You fall, and you land on the second sheet, which shatters also, with an even greater bang. Your plunge strikes the third, fourth, fifth sheet and so on, and with the acceleration of the fall the impacts chase each other closer and closer, like a drumbeat rising in rhythm and power. Ever more furious grows the plummet and its vortex, transforming into a mighty, rolling thunder that ultimately bursts the limits of consciousness.[41]

Clearly the references to a drumbeat (in German, *Trommelwirbel*, drum-roll, is close to *Trommelfeuer*, a barrage of gunfire) and mighty rolling thunder project machine-gun fire and canon thunder onto an urban scene, as the whole miniature is devised as a theatrical mise-en-scène. But this is where the miniature should have ended. What follows in both versions is an equally long explanatory paragraph that attempts to classify different terms in the semantic field of terror such as dread, fear, anxiety, horror, and fright—all of which were affects produced on the battlefield—before it ends with a rhetorical question about a real rather than only imagined collapse of consciousness in a situation of an anticipated total doom. This rather talkative and schoolmasterly exercise takes away from the power of the imagined scene. Even though the texts are practically identical in both versions, it is only in the 1929 version that this miniature appeared in the context of multiple references to the epoch of war and to the experiences on the technological battlefield, all of which were purged in the later version.[42]

Technology rather than a theatrical contraption conjures up similar experiences in "Song of the Machines" The narrator on a nightly walk in the city is confronted with a "dark and forsaken image."[43] Through a basement window he sees a machine whose gigantic flywheel spins inexorably on its axis, independent of any human presence or activity. The narrator then moves from this concrete observation to a more general description of the power of the roaring engines that lift airplanes into the sky or the bursts of fire that shoot out of blast furnaces as a train speeds past in an industrial landscape. Positive though this celebration of technology is, it also seems to hide inherent danger in ways that resemble the ambivalent representation of technology in Fritz Lang's *Metropolis*, though without the gendered dimension of Lang's film.[44] This danger emerges in surreal dreamlike ways in another urban scene in "In the Utility Rooms":

> I was sitting in a large café, in which a band was playing and many well-dressed guests were evidently bored. In order to find the toilets, I went through a doorway hung with red velvet, but then soon got lost in a maze of stairways and corridors and ended up leaving the elegantly decorated rooms for a badly run-down annex. I thought that I had come out at the bakery; the bleak corridor I walked through was dusted with flour and black cockroaches crept around on the walls. It seemed that someone was still working, since I came to a spot where a wheel was driving a belt with slow, jerky rotations; next to it, a leather bellows once in a while moved up and down. To see into the baking room, which probably lay below, I leaned far out of a blackened window that opened onto an overgrown garden. But the space that I then saw looked more like a blacksmith's shop. Each spark of the bellows sparked up a coal fire that had red-hot tools lying in it, and

each revolution of the wheel drew in all sorts of machines. I saw that they had seized two guests, a man and a woman, and wanted to force them to take off their clothes. They resisted vigorously, and I thought to myself: "Well, as long as they still have their good things on, they'll be safe." But it seemed a sinister omen that the fabric began to give here and there from the grabbing and that the flesh was visible through the tears. I quietly withdrew and was able to find my way back to the café. I sat back down at my table, but the band, the waiter, and the pleasant rooms now appeared to me in a completely different light. I also understood that it was not boredom that the guests felt, but fear.[45]

This miniature resembles a technological version of Baudelaire's "The Double Room," except that in Jünger we have two very different spaces under one roof—one public, the other hidden—rather than just the reimagination of one and the same room from divine to hellish under the impact of the spleen. The red and black color scheme suggests the colors of Nazi flags. In contrast to Baudelaire's alternately ecstatic and depressed narrator, Jünger's narrator remains unaffected by what he coldly observes. The machines suggest tools of torture, ultimately threatening all the seemingly oblivious guests in the urban café—again a displacement of the threat of the mechanized battles of the Great War into a civilian metropolitan context under the sign of technology, but this time with connotations of Nazi rule in the metropolis. The narrator, with perfect *désinvolture* (offhandedness), understands that it is fear that plagues the guests in the café rather than bourgeois boredom. But it does not seem to affect him, as he remains aloof in his understanding.

Fear, however, is absent from another explicitly metropolitan miniature called "Violet Endives," also a new addition to the later version. It lends itself well to problematizing Jünger's *Haltung* (comportment) in the face of barbaric violence and to critically reassessing Karl Heinz Bohrer's interpretation of Jünger as a writer whose work transcends politics through its aesthetic strategies and its focus on perception. In contrast to black romantic miniatures such as "The Black Knight," "The Stranger Visits," and "The Cloister Church," where the protagonist and narrator is himself overwhelmed by the effect

of horror, "Violet Endives" pursues a strategy of maximizing the
horror of the reader by avoiding any display of horror by the narrator in the face of the unspeakable: cannibalism subjected to capitalist commodity culture. The miniature is short enough to quote it
in toto:

> *Violet Endives*
> Steglitz
>
> Noticing a most particular kind of violet endive in the show
> window of an opulent gourmet shop, I went in. I was not sur-
> prised when the shopkeeper explained to me that the only meat
> that could be considered as an accompaniment to this dish was
> human flesh—I had already darkly suspected as much.
>
> A long conversation ensued on the manner of its preparation,
> after which we descended into the cold rooms, where I saw the
> humans hanging on the walls like hares in front of a game butch-
> er's shop. The shopkeeper was pointing out that I was looking
> exclusively at hunted specimens and not at those bred and fat-
> tened in captivity: "Leaner, but—I'm not saying this just to sell
> them—much more aromatic." The hands, feet, and heads were
> arranged in special bowls and had little price tags attached.
>
> As we went back up the stairs, I remarked: "I didn't know that
> civilization had come so far in this city"—upon which the shop-
> keeper appeared taken aback for a second, but then took his leave
> with a most engaging smile.[46]

The narrator's *désinvolture*, the absence of moral judgment, and his
cold, matter-of-fact interest in the face of what seems to be a modern
regression to the archaic and the atavistic, gets its poignancy from
his ironic comment on cannibalism as progress in civilization. Or is
it ironic? How are we to read the sentence "I didn't know that civilization had come so far in this city"? Is it really a metaphor critical
of fascist rule, a metaphor already pointing to what Bohrer describes
as the "explicit representation of the emerging SS-world" in the description of Köppels-Bleek in the *Marblecliffs?*[47] Reading Jünger as a
modernist master of slave language evading censorship obviously
makes it possible to validate his texts as anti-fascist. Then we might

even suggest that "Violet Endives" anticipates Adorno and Horkheimer's critique of the fateful and fatal dialectic of enlightenment
and barbarism. But things remain more ambiguous. In contrast to
Horkheimer and Adorno's *Dialectic of Enlightenment*, Jünger does not
see the dialectic of civilization and barbarism, reason and myth as a
dangerous aberration from Enlightenment ideals that he, like the
Nazis, continues to criticize as part of a bourgeois world to be overcome. The position of the narrator in the text invalidates any such
comparison. The text does not critically reveal that archaic and barbaric violence is always already inscribed in a commodified modernity and has only been set free in National Socialism. It rather expresses a conscious acquiescence to cannibalism as an advancement
of civilization, an acquiescence that does not, to be sure, participate
actively in the cannibalistic hunt but that takes it as an unavoidable
fate. How adequate really is this metaphor of commodity cannibalism
as a critique of fascist modernity, if that is what it was meant to be?

The text does not allow us to read it simply as criticism of what it
describes, as a diagnostic allegory of National Socialism. I have no
doubt that Jünger by 1938 intended to maintain his distance from
the Nazis, though that did not prevent him from serving as army officer in the occupation of Paris a few years later. Similar to Gottfried
Benn, he saw his service in the army as a kind of internal refuge from
Nazi rule, another German fantasy that is all too obvious in retrospect. While he served in Paris, *désinvolture* proved its practical side,
as the diaries from the occupation years testify. But the narrative
strategy in "Violet Endives," textually manifest in the apparently distant and sovereign subject position of the narrator, speaks a different
language. It betrays Jünger's continuing affinity for that heart of darkness in the midst of European civilization. Several phrasings reveal,
possibly against Jünger's intention, that the narrator's *désinvolture* is
a sham. Underlying is a dialectic of fascination and distance, participation and *désinvolture*, desire and repression in which the latter terms
(distance, *désinvolture*, repression) are fully constituted by and dependent on the former (fascination, participation, desire). In true
Mirbeau-like fashion (Jünger had read Mirbeau's sadomasochistic
Jardin des supplices in 1937[48]), the visual lure of the violet endives, similar to that of the "Tiger Lily," the lead miniature of the collection,

is explained by the fact that the narrator had already had some dark inkling that this delicacy should be accompanied by human flesh. Thus, he knew all along in which direction civilization was progressing. At the surface level, "Violet Endives" may be read as a critique of fascist barbarism, but at a hermeneutically deeper level things are much more ambiguous. This miniature, as others in the collection that portray slaughter, torture, and base violence, requires another kind of stereoscopic reading, one that simultaneously perceives the narrator's surface distanciation and his in-depth participation.

Stereoscopic Vision

Two aspects of Jünger's thought are usually foregrounded in assessments of his literary achievement in *The Adventurous Heart* as modernist: his interest in stereoscopic vision and his claim of a "second colder consciousness that brings with it the ability to see oneself as object."[49] Both aspects have to do with vision and thus raise the question of how Jünger's writing relates to modern visual media. This second consciousness, anti-sentimental and anti-psychological as it is, is said to characterize a human being "standing outside the zone of pain," and as such it is linked to photography:

> The photography stands outside of the zone of sensitivity. It has a telescopic quality; one can tell that the event photographed is seen by an insensitive and invulnerable eye. It records the bullet in mid-flight just as easily as it captures a man at the moment an explosion tears him apart.[50]

There is no question that the invulnerable camera eye must have been an ideal when faced with daily destruction of human life in the trenches. And it is turned on the self in the act of seeing oneself as object. This "second and colder consciousness" is related to Jünger's celebrated *désinvolture* toward others and the world.[51] *Désinvolture* objectifies the world like the camera eye does, and the second, colder consciousness extends *désinvolture* to the subject itself. Only through such a colder consciousness does a deeper understanding become possible for Jünger. Rather than a form of indifference or narcissistic distraction, self-conscious *désinvolture* must be seen as an extreme form of attentiveness in the face of danger. *Désinvolture* is the principal *dispositif* of the adventurous heart that embraces the dangers generated by modernity.

As such it involved the doubling of vision into surface and depth to be grasped simultaneously. This was the pop-philosophy dimension of Jünger's much-celebrated stereoscopic vision, which Jünger would claim to be at stake in all representations of violence in *The Adventurous Heart*. He viewed *désinvolture* as simultaneous recognition of surface and an understanding of some hidden deeper meaning. But it also had a defensive dimension because it functioned as a defense against traumatization. It was, after all, the constant fear of exploding shells and grenades in the trenches that led to *désinvolture* in the first place. And yet in the 1920s Jünger never ceased to celebrate war and heroic battle, as if trying to "win" the war by retrospective imagination. *Désinvolture* in his early writings was not simply indifference to the mass death on the battlefields around him; instead, it can be read as a traumatic reaction, a protection against shell shock. In contrast to Benjamin, however, Jünger quite understandably never privileged the rupture of *Reizschutz* (Benjamin's term for the protection against shock) as a means to arrive at a deeper aesthetic understanding. And yet it would be one-sided to read him as armored ego only, as completely unaffected by what he experienced. The war writings always acknowledged fear, anxiety, even nervous breakdown. Everywhere lurked the dread of war, and only steely discipline and self-control including conscious self-numbing—could protect against it. This is how that colder second consciousness emerged as a feature of the new age, shaping the gestalt of the anticipated new man of twentieth-century planetary modernity that Jünger conjured up in *The Worker*. Writing the diaries in World War I, one assumes, helped him deal with the daily assault on the senses and on the body. That is why the multiple rewritings of key passages of *Storm of Steel* can be read as a never-ending sequence of traumatic deferral symptoms transferred to writing.

Clearly, stereoscopic vision functions as a metaphor more than as an engagement with contemporary visual media or the science of vision. And when it comes to his literary notion of stereoscopy itself, it is hardly more than a specific form of an aesthetic gaze that combines vision and tactility, tactility and taste, taste and color. Stereoscopy, as described in "Stereoscopic Pleasure" in *The Adventurous Heart* appears as an updated kind of romantic synaesthesia expanded toward an understanding of the world at large.[52] It is closer to the symbolism of the Baudelairean "Correspondances" than to any form of media history or theory. Thus, it is not surprising that Jünger's notion of stereoscopic vision lacks the estranging and troubling conjuncture of temporality and spatiality that pervaded Kafka's early prose pieces, Benjamin's considerations of the Imperial Panorama, or Kracauer's street scenes. Rather than seeing the potential of aesthetic strategies to break through the protection against stimuli, Jünger was primarily interested in strengthening his mental and bodily armor and drawing pleasure from aesthetic perception. Instead of disrupting conventional regimes of seeing, stereoscopic vision provided a new wholeness of the senses and thus remained largely a protective metaphor in Jünger's writing, a traditional humanist trope that fused surface perception with depth and insisted on the simultaneity of all sense perceptions. With Helmholtz, one might call it Jünger's stereoscopic delusion.[53] Jünger never discussed stereoscopy in its materialist physiological dimension nor did he actively relate it to technical apparatuses such as the stereoscope itself. Nor are Jünger's miniatures, in contrast to those written by other miniaturists of the time, guided by an attempt to create images that were intended and able to compete with photography and film. In *On Pain*, he did call for such a "new kind of precise, objective description" in literature in tune with the new visual media, but he himself did not deliver.[54] His literary images, especially the dream images, remained mostly at the level of cliché versions of black romanticism and the literature of horror and the occult. He offered allegories of the emergence of a world of torture and base violence, to be sure, but remained oblivious to the question of whether such nineteenth-century literary devices were adequate to a representation of fascism or any other form of totalitarianism in the twentieth century. And when he addressed photography as *Lichtschrift* (writing in light) he saw it only as an addendum to writing instead of as a medium that as another kind of *Schrift* challenged writing itself.[55]

In the end it is not surprising that *The Adventurous Heart* is devoid of direct or indirect reflections on photography or film. More important, and in contrast to Kafka, Kracauer, Benjamin and Musil, there is never any substantive negotiation between literature and the visual media. Helmut Lethen has recently argued that the studied coldness of Jünger's descriptions of torture, violence, and dread is due less to modern technologies of vision than to the archive of nineteenth-century natural science and its culture of evidence and distanced observation.[56] The violence of war, which was discursively explicit in Jünger's writing in 1929, had become implicit and ever more hidden in ekphrastic descriptions of strangely beautiful flowers, dangerous plants, and destructive insects by 1938. Even this turn to nature remained embedded in the discourse of violence and danger. The war diary told us that when storm trooper Jünger was not leading an attack on English troops, he kept himself busy at the front as a botanist and bug collector. His turn toward nature in these texts and elsewhere was steeped in a nineteenth-century belief in positive science and classification, reflecting that period's belief in natural selection and the inevitable destructiveness of nature. Ultimately it served Jünger both to naturalize military violence and to present nature itself as violent in miniatures such as "Aus den Strandstücken 2." Jünger's unreflective uses of science (in contrast to Benn's or Musil's, for example) proves that the nineteenth century was deeply ingrained in his language, thought, and literary imagination in ways that make any comparison with the major modernist writers problematic. It also makes it difficult to see Jünger's cold gaze as substantively related to technological media, even though the camera gaze may well feed into the need for *désinvolture*. But it is especially in his extant comments on photography and his practice as an editor of and contributor to photo books that the limitations of Jünger's understanding of the new visual technologies become evident.

The Photo Books of the Early 1930s

There is practically no engagement with photography and film in *The Adventurous Heart* except for one deprecating comment in the 1929 version:

That is why photographs from the war become ever more hateful to me, just as photography in general represents one of the most disagreeable attempts to bestow an unbecoming validity to that which is temporal and transitory—photography as creator giving birth to material copies that remain deprived of the dark rays of the spiritual sun Swedenborg speaks of.[57]

The phrasing is revealing. To speak of "an unbecoming validity [of] that which is temporal and transitory" flies in the face of any modernist aesthetic that privileges the transitory. In the context of the late 1920s, this rejection of photography was a reaction to the increasing number of commercialized photo books about the war that were published at the time. He saw only frozen surfaces in these photos, no deeper meaning whatsoever. He hated them because they lacked what he called, with an erudite reference to Swedenborg, "the dark rays of the spiritual sun." But then a year later there was a full U-turn when he wrote the introduction and several essays for the photo book he himself edited as *Das Antlitz des Weltkrieges* (The face of the world war; 1930). In the publisher's introduction we read:

> In more immediate ways than words, photographs, taken at all fronts, can report of the time of war whose necessity and greatness only now appears before our eyes.[58]

Clearly, this celebration of immediacy and authenticity represents Jünger's own view. For rather than drawing on the nature of photography as artifice and technology, split between negative and positive, in "Krieg und Lichtbild" (War and photography), Jünger's introductory essay of *Das Antlitz des Weltkrieges*, he himself naturalized photography by comparing it to a geological phenomenon:

> It is similar to the imprints the existence of strange animals has left in rock formations.[59]

Temporal depth and distance are naturalized. The geological imprint guarantees evidence and authenticity, just as the claim for photography's immediacy allegedly does. Photography is assimilated to a natural process, thus erasing the technological dimension of the photographic apparatus from view. And when he discussed photography as a technology at all, it was invariably related to the technological battlefield of World War I. Thus, in that same introductory essay we read:

> Apart from the muzzles of rifles and canons, optical lenses were directed at the field of battle day in day out; as instruments of a technical consciousness they preserved the image of these devastated landscapes which the world of peace has long since reclaimed.[60]

Indeed, images of devastated landscapes seemingly devoid of human life are what we remember when we think of photographs from World War I—pictures taken from the trenches or from airplanes. And yet Jünger's photo book is chock-full of soldiers on the march or on the attack, with canons and tanks, with dead enemy soldiers and horses littering the battlefield, while dead Germans are nowhere to be seen. Populating the devastated landscape certainly dramatizes and stirs memory and imagination, a strategy that is further enhanced by the deliberate retouching of photographs to increase dramatic effect. Julia Encke, who compared the reproductions of war photography in Jünger's photo books with the original previously published photographs, has persuasively shown that "the dark rays of the spiritual sun" can be read as an apt metaphor for the hidden practice of retouching the original photos.[61] It is a practice dominant in *Das Antlitz des Weltkrieges*, where explosions are added in the interest of increasing drama, violence, and the sense of danger. Ironically, this is the only instance where photography and writing came together in Jünger's practice, since retouching as a rewriting for aesthetic effect was also his strategy with editions of *Storm of Steel* subsequent to the 1920 version. Needless to say, the practice of retouching photographs, which was widespread at the time, contradicted Jünger's claim that photography was unmediated and authentic, a claim that stands at the opposite end of Kafka, Kracauer, and Benjamin's understanding of photography.

But then Jünger's investment in photography did not simply aim at preservation and memory of the war. Nor was the camera only a tool of objectifying vision to preserve *désinvolture*. In *The Worker* (1932), he lauded photography as a weapon of political attack, and in

On Pain (1934), he described vision itself as an act of aggression in the modern world.[62] He thus turned against the popular notion that photography was neutral and objective. He attributed a form of "magical possession" to photography, which he now interpreted as a "form of the evil eye," an expression of the merciless "very cruel" gaze of the worker-warrior type.[63] This notion of an attack through optical means circles us back to Benjamin's cutting critique of the 1930 essay book *Krieg und Krieger*, edited by Jünger:

> What developed here, first in the guise of the world war volunteer and then in the mercenary of the *Nachkrieg*, is in fact the dependable fascist class warrior.[64]

Jünger's extreme definition of the photograph as weapon does not prevail everywhere in his writing. In his introduction to the 1933 photo book *Die veränderte Welt*, edited by Edmund Schultz—a book that offered a repertoire of images of international modernization rather than nationalist propaganda—Jünger correctly described the technical procedure as a "filter porous only for a certain dimension of reality." He pointed out that the very act of taking a picture already implied a *"Wertung,"* a validation, even before the photograph would become a means of battle.[65] This can be seen as a correction of the claims made in *Das Antlitz des Weltkrieges* that photography was immediate, authentic, and therefore objective. The claim of objective reportage ultimately didn't fit his desire to associate seeing and photography not just with aggression but with acts of danger. Thus in his essay "On Danger," which introduced yet another photo book, Ferdinand Bucholtz's *Der gefährliche Augenblick* (The dangerous moment; 1931), Jünger celebrated the ability of photography to capture the dangerous moment, whether it was the eruption of a volcano, an earthquake, an accident at the car races, a revolutionary demonstration, or a terror bombing attack.[66] Though images of war played only a subordinate role in this edition, the editor's choice of Jünger as the writer of the introduction made it quite clear that the experience of war lurked in the background of the dangerous moments documented in the book. Once again the realms of war and the city, military and civilian life appear not just next to each other but are presented in their fundamental and naturalized affinity. Danger was in the center of Jünger's attention, the danger always sought out by the adventurous heart. For danger and risk stood against reason and enlightenment, those despised markers of the insidious boredom of bourgeois culture. Today, Jünger's introduction reads like a posthumous justification of the spirit of 1914. The embrace of risk and danger questioned all systems of insurance invented to protect the bourgeois world from myth and fate. And it was World War I that restored danger, risk, and fate to their central position in all life.

What to conclude from all of this? Contrary to what one might expect, the second edition of *The Adventurous Heart* was not touched by the massive investment in photography Jünger had engaged in since publishing the first version in 1929. To be sure, there are titillating and dangerous moments in some of the miniatures, but style and narrative strategy are safely traditional. His claim in "On Danger" that the times demanded a new style in language that would use technical means in literature stands in contrast to the photo book's explicit goal of creating "a new kind of unsentimental and *unliterary* picture book for reading."[67] Jünger's formulation suggests the reverse: he looked for a writing style that could be accompanied by or match technical means such as photography. But this is precisely what he did not do in his miniatures. Photography and literary writing remained separate in his work, belonging to different registers. Jünger wrote about photography in his essays and photo books, but he did not write photographically in *The Adventurous Heart*. Missing is what the modernists attempted: to engage image media with literary means, to problematize the relation between the literary and the visual in the literary text. Jünger, in contrast, editorialized in his writing and falsified evidence by retouching in his use of photography. In his work the photograph remained external to literary writing. He valued it as a documentary but at the same time highly affective and propagandistic addendum to literary language. Jünger's reluctant and contradictory engagement with photography in the early 1930s did not lead him to question literature as a medium in a way that would make him comparable to Kafka, Kracauer, Benjamin, or Musil. This is another dimension of his writing in *The Adventurous Heart* that simply does not measure up to the literary experiments that were central to the metropolitan miniatures of the modernists.

8

———◈◈◈———

Musil's Posthumous Modernism

ROBERT MUSIL published his *Posthumous Papers of a Living Author* in late 1935 with the imprint date of 1936. This last major publication during Musil's lifetime thus falls right between the 1935 Congrès pour la défense de la culture in Paris, in which he participated, and the 1937 Paris World Exposition, which was infamous for the two monumental pavilions of the Third Reich and the Soviet Union facing each other across the midway under the Eiffel Tower and famous for the Spanish pavilion with its pièce de résistance, Picasso's *Guernica*, right next to Albert Speer's monstrosity.

To understand the project of Musil's *Posthumous Papers*, I will sidestep the aesthetics embodied in these three World Expo phenomena: heroic socialist realism, national-socialist monumentalism, and the political modernism of the committed left avant-garde. All of these form the contemporary backdrop to what I call here, drawing on Musil's title, a posthumous modernism. With his collection of short prose pieces, Musil occupies a space outside this triangle, which dominated the mid-1930s and lived on in so many retrospective assessments, often based on Benjamin's rhetorically brilliant but false opposition between the aestheticization of politics and the politicization of the aesthetic. Written mostly in the 1920s for the feuilleton and reworked in 1935, these miniatures embody a vibrant afterimage of interwar modernism at a time when modernism was officially ostracized in Germany and the Soviet Union, a politically highly precarious moment just before the Moscow show trials, the Civil War in Spain, and the Austrian *Anschluss*.[1] At the 1935 congress, pressures on intellectuals and writers were mounting to take a supportive political position vis-à-vis the Soviet Union and to embrace the popular front politics of the mid-1930s as the only hope for stemming the rising tide of fascism. At the same time, as an Austrian author writing in German, Musil in the mid-1930s did not belong to the literature of exile (like Brecht or the Mann brothers) or to that of the German inner emigration (like Jünger or Wiechert). Still free from the debilitating pressures of exile and from any compromises with the Nazi state, he was able to assert an aesthetic in which the literary dimension functioned, to paraphrase Adorno, both autonomously and as social fact, never captive to either side of the dialectic.[2] And certainly not captive to any specific party line.

Only recently has the broad spectrum and ambition of Musil's short prose been properly recognized. It ranged from social satire and poetic rendering of liminal states of perception that suggest certain analogies to Gottfried Benn's cultural anthropological reflection and Kafka's confrontation with the nonhuman in his animal stories; from the symptomatology of modern everyday life reminiscent of Kracauer's gaze at the surfaces of urban life to an incisive critique of the business of high culture that is similar to Benjamin's critique in *One-Way Street;* and to questions of the right life that finally connect Musil with Adorno. *Posthumous Papers of a Living Author* can indeed be seen as a literary analog of Adorno's philosophical *Minima Moralia*—a kind of *minima aesthetica*, a *littérature mineure* in a sense quite different from that of Deleuze and Guattari.[3]

This breadth of possible intellectual and literary linkages invalidates the widespread thesis that Musil's writing strategies were inherently privatistic, an argument that has been made especially vis-à-vis his notion of *"der andere Zustand"* (the other condition) in *The Man without Qualities.* The rupture of "normal" perceptions of the world that characterizes "the other condition" cannot simply be read as a kind of epiphanic mysticism. At stake is a mode of perception that allows enlightened rational thought to become aware of its own limitations. In an age of politics that was shrinking the breathing space of the arts and demanding surrender to prescriptive models, Musil's miniatures maintain a realm, however small, that transcends the political demands of the day by remaining rigorously opposed to any and all political instrumentalization. They attempt to articulate another condition in and of literature beyond the conventions of the novel and other forms of traditional narrative. At the same time, they very much fulfilled another demand of the day. They were written mainly in the 1920s for various newspapers and feuilletons, "with their inattentive, motley, amorphously large readerships," and were collected into a volume in 1935 in order to guarantee some minimal income for its author, whose major publication project, *The Man without Qualities*, was stalled at the time.[4] The first volume of *The Man without Qualities* had been published in 1931, but by the mid-1930s there was little hope for a timely conclusion of the novel or for the prospect of publishing a second volume in Hitler's Germany. *Posthumous Papers of a Living Author* are thus indeed posthumous in Musil's own mind, posthumous to his incomplete project, which he saw as a failure in those years just before the *Anschluss* that drove Musil too into exile.

Musil's address to the 1935 Congrès pour la défense de la culture was part of the congress's very first session on tradition and literary legacies, which was introduced by André Gide and a greeting from Romain Rolland. Musil spoke after E. M. Forster, who criticized British class politics and colonialism but defended the freedom of literature, and Julien Benda who insisted against the Comintern line that the realm of literature and the spirit cannot be deduced from economic determinations. Benda had become persona non grata in the intellectual left since the publication of his 1928 book *La trahison des clercs* (*The Treason of the Intellectuals*), and Musil's intervention in this session must indeed have appeared very traditional, apolitical, and even reactionary in its insistence on the separation of state and culture, politics and literature—even more so if one were to approach it with a Brechtian or Benjaminian aesthetic in mind. But a close reading reveals that Musil was not just advocating the positions of a conservative literary and cultural elite, the *Bildungsbürgertum*. Instead, he articulated a position that rejected any move that would shackle literature and culture to the identity politics of nation, class, religion, or race. His was a search for a political aesthetic in another key. This, I would argue, is his legacy to us. His text is spiked with cutting comments about Nazi cultural politics and other prevalent tendencies at the time to bind writers and artists to identitarian projects of nation or class. Though he made a point of recognizing different forms of the contemporary trends toward collectivism (i.e., his was not a theory of totalitarianism), he rejected the congress's goal of mobilizing culture for political ends:

> I doubt that one can improve the world by influencing its spirit; the engines that drive events are of a cruder nature.[5]

Ironically, it is in this double critique of the implicit idealism of the congress and the cruder nature of the Comintern's not-quite-successful attempts to turn the proceedings into a loyalty oath to the Soviet Union that Musil can be said to have been on the same page, though for different reasons, with others who criticized the politics of the Congress. These included Brecht, who admonished the congress from afar to focus on property relations; Benjamin, who followed the event "in silent disagreement"; and Breton, who attacked the idea of a defense of culture as platonic.[6] As did some others who spoke at the congress, Musil took a position in radical opposition to the goals of the Comintern and the popular front, which were in uneasy alliance at the time. He stated explicitly at the outset that his goal was to speak "unpolitically," since culture, he argued (and, he could have added, literature) "is not bound to any political form."[7]

The Project of *Posthumous Papers of a Living Author*

If in his address to the congress Musil insisted on keeping culture and the aesthetic free from current collectivist political pressures, *Posthumous Papers*, which was published only a few months later, offer a political aesthetic in their own right—one that remains very much in sync with Musil's earlier modernist trajectory instead of bowing either to the left historical avant-garde (Brecht, Eisenstein, Benjamin, Tretyakov) or to the tenets of a politically uncritical and largely affirmative version of literary *Neue Sachlichkeit*, which had by and large displaced the avant-garde as early as the late 1920s in Germany.[8] It is the time of this publication that made these miniatures political precisely in their avowed "unpoliticality."

In the foreword to his collection, Musil spoke of "little works," a literature in a minor mode:

> To publish nothing but little tales and observations amidst a thundering groaning world; to speak of incidentals when there are so many vital issues; to vent one's anger at phenomena that lie far off the beaten track: this may doubtless appear as weakness to some, and I will readily admit that I had all kinds of doubts regarding the decision to publish. (n.p.)

Actually, such little tales and observations were anything but a literary sideshow in the interwar period. As I argue in this book, they were one of the major modes of literary experimentation and invention in that period, more novel as a key element in metropolitan modernism than traditional genres such as the novel or poetry or drama. Thus, despite his doubts, Musil justified the publication by saying that these little tales and observations "were after all more durable than I had feared" (n.p.). He even attributed to them a certain anticipatory "look ahead" that is

> likely to occur to every man who observes human life in the tiny traits by which it carelessly reveals itself, to every man who pays attention to the 'loitering' sensibilities [*sich den "wartenden" Gefühlen überlässt*], which, apparently, up until a certain hour that stirs them up "have nothing to say," and harmlessly express themselves in our actions and our choice of surroundings. (n.p.)

It is hard not to think here of Kracauer's methodological suggestion in his essay on the mass ornament to identify the surface traces of modern life in order to get to the core of capitalist culture. Similarly, it is precisely in the "off the beaten track" dimension of these miniatures that we can locate their incisive critique of a certain habitus of modern life, even if it is not articulated here, as it is in Kracauer, as a Marxist critique of capitalist rationalization. Musil did not use the language of alienation (Marx) or anomie (Durkheim). But he had exactly that in mind when he lamented the ossified world of the *"Normalzustand"* (normal state of affairs) of social and cultural convention, the lack of human gestalt, and what he labeled *"seinesgleichen geschieht"* (the like of it happens) in *The Man without Qualities*.[9]

MUSIL'S POSTHUMOUS MODERNISM

Posthumous Papers is a carefully constructed collection based on a much larger number of available texts from earlier years, some of them going back to the diaries Musil kept in the years of World War I when he served as captain in the Austrian army in the Alps near the Italian border. The major change from earlier versions consists in the addition of poetological and aesthetic reflections. They are typically found in the new framing of the miniatures and point to Musil's goal of developing a new literary aesthetic. If the texts themselves are not an immediate reaction to the 1930s, they nevertheless tell us much about that broader crisis of culture that was consummated by the events of that decade, confirming Musil's comment about their anticipatory and durable dimension.

The collection has four sections, entitled "Pictures" ("Bilder"), "Ill-Tempered Observations," "Unstorylike Stories," and the concluding story "The Blackbird," a kind of narrative telos of the earlier sections. In different ways, all texts focus on issues of sensual perception, on the (im)possibility of narration, on obsolete and bizarre conventions, whether social or literary. I will focus here primarily on "Pictures" for two reasons. The texts collected in "Pictures" are the most challenging and ambitious ones of the collection, and it is significant that Musil placed them up front rather than beginning with the much easier to understand "Ill-Tempered Observations" or "Unstorylike Stories." In a way, these later texts gain their symptomological and satirical dimension only because they follow rather than precede "Pictures." The second reason to focus on "Pictures" involves their media-specific dimension in a changing literary context. The talk of *Bilder* highlights how Musil rethought the project of literature in light of contemporary media that did not leave the realm of the literary untouched.[10] The prevalence of *Bilder* in modern metropolitan society kept disturbing the realm of the literary. Instead of lamenting this fact, as Hofmannsthal did in his reflections on the cinema as a substitute for dreams, Musil welcomed the challenge.[11] This is where his texts connect with the short prose by other writers who experimented with new modes of perception and representation in the interwar period. The impact of the spread of mass photography and film had raised new questions, especially for someone as analytically inclined as Musil: How can language approach the act of seeing? How can a nonlinguistic visual experience be transformed into language? What is gained and what is lost in the transition from script to picture and from picture to script?

It is striking to see that unlike Baudelaire, Rilke, Benjamin, Aragon, and Kracauer, who place urban perception in the center of their texts, the city is only marginally present in that first section of *Posthumous Papers*. The opposite of course is true for *The Man without Qualities* which begins with a car accident and is centered on Vienna throughout. By contrast, key spaces of the miniatures are decidedly nonurban—the Baltic coast, an island, the high Alps, a Slovenian village—and the "Pictures" section focuses almost exclusively on the relationship between human and animal life in decidedly nonurban environments.[12]

How then can we think about this simultaneity of a concern with animal life and the reflection on modern visual media and their techniques of animation? Both, I will argue, are the product of a very specific constellation in interwar modernity: older definitions of the human had already been dislodged by Darwin and Nietzsche in the nineteenth century. But as the experiences of World War I appeared to signal a regression of the human to barbarism and animal behavior, a new post-Cartesian anthropology emphasizing *Leiblichkeit*, the body and the senses, led to new questions about the human relation to animal life. Just as the new media posed fundamentally new questions about the historicity of human perception in a rapidly changing metropolitan world, the heretofore stable borders between animals and humans became porous and led to untold representations of animals in literature and the visual arts (from Rilke's animal poems; Kafka's mice, monkey, dog, and mole; and Franz Marc's blue horses and yellow cow to Max Ernst's birdmen and Döblin's slaughterhouses). None of these modernists used animals primarily in order to represent human features and actions allegorically, as an older animal literature had done. They rather explored the porous boundaries between the human and the animalistic at a time when the human mode of sensual perception was undergoing a historical reconstruction that pointed beyond a philosophy of consciousness based on the rigorous separation of mind and body and the privileging of verbal language.

Digression: "Binoculars" and the Aesthetics of *Abspaltung*

The juxtaposition of media practices and animal life is palpably present in Musil's use of metaphor. Thus, in a key essay of 1925, "Toward a New Aesthetic," a review essay of Béla Balázs's *Visible Man*, Musil reflected on the role of film—silent film at the time—for a theory of the arts. Using an animal metaphor, he focused on how silent film isolates the visual from sound, color, and language:

> Silent like a fish and pale like something subterranean, film swims in the pond of the only-visible.[13]

The nature of film as isolation from language is described as an *Abspaltung* (a splitting off), a medial aspect that Musil claimed it shared with all other arts. But it was superimposition, condensation, displacement, and the close-up that for him played a key role in the blurring of boundaries between the human and the nonhuman. And yet, as Musil developed his cinematic aesthetic in *Pictures*, he did more than simply transfer cinematic codes into literature. Instead, his focus was on how sensory experience was being transformed by the new media and what effect such processes had in the arts:

> How is it that such a fundamentally strange splitting off from the fullness of life becomes art? Today we can already touch on the answer, but we do not yet possess it completely. It is probably connected to those processes (closely related to each other) that psychology calls condensation and displacement, whereby either heterogeneous images stimulated by the same affect are lumped together in masses, to which the sum of the affect attaches itself (for example, the animal people and multiple animals of primitive cultures, dreams, hallucinations, in which two or more people simultaneously appear as one), or the other way around, a single image (part) appears as representative of a complex and seems laden with the inexplicably high affective value of the whole (the magical role of hair, fingernails, shadows, reflections in the mirror, and the like).[14]

Abspaltung, however, not only characterizes the specific arts and their respective use of a chosen medium. It can also be located in everyday life when a technological device offers a different and estranged form of perception. "Binoculars," a miniature from "Ill-Tempered Observations" that critics have often seen as central to *Posthumous Papers*, thematizes such a splitting off from full life. As the narrator looks at the city through binoculars, he experiences a deautomatized perception. In the binoculars, the city looks strangely deformed and uncannily threatening. It appears in an opaque otherness, as it also does in silent film, thus enabling the narrator to relate differently to what he sees: with surprise, shock, apprehension, irony. There is no doubt that Musil attributed a critical function to this disruption of routine vision, but at the same time it was threatening, uncanny.

In its 1936 version, "Binoculars" ("Triëdere") begins with a reference to film:

> Slow motion pictures dive beneath the agitated surface, and it is their magic that permits the spectator to see himself with open eyes, as it were, swimming among the objects of life. Movies may have popularized this phenomenon; but it has long been available to us by a means still to be recommended nowadays because of its convenience: by looking, that is, through binoculars at objects that one would usually not watch through binoculars. (81)[15]

As the narrator trains his binoculars from his apartment window at street scenes and architectural detail across and all along the street, isolated aspects of reality appear grotesque and bizarre as they are estranged from the habitual gaze. The result of such *Abspaltungen* is summarized in the essay on Balázs:

> If the formal relations of an art suddenly emerge in isolation, there arises that frightened astonishment at an irrational world which I spoke of earlier, half in jest.[16]

The very same idea reappears expanded in "Binoculars" itself:

> The best way to insure against an obscene misuse of this philosophical tool is to ponder its theory, "Isolation." We always see

things amidst their surroundings and generally perceive them according to what function they serve in that context. But remove them from that context and they suddenly become incomprehensible and terrible, the way things must have been on the first day after creation, before the new phenomena had yet grown accustomed to each other and to us. So too, in the luminous solitude of our telescopic circle, everything becomes clearer and larger, but above all, things become more arcane and demonic. (83–84)

Horrified amazement about a world gone mad is described in the Balázs essay as the kind of "disequilibrium in our awareness of reality" that Musil privileges in all art.[17] When the consciousness of reality is shaken and its equilibrium lost, we are far from a metaphysical fusion experience à la Jünger, but we are also not quite in the realm of what Helmut Lethen has so persuasively described as cold conduct in the male habitus of the interwar period.[18] What is the status of such a "disturbance of equilibrium"? What are its implications for the reader? Since Brecht, we have become used to attributing a politically critical progressive function to estrangement, but for Musil it wasn't so easy.

The visual *Abspaltung* produced by looking through the binoculars produces uncanny effects in two major instances taken up in "Binoculars." A disturbance of equilibrium in the perception of reality occurs when an inanimate object returns the observer's gaze in that typically threatening way that Lacan's evil eye theory claims is constitutive of all vision. As the observer points his binoculars at a neighboring palais, he is

struck by how clearly this support structure, these windows and cornices had positioned themselves in the circle of his looking-glass; now that he had taken it all in with a single glance, he was almost startled at the stony perspectival exactitude with which it all returned his gaze. He suddenly realized that these horizontal lines that conjoined at some point toward the back of the building, these contracting windows that became all the more trapezoid the farther to the side they were situated—indeed, this entire avalanche of reasonable, familiar limitations into a funnel

for foreshortening located somewhere to the side and to the
rear—that all this had until now struck him as a Renaissance
nightmare; an awful painter's legend, actually, of disappearing
lines, reputedly exaggerated, though there may also be some
truth to it. But now he saw it before his very eyes, magnified to
more than life-size, and looking far worse than the most un-
likely rumor. (82)

The Renaissance representational convention of foreshortening uncannily takes on real life in the binoculars and becomes threatening,
just as the experience of geometry in urban space could become oppressive in Kracauer's miniatures.

As the observing narrator directs his binoculars at a trolley car
passing by, spatial reality is radically and at first rather violently destabilized before the threat is domesticated at the end of the passage:

And if you don't believe that the world is really like this, just
focus on a streetcar. The trolley made an S-shaped double curve
in front of the palace. Countless times from his second story
window, the observer had witnessed it approaching, seen it make
this very S-shaped double curve and drive away again: at every
stage of this development the same elongated red train. But when
he watched it through the binoculars, he noticed something
completely different: an inexplicable force suddenly pressed this
contraption together like a cardboard box, its walls squeezed ever
more obliquely together (any minute it would be completely flat);
then the force let up, the car grew wide to the rear, a movement
swept once again over all its surfaces, and while the flabbergasted
eyewitness released the breath he had held in his breast, the
trusty old red box was back to its normal shape again. (82-83)

While there is a comforting return to visual normalcy at the end of
this passage, the sense of disturbance lingers with the reader.

It is important to note that the estranging gaze in Musil has two
contrary dimensions: on the one hand, the observer opens himself
up to a deautomatized perception made possible by the binoculars,
as in the passages just quoted. Even if this produces a nightmarishly

new experience, this is the positive notion of estrangement the modernist arts privileged—the kind of perception that trains the imagination, pushing it toward a more critical assessment of the world of social and cultural conventions, a bourgeois world that had been reconstructed willy-nilly after the disaster of the Great War. On the other hand, the binocular gaze, isolated from any linguistic or communicational context, also displays an inherent violence visible in other seemingly harmless observations:

> A Woman's charm is fatally undercut [*tödlich durchschnitten*] as soon as the lens perceives her from the hem of her skirt upwards as a sack-like space from which two twisted little stilts peer forth. (84)

In contrast to film, which "makes every effort to beautify its [life's] deficiencies," the binoculars

> persist unrelentingly in showing us how ridiculously the legs disengage themselves from the hips and how clumsily they land on the heel and sole; not only does this organ swing inhumanly and land fat end first, but it likewise manages meanwhile to effect the most revealing personal grimaces. (85)

Inevitably, estranged and split-off perception produces verbal aggression toward what is being perceived now as "abnormal" and grotesque. It is no coincidence that such aggression is directed at women and their fashions. While the earlier experiences of looking through the binoculars produced a deautomatized perception that challenged normative rational understanding, it now seems that a very conventional male voyeurism is trying to regain the high ground at the expense of the objects looked at. The results of this kind of estrangement cannot be taken to be altogether beneficial as enabling a critical or alternative view of the world. But it may give the inscribed male spectator a feeling of superiority, thus protecting him from the uncanny threats generated by the gaze through the binoculars.

The question remains why Musil in this miniature shifted from the moving image of film—the slow motion mentioned in the beginning—to the fixed image of the binoculars.[19] I would suggest that his concern was not the most modern technology of *Abspaltung*, which at the time was silent film, but the phenomenon of *Abspaltung* itself, which was key to his aesthetics of perception and which could also be achieved with an older technology, that of the binoculars. While it was only silent film that made the phenomenon of *Abspaltung* broadly accessible in new ways by separating vision from sound and from color, an added advantage of the binoculars was that they offered a kind of stereoscopic, almost tactile vision that deprived an observed reality of its context and environment. Its visual effects of *Abspaltung* were three- rather than two-dimensional as in film. Actually, the original German title of "Binoculars" included an exclamation mark that changed the word *"Triëdere"* from noun to verb, asking the reader to mimic the experience of the narrator by looking through binoculars at the city. It challenged readers to train themselves in an alternative mode of perceiving the world.

Animals in *Posthumous Papers*

The digression through "Binoculars" prepares us to analyze the effects of *Abspaltung* on the relationship between humans and animals. At stake here is a radical turning away from the ways animals have been represented in an earlier literary tradition. A dialectic of positive (utopian) and negative (dystopian) moments, similar to that analyzed in the reading of "Binoculars," haunts Musil's deployment of animals, which present anything but an air-brushed idyll of animal interaction with humans. The dystopian moments appear most strongly in "Flypaper," "Monkey Island," and "Rabbit Catastrophe," texts that have often been read as satire of human behavior, although satire clearly does not exhaust their unusual fascination. The utopian moment is strongest in "Can a Horse Laugh?," "Sheep, Seen in Another Light" (better: seen otherwise), and "The Mouse."

But how concretely is the deployment of animals in *Pictures* related to Musil's focus on media, and what is their political dimension? At stake in each one of these pictures is the attempt to see animals differently, and this is when *Bild* as picture turns into *Bild* as image. At the same time, and without pushing it, one could say that the writing strategy in "Flypaper" draws specifically on the close-up, "Sheep Seen in Another Light" on freeze-motion photography, and "The Mouse" on superimposition. The subtitle "Seen in Another Light" of the miniature about sheep gives a cue to the reader. Again we are confronted with a technique of *Abspaltung* that disturbs and estranges conventional, "normal" perception, what Musil attributes to the *Normalzustand*, the normal state of affairs. Seeing animals differently involves seeing the animal-human relationship differently, thus representing a challenge to the differentiated object-subject or body-mind relation that had been codified since Descartes and Kant in anthropocentric enlightened and scientific thought. The animal world suddenly and unexpectedly invades mind and body, blurring the assumed stable boundaries between subject and object, the human and the nonhuman.[20] It is persuasively portrayed in "Rabbit Catastrophe," in which the civilized observers identify physically with the murderous instinct of the little lap dog who hunts down and kills a baby rabbit, before they collect themselves again and reestablish a safe distance between themselves and the animal world. This is the anthropological dimension of what Giedion has celebrated as *Durchdringung* (interpenetration) in relation to urban space, which appears here in highly ironic fashion as a *Durchdringung* of nature and culture, violence and civilization.

Durchdringung operates in Musil's text not just in the relationship between animals and humans; there also is interpenetration in form of a superimposition of seascapes and mountainscapes ("The Mouse"; "Rabbit Catastrophe") and of interiors and mountainscapes ("Slovenian Village Funeral"). In all these cases, there is a touch of the surreal, the unexpected, the alternate perception in passages that describe shell shots sailing silent as ships, like a school of fish across a mountain valley ("The Mouse") or that describe the dunes of an island resembling the peak of a mountain submerged in the sea ("Rabbit Catastrophe"). *Durchdringung* also pertains to the relation with objects. Thus it is no coincidence that Musil cites Lévy-Bruhl and other anthropologists who tried to capture that other relationship to things that Lévy-Bruhl called participation. Things are the other dimension of the nonhuman besides animals.[21] Film is of use to Musil because it highlights that "exotic life described in Balázs's book, a life in which things gain in visual isolation."[22] Optical solitude in silent film also means absence of language. Muteness is what things, seen in traditional anthropocentric perspective, have in common with animals. And here we touch upon that other premise of Musil's miniatures: the "Pictures," which, though written in language, describe phenomena (animals and things) that are lacking in language and push the reader toward another kind of mute communication, another state of perception. At stake is a participatory relationship between the human and the nonhuman, with participation working not through the mind but, more importantly, through the body and the senses. Ultimately, it is a *Durchdringung* of world and self, as Musil describes it in one of his key texts from the 1920s, "The German as Symptom":

> Whereas ordinarily the self masters the world, in the other condition the world flows into the self, or mingles with it or bears it, and the like (passively instead of actively). One participates in things (understands their language). In this condition understanding [*Verstehen*] is not impersonal (objective), but extremely personal, like an agreement between subject and object.[23]

Ultimately, the concern with film and technological media connects to the genealogy of Musil's literary deployment of animals. Given the fact that *Posthumous Papers* begins with a text on flies ("Flypaper") and ends with a story on a bird ("The Blackbird"), there can be no doubt that it is Nietzsche's "On Truth and Lies in a Nonmoral Sense" that frames the collection. In his critique of language, Nietzsche introduced animals to suggest that man has great difficulty

> to admit to himself that the insect or the bird perceives an entirely different world from the one that man does, and that the question of which of these perceptions of the world is the more correct is quite meaningless, for this would have to have been decided previously in accordance with the criterion of the *correct perception*, which means, in accordance with a criterion which is *not available*.[24]

When Nietzsche addressed the origins of language, he suggested that the first reaction to the amorphous world of things must be thought of as a movement from nerve stimulus to image to sound:

To begin with, a nerve stimulus is transferred into an image [*Bild*]: first metaphor. The image, in turn, is imitated in a sound: second metaphor.[25]

Here too Nietzsche seems to have given a cue to Musil. "Pictures" is placed at the beginning of Musil's collection of miniatures, whereas the concluding story focuses on sound, the song of the blackbird. And both mute seeing and hearing beyond language and eyesight are central to many of the miniatures. Nietzsche and film then: both led Musil to his critique of anthropocentric conventions and energized his search for some other mode of communication beyond, say, the modernist dreams of another language or a pure visuality. Another purer language à la Rilke or some uncontaminated visuality à la Kandinsky would precisely not be of interest to Musil who always worked at the thresholds between language and nonlanguage, the human and the nonhuman, the transcendent and the real. This is also what separates his epiphanic moments from the metaphysics of the dangerous moment in Jünger and approximates him more to Joyce or Proust, for whom the "mystical" moment never loses its ground in the real. Testing the limits of the aural and the visual in perception, Musil focused on their intersection just as he was aware of the limits of anthropocentrism in his deployment of animals in the miniatures.

Musil's animal pictures are not allegories of human behavior in the tradition of the fable, which usually endows animals with human speech. Instead, they stage an encounter between humans and animals that challenges conventional human perceptions of the animal world as coded in the opposition between nature and culture, an encounter made possible by the fact that human beings too are constituted by natural biology, a theme that would be powerfully articulated a decade later in Adorno and Horkheimer's *Dialectic of Enlightenment* in their reflection on the dialectics of mimesis in nature and in language. For Musil, as for Adorno and Horkheimer, the constitution of the human by nature brings with it violence and barbarism, not as regression to some animal state but rather as something produced or re-produced by humans within modernity itself. This is a fundamentally political insight. To be writing about porous borders between animals and humans is itself an act of political intellectual resistance to the kind of race theory that treated colonial subjects as not fully human, lamented the white man's burden in relation to the colonized, and that later divided the world into Aryans and subhumans, using animal metaphors and images to denigrate and eventually liquidate whole peoples and ethnicities. Like writers on the Marxist left, Musil had become suspicious of traditional forms of bourgeois humanism that had really veiled and continued to veil the human capacity for violence and destruction. At the same time, the genealogical context for Musil's animal images is not just its opposition to Nazi ideology, which was invested in rapacious biopower, but also World War I and the long-standing racialized discourse of Jews and Slaws as somehow less than human, later in Nazi ideology as vermin or rats.[26] The genealogy of *Posthumous Papers*, then, moves us indeed from World War I into the 1930s, and this is precisely what allowed Musil to claim their "durability."

While the crisis of language and perception and the search for some alternative perception, underlying all of interwar European culture, had already been powerfully articulated in the decade before World War I in Hofmannsthal's "A Letter," its political dimensions were revealed and exacerbated by the experience of World War I, in which Musil participated as an Austrian captain stationed in the Alps. In 1934, he wrote in "Der Dichter in dieser Zeit" ("The Poet in Our Time"):

> Whether the age in which we live is prodigious [*gewaltig*] is a question I would modestly prefer to leave unanswered; but it is most certainly an age of violence [*Gewalt*]. It began, rather abruptly, in the summer of 1914. Suddenly violence appeared, and since that time it has not abandoned mankind again but has been assimilated into it to a degree that, before that summer, would have been considered un-European. And its first appearance, even at that time, was already accompanied by two remarkable emotions: first a paralyzing feeling of catastrophe. What was called European culture suddenly had a crack, became the plunder of peace. Secondly, there arose simultaneously the even more astonishing feeling of a firm new solidarity within the smaller framework of individual nations, and this occurred as

strongly and indiscriminately as a previously mystical emotion rises up from primeval depths.[27]

Not culture but violence; not rational civilization but national myth—and yet postwar life, Musil suggested, was lived as before, if in a weakened state. As early as 1922, in "Das hilflose Europa" ("Helpless Europe"), Musil had concluded:

> First we were bustling good citizens, then we became murderers, killers, thieves, arsonists, and the like, but without really experiencing anything. . . . So we have been many things, but we haven't changed; we have seen a lot and perceived nothing. I think there is only one explanation for this: we were lacking the concepts with which to absorb what we experienced; or perhaps lacking the feelings whose magnetism sets the concepts in motion.[28]

And a few pages later in the same essay he wrote:

> Psychology demonstrates that the spectrum of human types spreads smoothly and seamlessly from super- to subnormal, and the war demonstrated to all of us in one monstrous mass experiment how easily human beings can move to the most radical extremes and back again without experiencing any basic change. They change—but what changes is not the *self*.[29]

This inability to experience and the desire to perceive differently resonate of course with that other crisis of the inability to narrate, which was already central in Rilke's *Malte* before the war but was later related directly to the experience of war in Walter Benjamin's "The Storyteller." The emergence and prevalence of the modernist miniature is a direct result of this aporia and the insistent desire to narrate, to tell, and to write differently. Already in Bergson and in *Lebensphilosophie* (vitalism) there had been the longing for some alternative, unmediated, and uncontaminated perception.[30] Helmut Lethen has persuasively argued that the recourse to some immediacy of perception is always a symptom of periods in which a traditional

frame of interpretation has broken down.[31] Narration does depend
on extant frames of interpretation, but of course it can also provide
refuge in times of chaos, as the history of the novella from Boccaccio
to Goethe demonstrates. The striking obsession with new forms of
narration, authenticity, and immediacy around 1900 already pointed
to the crisis in the frames of interpreting the world. But even though
interpretive frames had come under pressure before 1914, it was the
Great War that, in an orgy of national madness, exploded all previous
frames of meaning and made manifest what had been latent for several decades before. From its beginning in Baudelaire, the metropolitan miniature had attempted to do without such stable frame-
works of narration and interpretation and to account for alternative
forms of perception as they arose in the wake of ever more rapid
urbanization and technological developments.

War, Dystopia, "Flypaper"

War, indeed, is much more central to Musil's animal miniatures than
the reader suspects at first sight. "Flypaper," the very first and perhaps best known of the miniatures, is prefigured in a diary entry of
1915: "Late July. A fly dies; World War."[32] The miniature, first published in its extended version in 1914 and revised for *Posthumous
Papers*, describes how flies get fatally stuck on Tanglewood flypaper,
mainly "out of convention, because so many others are already there"
(5) and how every move to liberate themselves pulls them deeper
down, bringing them closer to death. Of course one can read this as
an allegory of thoughtless group behavior, a type of blind confor-
mity that ends in captivation and death: nationalism leading to war
and *völkisch* ideology locking people into deadly determinations. But
then the text could end after the first paragraph. An allegorical reading
depends on the one-to-one relationship of image and meaning, but
this easy translatability is precisely denied in the way the miniature
unfolds. Instead, the text moves through a whole series of ever more
frenzied similes that supplement the detailed description and add
levels of blurring and imprecision instead of clarifying allegorical
meaning. At stake here is thus not an allegorization of the human
condition but rather the attempt of the observing narrator to unfold
his thoughts as they are translated into moments of the narrative. In

the process the gap that separates the human observer from the trials of the flies caught on Tanglewood flypaper is bridged, and the reader gets caught in an attempt to articulate a new way of seeing in which descriptive precision meets parabolic fantasy, a kind of reciprocal *Durchdringung* of the human and the animal worlds. To put it differently: the relationship to human behavior is not allegorically implied, as in older forms of animal literature but it is time and again made explicit, beginning with the key sentence expanding on the fly's legs getting stuck on the poison paste:

> A very quiet disconcerting sensation, as though while walking in the dark we were to step on something with our naked soles, nothing more than a soft, warm, unavoidable obstruction, and yet something into which little by little the horrifying human essence [*das grauenhaft Menschliche*] flows, recognized as a hand that just happens to be lying there, and with five ever more decipherable fingers, holds us tight. (5; translation modified)

This horrifying passage conjures up empathy with the plight of the flies. The objectifying separation of animal description from human meaning that allegory requires is precisely denied here, resulting in a blurring of boundaries. It is as if these flies *are* humans instead of *referring to* humans or as if we, the human beings, are the flies getting caught in "*das grauenhaft Menschliche.*" And the similes continue:

> Here they stand all stiffly erect, like cripples pretending to be normal, or like decrepit old soldiers (and a little bowlegged, the way you stand on a sharp edge). (5)

Their exertion in their struggle to get free is compared to Laokoön, to the mountain climber in distress, the hunted man giving up. But inexorably "an *it* draws them in" (6). The more the flies' movements are restricted and paralyzed, the more the text moves into a frenzy of similes, many of which now don't even relate to the world of humans; they relate to objects and to other animals. Images abound that recall post-battle battlefields:[33]

This is how they lie there. Like crashed planes with one wing reaching out into the air. Or like dead horses. Or with endless gesticulations of despair. Or like sleepers. (6)

Allegory, however, works in this miniature in a different sense. If one were to ask: What might the fly landing on flypaper conjure up?, if one were to consider the visual dimension of small black bodies lying immobilized on the paper, then one might want to see an allegorical reference to the problematic of language and writing. Nietzsche and Mauthner had taught Musil to see language as an imprisoning space of convention. So what happens when words get down on paper? Words are like flies: it is convention that sets them down on paper, where they will die sooner or later. To see print language as dead has of course been a trope since Plato, but it took on new and strong resonances in the context of *Lebensphilosophie* and the vitalist search for immediacy and authenticity. Despite its frenzy of similes, however, the text leaves out any such direct reference to the literary, and this is precisely what adds an allegorical dimension after all. It functions as something like a second voice underneath the surface refusal of the traditional allegorical deployment of animals. And it is this allegorical reading alone that gives some meaning to the mysterious ending of this miniature:

> And only on their side, near their leg sockets, is there some tiny flickering organ that still lives a long time. It opens and closes, you can't describe it without a magnifying glass, it looks like a miniscule human eye that ceaselessly opens and shuts. (7; translation modified to "flickering" instead of "wriggling")

Much speculation has surrounded this ending, including some bizarre discussions of the anatomy of flies. Of course this ending returns us to the simile structure of the story—the flickering organ looks like a human eye but is not. The threshold between human and nonhuman is again blurred. But what sense can this miniscule human eye that is not a human eye possibly make? What, if anything, does it see? Kafka once suggested that one had to get very close to the miniatures of *Meditation* to see anything at all. The same pertains here: only if one gets very close will the text reveal a dimension of life, the eye that ceaselessly opens and shuts just as the reader's eye does when reading the text, which only comes to life, as it were, in close reading. Interpreting this passage as a transference or projection of the reader's eye onto the fly may indeed make sense if one assumes that only in being read does a literary text gain a new life. At the same time, this may be an all-too-rational reading that does not quite do justice to the surprising corporality of the dying fly's anatomy that the text suggests as simple fact and that strikes the reader in gruesome surreality, a veritable *punctum*, not in photography, as in Barthes, but in a literary text.

Kafka may well have known the early version of Musil's "Flypaper," which was published in 1914 with the title "Römischer Sommer" (Roman summer).[34] Toward the end of *The Trial*, shortly before Josef K. is killed, we read: "He pictured flies, tearing their tiny legs off as they struggled to escape the flypaper."[35] And then we remember that death, after all, is also suggested with the title *Posthumous Papers*, death of an author in this case. And yet there is that tiny utopian flicker at the ending of Musil's "Flypaper" that one is tempted to project onto the whole collection all the way to the final story "The Blackbird." Horrific and horrifying as the plight of the flies is described—and this horror has parallels in the plight of the worms being torn into pieces in "Fishermen on the Baltic" or that of the rabbit in "Rabbit Catastrophe"—there is indeed often also a miniscule utopian dimension that emerges from Musil's animal pictures as they attempt to explore a new way of seeing, hearing, or feeling.

War, Utopia, "The Mouse"

That utopian dimension—a dimension that transcends space and time of the present while maintaining an umbilical cord to reality—is especially strong in the miniature "The Mouse," first published in *Prager Presse* in 1921. Like "Flypaper" and analogous to many of Kafka's miniatures, it is prefigured in Musil's diaries in the context of an earlier planned book of animal sketches to be entitled *Tierbuch*, a book that never materialized.[36] The text opens with a narrative comment:

This miniscule story, that in fact is nothing but a punchline, a single tiny tip of a tale, and not a story at all, happened during the First World War. (29)

The space is defined as the high Alps above any habitation, near the Italian front, where, "in a wide, right hollow," somebody had put up a bench in peacetime. The alpine landscape then morphs into a seascape, which creates an eerie effect of deterritorialization, a narrative metamorphosis Musil used several times in the collection:

The shots sailed over it [the hollow with the bench]. Silent as ships, like schools of fish. They struck far back where nothing and no one was, and for months, with an iron perseverance, ravaged an innocent precipice. No one knew why anymore. (29)

War is present, yet somehow irrelevant. Instead of a personal observer, we get the impersonal German "man" ("Whoever sat on this bench sat firm"; 29) whose body parts fall asleep as if separated from each other, with breathing becoming estranged "in a steady, mindless motion of the breast" (29) inflicted on the man by "the blue colossus of the atmosphere, something like a pregnancy" (30). All of it takes place under an empty light above the jagged cliff that "was so savage and so inhumanly beautiful, as we imagine in the ages of the creation" (30). This is the Nietzschean high noon. From cosmic gaze upward toward the overhanging cliff, "your glance retreated, shattered into a hundred vistas." (30) The sublime Nietzschean—better, Zarathustran—noontime moment, the *Augen-Blick*, is then rewritten as the text turns to a little mouse scurrying around near the bench in "terrible silence." And now another eye asks for the reader's attention, the eye of the mouse, "as small and black as the head of a spinning needle" (30), and this eye, looking toward the bench, encounters the eye of the depersonalized narrator, estranging him from his already timeless and spaceless, almost disembodied reality and plunging him into what one can only call an epiphany:

And for an instance you had such a strange twisted feeling, that you really no longer knew: was it this tiny, living black eye that

turned? Or was it this monstrous immobility of the mountains
that moved? You just didn't know anymore: had you been touched
by the will of the world, or by the will of this mouse that glowed
out of a little, lonesome eye? You [*man*] didn't know: was war
still raging or had eternity won the day? (30; translation
modified)

An epiphanic moment it is, but it is not a transcendent epiphany. The
emphatic moment hovers in the undecideability between eternity and
the historical reality of the war. At stake is a perception beyond knowledge, but it is a transformation of knowledge rather than its mystical irrational other that interests Musil. A mouse, after all, does not
lend itself well as the subject or even the origin of a sublime mystical experience. In the presence of a mouse, flies, worms, and other
small animals that populate these texts, we are literally faced with a
minor literature in a different key. Scale is central both for the content and form of Musil's miniature "Pictures." Thus, the text turns
back to its narrative frame and concludes:

So you might have continued at length to ramble on about something you felt you could not know; but this is already all of this
little story, for in the meantime it had come to an end every time
before you could say exactly where it ended. (30; translation
modified)

Faced with what one cannot know, one can either ramble on or fall
silent. Like "Flypaper" or "Rabbit Catastrophe," "The Mouse" is another minor war text beyond war. Here too the goal is to gain another experience, another nonpossessive relationship to the world;
it is not just about the flash of an epiphany drawn from the encounter
with the gaze of the mouse. The miniature has moved from an exhausted immobilized and depersonalized body on a mountain bench
(breathing as if impregnated by the blue colossus) to the mirroring
experience with the eye of the mouse rushing around in its trenches.
Key is the difference of the gazes: the gaze of the protagonist goes
up toward the overhanging cliff but runs down like water and shatters into a hundred vistas. The mixed metaphor is clearly intended:

it speaks again to the *Durchdringung* of mountainscape and seascape. The mouse in turn seems to be able to capture some total view that remains alien to the nameless protagonist—at least he doesn't understand fully. While there is an encounter between animal and human consciousness, which actually reconstitutes the protagonist's subjectivity, there is no mystical union of the two. It is an alternative experience but without mystical fulfillment. The war appears strangely pacified in the image of the grenades and shells flying above like a school of fish (fish being the Christian symbol of peace), but it is also suggested, however subtly, in the *Gräben* (trenches) of the mouse, which easily conjure up the trenches, the *Schützengräben* of the war.[37]

How, then, can we describe a politics of Musil's miniatures, especially of the section called "Pictures"? The politics lies obviously not in any position taken toward concrete political developments in Austria, Germany, or Europe. Times and places are defined only in the most generic ways in these texts. The politics of *Posthumous Papers* operates at a much subtler level that does, however, remain linked to the realities of the 1930s. These miniatures reflect on new media, especially on film, as a means of constructing and experiencing new modes of perceiving the world beyond conventional norms and of representing it beyond the traditional literary genres. The aesthetics of *Abspaltung*, which was based on silent film and had already developed in the 1920s, is key in opening up possibilities of seeing the world differently and, as Musil would hope, acting differently in it. To be sure, with the coming of sound, color, and ever-longer narrative forms to the movies by the late 1920s, the estrangement of *Abspaltung*, as it characterized early cinema, was increasingly diminished and its uncanny effects were domesticated. While taking his cue from early cinema, Musil insisted on the *Eigensinn* of the literary in relation to film in ways that are comparable to the short prose experiments of Kracauer, Kafka, Benjamin, and other modernists. In Musil too the feuilleton miniature represents a literary project energized by the new image media. Here too one can speak of remediation. It is not only a remediation of film and photography in the miniature but remediation in a different and extended sense: Musil's "Pictures" represent a remediation of the relationship between human and animal worlds, a remediation that had been obscured if not erased by an earlier instrumental modernity. This is a dimension of his writing that connects him deeply to Kafka's longer animal stories. There too the world is no longer, as in traditional humanism, just the human world but a world where a different, noninstrumental relationship pertains between humans, animals, objects. This is not some sentimental "animal humanism," since the animals are not simply appropriated for allegory or for a view critical of anthropocentrism. It is the search for a new understanding of the "bio," which, as we know from scores of works since Foucault, is never absent from the political. On the contrary, it is a constituent part of the political. Musil's politics in this last major publication of his lifetime is a politics in minor key, *une politique mineure*. As such it is coupled with the aesthetic value of Musil's miniatures, their very nature as a minor literature in a decade of the political grand narratives of fascism, communism, and capitalist modernization, but this literature in a minor key and minor scale is still looking forward to some alternative world. In that sense it is posthumous to interwar modernism at one of the darkest moments of twentieth-century history, but it opens up questions that have only recently come fully to the fore.

Coda
Diving into the Wreck: Adorno's
Minima Moralia

I came to explore the wreck. / The words are purposes. /
The words are maps. / I came to see the damage that was done / and
the treasures that prevail.

     —Adrienne Rich

*T*HEODOR W. ADORNO's aphorism book *Minima Moralia* is read here in a double way: first as an exilic text par excellence written at the outer limits of the Western world and locating itself at the edge of philosophy and knowledge; and second, as a coda to the trajectory of the metropolitan miniature in the age of classical modernism. Its writing strategy is thoroughly literary in ways that test and transgress the limits of logical argument and conceptual thought. Those limits were starkly at stake for Adorno after he had been driven into exile by Nazi rule, and thus in its literariness, this book marks a limit of Adorno's own writing trajectory, in which *Minima Moralia* stands as the exception rather than the rule.[1] When Adorno's German publisher Peter Suhrkamp suggested that some of the aphorisms reminded him of Benjamin's literary experiments—and he must have had *One-Way Street* and *Berlin Childhood around 1900* in mind—Adorno objected strenuously. But then he concluded: "But such things, at a certain time, may just be in the air."[2] Indeed, the texts may resonate less with Benjamin's *One-Way Street* or Kracauer's street texts than with the aphoristic tradition from the enlightened French moralists and the Jena romantics to Nietzsche who, with his *Gay Science*, must be regarded as the main inspiration for Adorno's conveying of his thoughts in the form of aphorisms. And yet Suhrkamp was not entirely wrong. Even though conceptual thought, even at its limits, remained the major concern of the philosopher, like Benjamin he privileged the micrological gaze at concrete phenomena of life and mobilized literary strategies to keep his writing from veering off into abstract idealism or metaphysics. The micrological gaze is incisively captured in *Minima Moralia*, which, as message in a bottle, marks a certain ending of the trajectory of miniature writing since Baudelaire. Actually, Adorno himself gave a wonderful description of his writing strategy that succinctly characterizes the modernist miniature as I have analyzed it in this book:

> Properly written texts are like spiders' webs: tight, concentric, transparent, well-spun and firm. They draw into themselves all the creatures of the air. Metaphors flitting hastily through them become their nourishing prey. Subject matter comes winging toward them. . . . In the light that it [thought] casts on its chosen object, others begin to glow.[3]

While aesthetic issues are not thematized as such elsewhere in *Minima Moralia*, which deals primarily with the unattainability of the right life, the modernist aesthetic of the feuilleton miniature is present in its style of writing: changing tempi, condensation, provocative exaggeration, hyperbole, perspectivism, and a liberal use of metaphors and images. The thematic focus is impatience with the banalities of what Musil called the *Normalzustand* of social convention and what Lukács described as the reification of second nature, all of which had been turned upside down by the rise of Nazism and the experience of life in exile.

On Exile, the Metropolis, and Los Angeles

When it comes to literary or intellectual exile, we always have to distinguish two dimensions. There is the representation of real lived exile and there is exile as a metaphor for artistic and intellectual endeavors, often universally ontologized as the human condition from Adam and Eve to Salman Rushdie or Joseph Brodsky. Against that latter tendency, every case of exile should be located within its specific historical frame and conditions. The Romantic exile of Shelley or Byron differs from that of refugees from fascism and again from the multiple kinds of displacement and migration in our own world. We must always consider the fate of the exile in relation to a whole web of related terms, such as refugee, migrant, deportee, émigré, immigrant, expatriate, and returnee. Edward Said has well described the dialectic of these two dimensions—exile as reality versus exile as metaphor. He has given due weight to both but has rejected a merely universalizing metaphorical usage that forgets the realities of exiled life. It is no coincidence that *Minima Moralia*, which combines both dimensions imaginatively for cognitive gain, was one of his favorite books. Exiles, with what Said called their contrapuntal awareness, can train others in a plurality of vision.[4] This is the quasi-redemptive version of the benefits of exile, which was stated in different words by Bertolt Brecht in his *Refugee Conversations* of 1940:

> Emigration is the best school of dialectics. Refugees are the sharpest dialectical thinkers.[5]

Clearly, this is a best-case scenario. But it may well be truer for Adorno than for most of the other German exiles in California, including Brecht himself, whose phrasing here strikes me as a bit pat and close to wishful thinking. While Adorno would agree that there is cognitive gain to be had in exile, he also acknowledged the inescapable wound of exile when he wrote in "Dwarf Fruit":

> The splinter in your eye is the best magnifying glass. (50)

Said recognized this subjective side of *Minima Moralia* when he suggested that these aphorisms give us the most rigorous example of the exile, who

> must cultivate a scrupulous (not indulgent or sulky) subjectivity.[6]

This indeed was the project of *Minima Moralia* as Adorno himself defined it in the last sentences of the dedication:

> The specific approach of *Minima Moralia*, the attempt to present aspects of our [Adorno's and Horkheimer's] shared philosophy from the standpoint of subjective experience, necessitates that the parts do not altogether satisfy the demands of the philosophy of which they are nevertheless a part. The disconnected and non-binding character of the form, the renunciation of explicit theoretical cohesion, are meant as one expression of this. (18)

It is puzzling that *Minima Moralia* has rarely been analyzed in relation to its express commitment to subjective experience.[7] Adorno of course is better known as the theoretical gravedigger of bourgeois subjectivity whose crisis has been the topic of so many modernist literary works, from Hofmannsthal and Rilke, from Kafka and Musil to Eliot, Mann, and Joyce all the way to Beckett. Language politics in its relation to identity and subjectivity played a big role for all of these writers, as it did for Adorno, who sprinkled his text with words and sentences from other languages and with so-called *Fremdwörter*, thus undermining the monolingualism that was dominant in German discussions.[8] In "Second Harvest" he wrote:

> German words of foreign derivation [*Fremdwörter*] are the Jews of language. (110)

This is precisely why *Minima Moralia* as an exilic text questioning subjectivity can be linked to the modernist miniature. Modernism in literature, music, and the visual arts has been defined to a large extent by exiles, expatriates, and émigrés. The experience of an exiled life of alienation, language loss, and displacement and the creative critical impetus that came from it can stand as a cipher of modernism and its cosmopolitan, internationalist dimension. Thus, in an influential essay of 1987 entitled "When Was Modernism?" Raymond Williams attributed the creative impetus behind aesthetic modernism to exile, in addition to the rise of the new media and the international metropolitan city.[9] Of course, not every modernist was an exile. But Adorno was, and he wrote from within that tradition rather than from the position of an outside observer. *Minima Moralia*, his collection of miniatures, belongs very much in this context of metropolitan modernism as exile in its double sense.

Thus, I read *Minima Moralia* as part of a continental European tradition of metropolitan miniatures that began with Baudelaire and ended with Adorno at a time when the metropolis was entering its new post–World War II configuration. At first sight, such a reading may pose two seemingly insuperable problems. First, none of the aphorisms was first published alone or in groupings in some feuilleton. Because they were written in German, there simply was no feuilleton available in exile in California. These texts were rather written as a kind of soliloquy with interruptions or rather as an interior dialogue with Adorno's fellow refugee Max Horkheimer, to whom he dedicated the book. Actually, their prepublication history points to a key feature of exile: the difficulties of publishing and the limits of communication that come with displacement into a different linguistic realm. Part One of the German text was first mimeographed and offered as tribute to Horkheimer on his 50th birthday, in February 1945. Thus, it stands as an homage to Horkheimer's own aphoristic reflections on morality, values, and the right life that were collected in the volume *Dämmerung* of 1934. And it is an homage to their collaboration on the *Dialectic of Enlightenment*, which was finished and similarly distributed in mimeographed form in that same year of 1944 that is given as the date of origin for Part One of *Minima Moralia*. Needless to say, my concern here is more with "minima" and literature than with "moralia" and moral philosophy, concerns that prevailed in earlier readings. Approached from that angle, *Minima Moralia* shows clear affinities with earlier miniature collections.

A second and more important question, however, is this: Where, after all, is Los Angeles, the metropolis, in *Minima Moralia*? Here the argument about a structure of absence, which I posited in my reading of Kafka and Musil's miniatures, comes into play again, and perhaps even more forcefully than in those earlier instances. As I have argued throughout, one common feature of the metropolitan miniature is that its authors avoid and shun the mimetic strategies of nineteenth-century realisms and of the urban sketch. As a result, these texts are symptomatically devoid of ekphrastic descriptions of urban scenes and sites as we find them in the urban feuilleton from Louis Sébastien Mercier's *Tableau de Paris* through the feuilleton texts of Robert Walser and Joseph Roth all the way to the present. Thus, the absence of the real Los Angeles of the 1940s from *Minima Moralia* matches the absence of robust ekphrastic descriptions of Paris in Baudelaire's miniatures, Prague in Kafka's, Brussels in Benn's, Berlin in Benjamin's in *One-Way Street* (though not in *Berlin Childhood around 1900*), and Vienna in Musil's. Adorno's critique of the American culture industry coupled with his reflections on writing and visual media codifies in theoretical terms what all these authors have been struggling with in their attempts to render the new urban imaginary in literary language.

As we look at Adorno's writing of the 1940s, the structure of absence seems to be in play not only in relation to the city of angels but even in his reflections on exile. It was in Los Angeles as a refugee from Hitler that Adorno, together with Max Horkheimer, wrote their arguably most influential book, the *Dialectic of Enlightenment*, a book that contains one of the most radical critiques of Western modernity and that still grounds his later, posthumously published *Aesthetic Theory*. But exile in the literal sense did not figure in it. Nor did exile figure in that other major work written in Los Angeles, *The Philosophy of New Music*, a book that treats, after all, two exiled composers, Schönberg and Stravinsky. On the other hand, it was also here on the Pacific Coast that he wrote his *Minima Moralia*, a literary work in its own right that eventually turned out to be his most popular book "back home"—popular in the sense of its accessibility, the number of copies sold, and its impact on several generations of German readers. *Minima Moralia* stands out in Adorno's production in the 1940s in that it is very much a book of and about the experience of exile, in both its literal and metaphoric senses. Given, however, that Los Angeles itself, the place of his exile for eight years, is largely absent from this writing, it is hardly surprising that a recent

German book with new readings of *Minima Moralia*, published on the occasion of the 100th anniversary of the philosopher's birth in 2003, does not bother to mention Los Angeles or the importance of exile in its genealogy.[10] And yet this collection of miniatures must be taken to be an exilic text par excellence, both in its content and in its form. Los Angeles, I would claim, is an absent presence throughout the book because it shaped Adorno's micrological observations on America and his concept of the culture industry.[11]

It is an absent presence of a different kind than the one we get in Kafka, Benjamin, and Musil, who were all strongly inscribed in their home cities of Prague, Berlin, Vienna. Adorno came to the American metropolis from Oxford and Frankfurt, smaller and rather provincial towns. Thus, the absence of empirical references to Los Angeles in *Minima Moralia*, while clearly a writerly choice, may also be attributed to his general dislike of big cities. Given this biographical background, it is not surprising to find the usually conservative reflex against the horrors of the metropolis manifest itself in the letters to his parents he wrote in those years. He advised his parents, who had come as refugees to the United States via Havana, to avoid Miami, "one of the most ghastly places I have ever seen, a desert littered with house palm-trees and rip-off bars."[12] Chicago, apart from its lakefront, "made a rather ghastly impression" on him, and, in the context of his life in New York from 1938 to 1941, he spoke in general of the "horror of the [big] city."[13] Most of his American years, however, were spent in Los Angeles, first Brentwood Heights and later Pacific Palisades, to be precise. The letters to his parents contain many positive comments about the beauty of the landscape of southern California, excursions by automobile, the intense colors at sunset, the southern style of architecture, the mountainous Pacific Coast as a superimposition of the Riviera and the Toscana.[14] He even spoke of a "cultural landscape" (*Kulturlandschaft*), but as if to catch himself, he continued:

> One actually has the feeling that this part of the world is inhabited by humanoid beings, not only by gasoline stations and hot dogs.[15]

In that same letter, he spoke of his new vicinity as a mix of country and city, comparing it somewhat implausibly to Oberrad, a green-

and-garden–oriented district of Frankfurt. Of course, his spatial environment west of downtown Los Angeles was much less urban than Manhattan, where in his first years of U.S. exile he lived on Riverside Drive, and the multiple references to the California landscape in *Minima Moralia* and in the letters reflect that. At the same time, I am tempted to speculate that it may well have been the sprawl of Los Angeles that led him to see metropolitan existence as oozing into all social and geographic space, erasing an earlier clear-cut border between country and city life that was the unspoken backdrop of the metropolitan miniature in earlier decades. Miniature 91, entitled "Vandals," points in that direction, without, however, mentioning Los Angeles explicitly:

> The haste, nervousness, restlessness observed since the rise of the big cities is now spreading in the manner of an epidemic, as did once the plague and cholera. (138)

It was this spread and sprawl as the spatial expression of urban habits, consumerism, and the culture industry to the far corners of the country that grounded his homogenizing critique of mass culture, a development that indeed anticipates post–World War II European transformations. Indeed, Los Angeles as urban space already then differed significantly from the cities treated in the metropolitan miniature of the preceding decades. This is yet another reason to see *Minima Moralia* as a coda to this experimental mode of writing tied to a very specific stage of urban development that had changed its shape by the 1940s.

The Genealogy of the Text

Minima Moralia: Reflections from a Damaged Life, a collection of 153 short prose texts, was first published in its original language six years after the end of World War II to great success at a time when the jargon of authenticity and other Heideggerisms were still widespread in postfascist West Germany and Ernst Jünger's postwar writings were embraced by the younger generation. Each of its three parts, written in 1944, 1945, and 1946–1947, respectively, has a motto: "Life does not live," by Ferdinand Kürnberger, a nineteenth-century Austrian radical who wrote the novel *Der Amerikamüde*, which portrays

America as a seedbed of depravity, greed, and brutality; "Where everything is bad it must be good to know the worst," a saying by the British idealist philosopher F. H. Bradley; and finally *"Avalanche, veux-tu m'emporter dans ta chute?"* (Avalanche, will you sweep me along in your fall?), a quote from "Le Goût du néant" (The Taste for Nothingness) in Baudelaire's *Flowers of Evil*, which, like the other two mottos, is not apt to provide a brighter horizon than the others. The mottos are in tune with the characterization of the book as a "melancholy science," a deliberate retraction of Nietzsche's "gay science" at a time when philosophy's most noble calling, "the teaching of the good life," had "lapsed into intellectual neglect, sententious whimsy, and finally oblivion" (15). Adorno held philosophy's "conversion into method" responsible and, more important, he grasped the impossibility of thinking the good/right life at a time when Europe had lapsed into fascist barbarism. He pointed out in the dedication that each section of the book begins with "the narrowest private sphere, that of the intellectual in emigration" (18). The subsequent miniatures give "considerations of a broader social and anthropological scope" (18). Among other things, they discuss political economy, the sociology of the modern family, science, Freud and psychoanalysis, marriage and divorce, sex, eros, and love. The final miniatures turn toward philosophy "without ever pretending to be complete or definitive" (18). But then the dedication turns activist and transcends its melancholy beginnings:

> They are all intended to mark out points of attack or to furnish models for a future exertion of [conceptual] thought [*Anstrengung des Begriffs*]. (18; intervention would be a better translation instead of "attack")

Some alternative future is intimated in the idea that critical theory was a message in a bottle that was tossed into the sea and, as the metaphor requires, was to be read, understood, and acted on at some point in the future. This famous metaphor of the *Flaschenpost* addressed to some unknown future recipient points again to the isolation of exile, highlighting the fact that Adorno and his colleagues lacked access to any German-language feuilletons or publishers at the time.

A Mosaic of Exile: The Turn toward the Subject

We must read *Minima Moralia* as a literary work of exile, not as a social scientific analysis of American society and culture. The first cue is the subtitle: The damaged life, of course, refers to the exilic condition of the critical theorists at the time, and some of the most moving miniatures, especially in Part One, analyze the displacements and dispossessions of life in exile. Emphasizing lived experience, Adorno wrote reflections *from* rather than *about* a damaged life. But as the book grew beyond its first part in the second half of the 1940s, exile took on a broader meaning as a metaphor not just for an aesthetic modernism under siege but also for life in capitalist modernity tout court. The damage affects more than the refugees from Nazism; it has become general: thus Ferdinand Kürnberger's motto "Life does not live" and Adorno's outrageous, yet deeply felt claim: *"Es gibt kein richtiges Leben im falschen,"* translated as "wrong life cannot be lived rightly" (39). What he came to call the *"universaler Verblendungszusammenhang"* (universal context of deception) of life under capitalism also finds expression in a similar rhetoric of exaggeration, when he said, inverting Hegel, "the whole is the false" (50).[16] Or when he claimed that "there is nothing innocuous left," in analogy to Brecht's famous exile poem "To Those Who Follow in Our Wake," which suggested that a conversation about trees is almost a crime since it includes silence about so many misdeeds.[17] The rhetoric itself undermines what seem to be universalizing truth claims. Thus, what appears as outrageously grim generalization is never to be read literally as statement of fact. As Alexander Düttmann has persuasively argued, exaggeration gives neither truth nor untruth; instead, it functions as transgression of a limit, pushes beyond rational argument, and embodies an excess that cannot be recovered conceptually.[18] Its very formulation provokes a resistance in the reader, a resistance to accepting what playwright Friedrich Dürrenmatt later described as "the worst possible turn of events" as the key to his concept of postwar comedy. There was nothing comical about Adorno's worst possible turns, but there was a sliver of hope when he pointed to the dialectic inherent in the "universal context of deception":

Every individual feature of the context of deception is actually
relevant to its potential end.[19]

Adorno shunned ontological universalism. What at first sight may
look like a universal claim reveals itself as thoroughly post-ontological
when one takes the literary dimension of articulation into account.
The post-ontological dimension of the text emerges forcefully in the
frequently used rhetorical structure of an extreme statement followed
by its immediate retraction. It is a rhetoric that creates equivocation
and paradox. The reader can never be quite sure if exaggeration serves
Adorno to open up questions or to close them down. There is no way
of escaping the contradiction, for it does both at the same time.

There is no question that Adorno's feeling of being damaged by
exile was real. It was the experience of exile that made Adorno dive into
what to him had become the wreck of capitalism and human history.
The historical conjuncture of Europe under fascist rule did not seem
to allow for anything but radical negativity, and thus Nietzsche's gay
science has been inverted into a melancholy science in light of the news
about the death camps; the untold millions of war dead; the reckoning
with bombed-out cities all over Europe, from Guernica to Rotterdam
and Dresden; the nuclear devastation of Hiroshima and Nagasaki; and
the beginning of a new superpower conflict between the United States
and the Soviet Union and potential worldwide nuclear catastrophe on
the horizon. None of this inspired confidence in the moral human
condition or in the possibility of a right life. Adorno's letters to his
parents from those years testify how profoundly shaken and disoriented he was by Europe's collapse into fascist barbarism. This is
what primarily motivated Adorno's radical critique of modernity.

However, the miniatures of *Minima Moralia* do not focus directly
on the big historical events that can only be intimated in the text, as
if seen through a thickly woven scrim. They focus instead on small,
surface phenomena of everyday life in the United States, experienced
by a European intellectual displaced into the urban and cultural
sprawl of Los Angeles. And then they draw broad conclusions, often
without adequate mediation about the state of the capitalist world.
Here Adorno's critique of Benjamin's work on Paris and Baudelaire
as lacking mediations hits him like a boomerang. The "melancholy
science" of *Minima Moralia* does not rejoice jubilantly in the Allies'

victory over the Axis powers, perhaps understandably so, given all
that had happened under fascist rule. Instead it gives a radically critical analysis of mid-twentieth-century capitalism as a form of life.
Differences we would want to see acknowledged between Hitler's
Germany and Roosevelt's New Deal are given short shrift in an analysis that saw America, not unlike that of many other leftist analysts
at the time, as the epitome of twentieth-century capitalist modernity and its destructive anti-human potential at a time when America
was about to save Europe from fascism. Life under consumer capitalism, according to Adorno, spelled the endgame of subjectivity, the
end of human autonomy as it once was imagined in an enlightened
liberal age and as Beckett was to give it artistic shape a decade later.
Actually, this analysis was not so very different from the cultural
critique of United States mass culture articulated by the New York
intellectuals in the late 1940s and 1950s, a historical fact often and
conveniently forgotten by those who reduce Adorno's thought to
elitist Eurocentrism.[20]

But here too there was a contradiction: under the rubble and in
the ruins of life in postwar Germany, Adorno tried to locate the residue of some countervailing force, emerging from relentless negativity itself. And this is the paradox: he found it under the extreme
pressure of intellectual exile in the need for enlightenment about enlightenment, the main impetus behind the writing of the *Dialectic of
Enlightenment*. Such enlightenment depends on what he later, in his
famous 1959 radio address "What Does Coming to Terms with the
Past Mean?," called the *turn toward the subject:* reinforcement of a person's self-consciousness and, with that, of a sense of self.[21]

The context of this 1959 essay, to be sure, is different, but this turn
toward the subject, which so clearly contradicts the notion of Adorno
as doomsday prophet of any and all subjectivity, is already foreshad-
owed in *Minima Moralia*. It was brought about by the very experience of exile.

Key to my reading of *Minima Moralia* is its explicit focus on that
"narrowest private sphere" that marks an existential turn toward subjectivity quite different from the world-historical analysis of the subject we find in his reading of Odysseus in the *Dialectic of Enlightenment*. I will limit myself here to the miniatures of the first part, which
were written before 1945, before an end to exile had become a real

possibility. Not surprisingly for Adorno, the private sphere is immediately expanded toward a broader public context. The first miniature, entitled "For Marcel Proust," conjures up remembrances of a pre–World War I happy childhood and belonging that haunts the text throughout in a "counterpuntal" (Said) fashion. But it also offers a hard-nosed assessment of his own position as privileged "son of well-to-do parents who . . . engages in a so-called intellectual profession" as an artist or a scholar and who acknowledges being subjected to a division of labor that ultimately "presses [the demands of bourgeois society] home in the very domain where the deserter takes refuge" (21). This critical self-positioning loosely corresponds to the self-doubt of the narrator in the modern novel, and it also resonates with the ironic inscriptions of perspectivalism in Nietzsche and in the literary miniature since Baudelaire, who was as much a "herald of modernity" for Adorno as he was for Benjamin.[22]

A mosaic of exilic experience emerges as the reader encounters references to exile strewn across the wide path of the miniatures. Before exile even becomes an explicit theme, Nazism as the cause of exile and its effect on generational relations and on the very notion of privacy is explored in several miniatures. The "Grassy Seat" in the title of the second miniature calls up a stanza in a highly ironic Brecht poem about the cherished spot near the parents' grave. It is almost as if Adorno anticipated the death of his parents, who at the time were refugees in New York, when he spoke of "a sad, shadowy transformation" of "our relationship to parents" (22). What he had in mind was the cult of youth in an antagonistic society that privileged aggressive competition and the resulting disempowerment of the aged. He then turned to the specificity of Nazi Germany within this capitalist world:

> But today it is beginning to regress to a state, versed not in the Oedipus complex, but in parricide. One of the Nazis' symbolic outrages is the killing of the very old. (22)

Movingly and clearly hinting at the Nazis' anti-Semitic pogroms, he continued:

> Such a climate fosters a late, lucid understanding with our parents, as between the condemned, marred only by the fear that

we, powerless ourselves, might now be unable to care for them as well as they cared for us when they possessed something. (22)

Adorno's extensive correspondence with his parents throughout those years testifies vividly to a cross-generational solidarity that resisted the (to him) relentless trends of the age toward destroying intimacy, privacy and intergenerational bonds of love. His parents came to New York after having lived through the pogrom of 1938 and having been themselves dispossessed. More than implied here is not just the condition of exile, but that of the concentration camp that his parents barely escaped.

Adorno's description of what he always called emigration rather than exile hits all the well-known themes listed in Said's "Reflections on Exile." In "Protection, help and counsel," we read:

> Every intellectual in emigration is, without exception mutilated ["damaged" would be more accurate since *"beschädigt"* repeats the subtitle's phrasing], and does well to acknowledge it to himself. . . . He lives in an environment that must remain incomprehensible to him. . . . He is always astray. Between the reproduction of his own existence under the monopoly of mass culture, and impartial, responsible work, yawns an irreconcilable breach. His language has been expropriated, and the historical dimension that nourished his knowledge, sapped. (33)

The theme of expropriation concerns more than language, as miniature 25 suggests with its title "To them shall no thoughts be turned," a slightly modified line from Heine, a lifelong exile in Paris:

> The past life of emigrés is, as we know, annulled. Earlier it was the warrant of arrest, today it is intellectual experience that is declared non-transferable and un-naturalizable. Anything that is not reified, cannot be counted and measured, ceases to exist. (46–47)

Because the émigré's past is listed simply as "background" on questionnaires,

even the past is no longer safe from the present, whose remembrance of it consigns it a second time to oblivion. (47)

Such immaterial expropriations of exile, following on the expropriation of citizenship and property, conjure up a dystopian image, "the
horrifying spectre of a mankind without memory" (*das Schreckbild
einer Menschheit ohne Erinnerung*).[23] Radical isolation of the intellectual comes to be the result, especially since the relationship with most
fellow émigrés belies ideals of diasporic community:

> Relations between outcasts are even more poisoned than between
> long-standing residents. All emphases are wrong, perspectives
> disrupted. Private life asserts itself unduly, hectically, vampire-
> like, trying convulsively, because it really no longer exists, to
> prove it is alive. (33)

A realistic statement indeed, as we remember the resentments, power
plays, and infighting among the German exiles in California. It is
not only that there is no longer any community. In exile, the transcendental homelessness Lukács analyzed in the nineteenth-century
novel, has become real homelessness. This issue is addressed in
"Refuge for the homeless," which powerfully interlaces the real and
the metaphoric dimensions of exile:[24]

> The predicament of private life today is shown by its arena.
> Dwelling, in the proper sense, is now impossible. (38)

After a radical critique of traditional bourgeois residences as sites of
family oppression and of "functional modern habitations" as "factory
sites that have strayed into the consumption sphere" (38), Adorno
mentions the hotel or the furnished apartment as practical evasions
from dwelling. But then the exile situation is extrapolated again toward modernity at large:

> The house is past. The bombings of European cities, as well as
> the labour and concentration camps, merely proceed as execu-
> tors, with what the immanent development of technology had

long decided was the fate of houses. These are now good only
to be thrown away like old food cans. . . . No individual can resist this process. . . .The best mode of conduct, in face of all this,
still seems an uncommitted, suspended one: to lead a private life,
as far as the social order and one's own needs will tolerate nothing
else, but not to attach weight to it as something still socially sub-
stantial and individually appropriate. (39)

After quoting Nietzsche, who had praised his good fortune not to
be a house-owner, Adorno concluded:

It is part of morality not to be at home in one's home. (39)

Yet according to the later miniature "Memento," there seems to be
one exception—in writing:

In his text the writer sets up house. Just as he trundles papers,
books, pencils, documents untidily from room to room, he creates the same disorder in his thoughts. They become pieces of
furniture that he sinks into, content or irritable. He strokes them
affectionately, wears them out, mixes them up, re-arranges, ruins
them. For a man who no longer has a homeland, writing becomes
a place to live. (87)

But even this homecoming in writing is inherently threatened in
exile:

In it [the place of writing] he immediately produces, as his family
once did, refuse and junk. But now he lacks a store-room, and
it is hard in any case to part from left-overs. So he pushes them
along in front of him, in danger of finally filling his pages with
them. (87; translation of "junk" is a modification of "lumber"
for "Bodenramsch")

Clearly, this is a reflection on the process of composing his volume
of miniatures. How then to ban the danger of just muddling along?
Self-discipline and rigor are the answer:

> The demand that one harden oneself against self-pity implies
> the technical necessity to counter any slackening of intellectual
> tension with the utmost alertness, and to eliminate anything that
> has begun to encrust the work or to drift along idly, which may
> at an earlier stage have served, as gossip, to generate the warm
> atmosphere conducive to growth, but is now left behind, flat and
> stale. In the end, the writer is not even allowed to live in his
> writing. (87)

This is of course another example of Adorno's writing strategy
throughout: statement leads to counterstatement, which in turn leads
to retraction confirming the original statement instead of some kind
of Hegelian synthesis. It does not make sense to ask which of the irreconcilable statements is true. Truth here is not in any of the statements themselves but in the mise-en-scène of a process of arguing
that deliberately embraces different perspectives but never a
wholesome, merely positive conclusion.

The same is true for the very last miniature, entitled "Finale,"
which begins with a statement about responsible philosophy in double
subjunctive, thus casting doubt about its very feasibility:

> The only philosophy that can be responsibly practiced in face
> of despair would be the attempt to contemplate all things as they
> would present themselves from the standpoint of redemption.
> (247; my modification of the translation of "despair is" to "de-
> spair would be")

Clearly this is a phrasing that calls up Benjamin's last work, but for
Adorno any standpoint of redemption was entirely virtual. Instead,
uncompromising insistence on negativity is demanded by the state
of affairs,

> because consummate negativity, once squarely faced, delineates
> the mirror image of its opposite. (274)

Lest this sound too utopian, pointing to a rupturing or even overcoming of the context of deception, the text continues:

But it is also the utterly impossible thing, because it presupposes a standpoint removed, even though by a hair's breadth, from the scope of existence, whereas we well know that any possible knowledge must not only first be wrested from what is, if it shall hold good, but is also marked, for this very reason, by the same distortion and indigence which it seeks to escape. (247)

The most famous example of this kind of *mise en abyme* is perhaps the statement in *Negative Dialectics* where Adorno retracted his earlier suggestion that it is barbaric, even impossible to write poetry after Auschwitz, only then to go into overdrive, asking the even more radical, though less cultural question

whether after Auschwitz you can go on living—especially whether one who escaped by accident, one who by rights should have been killed, may go on living. His mere survival calls for the coldness, the basic principle of bourgeois subjectivity, without which there could have been no Auschwitz; this is the drastic guilt of him who was spared. By way of atonement he will be plagued by dreams such as that he is no longer living at all, that he was sent to the ovens in 1944 and his whole existence since has been imaginary, an emanation of the insane wish of a man killed twenty years earlier.[25]

Such dreams of course articulated existential, post-exilic survivor guilt, an extreme case of a feeling of unreality, which, as Adorno went on to say, was shared by many modernist artists, a feeling of the world as an "as if," of not being quite themselves, of standing outside themselves and observing from a distance. It is like exile from oneself, again exile as metaphor but existentially grounded in Adorno's consciousness of having been destined for Auschwitz. With this kind of consciousness, there could never be a comfortable being at home in or with oneself. After Auschwitz, there could be no redemption.

In *Minima Moralia*, the demand not to be at home in one's home even affects the relation to things that can no longer be considered private property under conditions of mass production. And now Adorno mobilized certain differences between Europe and the United States that only made sense to the suspicious eye of the disoriented exile who held technification responsible for the increasing brutality in the world. Technical modernity, he suggested in an overwrought comparison, required that doors of cars and refrigerators have to be slammed rather than discreetly closed:

> The new human type cannot be properly understood without awareness of what he is continuously exposed to from the world of things about him, even in his most secret innervations. What does it mean for the subject that there are no more casement windows to open, but only sliding frames to shove, no gentle latches but turnable handles, no forecourt, no doorstep before the street, no wall around the garden? (40)

To see in such simple markers of cultural difference the hauntings of fascist violence demonstrates a tendency toward homogenization that we don't expect from the theorist of non-identity. But then, here too, the reader confronts that rhetoric of exaggeration best encapsulated in the aphorism in "Dwarf Fruit":

> In psychoanalysis nothing is true except the exaggerations. (49)

The title "Dwarf Fruit" itself casts an ironic light on this aphorism. Dwarfed in this case refers to the fruit's stunted growth. Thus, exaggeration itself is an effect of the mutilations of modernity and its rhetoric as a style of writing is part of a modernist aesthetic that was first practiced in Nietzsche and reverberated throughout the interwar period.[26]

Two Modernisms

Indeed, *Minima Moralia* as an exilic text embodies a tradition of radical thought and modernist writing that questioned the systematic philosophical treatise, just as the metropolitan miniature questioned the grand social novel. In its very form it questioned the assumptions of continuity that shaped the philosophy of history that had been so powerfully developed from Lessing and Herder all the way to Freud and Adorno. This becomes very clear as one considers Adorno's relationship to Thomas Mann, his fellow exile in Pacific Pali-

sades. In his diaries, Mann mentioned a dinner at the Adornos' in
an entry dated December 5, 1945:

> He read from his aphorisms . . . entangled intellectual lyri-
> cism . . . annihilating and sad.[27]

Elsewhere in Mann's diaries we encounter the telling reproach
of cerebralism and formlessness, allegedly features of Adorno's
writing:

> That which is thought is then being un-thought, re-thought,
> rolling on formlessly but with great precision of language.[28]

Mann, of course, always felt threatened by formlessness. Thus, he
stayed with key aspects of the traditional novel, however ironically
fractured and subjected to montage, when he wrote *Doctor Faustus*
in Pacific Palisades at the same time Adorno wrote *Minima Moralia*.
Actually, we know that Mann and Adorno met several times on social occasions when they read from their work: Mann from the draft
novel, Adorno from the manuscript of *Minima Moralia*. We also know
how Mann benefited hugely from Adorno's advice regarding modernist music; many of Adorno's ideas about Beethoven, orchestral
music, Schönberg, and avant-gardism entered into the fabric of Mann's
Faustus novel, many of them verbatim.[29] In the protagonist Adrian
Leverkühn's encounter with the devil, the devil sounds aesthetic ideas
we know from Adorno's *Philosophy of New Music:*

> Today, the only works that count are those that are no longer
> works.[30]

In Mann's novel, the devil says:

> What is art today? A pilgrimage on peas. . . . Composing itself
> has got too hard, devilishly hard. Where work does not go any
> longer with sincerity how is one to work? But so it stands, my
> friend, the masterpiece, the self-sufficient form, belongs to tra-
> ditional art, emancipated art rejects it.[31]

Adorno, not unlike Georg Lukács, admired Thomas Mann greatly
throughout his life. But given the temporal and spatial proximity of
Doctor Faustus with *Minimal Moralia*, what strikes me is the difference in their respective aesthetic ethoses. Though Mann problema-
tized the notions of the masterpiece and traditional art, he still
couched his skepticism in a novel about the life of an artist and in
the shape of a very national German myth. Mann's novel still is a
work oriented toward a traditional form in a way that *Minima Moralia*
is not. More than that: *Minima Moralia* questions the very possibility
of philosophical form, just as it questions the possibility of the right
life, which, after all, had always been a major theme of the modern
novel.

At the same time, Mann's novel has often been accused of having
its own rhetoric of exaggeration: the trajectory of German music
being analogized with the trajectory of national German history from
Luther via Nietzsche to Hitler. This was a different philosophy of
history, to be sure, from Adorno's, and yet there is an undeniable affinity: thinking the development of musical technique in relationship to broad historical and cultural developments was key to Adorno's reading of music from Beethoven to Schönberg and beyond. But
in contrast to Mann's narrative, Adorno's *Minima Moralia*, like the
metropolitan miniature in general, displays a kind of radical writing
strategy that counteracts or subverts the very continuity posited by
its own reliance on the philosophy of history, modernity, and capitalism. Thereby it also disproves a claim often made by scholars of
German exile literature that interwar exile led invariably to an abandonment of an avant-gardist ethos and to a regression to traditional
forms such as nature poetry, the sonnet, and the historical novel. This
thesis has come in for legitimate critique in recent years, and it does
not hold up vis-à-vis *Minima Moralia*, a literary text that continues
and expands on one the most radical traditions of modernist prose
writing, that of the metropolitan miniature.[32] But it offers, as it were,
an afterimage of that metropolitan writing. Damaged life as experienced and observed in the city of angels is no longer specific to the
metropolis alone. It has permeated all of capitalist society in the form
of consumerism, alienation, and media penetration. In that respect,
Minima Moralia already points forward to the postwar period in which

the metropolis was no longer an island of modernization and the only
magnet for experimental artistic practices, as it had been in earlier
decades. The death camps and the bombed-out cities had taken away
for good the glow of promise and excitement that lit the urban imaginaries of those earlier decades, even when they too focused on the
damages of modernization. For Adorno, by 1940 history had "taken
on the character of catastrophe"[33] and World War II was no longer
just war, but signified

> the collapse of a form of culture that had been alive in the world
> since the migration of peoples.[34]

As many observers have claimed, something indeed ended in the
mid-twentieth century, and that end also spelled the ending of the
metropolitan miniature as it had developed in Europe since
Baudelaire.

In that sense, *Minima Moralia* stands as the coda to that tradition
and, in a more personal vein, as an epitaph to Walter Benjamin's
suicide.

After Exile—Afterthoughts

One last important point needs to be registered. What happened to
the message in the bottle once it reached its destination: post-fascist
Germany? How was the rhetoric of exaggeration received there? The
book quickly found a growing audience, and it has remained popular. But all too often *Minima Moralia* was read literally as offering
a set of propositions, and as such it fed into the student movement
and the New Left in the 1960s. The apodictic statement that there
is no right life in the wrong one became something of a slogan of
anti-capitalist protest at the time.[35] Others saw *Minima Moralia* as
being marred by nostalgia and by a conservative European *Kulturkritik* that had made America and Americanization its favorite
target. But Adorno's over-the-top analogies between fascism and
America in the 1940s that proved so influential in the West German
anti-Vietnam protests of the 1960s are counteracted in a whole series
of more sober statements in which Adorno actually praised America
for having given him a new outlook on life, deprovincialized him,

and allowed him to look at German culture from the outside. As he put it in 1968 in "Scientific Experiences of a European Scholar in America":

> In America I was liberated from a naïve belief in culture, acquired the ability to see culture from the outside.[36]

That dimension of self-critique was, however, not matched by equal insight into the realities of New Deal America, not in *Minima Moralia* or in his postwar writings. His focus on anti-semitic evangelical preachers and later on McCarthyism may have prevented him from differentiating. Actually Adorno was curiously disinterested in the social and political developments of the New Deal and in American political parties and institutions in general. Instead, he turned his own experience of homelessness into a general diagnosis of the world-historical moment. As critics have pointed out, social scientific and political analysis of America in the tradition of Tocqueville or Max Weber took a culturalist and sociopsychological turn in Adorno's work in the 1940s.[37] In retrospect it is easy to see the limitations of his approach. He was always and stubbornly wrong about jazz, as in that notorious article that was written in Oxford in 1936 prior to his exile years and thus has very little to do with his American experience.[38] On the other hand, his political fear that America was not immune to anti-semitism was quite accurate at the time and was borne out by observation and research on the authoritarian personality, the book that identified him to American readers until the late 1960s.[39] Clearly he was wrong to think that America might fall for the temptations of a totalitarian state that were presaged in the American culture industry. But the misapprehensions of American politics must be read in light of the exilic experience, the pressures of early knowledge about the death camps, and the barbarism that had come to rule Europe. His was a melancholy imagination caught in the vise of a philosophy of history that saw the whole course of history rushing toward disaster—not exactly a view unknown in California or America at large. And yet his empirical and practical work in New York in the context of Paul Lazarsfeld's Radio Research Project and his extensive encounters with Hollywood gave him much deeper insights into the inner workings of the American culture industry than Bertolt Brecht ever had.[40]

At the same time, Adorno was always grateful to the land that saved him. If he changed his views about America in the postwar period, especially in the late 1960s, that should not be seen as simply irreconcilable with those earlier negative views.[41] It just reflects a changed historical situation after the defeat of fascism. From the viewpoint of the returnee, the American experience could be rearticulated and acknowledged as having given him a unique experiential perspective from which to carry on the task of critique in post-fascist Germany. Critical theory was no longer a message in a bottle but had begun to shape public intellectual discourse, ironically via the medium Adorno had impugned as fascist in the 1940s: the radio. It was in his many radio lectures from the 1950s on that Adorno established himself as a public intellectual in West Germany.

But his recognition of American political life went farther and was not limited to the post-exile period. In the *Introduction to the Sociology of Music*, written in exile in the United States, we read:

> In America, the self-evident reification recoils at times, unforced, into a semblance of humanity and proximity—and not just into semblance.[42]

This view, which might strike some as condescending, is expanded in the astonishing passage from the 1968 essay first published in English as "Scientific Experiences of a European Scholar in America":

> More important and more gratifying was my experience of the substantiality of democratic forms: that in America they have seeped into life itself, whereas at least in Germany they were, and still are, nothing more than formal rules of the game. Over there I became acquainted with a potential for real humanitarianism that is hardly to be found in old Europe. The political form of democracy is infinitely closer to the people. American everyday life, despite the often lamented hustle and bustle, has an inherent element of peaceableness, good naturedness

and generosity, in sharpest contrast to the pent-up malice and envy that exploded in Germany between 1933 and 1945. Surely America is no longer the land of unlimited possibilities, but one still has the feeling that anything could be possible.[43]

In a short piece of 1954, entitled "Im Flug erhascht" (Captured in flight) and written after what seems to have been his first flight ever, from Los Angeles to New York during his final short stay in the United States in 1953, he had this to say about the experience of temporality plaguing the former exile:

> In any case, the temporal order has become disorder for the emigrant. The years of the fascist dictatorship have been blasted out of the continuity of his life; what happened in those years hardly blends in with that other life. When he returns, he has aged, but simultaneously remained as young as he was in the moment of banishment, somewhat similar to the dead who always keep the age in which one last knew them. He imagines to be permitted to continue where he ended; those who are as old today as he was in 1933 appear as peers to him, and yet he has his real age which interlaces itself with the other, breaks through it, lends it a secret meaning, belies it. It is as if fate had displaced those to whom it happened and who were permitted to survive into a temporality simultaneously multi-dimensional and shot through with holes.[44]

Perhaps Adorno's need to move from the micro-experiences of exile in *Minima Moralia* to the metalevel or grand narrative of a philosophy of history and a universalizing account of advanced capitalism can be read as a last-ditch attempt of the exile to plug the holes of that shot-through temporality at a time when he himself intimated that the bell had tolled on the philosophy of history. The very fragmented literary form of *Minima Moralia* testifies to that insight more powerfully than his philosophical opus magnum, *Negative Dialectics*. And so does his fragmentary, posthumously published *Aesthetic Theory*, which questions the very possibility of normative aesthetics after modernism.

To return to the Adrienne Rich quote with which I began: Adorno will of course be remembered better as the seismograph of the damage that was done than as a purveyor of the treasures that prevail. But there is a legacy in *Minima Moralia* as a literary text that can still provide a starting point for contemporary reflections on the aesthetic dimension in the experience and art of exile, even if the miniature as his chosen form no longer prevails. Adorno never ontologized his exile. That is why he could maintain his critical project under different circumstances and with different political parameters in post-fascist Germany. That is also why as a returnee he could become an effective public intellectual in a society in transition to democracy.

Unlike Kracauer or Benjamin, Adorno is not known as a theorist of urban life. As I have suggested, the absence of the city in *Minima Moralia* can be explained in several ways, but on some fundamental historical level it is different from that of the earlier metropolitan miniatures. Having grown up in a medium-sized city in Germany, Adorno shared a widespread aversion to the real metropolis, as his letters to his parents make clear enough. As the place of forced exile, Los Angeles was never home to him as Paris was to Baudelaire, Prague to Kafka, or Berlin to Benjamin. In Los Angeles he did not live downtown but on the coastal margins and in relative comfort and isolation from the larger urban streams of American life as they characterized New York, Detroit, or Chicago at the time. But the most important aspect of the absent presence of Los Angeles in *Minima Moralia* must be explained differently. It is no longer simply the conscious avoidance of realistic city description that characterized the earlier miniatures. Los Angeles of the 1940s already represents a new amorphous form of a metropolitan agglomeration in which the urban bleeds into suburbia and country life and in which urban culture, technology, and lifestyle have migrated outward, pervading parts of the country heretofore untouched by metropolitan culture. Los Angeles, center of the American film industry, thus came to be the implicit model for an all-pervasive culture industry. Film as a form of vernacular modernism, after all, was the key medium that made the metropolitan experience pervasive beyond the metropolis itself.[45] In that sense, Los Angeles in the 1940s was already in the vanguard of urban and cultural developments that were to characterize the postwar period in the United States and in Europe as well. This is why I argue that with Adorno the metropolitan miniature has come to an end. Its very condition of possibility—the metropolis as island of modernization in a largely agricultural and provincial environment as it characterized European developments from the mid-nineteenth century through the interwar period—had disappeared for good.

NOTES

INDEX

Notes

Introduction

1. David Harvey, *The Condition of Postmodernity* (Cambridge, Mass.: Blackwell, 1989).
2. Anton Kaes has documented and analyzed the symptomatic struggle between cinema and literature for the period 1909–1929 in his *Kino-Debatte: Texte zum Verhältnis von Literatur und Film* (Tübingen: Max Niemeyer Verlag, 1978).
3. On the issue of perception and attentiveness in the late nineteenth century, see Jonathan Crary, *Suspensions of Perception: Attention, Spectacle, and Modern Culture* (Cambridge, Mass.: MIT Press, 2001); Christoph Asendorf, *Batteries of Life: On the History of Things and Their Perception in Modernity* (Berkeley: University of California Press, 1993). On my use of the idea of an urban imaginary, see Andreas Huyssen, ed., *Other Cities, Other Worlds: Urban Imaginaries in a Globalizing World* (Durham, N.C.: Duke University Press, 2008), 3.
4. Walter Benjamin, "Paris, the Capital of the Nineteenth Century," in *Selected Writings*, vol. 3, *1935–1938*, ed. Howard Eiland and Michael Jennings, trans. Edmond Jephcott, Howard Eiland, and Others (Cambridge, Mass.: Harvard University Press, 2002), 32.
5. On the issue of acceleration as a key criterion of classical modernity and contemporary globalizing tendencies, see Hartmut Rosa, *Weltbeziehungen im Zeitalter der Beschleunigung* (Frankfurt am Main: Suhrkamp, 2012), esp. chapter 5.
6. Ilya Ehrenburg, *Life of the Automobile*, trans. from the Russian by Joachim Neugroschel (New York: Urizen Books, 1976). The German version of 1973, published by Paco Press in Amsterdam, lacks this first chapter that opens the English version.

7. Rilke, Kafka, and Musil are three of my authors who address this issue of
   urban sound and noise time and again in their writings about the city. If
   it remains by and large outside of my readings, it is because prose miniature, photography, and early film are all silent media.

8. The notion of *Eigensinn* is taken from Oskar Negt and Alexander Kluge's
   book *Geschichte und Eigensinn* (Frankfurt am Main: Zweitausendeins, 1981).
   A shortened and updated English translation has just been published as
   History and Obstinacy, ed. with an introduction by Devin Fore (New York:
   Zone Books, 2014). Negt and Kluge discuss *Eigensinn* in social life not as a
   natural human quality, but as a condensed protest against the expropriation of a human being's five senses. Ever since Marx we have known that
   human senses and perceptions are subject to historical change, not the
   least by change in media technologies. To project *Eigensinn* onto literature and the media departs from Negt and Kluge's use and raises other
   questions. But it matches their anti-ontological definition of *Eigensinn*
   and their focus on perception and embodiment. Sam Weber's notion of
   "differential specificity" developed in relation to contemporary media developments, and taken up in Rosalind Krauss's work in the visual arts
   captures the anti-ontological meaning of the term as well. Similar to the
   differential specificity of a medium, the *Eigensinn* of a medium is not an
   ontological but a relational category. It points to the self-reflexive specificity of a medium in relation to other media. Sam Weber, "Television:
   Set and Screen," in *Mass Mediauras: Form, Technics, Media* (Stanford,
   Calif.: Stanford University Press, 1996) 108–128; Rosalind Krauss, *A
   Voyage on the North Sea: Art in the Age of the Post-Medium Condition* (New
   York: Thames & Hudson, 2000).

9. For both pragmatic and substantive reasons I base my readings on the book
   versions. Seeking out earlier feuilleton versions is desirable in certain instances, but my focus is on the principles of composition and de-composition
   that guided the various authors in their final assembly of their mosaics of
   miniatures. The often tentative and arbitrary arrangement of texts in the
   feuilleton assumed greater purpose and ambition in their collection into
   the book format.

10. Among the authors treated here, Rilke as a transitional figure between,
    say, Baudelaire and Kafka may be the one exception. But even in his novel,
    Malte's learning how to see is an attempt to overcome the crisis of narra-
    tion, not of language as such.

11. McLuhan's *Understanding Media* is a once-popular book that posited a
    teleological development of media technologies from oral to written and ul-
    timately back to oral at a higher level—a three-step history of salvation in
    which orality was writ large and as such a kind of creationist theory of the
    media. This very catholic theological dimension is the weakest part of
    McLuhan's project. See Andreas Huyssen, "In the Shadow of McLuhan:
    Baudrillard's Theory of Simulation," in *Twilight Memories: Marking Time
    in a Culture of Amnesia* (New York: Routledge, 1996), 175–190. Other as-
    pects of the book, however, may still lay claim to our attention, as Fried-

rich Kittler's media theory has shown; see his *Gramophone, Film, Typewriter* (Stanford, Calif.: Stanford University Press, 1999).

12. Thus, triumphalists of the Internet keep making all kinds of overblown claims about other media presumably having become obsolete (photography, film, not to mention the book). Especially in the 1990s, the Internet was often seen as a radical break with the past, as a harbinger of entirely new forms of direct democracy, cyberfreedom, and unlimited global communication. This was Californian New Ageism in digital guise before the revelations about the National Security Agency sounded a wake-up call.

13. David Bolter and Richard Grusin, *Remediation: Understanding New Media* (Cambridge, Mass.: MIT Press, 2000). The authors recognize that "older media can also remediate newer ones" (p. 55), but for them this move somehow seems to lack the legitimacy of the unidirectional causality of remediation in McLuhan's sense. There is an extensive literature that discusses the modernist city novel in terms of cinematic narrative and technique, i.e., as a form of retrograde remediation. The relationship of modernist literary texts to photography, on the other hand, has been much less discussed. Unlike Bolter and Grusin, Pavle Levi has turned retrograde remediation into a positive term in his discussion of "Cinema by Other Means," *October* 131 (Winter 2010): 65-68. Levi's starting point is the cinema, and thus his notion of retrograde remediation is different from my use of remediation in reverse, the starting point of which is the older medium of literature.

14. Lessings's programmatic separation of literary works from works in the visual arts was of course itself engaged in a specific historical struggle to validate the ambitions of German literature at the time and should not be taken as timeless truth.

15. Franco Moretti, *Modern Epic: The World System from Goethe to García Marquez* (New York: Verso, 1996).

16. Ernst Bloch, *Briefe: 1903–1975*, vol. 1 (Frankfurt am Main: Suhrkamp, 1985), 278, my translation.

17. Franz Kafka, *Tagebücher*, ed. Hans-Gerd Koch, Michael Müller, and Malcolm Pasley (Frankfurt am Main: Fischer, 2002), 427, 429; Franz Kafka, *The Diaries of Franz Kafka*, ed. Max Brod (New York: Schocken Books, 1965), 165, 167; Franz Kafka, *Briefe, 1900–1912*, ed. Hans-Gerd Koch (Frankfurt am Main: Fischer, 1999), 222; *Letters to Felice*, ed. Erich Heller and Jürgen Born, trans. James Stern and Elisabeth Duckworth (New York: Schocken Books, 1973), 33.

18. Walter Benjamin to Gershom Scholem, December 22, 1924, in *The Correspondence of Walter Benjamin, 1910–1940* (Chicago: University of Chicago Press, 1994), 257.

19. Robert Musil, "Literarische Chronik," in Robert Musil, *Gesammelte Werke*, Band 9, ed. Adolf Frisé (Reinbek: Rowohlt, 1978), 1468, my translation.

20. It would be interesting to explore why the urban prose miniature is also widespread in Latin American literature during the period of the rapid

modernization of urban centers such as Buenos Aires, Rio de Janeiro, São Paolo, and Mexico City. The influence of Baudelaire and French literature has certainly been a major factor. See the collection of texts from different Hispanic countries David Lagmanovich, ed., *La otra mirada: Antología del microrelato hispánico* (Palencia: meno**scuarto,** 2005).

21. On the differences in perceptions of Berlin as compared with Paris or London, see Erhard Schütz, "Wo liegt Europa in Berlin? Berlin-Darstellungen als Paradigma für eine europäische Moderne," in *Europa. Stadt. Reisende: Blicke auf Reisetexte 1918–1945*, ed. Walter Fähnders, Wolfgang Klein, and Nils Plath (Bielefeld: Aisthesis Verlag, 2006), 11–40.

22. On the question of the miniature in relation to contemporary digital media, see Sabine Haenni, "Intellectual Promiscuity: Cultural History in the Age of the Cinema, the Network, and the Database," *New German Critique* 122 (Summer 2014): 189–202.

23. On Kluge's recent expansion of story space toward globalization, see the recent work by Leslie Adelson, "Horizons of Hope in Times of Despair: Alexander Kluge's Cosmic and Global Miniatures for the 21st Century," lecture given at the Institute for Comparative Modernities, Cornell University, April 2, 2013; Harro Müller, "Die authentische Methode: Alexander Kluge's anti-realistisches Realismus Realismusprojekt," in *Gegengifte: Essays zu Theorie und Literatur der Moderne* (Bielefeld: Aisthesis Verlag, 2009), 97–121.

24. For an attempt to grapple with this issue, see Andreas Huyssen, ed., *Other Cities, Other Worlds: Urban Imaginaries in a Globalizing Age* (Durham, N.C.: Duke University Press, 2008).

25. On the issue of *Bilderangst*, see especially Horst Bredekamp, *Theorie des Bildakts* (Frankfurt am Main: Suhrkamp, 2010). On Bredekamp's theory, see Reimut Reiche, "Vom Handeln der Bilder. Horst Bredekamps Frankfurter Adorno-Vorlesungen 2007," in *West End: Neue Zeitschrift für Sozialforschung* 5 (2008): 174–181.

26. Miriam Hansen, "Mass Culture as Hieroglyphic Writing: Adorno, Derrida, Kracauer," *New German Critique* 56 (Spring-Summer 1992): 43–73. Later reworked in *Cinema and Experience* (Berkeley: University of California Press, 2011).

27. On Hofmannsthal and Schnitzler, see Andreas Huyssen, "The Disturbance of Vision in Vienna Modernism," *Modernism/Modernity* 5, no. 3 (1998): 33–48.

28. Sigfried Giedion, *Bauen in Frankreich, Eisen, Eisenbeton* (Leipzig: Klinkhardt und Biermann, 1928), translated as *Building in France, Building in Iron, Building in Ferroconcrete* (Santa Monica, Calif.: Getty Center for the History of Art and the Humanities, 1995). The notion of *Durchdringung*, and not only in Giedion's sense, is a leitmotif in the superb study by Heinz Brüggemann, *Architekturen des Augenblicks: Raum-Bilder und Bild-Räume einer urbanen Moderne in Literatur, Kunst und Architektur des 20. Jahrhunderts* (Hannover: Offizin Verlag, 2002).

29. On this aspect of Italian futurism, see Heinz Brüggemann, *Architekturen des Augenblicks* (Offizin: Hannover, 2002), 95–196.

30. Hilde Heynen, *Architecture and Modernity* (Cambridge, Mass.: MIT Press, 1999), 35.

31. This point about scale owes a lot to a conversation with Reinhold Martin.

32. See the first section entitled "Lead-in: Natural Geometry" in Siegfried Kracauer, *The Mass Ornament* (Cambridge, Mass.: Harvard University Press, 1995). Chapter 4 of this book reads two of the miniatures from this section.

33. Georg Simmel, "The Metropolis and Mental Life," in *The Sociology of Georg Simmel*, trans. and ed. Kurt H. Wolff (New York: The Free Press, 1950), 409–426.

34. "Dass das Raumproblem zum Ausgangspunkt einer neuen Selbstbesinnung der Ästhetik werden könne"; Ernst Cassirer, *Symbol, Technik, Sprache: Aufsätze aus den Jahren 1927–33* (Hamburg: F. Meiner, 1985), 95.

35. The Kafka example is discussed in the chapter on Kracauer and Benjamin; for the other example, see the chapter on Jünger.

36. Gayatri Spivak's felicitous phrase "affirmative sabotage," developed for a different context, pushes against and beyond the old opposition of affirmative vs. critical culture (Marcuse) that was central to earlier forms of ideology critique. It suggests that affirmation can have a critical dimension and vice versa; a binary is turned into a subtle dialectic. See Gayatri Chakravorty Spivak, *An Aesthetic Education in the Era of Globalization* (Cambridge, Mass.: Harvard University Press, 2013).

37. Inka Mülder-Bach, *Kracauers Blick: Anstösse zu einer Ethnographie des Städtischen* (Hamburg: Europäische Verlagsanstalt, 2006), 45; Egon Erwin Kisch, *Der rasende Reporter* (Cologne: Kiepenheuer und Witsch, 1985), 7-8 ("*unretouchierte Zeitaufnahme*").

38. Theodor W. Adorno, *Aesthetic Theory*, trans. Robert Hullot-Kentor (Minneapolis: University of Minnesota Press, 1997), 5.

39. Theodor W. Adorno, "Kunst und die Künste," in *Ohne Leitbild: Parva Aesthetica* (Frankfurt am Main: Suhrkamp, 1967), 158–182. On Adorno's notion of fraying (*Verfransung*), see Juliane Rebentisch, *Ästhetik der Installation* (Frankfurt am Main: Suhrkamp, 2003), 101–145. English translation as *Aesthetics of Installation Art* (Berlin: Sternberg Press, 2012), 99–140.

40. Friedrich Kittler, *Discourse Networks 1800/1900* (Stanford, Calif.: Stanford University Press, 1990), 250.

41. See, for instance, the marvelous polemic in Jonathan Crary, *24/7: Late Capitalism and the Ends of Sleep* (London and New York: Verso, 2014).

42. See most recently Evgeny Morozov, *To Save Everything, Click Here: The Folly of Technological Solutionism* (New York: Public Affairs Publishing, 2013).

43. The soundscape of metropolitan life, an important topic in itself, has to remain outside of this investigation. Indeed, one could argue that disorientation by sound, the directionality of which often cannot be determined, is even more important in the metropolis than sight. For an excellent analysis of sound in modernist literature and culture, see Tyler Whitney, "Spaces of the Ear: Literature, Media, and the Science of Sound, 1886–1928" (PhD diss., Columbia University, 2012).

CHAPTER 1   *Urban Spleen and the Terror of Paris*
             in Baudelaire and Rilke

1. See Hartmut Engelhardt, ed., *Materialien zu Rainer Maria Rilke: Die Aufzeichnungen des Malte Laurids Brigge* (Frankfurt am Main: Suhrkamp, 1974), 164.

2. Charles Baudelaire, *The Parisian Prowler: Le Spleen de Paris. Petits Poèmes en prose*, 2nd ed., trans. Edward K. Kaplan (Athens and London: University of Georgia Press, 1997), 129. All further references are given with page numbers in the text.

3. Karl Heinz Stierle, *Der Mythos von Paris: Zeichen und Bewusstsein der Stadt* (Munich: Deutscher Taschenbuchverlag, 1998), 900.

4. "The Metropolis and Mental Life," in *The Sociology of Georg Simmel*, trans., ed., and intro. Kurt H. Wolff (New York: Free Press, 1964), 409–424.

5. Charles Baudelaire, "The Painter of Modern Life," in *The Painter of Modern Life and Other Essays*, trans. and ed. Jonathan Mayne (New York: Da Capo Press, 1986), 1–40.

6. Charles Baudelaire, "The Salon of 1859," in *Art in Paris 1845–1862: Salons and Other Exhibitions*, trans. and ed. Jonathan Mayne (Ithaca, N.Y.: Cornell University Press, 1965), 153.

7. Walter Benjamin, "Paris, the Capital of the 19th Century," in *Selected Writings*, vol. 3, *1935–1938* (Cambridge, Mass.: Harvard University Press, 2002), 43. Benjamin probably had the feuilleton novel in mind rather than the Baudelairean miniatures, texts he never had much to say about because his reading of Baudelaire focused primarily on the poetry. But the quote fits the miniature even better than the publication of novels in installments.

8. David Harvey, *The Condition of Postmodernity* (Cambridge, Mass.: Blackwell, 1989).

9. See Lise Sabourin, "De *Gaspard* à ses illustrations," in *Gaspard de la nuit: Le Grand Oeuvre d'un petit romantique*, ed. Nicolas Wanlin (Paris: Presse de l'université Paris-Sorbonne, 2010), 219–240.

10. Charles Baudelaire, "My Heart Laid Bare," in *My Heart Laid Bare and Other Prose Writings*, trans. Norman Cameron (London: Soho Books, 1986), 175.

11. "*Mais c'est lui qui lui donne ses lettres de noblesse, qui l'introduit dans l'horizon de ses contemporains et de ses successeurs, qui en fait un modèle d'écriture.*" Tzvetan Todorov, *Les genres du discours* (Paris: Editions du Seuil, 1978), 119, my translation.

12. See Suzanne Bernard, *Le poème en prose de Baudelaire jusqu'à nos jours* (Paris: Librairie Nizet, 1959), 113; and André Gide, *Journal 1939–1949: Souvenirs* (Paris: Gallimard, 1972), 16. Gide speaks of "*des décevantes gaucheries et insuffisances*" (the deceptive awkwardness and insufficiency). Even Benjamin underestimated Baudelaire's prose poems when he suggested that Baudelaire displayed his "productive capacity almost entirely" in his versified poetry. Walter Benjamin, "On Some Motifs in Baudelaire," *Selected Writings*, vol. 4, 1938-1940 (Cambridge, Mass.: Harvard University Press, 2003), 341.

13. Charles Baudelaire to his mother, March 9, 1865, in *Correspondance. Texte établi, présenté et annoté par Claude Pichois, avec la collaboration de Jean Ziegler* (Paris: Gallimard, 1973), 2:473, my translation.

14. Baudelaire to Troubat, February 19, 1866, in *Correspondance*, 2:615, my translation.

15. Karlheinrich Biermann, *Literarisch-politische Avantgarde in Frankreich 1830–1870: Hugo, Sand, Baudelaire und andere* (Stuttgart: Kohlhammer, 1982).

16. See also Karlheinrich Biermann's earlier essay "Baudelaires *Petits poèmes en prose:* Ein Diskussiosbeitrag zum Verhältnis zwischen Hoch- und Trivialliteratur," *lendemains* 10 (May 1978): 117–124.

17. On the role of photography in Rilke, see the Malte chapter in Stefanie Harris's incisive study *Mediating Modernity: German Literature and the "New Media," 1895–1930* (University Park: Pennsylvania State University Press, 2009), 21–53.

18. Rainer Maria Rilke to Lou Andreas-Salomé, July 18, 1903, in *Rainer Maria Rilke and Lou Andreas-Salomé: The Correspondence*, trans. Edward Snow and Michael Winkler (New York: W. W. Norton, 2006), 50.

19. Ibid.

20. Rilke, *The Notebooks of Malte Laurids Brigge*, trans. Stephen Mitchell (New York: Vintage, 1985), 72. All other page references in the text.

21. On the dimension of visual crisis in the Hofmannsthal's Chandos letter, see Andreas Huyssen, "The Disturbance of Vision in Vienna Modernism," *Modernism/Modernity* 5, no. 3 (1998): 36ff.

22. My reading of Rilke's novel, as of the miniature in general, has close affinities with Carsten Strathausen's incisive recoding of the relationship between the verbal and the visual in German poetry around 1900. See especially the chapter on Rilke's *New Poems* entitled "Rilke's Stereoscopic Vision," in Strathausen, *The Look of Things: Poetry and Vision around 1900* (Chapel Hill: University of North Carolina Press, 2003), 190–236.

23. Siegfried Kracauer, *Jacques Offenbach und das Paris seiner Zeit* (Frankfurt am Main: Suhrkamp, 1976), 83. Translated as *Jacques Offenbach and the Paris of His Time*, trans. Gwenda David and Eric Mosbacher (New York: Zone Books, 2002). This telling formulation is missing from the English translation. The German reads: *"ein dem Zugriff der gesellschaftlichen Realität entrückter Ort. Ein neutraler Treffpunkt. Ein unwirkliches Gelände."*

24. Snow and Winkler, *Rainer Maria Rilke and Lou Andreas-Salomé*, 224. I owe this reference to Stefanie Harris, who in her chapter on Rilke goes on to relate Rilke/Malte's urban experience and the technology of photography to the experience of the artisanal stained-glass windows inside the Rouen cathedral. To be sure, there are no such statements about photography uttered by the novel's protagonist, but the affinities between the novel's protagonist and his author are strong enough to make this interpretation plausible. Harris, *Mediating Modernity*, 21-53.

25. Harris, *Mediating Modernity*, 33.

26. *Letters of Rainer Maria Rilke*, vol. 1, *1892–1910*, trans. Jane Bannard Greene and M. D. Herter Norton (New York: W. W. Norton, 1945), 124.

27. See my reading of the famous mirror scene in my earlier essay "Paris/Child-hood: The Fragmented Body in Rilke's *Notebooks of Malte Laurids Brigge*," in *Twilight Memories: Marking Time in a Culture of Amnesia* (New York: Routledge, 1995), 117–121.

28. Stierle, *Der Mythos von Paris*, 891ff.

29. Jean Jacques Rousseau, *The Confessions of J. J. Rousseau with the Reveries of a Solitary Walker*, vol. 2, trans. from the French (London: Printed for J. Bew, 1783), 144.

30. Charles Mauron, *Le dernier Baudelaire* (Paris: J. Corti, 1966). Lucien Gold-mann similarly posits Baudelaire's solidarity with the oppressed; see Agnes Krutwig Caers, "La vision du monde dans *Les petits poèmes en prose* de Baude-laire," *Revue de l'Institut de Sociologie* 46 (1973): 625–639.

31. See Richard Terdiman, *Discourse/Counter-Discourse: The Theory and Prac-tice of Symbolic Resistance in 19th-Century France* (Ithaca, N.Y.: Cornell Uni-versity Press, 1985), 315.

32. See especially the work of Dolf Oehler in *Pariser Bilder* (Frankfurt am Main: Suhrkamp, 1979); and *Ein Höllensturz der alten Welt* (Frankfurt am Main: Suhrkamp, 1988); and Wolfgang Fietkau, *Schwanengesang auf 1848* (Re-inbek: Rowohlt, 1978).

33. Baudelaire, "My Heart Laid Bare," 175. Here the translation of "*De la va-porisation et de la centralisation du Moi*" reads "The distillation and central-ization of the ego." The French "*vaporisation*," however, points to a kind of dispersal that is not caught by "distillation," which is too much like "cen-tralization" instead of its opposite.

34. On the relationship between metropolitan terror and childhood experi-ences in Rilke's novel, see my essay "Paris/Childhood" in *Twilight Memories*.

35. Ulrich Baer, *Remnant of Song: Trauma and the Experience of Modernity in Charles Baudelaire and Paul Celan* (Stanford, Calif.: Stanford University Press, 2000).

36. The French text with its phrasing of "*épouser la foule*" clearly suggest an erotic sexual relationship.

37. Georges Blin, *Le sadisme de Baudelaire* (Paris: J. Corti, 1948), 143, 176.

CHAPTER 2   *Kafka's* Betrachtung *in the Force Field of Photography and Film*

1. Diary entries for May 6, 1912, and September 11, 1912, in Franz Kafka, *Tagebücher, Kritische Ausgabe* (Frankfurt am Main: Fischer Verlag, 2002), 419 and 436. Translated as *The Diaries of Franz Kafka*, vol. 1, *1910–1913*, ed. Max Brod, trans. Joseph Kresh (New York: Schocken Books, 1965).

2. Kafka to Oskar Pollak, December 20, 1902, in Franz Kafka, *Briefe 1900–1912. Kritische Ausgabe. Schriften, Tagebücher, Briefe*, ed. Hans-Gerd Koch (Frankfurt am Main: Fischer, 1999), 17. Translation in Franz Kafka, *Let-ters to Friends, Family, and Editors*, trans. Richard Winston and Clara Win-ston (New York: Schocken, 1977), 5.

3. See Veronika Tuckerova, "Reading Kafka in Prague: The Reception of Franz Kafka between the East and the West during the Cold War" (PhD diss., Columbia University, 2012), esp. Chapter 1, "Translator's Visibility: Pavel Eisner's Translation of *The Trial*."

4. It is the great merit of Mark M. Anderson's *Kafka's Clothes* (Oxford: Oxford University Press, 1992) to have located Kafka on the French-German cultural axis linking him to Baudelaire and Huysmans, Rilke and Benjamin and to have brought into view the early Kafka's relationship to ornament and aestheticism as a key concern of his early writing. While this is no doubt true, I will gently disagree with Anderson's reading of Kafka's first book publication, *Betrachtung*, as a predominantly aestheticist text invested in impressionist prose poetry. Relying on Anderson's overall argument about Kafka's shift away from turn-of-the-century aestheticism, however, I would suggest that Kafka already overcomes aestheticist tendencies with the miniatures of *Betrachtung*, moving toward an anti-ornamental, streamlined, cold modernism. Anderson himself observes that this anti-aestheticist and anti-ornamental shift in Kafka's writing happens between 1907 and 1910, when many of the miniatures were written (p. 8 of his study). And when Kafka later rewrites Octave Mirbeau in *The Penal Colony*, his "source" will be completely transformed.

5. Walter Benjamin, "On Some Motifs in Baudelaire," in *Selected Writings*, vol. 4, *1938–1940*, ed. Howard Eiland and Michael W. Jennings (Cambridge, Mass.: Harvard University Press, 2003), 323, 321.

6. Quoted after Hartmut Binder, *Kafka in neuer Sicht* (Stuttgart: Metzler, 1976), 105, my translation. Binder elaborates extensively on the importance of the circle in Kafka's imagination.

7. Max Brod, ed., *The Diaries of Franz Kafka 1914–1923* (New York: Schocken, 1949), 208-209.

8. In several books about Kafka and Prague one looks in vain for a contribution that would focus on Kafka's urban imaginary as it manifests itself in his texts. The most recent example is Peter Becher, Steffen Höhne, and Marek Nekula, eds., *Kafka und Prag: Literatur-, kultur-, sozial- und sprachhistorische Kontexte* (Cologne: Böhlau, 2012).

9. Walter Benjamin, "Conversations with Brecht," in Theodor Adorno, Walter Benjamin, Ernst Bloch, Bertolt Brecht, and Georg Lukács, *Aesthetics and Politics* (London: Verso, 1977), 90–91.

10. It remains surprising that the many current Kafka handbooks lack a dedicated article on Kafka and urban space.

11. Benno Wagner's work on Kafka's official writings has shown how during his student days, Kafka came in touch with Heinrich Rauchberg's work on statistics and Alphonse Quételet's sociological notion of the "average man." See Stanley Corngold and Benno Wagner, *Franz Kafka: The Ghosts in the Machine* (Evanston, Ill.: Northwestern University Press, 2011), 18–20, 41–42.

12. For details, see Gerhard Kurz, "Lichtblicke in eine unendliche Verwirrung: Zu Kafka's 'Betrachtung,'" in *Franz Kafka*, ed. Heinz Ludwig Arnold (Munich: Text und Kritik, 1994), 49–65; Manfred Engel, "*Betrachtung*," in *Kafka*

Handbuch: Leben—Werk—Wirkung, ed. Manfred Engel and Bernd Auerochs (Stuttgart: Metzler, 2010), 111–126. Engel also provides a detailed
bibliography.

13. A good reception history is given in Sophie von Glinski, *Imaginationsproz-
esse: Verfahren phantastischen Erzählens in Kafkas Frühwerk* (Berlin: De
Gruyter, 2004), 1–25. Recent readings of *Betrachtung* include Hans Jürgen
Scheuer, Justus von Hartlieb, Christian Salmen, and Georg Höfner, eds.,
Kafkas Betrachtung: *Lektüren* (Frankfurt am Main: Peter Lang, 2003) and,
in the broader context of short prose around 1900, Manfred Engel and
Ritchie Robertson, eds., *Kafka und die kleine Prosa der Moderne/Kafka and
Short Modernist Prose* (Würzburg: Königshausen und Neumann, 2010).

14. One major exception being Mark M. Anderson in *Kafka's Clothes*, which
has inspired my attempt to read *Betrachtung* as city literature.

15. "*Grosse künstlerische Herrschaft über sich*," in Robert Musil, "Literarische
Chronik. August 1914," *Gesammelte Werke*, 9 (Rowohlt: Reinbek, 1978),
1468.

16. On the relationship of Kafka's short prose to that body of literature, see
the two introductory articles by Dirk Göttsche and Rüdiger Zymner in
Manfred Engel and Ritchie Robertson, eds., *Kafka und die kleine Prosa der
Moderne/Kafka and Short Modernist Prose* (Würzburg: Königshausen &
Neumann, 2010).

17. Benno Wagner, editor of Kafka's *Amtliche Schriften*, has analyzed the impact on Kafka's writing of other communication technologies, such as Hermann Hollerith's tabulating machine, which facilitated new forms of data
processing and statistics. He has also argued that Kafka in all likelihood
was familiar from his university days with Adolphe Quételet's statistical
concept of "the average man." Anonymity and depersonalization in Kafka
are always overdetermined. Wagner writes persuasively: "Given his poetic
powers, Kafka can bathe the construct of the average man in something
different from an expectable humanistic pathos, a lament for lost personality." Stanley Corngold and Benno Wagner, *Franz Kafka: The Ghost in the
Machine* (Evanston: Northwestern University Press, 2011), 31-32; see 19 for
Quételet.

18. I will not take up here the often rather tedious scholarly debate about the
genres of the aphorism, the parable, the paradox, and other short forms, a
debate that marshals extensive historical knowledge but in the end misses
the specific historicity of Kafka's writing practice. Just as Kafka never developed a theory of visual media, he was felicitously insouciant regarding
definitions of literary genres.

19. I owe much insight to Carolin Duttlinger's seminal work on the relation
of film to photography in Kafka's works. My own contribution in reading
Betrachtung consists of linking this media aspect more closely to the urban
theme and thus to the development of the metropolitan miniature more
generally. Carolin Duttlinger, *Kafka and Photography* (Oxford: Oxford University Press, 2007). Also important is the earlier pioneering work by Hanns
Zischler, *Kafka geht ins Kino* (Reinbek: Rowohlt, 1996), translated as *Kafka
Goes to the Movies* (Chicago: University of Chicago Press, 2003); and Peter

André Alt, *Kafka und der Film: Über kinematographisches Erzählen* (Munich: Beck, 2009). Only Duttlinger, though, makes the relationship between film and photography central to her analysis. See also Duttlinger, "Film und Fotografie," in *Kafka Handbuch: Leben, Werk, Wirkung*, ed. Manfred Engel and Bernd Auerochs (Stuttgart: Metzler, 2010), 72–79.

20. On the presence of nonliterary media in Kafka's narratives, see, for instance, Stanley Corngold, "Medial Interventions in *The Trial*," in Corngold, *Lambent Traces: Franz Kafka* (Princeton, N.J.: Princeton University Press, 2004), 51–66.

21. My focus on the importance of the visual in Kafka's urban texts is not to deny the equally great interest he took in the aural dimension of city life. See for instance the diary entry of November 5, 1911, also published under the title "Grosser Lärm" in 1912 in Willy Haas's *Herderblätter*. On the intense debate about urban noise around 1900 and its reflection in Kafka's *Trial* and "The Burrow," see Tyler Whitney, "Spaces of the Ear: Literature, Media, and the Science of Sound, 1886–1928" (PhD diss., Columbia University, 2012).

22. The close and competitive relationship between literature and film in the early twentieth century was first discussed by Anton Kaes in his incisive introduction to his edited volume *Kino-Debatte: Texte zum Verhältnis von Literatur und Film 1909–1929* (Tübingen: Max Niemeyer, 1978), 1–35.

23. Alt and Duttlinger discuss these three early critics' insights in some detail.

24. Walter Benjamin, "Franz Kafka," in *Selected Writings*, vol. 2, part 2, *1931–1934*, ed. Michael W. Jennings, Gary Smith, and Howard Eiland (Cambridge, Mass.: Harvard University Press, 1999), 814.

25. Walter Benjamin, "Little History of Photography," in ibid., 507–530. See also Miriam Hansen, *Cinema and Experience* (Berkeley: University of California Press, 2012), 129.

26. Theodor Adorno to Benjamin, December 17, 1934, in Theodor Adorno and Walter Benjamin, *The Complete Correspondence 1928–1940*, ed. Henri Lonitz, trans. Nicholas Walker (Cambridge, Mass.: Harvard University Press, 1999), 70 (my modification of the translation of *"die letzten verschwindenden Verbindungstexte zum stummen Film"*) and 66.

27. See the analysis of the different dimensions of *Verkehr* in Anderson, *Kafka's Clothes*, esp. chapter 1.

28. *The Diaries of Franz Kafka 1910–1923*, ed. Max Brod, trans. Joseph Kresh and Martin Greenberg (London: Minerva, 1992), 9.

29. See Tom Gunning, "An Aesthetic of Astonishment: Early Film and the (In)credulous Spectator," *Art and Text* 34 (Fall 1989), reprinted in *Film Theory and Criticism*, ed. Leo Braudy and Marshall Cohen (Oxford: Oxford University Press, 2004).

30. The jointly written text was published in the journal *Herderblätter* in June 1912.

31. This is the way the film's plot is rendered in the text. Duttlinger has shown that this plot summary is based on a misremembering or a retrospective rewriting of the film. Carolin Duttlinger, "Film und Fotografie," in *Kafka*

Handbuch: Leben, Werk, Wirkung, ed. Manfred Engel and Bernd Auerochs (Stuttgart: Metzler, 2010), 72.

32. "Erstes Kapitel des Buches 'Richard und Samuel' von Max Brod und Franz Kafka," in Franz Kafka, *Kritische Ausgabe. Drucke zu Lebzeiten*, ed. Wolf Kittler, Hans-Gerd Koch, and Gerhard Neumann (Frankfurt am Main: Fischer Verlag, 2002), 429, my translation.

33. Gustav Janouch, *Conversations with Kafka*, trans. Goronwy Rees (New York: New Directions, 1971), 31. All further page numbers given in parenthesis in the text.

34. K. Eder and Alexander Kluge, *Ulmer Dramaturgien, Reibungsverluste* (Munich: Hanser, 1980), 48. Miriam Hansen cites Kluge's insightful quip, giving the broader context in her *Cinema and Experience* (Berkeley: University of California Press, 2012), xviii.

35. Kafka, *Diaries*, 430.

36. Theodor W. Adorno, *Prisms*, trans. Shierry Nicholsen Weber and Samuel Weber (Cambridge, Mass.: MIT Press, 1981), 246.

37. Adorno, *Prisms*, 246.

38. See Jonathan Crary, *Suspensions of Perception: Attention, Spectacle, and Modern Culture* (Cambridge, Mass.: MIT Press, 1999). On the related question of fatigue and the body in labor, see Anson Rabinbach, *The Human Motor: Energy, Fatigue, and the Origins of Modernity* (New York: Basic Books, 1990). For a systematic sociological analysis of processes of acceleration and their effect on changing structures of temporal experience, see Hartmut Rosa, *Beschleunigung: Die Veränderung der Zeitstrukturen in der Moderne* (Frankfurt am Main: Suhrkamp, 2005).

39. Max Brod, "Nachwort," in Franz Kafka, *Beschreibung eines Kampfes. Die zwei Fassungen. Parallelausgabe nach den Handschriften* (Frankfurt am Main: Fischer, 1969), 148-159.

40. See especially Tom Gunning, "The Cinema of Attraction: Early Film, Its Spectator, and the Avant-Garde," in *Film and Theory: An Anthology*, ed. Robert Stam and Toby Miller (Oxford: Blackwell, 2000), 229–235.

41. Kafka, *Diaries*, 238.

42. Kafka to Felice Bauer, January 3/4, 1913, in *Letters to Felice*, ed. Erich Heller and Jürgen Born, trans. James Stern and Elisabeth Duckworth (London: Secker and Warburg, 1974), 140, my italics.

43. Franz Kafka, *Drucke zu Lebzeiten: Apparatband*, ed. Wolf Kittler, Hand-Gerd Koch, and Gerhard Neumann (Frankfurt am Main: Fischer, 196), 34, my translation.

44. Kafka to Felice Bauer, December 29/30, 1912, in Kafka, *Letters to Felice*, 132. In the original: *"Lichtblicke in eine unendliche Verwirrung hinein und man muss schon sehr nahe herantreten, um etwas zu sehen"*; Kafka, *Briefe an Felice*, 218.

45. Franz Kafka, *The Complete Stories*, ed. Nahum N. Glatzer with a new foreword by John Updike (New York: Schocken, 1983), 388. Further page references in parenthesis in the text.

46. I owe this observation to Anderson's reading in *Kafka's Clothes*.

47. Siegfried Kracauer, "Photography," in *The Mass Ornament* (Cambridge, Mass.: Harvard University Press, 1995), 55. Fashion is key to what Klaus Scherpe has called Kafka's poetics of description in "Kafkas Poetik der Beschreibung," in *Kontinent Kafka*, ed. Klaus R. Scherpe and Elisabeth Wagner (Berlin: Vorwerk 8, 2006), 88–103.

48. Here the word *"Unglück"* links this miniature both to "The Bachelor's Ill Luck" ("Das Unglück des Junggesellen") and "Unhappiness" ("Unglücklichsein"), a linguistic linkage lost in translation.

49. See Stefan Andriopoulos, *Possessed: Hypnotic Crimes, Corporate Fiction and the Invention of Cinema*, trans. Peter Jansen and Stefan Andriopoulos (Chicago: University of Chicago Press, 2008).

50. Hal Foster, "Armor Fou," *October* 56 (Spring 1991): 85. Foster's Theweleit-inspired analysis mainly focuses on Max Ernst and Hans Bellmer, but Jünger becomes an important reference in the argument.

51. It is only one of the several pairings in this text. Pairings appear frequently in Kafka, both in textual form, as here, and in content, as with the two assistants in *The Castle*, the two agents who arrest Josef K in *The Trial* and the two others who kill him, the two celluloid balls in the *Blumfeld* fragment, and so forth. Such doublings, whether in content or in form, always challenge singular identity.

52. The translation in *Complete Stories* has "final peace of the graveyard" which loses the dimension of *Ruhe* as repose or stillness. *"Ruhe"* in its pairing with *"Unruhe"* is of course a key word in relation to *Betrachtung* and the media problematic.

53. Unless one sees heightened irony in the German reference to *"gehen"* in the last sentence: *"um nachzusehen, wie es ihm* geht" (my emphasis). The English translation "how he is getting on" tries to capture the double German meaning but is not very convincing. Only the German original has the kind of literalness that is in conflict with the basic meaning of this impersonal usage of *"gehen."*

54. Anderson, *Kafka's Clothes*, 32.

55. On animation and things in Kafka, see Brook Henkel, "Animistic Fictions: German Modernism, Film, and the Animation of Things" (PhD diss., Columbia University, 2013).

CHAPTER 3   *Benn in Occupied Brussels: The Rönne Novellas*

1. See Helmut Lethen, *Der Sound der Väter: Gottfried Benn und seine Zeit* (Reinbek: Rowohlt, 2006), 21.

2. Recent exceptions are Marcus Hahn, "Assoziation und Autorschaft: Gottfried Benns Rönne- und Pameelen-Texte und die Psychologien Theodor Ziehens und Semi Meyers," *Deutsche Vierteljahrsschrift* 80, no. 2 (2006): 245–316. Hahn's work is the first to locate Benn's texts rigorously in their constitutive relationship to scientific discourse of the times, thus enabling a new literary reading. Apart from Lethen's book (see note 1), it is arguably the most important contribution to Benn research of recent

years. See also Thomas Pauler, *Schönheit und Abstraktion: Über Gottfried Benns "absolute Prosa"* (Könighausen und Neumann: Würzburg, 1992). On the hermeticism of modernist short prose more generally, see especially Moritz Bassler, *Die Entdeckung der Textur: Unverständlichkeit in der Kurzprosa der emphatischen Moderne 1910–1916* (Tübingen: Niemeyer, 1994).

3. Unless otherwise noted, all translations from Benn's works are by Mark M. Anderson with the exception of the quotes from the fourth miniature, *The Birthday*, the only one that has been translated into English. Page numbers preceded by *P&A* refer to the German version of Benn, *Prosa und Autobiographie in der Fassung der Erstdrucke*, ed. Bruno Hillebrand (Frankfurt am Main: Fischer, 1984). Quotes from other volumes will be separately footnoted.

4. Gottfried Benn, "Wie Miss Cavell erschossen wurde," in Benn, *Essays und Reden in der Fassung der Erstdrucke*, ed. Bruno Hillebrand (Frankfurt am Main: Fischer, 1989), 65-66.

5. Ibid., 66.

6. Gottfried Benn, *Doppelleben* (1949) in Benn, *Prosa und Autobiographie*, 355–480. A good summary of the different positions regarding Benn's 1933–1934 commitment to the Nazi state is found in Lethen, *Der Sound der Väter*, 166–180. It is interesting to note that it was Benn's pro-Nazi stance that ultimately triggered the famous and influential debate of the later 1930s about expressionism and modernism, documented in Theodor Adorno, Walter Benjamin, Ernst Bloch, Bertolt Brecht, and Georg Lukács, *Aesthetics and Politics* (London: Verso, 1977).

7. Lethen, *Der Sound der Väter*, 16, 27.

8. In *Doppelleben* (1949), Benn himself spoke more appropriately of "absolute prose," which he saw prefigured in Flaubert, Carl Einstein, and certain works by André Gide. In Benn, *Prosa und Autobiographie*, 446.

9. I will only cursorily refer to this fifth miniature in my discussion, not just because Benn himself considered it inadequate but because it doesn't add anything to my theme of urban perceptions.

10. "Unheard-of event" (*"unerhörte Begebenheit"*) was part of Goethe's definition of the novella that became key for defining the genre.

11. For this view, see Will Müller-Jensen, "Gottfried Benns Rönnefigur und Autopsychotherapie," in *Gottfried Benns absolute Prosa und seine Deutung des "Phänotyps dieser Stunde": Anmerkungen zu seinem 110. Geburtstag*, ed. Wolfgang H. Zangemeister, Will Müller-Jensen, and Jürgen Zippel (Würzburg: Königshausen und Neumann, 1999), 89–94.

12. *"Seine wilden und grossen Anfänge"*; Theodor W. Adorno to Peter Rühmkorf, February 13, 1964, in Rühmkorf, *Die Jahre, die ihr kennt*, ed. Wolfgang Rasch (Reinbek: Rowohlt, 1999), 153.

13. On the debates with the Weimar left and later the exiles, see especially Joachim Dyck, *Der Zeitzeuge: Gottfried Benn 1929–1949* (Göttingen: Wallstein, 2006); and the biography by Gunnar Decker, *Gottfried Benn: Genie und Barbar* (Berlin: Aufbau Verlag, 2006).

14. Benn, *Prosa und Autobiographie*, 490, my translation.

15. Hahn, "Assoziation und Autorschaft," 250.

16. Lethen, *Der Sound der Väter*, 62ff. Apart from Hahn's work, see Ursula Kirchdörffer-Bossmann, *"Eine Pranke in den Nacken der Erkenntnis": Zur Beziehung von Dichtung und Naturwissenschaft im Frühwerk Gottfried Benns* (St. Ingbert: Röhrig Universitätsverlag, 2003).

17. See Lethen, *Der Sound der Väter*, 61ff.; and Hahn, "Assoziation und Autorschaft," 251ff.

18. "Wie kommt sein Wortschatz so ins Blühen?" in Gottfried Benn and Thea Sternheim, *Briefwechsel und Aufzeichnungen* (Göttingen: Wallstein, 2004), 7-8.

19. Benn to Dieter Wellershoff, November 22, 1950, in Gottfried Benn, *Ausgewählte Briefe* (Wiesbaden: Limes Verlag, 1957), 202.

20. Gotthart Wunberg, "Unverständlichkeit: Historismus und literarische Moderne," *Hofmannsthal Jahrbuch* 1 (Freiburg im Breisgau: Rombach, 1993), 309–350.

21. Analogously, the subsequent emergence of avant-gardist montage techniques in the work of Raul Hausmann and Hannah Höch has been linked persuasively to image practices of popular postcards and staged photographic practices of the Wilhelminian age and is therefore not as radically new as has often been claimed. See chapter 5 in this book.

22. See Pauler, *Schönheit und Abstraktion*, 63.

23. See Decker, *Gottfried Benn*, 63.

24. See Klaus Theweleit, *Male Fantasies*, vol. 2 (Minneapolis: University of Minnesota, 1989).

25. Famously, Lukács's misreading of Benn's poem *Songs*, which begins with the notorious lines "O that we were our primal ancestors / Small lumps of plasma in hot, sultry swamps." Georg Lukács, "The Ideology of Modernism," in *Realism in Our Time: Literature and the Class Struggle* (New York: Harper & Row, 1964), 32.

26. Gottfried Benn, *Briefe*, vol. 1, *Briefe an Oelze, 1932–1945*, ed. Harald Steinhagen and Jürgen Schröder (Stuttgart: Klett Cotta, 1977), 311. See also Pauler, *Schönheit und Abstraktion*, 79.

27. All quotes from "The Birthday" are taken from *Primal Vision: Selected Writings of Gottfried Benn*, ed. E. B. Ashton (London: Marion Boyers, 1976). This first quote from *Primal Vision*, 3. *The Birthday* seems to be the only Rönne text ever to be translated into English.

28. Gottfried Benn, *Briefe an F. W. Oelze 1932–1945*, ed. Harald Steinhagen and Jürgen Schröder (Wiesbaden: Limes Verlag, 1977), 237-238, my translation.

29. See Marcus Hahn's detailed discussions of these links. Hahn, "Assoziation und Autorschaft," see note 2.

30. Bruno Hillebrand, ed., *Über Gottfried Benn: Kritische Stimmen 1912–1956* (Frankfurt am Main: Fischer Verlag, 1987), my translation.

31. Gottfried Benn, "Epilog und Lyrisches Ich," in Benn, *Prosa und Autobiographie*, 271.

32. See Gottfried Benn, "Gespräch," in Benn, *Szenen und Schriften in der Fassung der Erstdrucke*, ed. Bruno Hillebrand (Frankfurt am Main: Fischer

Verlag, 1990), 19. See also Rainer Maria Rilke, *Rodin*, trans. Jessie Lemont and Hans Trausil (London: The Grey Walls Press, 1946).

CHAPTER 4 *Photography and Emblem in Kracauer and Benjamin's Street Texts*

1. Thus, Philippe Despoix reads Kracauer's miniatures exclusively in relation to film in "Zwischen urbaner Ethnographie und Heuristik des Films: Kracauers kinematographischer Blick auf die Stadt," in *Kracauer's Blick: Anstösse zu einer Ethnographie des Städtischen*, ed. Christine Holste (Hamburg: EVA/Philo, 2006), 63–80. Graeme Gilloch reads Kracauer's street texts similarly as fundamentally cinematic texts in his forthcoming *Siegfried Kracauer: Our Companion in Misfortune* (London: Polity Press, 2015). Miriam Hansen, on the other hand, has convincingly argued that "Kracauer does not posit the relationship between photography and film in evolutionary terms, but seeks to articulate an aesthetic of film in the interstices of the two media." Miriam Bratu Hansen, *Cinema and Experience: Siegfried Kracauer, Walter Benjamin, and Theodor W. Adorno* (Berkeley: University of California Press, 2011), 37–38. This is the approach that guides my reading of Kracauer's literary miniatures. The shortness of the miniature and the frequent focus on claustrophobic spaces approximates it to the photograph more so than to the cinematic motion of metropolitan street life.
2. For several pertinent quotations from the letters to Scholem, see Burkhardt Lindner, ed., *Benjamin Handbuch* (Stuttgart: Metzler, 2006), 363. On *One-Way Street* as a book of aphorisms, a view I do not share, see Friedemann Spicker, "Benjamins *Einbahnstrasse* im Kontext des zeitgenössischen Aphorismus," in *Benjamin Studien 2*, ed. Daniel Weidner and Sigrid Weigel (Munich: Wilhelm Fink Verlag, 2011), 273–294.
3. Theodor W. Adorno, "Benjamin's *Einbahnstrasse*," in *Notes to Literature*, vol. 2 (New York: Columbia University Press, 1992), 322.
4. Ibid., 323.
5. Siegfried Kracauer, *Strassen in Berlin und anderswo* (Berlin: Das Arsenal, 1987), 52.
6. "*Bildlichkeit*" does not have a good English equivalent. It refers to the visual dimension of phenomena that are not pictures, such as the visual dimension of script. As used by Benjamin, it is translated as 'figurativeness' in "Attested Auditor of Books," one of the miniatures of *One-Way Street*. The literal and technical translation of the German term "*Schriftbild*" is typeface. In the broader sense used here, the term refers to the fact that all script, in contrast to spoken language, first appears as image. Implied here is the notion of the hieroglyph.
7. Siegfried Kracauer, "On the Writings of Walter Benjamin," in *The Mass Ornament: Weimar Essays* (Cambridge and London: Harvard University Press, 1995), 259–264.
8. Ibid., 260.
9. Ibid., 263–264.

10. Bruno Reifenberg, "Gewissenhaft," *Frankfurter Zeitung*, July 1, 1929, my translation.

11. Siegfried Kracauer, *The Salaried Masses: Duty and Distraction in Weimar Germany*, trans. Quintin Hoare, intro. Inka Mülder-Bach (London: Verso, 1998), 32. The German subtitle is actually different with an ethnographic bent: From the Newest Germany.

12. Bruno Reifenberg, "Gewissenhaft," *Frankfurter Zeitung*, July 1, 1929. Quoted in Helmut Stalder, *Siegfried Kracauer: Das journalistische Werk in der <Frankfurter Zeitung> 1921–1933* (Würzburg: Königshausen und Neumann, 2003), 100.

13. Both quotes in Michael Bienert, *Joseph Roth in Berlin: Ein Lesebuch für Spaziergänger* (Cologne: Kiepenheuer und Witsch, 1997), 1415, my translation. Bienert gives no source.

14. I cite titles in German only when they have not been translated.

15. Kracauer, *Strassen in Berlin und anderswo*, 52. Note the suggestive closeness in German of *"Raumbild"* and *"Traumbild,"* which couples space and dream by the difference of just one letter.

16. See especially Inka Mülder-Bach, *Siegfried Kracauer: Grenzgänger zwischen Theorie und Literatur. Seine frühen Schriften 1913–1933* (Stuttgart: J. B. Metzler, 1985).

17. Siegfried Kracauer, "Exposé zur Reorganisation der *Neuen Rundschau*," July 18, 1928, Marbacher Nachlass, KN/DLA 3. Quoted in Dirk Oschmann, *Auszug aus der Innerlichkeit* (Heidelberg: Winter, 1999), 194.

18. Siegfried Kracauer, "Photography," in *The Mass Ornament*, 62.

19. Ibid., 61.The most incisive reading of this puzzling statement is found in Miriam Hansen, *Cinema and Experience* (Berkeley: University of California Press, 2011), 27–39.

20. On Kracauer and Benjamin's theories of photography in relation to memory and modernity see Jan Gerstner, *Das andere Gedächtnis: Fotografie in der Literatur des 20. Jahrhunderts* (Bilefeld: transcript Verlag, 2013), esp. 73–108, 143–198. On Benjamin, see especially Eduardo Cadava, *Words of Light: Theses on the Photography of History* (Princeton, N.J.: Princeton University Press, 1997).

21. See for instance Hermann Vogel, *Die chemischen Wirkungen des Lichts und die Photographie in ihrer Anwendung in Kunst, Wissenschaft und Industrie* (Leipzig: F.A. Brockhaus, 1884) 125.

22. Roland Barthes, *Camera Lucida* (New York: Farrar, 1981), 27.

23. Maurice Merleau-Ponty, *Das Auge und der Geist* (Reinbek: Rowohlt, 1967) 39.

24. Kracauer, "Aus dem Fenster gesehen," in *Strassen in Berlin und anderswo*, 41, my translation.

25. Ibid., 40, my translation.

26. Kracauer, "Photography," 61.

27. Ibid., 61–62.

28. Sigfried Giedion, *Bauen in Frankreich, Eisen, Eisenbeton* (Leipzig: Klinkhardt und Biermann, 1928), translated as *Building in France, Building in Iron,*

Building in Ferroconcrete (Santa Monica, Calif.: Getty Center for the History of Art and the Humanities, 1995).

29. Hilde Heynen, *Architecture and Modernity* (Cambridge, Mass.: MIT Press, 1999), 35.

30. Siegfried Giedion, *Building in France, Building in Iron, Building in Ferro-Concrete*, trans. J. Duncan Berry (Santa Monica: Getty Center for the History of Art and the Humanities, 1995), 90.

31. For much more on the concept of *Durchdringung* in the historical avant-garde in Italian futurism, Kafka, Le Corbusier, Benjamin, Joyce, Musil, and Giedion, see the brilliant book by Heinz Brüggemann, *Architekturen des Augenblicks: Raum-Bilder und Bild-Räume einer urbanen Moderne in Literatur, Kunst und Architektur des 20. Jahrhunderts* (Hannover: Offizin, 2002).

32. Siegfried Kracauer, *Strassen in Berlin und anderswo*, 40, my translation.

33. Ibid., 33, my translation. All further translations from this miniature are given with page number in the main text.

34. Kracauer, *The Mass Ornament*, 38–39. All further quotes given with page numbers in the text. The following reading of Kracauer's miniature owes much to Heinz Brüggemann's book *Das andere Fenster: Einblicke in Häuser und Menschen* (Frankfurt am Main: Fischer Verlag, 1989).

35. It is interesting to note that as of this writing, the old harborfront below the legendary Canebière is undergoing an urban renewal project ambitiously named Marseille-Euroméditerranée.

36. Walter Benjamin, *Briefe an Siegfried Kracauer* (Marbach: Deutsche Schillergesellschaft, 1987), 33, 44, my translation.

37. Siegfried Kracauer, *Das Ornament der Masse* (Frankfurt am Main: Suhrkamp, 1977), 12.

38. Franz Kafka, *Hochzeitsvorbereitungen auf dem Lande* (Frankfurt am Main: Fischer Verlag, 1966), 94. Of course, Kracauer could not have known this aphorism, which had not yet been published at the time.

39. Kracauer, *The Mass Ornament*, 38. All further page references in the text.

40. Anthony Vidler, "Agoraphobia: Spatial Estrangement in Simmel and Kracauer," *New German Critique* 54 (Fall 1991): 31–45. Volume 54 of *New German Critique* is a special issue on Siegfried Kracauer.

41. In *Siegfried Kracauer: Our Companion in Misfortune* (London: Polity Press, 2015), Graeme Gilloch draws attention to Kracauer's novel *Ginster*, which links automation to the effects of military discipline on the human body. Taylorized production, the entertainment industry, and the military regime of World War I thus converge in Kracauer's urban imaginary. In a very different constellation, war and metropolis will also converge in the work of Ernst Jünger; see my analysis in chapter 7 in this volume.

42. Kracauer, *Strassen in Berlin und anderswo*, 8. Further page references in text. Translations from this title are mine.

43. On the notion of *Strassenrausch* and the feuilleton, see Eckart Köhn, *Strassenrausch: Flanerie und kleine Form Versuch zur Literturgeschichte des Flaneurs bis 1933* (Berlin: Das Arsenal, 1989).

44. For a more extended discussion of the Freud-Hofmannsthal connection, see Andreas Huyssen, "The Disturbance of Vision in Vienna Modernism," *Modernism/Modernity* 5, no. 3 (1998): 33–48.

45. Franz Kafka, *The Diaries of Franz Kafka* (New York: Schocken Books, 1965), 291, translation modified.

46. Ernst Bloch, *Erbschaft dieser Zeit* (Frankfurt am Main: Suhrkamp, 1973), 212.

47. "Schreie auf der Strasse" and "Strasse ohne Erinnerung," in Kracauer, *Strassen in Berlin und anderswo*, 21–23 and 15–18.

48. Kracauer, *Schriften*, Band 5, Teil 2, *Aufsätze 1927–1931*, ed. Inka Mülder-Bach (Frankfurt am Main: Suhrkamp, 1990), 25. Here and in the following quotes, my translations.

49. Ibid., 26.

50. The very same contrast between Paris and Berlin, France and Germany also serves Benjamin as *point de départ* for his surrealism essay of that same time.

51. Kracauer, *The Mass Ornament*, 332.

52. Kracauer, *Schriften* 5, part 2, 19.

53. Kracauer, "Dielinterführung," *Strassen in Berlin und anderswo*, 38–39.

54. Kracauer, *Schriften*, Band 5, Teil 3, *Aufsätze 1932–1965*, ed. Inka Mülder-Bach (Frankfurt am Main: Suhrkamp, 1990), 211.

55. Bernd Witte, *Walter Benjamin: An Intellectual Biography* (Detroit, Mich.: Wayne State University Press, 1991), 92. Gerhard Richter describes *One-Way Street* as "lyrical-philosophical snapshots that are brought into a constellation by the montage technique." Gerhard Richter, "A Matter of Distance: Benjamin's *One-Way Street* through *The Arcades*," in *Walter Benjamin and The Arcades Project*, ed. Beatrice Hanssen (London: Continuum, 2006), 141. See also Richter's *Thought Images: Frankfurt School Writers' Reflections from Damaged Life* (Stanford, Calif.: Stanford University Press, 2007). On the reciprocal closeness between Benjamin and Kracauer's writing in the late 1920s, which Miriam Hansen has done so much to bring into focus, see most recently Michael Jennings, "Walter Benjamin, Siegfried Kracauer, and Weimar Criticism," in *Weimar Thought: A Contested Legacy*, ed. Peter E. Gordon and John P. McCormick (Princeton, N.J.: Princeton University Press, 2013), 203–219.

56. Ernst Bloch, "Erinnerungen," in *Über Walter Benjamin* (Frankfurt am Main: Suhrkamp, 1968), 17.

57. *Denkbild* is indeed the German term for emblem. But Benjamin himself did not use the term until later and never in relationship to the miniatures of *One-Way Street*. His later *Denkbilder* collection contains texts of a very different nature.

58. Walter Benjamin, *The Origin of Tragic German Drama* (London: NLB, 1977), 178.

59. See Detlev Schöttker, *Konstruktiver Fragmentarismus* (Frankfurt am Main: Suhrkamp, 1999).

60. Heinz Schlaffer, "Denkbilder. Eine kleine Prosaform zwischen Dichtung und Gesellschaftstheorie," in *Poesie und Politik*, ed. Wolfgang Kuttenkeuler

(Stuttgart, Berlin, Köln, Mainz: W. Kohlhammer, 1973), 137–154. More recently, Gérard Raulet spoke only of *inscriptio* as script and *pictura* as image in the metaphoric sense, remaining oblivious to the dimension of *subscriptio* and to any real visual dimension of the emblem. Gérard Raulet, "Einbahn-strasse," in Lindner, *Benjamin Handbuch*, 365–366.

61. Walter Benjamin, "Denkbilder," in *Gesammelte Schriften*, Band 4, Teil 1 (Frankfurt am Main: Suhrkamp, 1972), 305–438.

62. List and texts are published in the recent critical edition of Walter Ben-jamin, *Einbahnstrasse*, ed. Detlev Schöttker (Frankfurt am Main: Suhrkamp, 2009), 79–128. The *Gesammelte Werke*, Band 4, Teil 2, 911ff. contains the list but not the texts themselves.

63. Franz Hessel, "Von der schwierigen Kunst spazieren zu gehen," in *Er-munterung zum Genuss: Kleine Prosa* (Berlin: Brinkmann und Bose, 1981), 53–61.

64. The incongruity between titles and texts has been emphasized in the schol-arship, most recently by Patrizia McBride, who, in a wonderful metaphor, suggests that the shifting moods and patterns across the work's textual fabric are "unable to fill in all the potholes that make the ride down its street so jerky." She also offers several salient readings of specific minia-tures in their relationship to the constructivism of the 1920s. Patrizia Mc-Bride, "*Konstruktion als Bildung:* Refashioning the Human in German Con-structivism," *Germanic Review* 88, no. 3 (2013): 240.

65. Here I differ from Margaret Cohen's thesis that "proto-Chock" is the core of *One-Way Street.* Even as Benjamin describes the violence of social condi-tions, say in "Imperial Panorama," or the "paroxysms of genuine cosmic experience" in "To the Planetarium," his language is that of a commentator, not that of a subject experiencing street shock. Cohen's reading, however, is invaluable in that it shows in detail how Benjamin both adopts and rejects the surrealism of André Breton, a topic I will take up in the chapter about the presence of Aragon's surrealism in *Berlin Childhood around 1900.* Mar-garet Cohen, *Profane Illumination: Walter Benjamin and the Paris of Surrealist Revolution* (Berkeley: University of California Press, 1993), esp. 183–185.

66. Kracauer, "On the Writings of Walter Benjamin," 264.

67. Walter Benjamin, "One-Way Street," in *Selected Writings*, vol. 1, ed. Marcus Bullock and Michael W. Jennings (Cambridge, Mass.: Harvard Univer-sity Press, 1996), 466.

68. He only used a few images in his essays on children's books and on pho-tography, where they have a purely illustrative function.

69. Benjamin, *One-Way Street*, 444.

70. Ibid., 456.

71. Ibid., 444.

72. Ibid.

73. Walter Benjamin, "Little History of Photography," in *Selected Writings*, vol. 2, part 2 (Cambridge, Mass.: Harvard University Press, 1999), 527.

74. Walter Benjamin, "Letter from Paris (2)," in *Selected Writings*, vol. 3 (Cam-bridge, Mass.: Harvard University Press, 2002), 241.

75. Benjamin, *One-Way Street*, 104.

76. Ibid., 446.
77. Ibid., 444.
78. Ibid., 466.
79. Ibid., 478.
80. Ibid., 479.
81. Ibid.
82. Walter Benjamin to Gershom Gerhard Scholem, September 18, 1926," in *The Correspondence of Walter Benjamin, 1910–1940* (Chicago: University of Chicago Press, 1994).
83. Joseph Roth to Reifenberg, May 13, 1926, in catalog from *Ausstellung Deutsche Bibliothek* (Frankfurt am Main: Buchhändler Vereinigung, 1979), 116. Translation taken from Karsten Witte's unsurpassed essay on the types of Kracauer's literary reviews, " 'Light Sorrow': Siegfried Kracauer as Literary Critic," *New German Critique* 54 (Fall 1991): 77–94.

CHAPTER 5   *Double Exposure Berlin: Photomontage and Narrative in Höch and Keun*

1. See especially the recent work by Michael Cowan on the Querschnitt film: "Cutting through the Archive: *Querschnitt* Montage and Images of the World in Weimar Visual Culture," *New German Critique* 120 (Fall 2013): 1–40. See also Michael Cowan, "Advertising, Rhythm, and the Filmic Avant-Garde in Weimar," *October* 131 (Winter 2010): 23–50. On the novel, see Devin Fore, "Döblin's Epic Sense: Document and the Verbal World Picture," *New German Critique* 99 (Fall 2006): 171–208.
2. In her work on surrealist photography, Rosalind Krauss established the close relationship between the visual and writing in photomontage, an argument that was prefigured in Benjamin but not related there to surrealism. Rosalind Krauss, "The Photographic Condition of Surrealism," *October 19* (Winter 1981): 3–34.
3. See Klaus R. Scherpe, "The City as Narrator: The Modern Text in Alfred Döblin's *Berlin Alexanderplatz*," in *Modernity and the Text: Revisions of German Modernism*, ed. Andreas Huyssen and David Bathrick (New York: Columbia University Press, 1989), 162–179.
4. Quoted after Walter Benjamin, "Little History of Photography," *Selected Writings*, vol. 2, part 2, *1931–1934* (Cambridge, Mass.: Harvard University Press, 1999), 526.
5. On Heartfield's post-Dada political montages, Aragon, and the beginnings of socialist realism, see the chapter on Heartfield in Devin Fore, *Realism After Modernism: The Rehumanization of Art and Literature* (Cambridge, Mass.: MIT Press, 2012), 243–304, esp. 263.
6. Walter Benjamin, "Letter from Paris (2)," in *Selected Writings*, vol. 3, *1935–1938* (Cambridge, Mass.: Harvard University Press, 2002), 241.
7. See my discussion of Sasha Stone's photomontage in chapter 4.
8. On Höch's later work with the photo book and its relation to her political photomontages in the context of the Weimar debate about photography and photomontage, see Patrizia McBride, "Narrative Resemblance: The

Production of Truth in the Modernist Photobook of Weimar Germany," *New German Critique* 115 (Winter 2012): 169–198.

9. See Andrés Zervigón, *John Heartfield and the Agitated Image* (Chicago: University of Chicago Press, 2012), 12. Zervigón actually shows how Heartfield first turned to animation film as a result of his disgust with wartime photography; see especially his chapter 4.

10. Ibid.

11. Laszlo Moholy-Nagy, *Painting, Photography, Film* (Cambridge, Mass.: MIT Press, 1969), 29.

12. A more detailed comparison than I can offer here would be salutary, since it could highlight the *Durchdringung* of image and text, picture and words in the broader context of Weimar media culture. The role of montaged script in Höch's political photomontages, especially in *Cut with a Kitchen Knife*, has been amply analyzed.

13. Alice Rühle-Gerstel, "Back to the Good Old Days?" in *The Weimar Republic Sourcebook*, ed. Anton Kaes, Martin Jay, and Edward Dimendberg (Berkeley: University of California Press, 1994), 218–219.

14. Leah Dickerman, *Dada* (Washington: National Gallery of Art in association with D.A.P./Distributed Publishers, Inc., 2006), 90.

15. For readings of this work see Maud Lavin, *Cut with the Kitchen Knife: The Weimar Photomontages of Hannah Höch* (New Haven, Conn.: Yale University Press, 1993); Maria Makela, "The Misogynist Machine: Images of Technology in the Work of Hannah Höch," in *Women in the Metropolis: Gender and Modernity in Weimar Culture*, ed. Katharina von Ankum (Berkeley: University of California Press, 1997), 106–127; Matthew Biro, *The Dada Cyborg: Visions of the New Human in Weimar Berlin* (Minneapolis: University of Minnesota Press, 2009).

16. Lavin, *Cut with a Kitchen Knife*, 37.

17. The privileging of the dandy as male continued in work on urban culture by Simmel, Benjamin, Hessel, Marshall Berman, and Richard Sennett.

18. Janet Wolff, "The Invisible Flâneuse: Women and the Literature of Modernity," *Theory, Culture, and Society* 2, no. 3 (1985): 37–48; and Griselda Pollock, *Vision and Difference: Femininity, Feminism, and the Histories of Art* (New York: Routledge, 1988), esp. chapter 3.

19. For a superb critical take on this phenomenon of the New Woman, see Atina Grossman, "Girlkultur; or, Thoroughly Rationalized Female: A New Woman in Weimar Germany?" in *Women in Culture and Politics: A Century of Change*, ed. Judith Friedlander, Blanche Wiesen Cook, Alice Kessler-Harris, and Carroll Smith-Rosenberg (Bloomington: Indiana University Press, 1986), 62–80. On the New Woman in Weimar literature, see Kerstin Brandt, *Sentiment und Sachlichkeit: Der Roman der Neuen Frau in der Weimarer Republik* (Cologne: Böhlau Verlag, 2003).

20. See Gerd Kuhn, *Wohnkultur und kommunale Wohnungspolitik in Frankfurt am Main 1880–1930. Auf dem Wege zu einer pluralen Gesellschaft der Individuen* (Bonn: Dietz Verlag, 1998), 142–176.

21. Siegfried Kracauer, "The Mass Ornament," in *The Mass Ornament: Weimar Essays*, trans., ed., and intro. Thomas Y. Levin (Cambridge, Mass.: Harvard University Press, 1995). 76.

22. Identified in Biro, *The Dada Cyborg*, 215.
23. Here I disagree with Matthew Biro, who reads this hand as a female hand. Ibid., 217.
24. Katharina von Ankum, in her most welcome recent translation of the novel, renders "*Glanz*" as "star." But Doris never thinks she could be a real film star; she just wants to reproduce some of the glamour of the film world in her own everyday life.
25. Kracauer, "The Little Shop Girls Go to the Movies," in *The Mass Ornament*, 291–306.
26. In a later essay, "Mädchen im Beruf," Kracauer himself revised his condescending take on the little shop girls when he writes:" Indeed, the tension between the illusions generated by the films and reality has become so great that the majority of female employees will not be so easily enchanted." Kracauer, *Schriften*, Band 5, Teil 3, *Aufsätze (1932–1965)*, ed. Inka Mülder-Bach (Frankfurt am Main: Suhrkamp, 1990), 60, my translation. Even though Doris is not a girl with a job, she embodies that Weimar dialectic between enchantment and disenchantment, with disenchantment in the end winning the day.
27. Irmgard Keun, *The Artificial Silk Girl*, trans. Katharina von Ankum (New York: Other Press, 2002), 3. All further quotes by page number in text.
28. This is part of the "artificiality" of the artificial silk girl Klaus R. Scherpe has analyzed with great sympathy and insight in "Doris' gesammeltes Sehen: Irmgard Keuns kunstseidenes Mädchen unter den Städtebewohnern," in *Stadt. Krieg. Fremde: Literatur und Kultur nach den Katastrophen* (Tübingen: Francke Verlag, 2002), 37–48.
29. See Siegfried Kracauer, *The Salaried Masses: Duty and Distraction in Weimar Germany*, trans. Quinton Hoare, intro. Inka Mülder-Bach (London: Verso, 1998).
30. Kracauer, *The Salaried Masses*, 88. Indeed, the word "*Glanz*," referring in Keun to that which is not real but artificial silk or rayon, also occurs frequently in Kracauer's writing about Berlin's popular culture and its false appearances, sometimes translated as "splendor," other times as "glamour."
31. The most striking example is the passage where Doris describes herself as an equal to the artists and intellectuals who frequent the famous Romanisches Café: "*Da sassen wir als Künstler unter sich*" (67). The translation "We artists were hanging out together" (90) fails to render the fundamental discrepancy between "*wir*" and "*unter sich*" instead of "*unter uns*." So a literal translation would be: "We artists were sitting there among themselves." Clearly this would sound just wrong, not funny and grammatically distorted like the German.
32. Which is of course not Doris's case, since she doesn't have a job and is not married.
33. Simone de Beauvoir, *Das andere Geschlecht* (Reinbek: Rowohlt, 1968), 514. The passage did not make it into the English translation.
34. Irmgard Keun, "System des Männerfangs," *Der Querschnitt* (April 1932), reprinted in Irmgard Keun, *Das kunstseidene Mädchen*, ed. Stefanie Arend and Ariane Martin (Berlin: Claassen, 2005), 267–273.

CHAPTER 6   *Benjamin and Aragon: Le Paysan de Berlin*

1. Translated as "the marvelous suffusing everyday existence" in the English version of *Le Paysan*.

2. See the chapter on Kracauer and Benjamin. Josef Fürnkäs has best elaborated Benjamin's relationship to surrealism in *Surrealismus als Erkenntnis: Walter Benjamin—Einbahnstrasse und Pariser Passagen* (Stuttgart: Metzler, 1988). More recently, Detlev Schöttker, *Konstruktiver Fragmentarismus* (Frankfurt am Main: Suhrkamp, 1999) has underplayed surrealism's importance for Benjamin in order to make a case for Benjamin's constructivist tendencies in the 1920s and beyond. I see no reason not to acknowledge both as part of a fluid situation within the historical avant-garde, even as Benjamin was fully aware of certain differences between the two movements. The best study in English of Benjamin's relationship to surrealism still is Margaret Cohen's *Profane Illumination: Walter Benjamin and the Paris Surrealist Revolution* (Berkeley: University of California Press, 1993), but it focuses almost exclusively on Breton and has not much to say about Aragon at all; and while it reads *One-Way Street* in its ambivalent relationship to surrealism, it does not deal with *Berlin Childhood*.

3. Scholars have occasionally commented on the surrealist dimension of *Berlin Childhood*, but it has not been demonstrated in close reading; nor has it been contextualized properly in relation to Benjamin's very sparse comments on Aragon. In his magisterial yet sadly incomplete and posthumously published intellectual biography of Benjamin, Jean-Michel Palmier comes perhaps closest to acknowledging the link when he writes: "*Berlin Childhood* and *Paris Peasant* have many commonalities in ways of feeling and perceiving things." Jean-Michel Palmier, *Walter Benjamin: Lumpensammler, Engel und bucklicht Männlein. Ästhetik und Politik bei Walter Benjamin*, ed. Florent Perrier, trans. Horst Brühmann (Frankfurt am Main: Suhrkamp, 2009), 139, my translation. A chapter Palmier planned to include on Aragon and Benjamin was never written.

4. See Rolf Tiedemann, "Nachwort," in Walter Benjamin, *Berliner Kindheit um 1900. Giessener Fassung* (Frankfurt am Main: Suhrkamp, 2000). See also Anja Lemke's entry on *Berliner Kindheit um neunzehnhundert* in *Benjamin Handbuch: Leben—Werk—Wirkung*, in Burkhardt Lindner (Stuttgart: Metzler Verlag, 2006), 653–663.

5. Evidently Benjamin was still considering possibly including some other pieces that were appended to the 1938 manuscript but not listed in its table of contents. See Schöttker, *Konstruktiver Fragmentarismus*, 229ff. The English translation of the 1938 version is Walter Benjamin, *Berlin Childhood around 1900*, trans. Howard Eiland (Cambridge, Mass.: Harvard University Press, 2006). This is the version I will quote from unless otherwise indicated.

6. *Berlin Childhood* shares this tendency toward deindividuation in autobiography with Carl Einstein's then still unpublished second version of his *Bebuquin*. See Devin Fore, *Realism after Modernism: The Rehumanization of Art and Literature* (Cambridge, Mass.: MIT Press, 2012), 187–242. Deindi-

viduation was of course already a feature of Kafka's early miniatures, though not in the context of autobiography.

7. Walter Benjamin, *Berlin Chronicle*, in *Selected Writings*, vol. 2, part 2, *1931–1934*, trans. Rodney Livingstone and others (Cambridge, Mass.: Harvard University Press, 1999), 612.

8. Media issues, especially photography, are actually present in some of the miniatures deleted from the final version; the only instance left in the 1938 version is the miniature of the "Imperial Panorama." On the affinity between Benjamin's anti-autobiographical text to his anti-photographic treatment of images, especially in relationship to his "Doctrine of the Similar," see the wonderful essay on *Berlin Childhood* in Linda Haverty Rugg, *Picturing Ourselves: Photography and Autobiography* (Chicago: University of Chicago Press, 1997), 133–187.

9. Again, some earlier miniatures included such references, but they were deleted from the final version.

10. On Benjamin's complex relationship toward the Weimar left scene, see Palmier, *Walter Benjamin*, especially chapter 4, 381–444.

11. While the critical literature foregrounds Proust and the relationship to Baudelaire's urban imaginary as present in his poetry, the direct link to *Spleen de Paris* is rarely explored. This absence reflects Benjamin's own puzzling silence about his relationship to Baudelaire's prose miniatures.

12. "The Reading Box," in Walter Benjamin, *Berlin Childhood around 1900*, trans. Howard Eiland (Cambridge, Mass.: Harvard University Press, 2006), 140. All further quotes will be given by page number in the text. This edition of the 1938 version does include purged pieces, such as this one, from earlier groupings, in a separate section.

13. Adorno, "Looking Back at Surrealism," in *Notes on Literature I* (New York: Columbia University Press, 1991), 86–90.

14. Benjamin to Adorno, May 31, 1935, in Walter Benjamin, *The Correspondence of Walter Benjamin, 1910–1940*, trans. Manfred R. Jacobson and Evelyn M. Jacobson (Chicago: University of Chicago Press, 1994), 488.

15. My argument in this chapter builds on the work of Abigail Susik, who has given the best and most detailed account of Benjamin's long-lasting relationship to Aragon's work so far in "The Vertigo of the Modern: Surrealism and the Outmoded" (PhD diss., Columbia University, 2009). Some of this work has been published in essay form; see Abigail Susik, "Between the Old and the New: The Surrealist Outmoded as a Radical Third Term," in *The Great Divide? High and Low Culture in the Avant-Garde and Modernism*, European Avant-Garde and Modernism Studies, vol. 2 (Berlin: De Gruyter, 2011), 323–339. See also Susik, "Aragon's *Le Paysan de Paris* and the Buried History of Buttes-Chaumont Park," *Thresholds* (MIT), no. 36 (Winter 2009): 62–71. However, she does not read *Berlin Childhood* for traces of Aragon's work.

16. Walter Benjamin, "Surrealism: The Last Snapshot of the European Intelligentsia," trans. Edmond Jephcott, in *Selected Writings*, vol. 2, part 1, *1937–1940* (Cambridge, Mass.: Harvard University Press, 1999), 214.

17. Walter Benjamin, *The Arcades Project*, trans. Howard Eiland and Kevon McLaughlin (Cambridge, Mass.: Harvard University Press, 1999), 458.

18. See most recently the discussion in Miriam Hansen, *Cinema and Experience: Siegfried Kracauer, Walter Benjamin, Theodor Adorno* (University of California Press: Berkeley, 2012).

19. Louis Aragon, "Critique du *Paysan de Paris* (Une jacquerie de l'individualisme)," [1930], *L'Infini* (Paris) 68 (Winter 1989): 74–78.

20. While Fürnkäs has acknowledged Aragon's anti-Cartesianism, he has emphasized the continued presence of an Enlightenment impetus in Aragon's notion of modern mythology and his distance from a Romantic utopia of a new mythology and its embeddedness in a philosophy of history. See Fürnkäs, *Surrealismus als Erkenntnis*, 79ff.

21. One exception is Anna Stüssi, *Erinnerung an die Zukunft: Walter Benjamin's "Kindheit um neunzehnhundert* (Göttingen: Vandenhoeck und Ruprecht, 1977), especially 28–34. Even Jean Michel Palmier, who makes the point that Benjamin rediscovered the Berlin of his childhood by detour through his passion for Paris, mentions Aragon only marginally in his superb biography *Walter Benjamin: Lumpensammler, Engel und bucklicht Männlein. Ästhetik und Politik bei Walter Benjamin* (Frankfurt am Main: Suhrkamp, 2009), 138-142.

22. Walter Benjamin, "The Present Social Situation of the French Writer," in *Selected Writings*, vol. 2, part 2, 759-760.

23. Ibid., 760.

24. I owe the following observations to Susik, "The Vertigo of the Modern," 137.

25. Benjamin, "Surrealism," 209.

26. Walter Benjamin, *Gesammelte Schriften*, Band 2, Teil 3, ed. Rolf Tiedemann and Hermann Schweppenhäuser (Frankfurt am Main: Suhrkamp, 1977) 1025, my translation.

27. Benjamin, "Surrealism," 209.

28. See the excellent contextual reading of these scenes in Cohen, *Profane Illumination*, 77–119.

29. Benjamin, "Surrealism," 209.

30. Ibid., 211.

31. Walter Benjamin, "Little History of Photography," *Selected Writings*, vol. 2, part 2, 518.

32. On photography in *Nadja*, see Michel Beaujour, "Qu'est-ce que *Nadja?*" *La Nouvelle Revue Française*, no. 172 (April 1967): 780–799; Dawn Ades, "Photography and the Surrealist Text," in Rosalind Krauss, Dawn Ades, and Jane Livingston, *L'Amour fou: Photography and Surrealism* (New York: Abbeville Press, 1985), 155–192. See also Rosalind Krauss, "The Photographic Conditions of Surrealism," *October* 19 (Winter 1981): esp. 10–14.

33. Aragon does not appear at all in one of the most substantive readings of *Berlin Childhood*, Marianne Muthesius, *Mythos Sprache Erinnerung: Untersuchungen zu Walter Benjamins "Berliner Kindheit um neunzehnhundert"* (Frankfurt am Main: Stroemfeld Verlag, 1996) and only marginally in other writings, including Anja Lemke's essay on *Berlin Childhood* in the *Benjamin*

Handbuch. In *Konstruktiver Fragmentarismus,* Detlev Schöttker focuses on differences with Proust. In *Das andere* Fenster: *Einblicke in Häuser und Menschen* (Frankfurt am Main: Fischer, 1989), 255ff., Heinz Brüggemann focuses on Giedion, though he points to one important passage in Aragon as inspiration for the miniature "Loggias." Only Anna Stüssi draws on textual detail from *Le Paysan,* in a few pages of her study, *Erinnerung an die Zukunft: Walter Benjamin's "Kindheit um neunzehnhundert* (Göttingen: Vandenhoeck und Ruprecht, 1977), esp. 28–34. But her pathbreaking work has not been followed up.

34. Michael Jennings has attempted to construct a much closer relationship than I would between *One-Way Street* and *Berlin Childhood* in his essay entitled "Double Take: Palimpsestic Writing and Image-Character in Benjamin's Late Prose," in *Benjamin Studien 2,* ed. Daniel Weidner and Sigrid Weigel (Munich: Wilhelm Fink Verlag, 2011), 33–44. A very good discussion of both *One-Way Street* and *Berlin Childhood around 1900* can be found in Willi Bolle's comprehensive study of Benjamin's metropolitan imaginary, *Physiognomik der modernen Metropole: Geschichtsdarstellung bei Walter Benjamin* (Cologne: Böhlau Verlag, 1994).

35. For a longer discussion of Aragon's comments on Proust, see Susik, "The Vertigo of the Modern," 189ff. in the e-version.

36. Theodor W. Adorno, "Im Schatten junger Mädchenblüte," in *Dichten und Trachten,* Jahresschau des Suhrkamp Verlages 4 (Frankfurt am Main: Suhrkamp, 1954), 74. The quotation in English can be found in Peter Szondi, "Hope in the Past: On Walter Benjamin," in Benjamin, *Berlin Childhood,* 3.

37. As Peter Szondi has first pointed out, some of these motifs also appear in Rilke's *The Notebooks of Malte Laurids Brigge,* not surprisingly perhaps, since all these texts deal with the similar raw material—upper-class family life at the fin de siècle. Szondi, "Hope in the Past," 7-9.

38. This is not to say that space was not a concern for Proust. See Georges Poulet, *Proustian Space* (Baltimore, Md.: Johns Hopkins University Press, 1977).

39. Louis Aragon, *Paris Peasant,* 110, 13.

40. It would be tempting to relate *écriture automatique* to the radical associationism of Theodor Ziehen that Gottfried Benn critiqued. See chapter 3 in this volume.

41. Louis Aragon, *Treatise on Style,* trans. Alison Waters (Lincoln: University of Nebraska Press, 1991), 96.

42. Louis Aragon, *Je n'ai jamais appris à écrire* (Geneva: Skira, 1969), 54-55. This passage is translated in the introduction to Aragon, *Paris Peasant,* xi-xii.

43. Ibid., xi.

44. Curiously, this rather obvious formal reference to *Spleen de Paris* is rarely made in discussions of *Berlin Childhood.* Only the theme of Baudelaire's urban imaginary is cited time and again as inspiration.

45. In 1972, Tillman Rexroth followed Adorno's choice in his edition of *Berliner Kindheit* in the *Gesammelte Schriften,* Band 4, Teil 1, ed. Tillman Rexroth (Frankfurt am Main: Suhrkamp, 1972) 235.

46. Bernd Witte's valiant attempt to read a *"gestaltete Einheit"* into Benjamin's own 1938 version is questionable since the typescript found in the Bibliothèque Nationale included a note about further necessary reworkings and potential insertions of other pieces. Witte's essay preceded the publication of the contents of that note in *Gesammelte Schriften* VII:2, ed. Rolf Tiedemann and Hermann Schweppenhäuser unter Mitarbeit von Christoph Gödde, Henri Lonitz and Gary Smith (Frankfurt am Main: Suhrkamp, 1989) 695-705. Bernd Witte, "Bilder der Endzeit. Zu einem authentischen Text der <Berliner Kindheit> von Walter Benjamin," in *Deutsche Vierteljahrsschrift für Literaturwissenschaft und Geistesgeschichte* 58, no. 4 (1984): 570–592.

47. The so-called Giessener Fassung from 1932, on the other hand, still has many subjective comments, just as the preceding *Berliner Chronik* does. Overall, one can trace a process of deindividualization of the text, beginning with the early versions of *Berlin Childhood* in relation to *Berlin Chronicle* and coming to a head in several miniatures of the 1938 version that have been heavily reworked and condensed by elimination of biographical and anecdotal detail.

48. Charles Baudelaire, *The Painter of Modern Life and Other Essays*, trans. and ed. Jonathan Mayne (New York: Phaidon Press, 1964), 8.

49. Benjamin, *Berlin Childhood*, 37. Further page numbers given in text.

50. See Irving Wohlfarth, "Märchen für Dialektiker: Walter Benjamin und sein 'bucklicht Männlein,'" in *Walter Benjamin und die Kinderliteratur*, ed. Klaus Doderer (Munich: Juventa, 1988), 121–176.

51. See ibid., 135–138, 150–151.

52. Benjamin, *Gesammelte Schriften*, Band 4, Teil 1, ed. Tillman Rexroth (Frankfurt am Main: Suhrkamp, 1972) 304, my translation.

53. Theodor W. Adorno, "Nachwort zur *Berliner Kindheit um 1900*," in *Über Walter Benjamin* (Frankfurt am Main: Suhrkamp, 1970), 31, my translation.

54. Aragon, *Paris Peasant*, 9.

55. Ibid., 12, my italics.

56. Louis Aragon, *Der Pariser Bauer* (Frankfurt am Main: Suhrkamp, 1996), 17.

57. For an analysis of Benjamin's thresholds, see Winfried Menninghaus, *Schwellenkunde* (Frankfurt am Main: Suhrkamp, 1986).

58. Theodor W. Adorno, *Minima Moralia: Reflections from Damaged Life*, trans. E. F. N. Jephcott (London: Verso, 1974), 38.

59. See Adorno's more generalized comments on the impossibility of dwelling in modernity in *Minima Moralia*. See also the Coda in this volume.

60. On the link between Buttes Chaumont and the Tiergarten, see Christine Dupouy, "Passages—Aragon/Benjamin," *Pleine marge*, no. 14 (1991): 42.

61. Aragon, *Paris Peasant*, 13, 22; Benjamin, *Berlin Childhood*, 56.

62. In Aragon, this glaucous gleam is paralleled "with the special quality of pale brilliance of a leg suddenly revealed under a lifted skirt" (14), a phrasing that Benjamin excerpted in the *Arcades Project*, 539. Because of the child's perspective in *Berlin Childhood*, there are no such erotic references in this

327

text, but they are clearly present in Benjamin's other writing about arcades and boulevards.

63. Benjamin, *Selected Writings*, vol. 3, *1935–1938* (Cambridge, Mass.: Harvard University Press, 2002), 40.
64. "Aquarien der Ferne und der Vergangenheit," in Benjamin, *Gesammelte Schriften*, vol. 4, part 1, 240. This phrase is not found in the translated versions of "Imperial Panorama."
65. Charles Baudelaire, "The Salon of 1859," in *Art in Paris 1845–1862: Salons and Other Exhibitions*, ed. and trans. Jonathan Mayne (Ithaca, N.Y.: Cornell University Press, 1965), 200.
66. Benjamin, "Surrealism," 216.
67. Benjamin, "The Present Social Situation of the French Writer," 759-760.

CHAPTER 7   *War and Metropolis in Jünger*

1. For a summary see Helmut Kiesel, *Ernst Jünger: Die Biographie* (Munich: Siedler Verlag, 2007), 630ff.
2. George L. Mosse, "Two World Wars and the Myth of the War Experience," *Journal of Contemporary History* 21, no. 4 (October 1986): 491–513. In my earlier essay on Jünger, "Fortifying the Heart—Totally: Ernst Jünger's Armored Texts," in *Twilight Memories:Marking Time in a Culture of Amnesia* (New York: Routledge, 1995) 127-144, I argued that subsequent editions of *Storm of Steel* increasingly aestheticized his war experience, which was originally rendered in a rather objective matter-of-fact description without the later nationalist and ideological trappings. This reading finds confirmation in Eva Dempewolf, *Blut und Tinte: Eine Interpretation der verschiedenen Fassungen von Ernst Jüngers Kriegstagebüchern vor dem politischen Hintergrund der Jahre 1920 bis 1980* (Würzburg: Königshausen und Neumann, 1992), which was not accessible to me at the time of writing, and in Steffen Martus, "Der Krieg der Poesie: Ernst Jüngers 'Manie der Bearbeitungen und Fassungen' im Kontext der 'totalen Mobilmachung,'" *Jahrbuch der deutschen Schillergesellschaft* 44 (2000): 212–234.
3. See Helmut Lethen, *Cool Conduct: The Culture of Distance in Weimar Germany* (Berkeley: University of California Press, 2002).
4. Hal Foster, "Armor Fou," *October* 56 (Spring 1991): 64–97. See also Jeffrey Herf, *Reactionary Modernism: Technology, Culture, and Politics in Weimar and the Third Reich* (New York: Cambridge University Press, 1984).
5. Ernst Jünger, *Kriegstagebuch 1914–1918*, ed. Helmuth Kiesel (Stuttgart: Klett-Cotta, 2010).
6. "*Unvergleichliche Schule des Krieges.*" Ernst Jünger, *Das abenteuerliche Herz. Erste Fassung, in Sämtliche Werke*, Vol. 9, *Essays III* (Stuttgart: Klett-Cotta, 1979), 98, my translation. There is as yet no translation of this first version.
7. On Jünger's reactions to Adolf Hitler in the 1920s, see Kiesel, *Ernst Jünger*, esp. 269–274.
8. Karl Heinz Bohrer, *Die Ästhetik des Schreckens* (Munich: Hanser Verlag, 1978).

9. Only the second version is available in English; see Ernst Jünger, *The Adventurous Heart: Figures and Capriccios*, trans. Thomas Friese (Candor, N.Y.: Telos Press, 2012).

10. See the fair but persuasive critique of Bohrer's view of Jünger as a modernist in Karl-Heinz Kittsteiner and Helmut Lethen, " 'Jetzt zieht Leutnant Jünger seinen Mantel aus.' Überlegungen zur 'Ästhetik des Schreckens,' " *Berliner Hefte* 11 (1979): 20–50.

11. Ernst Jünger, "Der Kampf als inneres Erlebnis." I take the translation from Jeffrey Herf, *Reactionary Modernism* (New York: Cambridge University Press, 1984), 76. Herf gives a model analysis of these aspects of Jünger's reactionary modernism from the viewpoint of intellectual history.

12. Ernst Jünger, "Fortschritt, Freiheit und Notwendigkeit," *Arminius* 8 (1926): 8, my translation.

13. Walter Benjamin, "Theories of German Fascism," in *Selected Writings*, vol. 2, part 1, *1927–1930* (Cambridge, Mass.: Harvard University Press, 1999), 316.

14. Ibid., 314.

15. In an earlier essay on Jünger, which was a critical response to Bohrer's intriguing attempt to salvage Jünger for modernism, I argued against the 1980s revival of Jünger as a hero of modernism. I argued that compared to Kafka or Musil, Jünger is at best a B-level literary modernist, and I quoted with glee J. P. Stern's bon mot that Jünger wrote in "the style of a drill sergeant with a taste for philosophy." See J. P. Stern, *Ernst Jünger: A Writer of Our Time* (Cambridge, Mass.: Bowes and Bowes, 1953), 27; and Andreas Huyssen, "Fortifying the Heart—Totally: Ernst Jünger's Armored Texts," in *Twilight Memories: Marking Time in a Culture of Amnesia* (New York: Routledge, 1995), 127–144. Stern's comment may have been over the top, but given Jünger's many and often observed stylistic lapses, his pompous overwriting combined with an all-too-frequent slide into banality, I see no reason to retract my earlier argument, which I supported there with an analysis of language, narrative structure, and the early Jünger's pervasive reactionary imaginary rather than with the crude Marxist reproach that he was a fascist and a steppingstone for Hitler's rise to power. His documented distance from the Nazis in the 1930s was subjectively genuine, though it had less to do with any true opposition to Nazism than with the fact that he considered the Nazis not radical enough because they engaged in electoral politics.

16. Ernst Jünger, "Gross-Stadt und Land," *Deutsches Volkstum* 8 (August 1926), reprinted in Ernst Jünger, *Politische Publizistik 1919 bis 1933*, ed. Sven Olaf Berggötz (Stuttgart: Klett Cotta, 2001), 233-234, my italics, my translation.

17. Walter Benjamin, *One-Way Street*, in *Selected Writings*, vol. 1 (Cambridge, Mass.: Harvard University Press, 1996), 487.

18. Ernst Jünger, *Feuer und Blut*, in *Sämtliche Werke*, Erste Abteilung. Tagebücher, vol. 1 (Stuttgart: Klett-Cotta, 1978), 439–538, quote on 475-476, my translation.

19. Jünger, *Das abenteuerliche Herz. Erste Fassung*, 132. All translations from the first version are my own.

20. Ibid., 121-122.
21. Ernst Jünger, *Der Kampf als inneres Erlebnis*, in *Sämtliche Werke*, Zweite Abteilung, Essays I, vol. 7 (Stuttgart: Klett Cotta, 1980), 74, my translation.
22. Ibid., 50, my translation.
23. Ernst Jünger, "Der Wille," *Standarte*, May 6, 1926, my translation. Republished in *Grundlagen des Nationalismus: Vier Aufsätze von Ernst Jünger*, in *Stahlhelm-Jahrbuch 1927. Im Auftrage der Bundesleitung des Stahlhelm, Bund der Frontsoldaten*, ed. Frank Schauwecker (Magdeburg: Stahlhelm Verlag, 1927), 74-76. Also in Jünger, *Politische Publizistik*, 200ff.
24. This makes it different from the narrative strategies of Adolf Hitler's *Mein Kampf* as analyzed by Alfred Koschorke, "Ideology in Execution: On Hitler's *Mein Kampf*," *New German Critique* 124 (Winter 2015) forthcoming.
25. The German "*zersetzen*" was a key term in anti-semitic discourse. Ernst Jünger, "Der Geist," in *Grundlagen des Nationalismus*, 74-76, my translation; also in Jünger, *Politische Publizistik*, 321ff.
26. Siegfried Kracauer, "Gestaltschau oder Politik?" in Kracauer, *Schriften*, Band 5, Teil 3, ed. Inka Mülder-Bach (Frankfurt am Main: Suhrkamp, 1990), 122-123, my translation.
27. Klaus Theweleit, *Male Phantasies*, 2 vols. (Minneapolis: University of Minnesota Press, 1987 and 1989).
28. "*Den verwickelten Traumzustand der modernen Zivilisation*." Jünger, *Das abenteuerliche Herz. Erste Fassung*, 117.
29. See my reading of *The Black Knight* in "Fortifying the Heart," 139-140.
30. Such comparisons are key to Bohrer's attempt to salvage Jünger as a major modernist in his *Ästhetik des Schreckens*.
31. For a brief analysis of the difference between Jünger's torture scenes and Kafka's debts to Octave Mirbeau, see "Fortifying the Heart," 143.
32. Jünger, *Das abenteuerliche Herz. Erste Fassung*, 79.
33. Ibid., 80.
34. Ibid.
35. Ibid., 89.
36. Ibid., 90.
37. Ibid., 115.
38. Ibid., 98.
39. Ibid., 99.
40. Theodor W. Adorno and Thomas Mann, *Correspondence 1943-1955*, trans. Nicholas Walker (Cambridge, Mass.: Polity Press, 2006), 35, translation modified.
41. Ernst Jünger, *The Adventurous Heart*, 6-7.
42. See Bohrer, *Ästhetik*, 169ff. and 187.
43. Jünger, *The Adventurous Heart*, 37.
44. See Andreas Huyssen, "The Vamp and the Machine: Fritz Lang's *Metropolis*," in *After the Great Divide: Modernism, Mass Culture, Postmodernism* (Bloomington: Indiana University Press, 1986), 65-81.
45. Jünger, *The Adventurous Heart*, 54-55.
46. Ibid., 5.
47. See Bohrer, *Ästhetik*, 248ff.

48. Kiesel, *Ernst Jünger*, 454f.
49. Ernst Jünger, *On Pain*, trans. David C. Durst (Candor, N.Y.: Telos Press, 2008), 38.
50. Ibid., 38-39.
51. Ibid., 38.
52. Jünger, *The Adventurous Heart*, 15–18.
53. See Julia Encke, *Augenblicke der Gefahr: Der Krieg und die Sinne 1914–1934* (Munich: Wilhelm Fink Verlag, 2006), 97.
54. Jünger, *On Pain*, 39.
55. The translation of *"Lichtschrift"* as "images recorded in photographs" lacks the German coupling of photography with script. *On Pain*, 38.
56. "Helmut Lethen im Gespräch mit Stephan Schlak," in *Ernst Jünger: Arbeiter am Abrund*, marbacher catalog 64 (Marbach: Deutsche Schillergesellschaft, 2010), 249–261.
57. Jünger, *Das abenteuerliche Herz. Erste Fassung*, 118.
58. Ernst Jünger, ed., *Das Antlitz des Weltkrieges: Fronterlebnisse deutscher Soldaten. Mit etwa 200 photographischen Aufnahmen auf Tafeln, Kartenanhang sowie einer chronologischen Kriegsgeschichte in Tabellen* (Berlin: Neufeld und Henius Verlag, 1930), 7, my translation.
59. Ibid., 11, my translation.
60. Ibid., 9, my translation.
61. A full analysis is in Encke, *Augenblicke der Gefahr.*
62. Ernst Jünger, *Der Arbeiter: Herrschaft und Gestalt* (Stuttgart: Ernst Klett, 1981), 122; Jünger,*On Pain*, 39.
63. Jünger, *On Pain*, 40. For an excellent critique of *On Pain*, see Albrecht Koschorke, "Der Traumatiker als Faschist: Ernst Jüngers Essay 'Über den Schmerz,'" in *Modernität und Trauma: Beiträge zum Zeitenbruch des Ersten Weltkrieges*, ed. Inka Mülder-Bach (Vienna: WUV Universitätsverlag, 2000), 211–227.
64. Benjamin, "Theories of German Fascism," 319.
65. Edmund Schultz, *Die veränderte Welt: Eine Bilderfibel unserer Zeit* (Breslau: W. G. Korn, 1933), 7–8.
66. Ernst Jünger, "On Danger," introduction to *Der gefährliche Augenblick: Eine Sammlung von Bildern und Berichten*, ed. Ferdinand Bucholtz (Berlin: Junker und Dünnhaupt, 1931), 11–16.
67. Jünger, "Vorwort," in Bucholtz, *Der gefährliche Augenblick*, 5, my italics.

CHAPTER 8 *Musil's Posthumous Modernism*

1. Some of them actually go back to notes in Musil's diaries. On the publication history, see Helmut Arntzen, *Musil Kommentar sämtlicher zu Lebzeiten erschienener Schriften ausser dem Roman "Der Mann ohne Eigenschaften"* (Munich: Winkler Verlag, 1980).
2. Theodor W. Adorno, *Aesthetic Theory*, trans. Robert Hullot-Kentor (Minneapolis: University of Minnesota Press, 1997), 5.
3. Gilles Deleuze and Félix Guattari, *Kafka: Toward a Minor Literature* (Minneapolis: University of Minnesota Press, 1986). Deleuze and Guattari read

Kafka as a linguistically, socially, and literarily deterritorialized writer. This intriguing reading, based as it is on much preceding Kafka research, appears less convincing as one considers Kafka's canonical literary models: Goethe, Flaubert, Stifter, none of them writers of a minor literature.

4. Robert Musil, Foreword to *Posthumous Papers of a Living Author* (London: Penguin Books, 1995), n.p. Translation slightly modified. "Amorphously" is a better rendering of *"dämmerig-grossen Leserkreis"* than "inordinately." All further page numbers given in the text.

5. Robert Musil, "Vortrag in Paris. Vor dem internationalen Schriftstellerkongress für die Verteidigung der Kultur, Juli 1935, Korrigierte Reinschrift," in *Gesammelte Werke 8, Essays und Reden*, ed. Adolf Frisé (Reinbek: Rowohlt, 1978), 1265, my translation.

6. Sandra Teroni,. "Défense de la culture et dialogues manqués," in *Pour la defense de la culture: Les textes du Congrès international des écrivains. Paris, juin 1935*, ed. Sandra Teroni and Wolfgang Klein (Dijon: Editions universitaires de Dijon, 2005), 30.

7. Robert Musil, "Vortrag in Paris," 1263, my translation.

8. A critical practice of *Sachlichkeit*, objectivity or sobriety, is of course a key feature of Musil's thought and writing throughout. In general, *Neue Sachlichkeit* was much more multi-layered than the contemporary leftist critique made it out to be.

9. Robert Musil, *Gesammelte Werke 8*, "Ansätze zu Neuer Ästhetik," 1143 and "Der deutsche Mensch als Symptom," 1368ff. *Seinesgleichen geschieht* is the title of first book's second part.

10. The most comprehensive and incisive discussion of centrality of *Bild* in Musil can be found in Arno Russegger, *Kinema Mundi: Studien zur Theorie des "Bildes" bei Robert Musil* (Vienna: Böhlau, 1996).

11. Hugo von Hofmannsthal, "Der Ersatz für Träume," in *Gesammelte Werke. Reden und Aufsätze II. 1914–1924* (Frankfurt am Main: Fischer Verlag, 1979), 141–145. Stefanie Harris reads Hofmannsthal's engagement with film more positively in her book *Mediating Modernity: German Literature and the "New" Media, 1895–1930* (University Park : Pennsylvania State University Press, 2009), 72–78.

12. When the locale in the miniatures of the other sections is urban, more often than not it is an urban scene located in an inside or an outside perceived from the inside (e.g., "Boardinghouse Nevermore"; "Awakening"). And yet all these miniatures revolve around that crisis of sensual perception that cannot be thought without considering the late nineteenth century's rapid urbanization and the accumulating impact on the senses of new visual and aural media.

13. Robert Musil, "Toward a New Aesthetic: Observations on a Dramaturgy of Film" (1925), in *Precision and Soul: Essays and Addresses*, ed. and trans. Burton Pike and David S. Luft (Chicago: University of Chicago Press, 1990), 194.

14. Ibid., 194–195.

15. Translation modified: "telescope" replaced by "binoculars." Linguistically the use of "telescope" for the German *"Fernrohr"* is correct, but a *Fernrohr*

is always monocular, not binocular. Musil's use of *"Fernrohr"* for
"Trieder" is thus misleading.

16. Musil, "Toward a New Aesthetic," 195.

17. Ibid., 196.

18. Helmut Lethen, *Cool Conduct: The Culture of Distance in Weimar Germany*
(Berkeley: University of California Press, 2002).

19. Of course the objects seen through the binoculars may still move, such as
the trolley, which changes its shape uncannily when it is observed moving
through a sharp S-curve in the street below. Nevertheless the binoculars
do not scan but remain trained on one single space.

20. On this blurring of boundaries between animals and humans, see Kári
Driscoll, "Toward a Poetics of Animality: Hofmannsthal, Rilke, Pirandello,
Kafka" (PhD diss., Columbia University, 2013). Driscoll puts it succinctly
when he says that around 1900, animals in literature begin to behave badly.

21. On the animation of things in early cinema and its effects in literature,
especially in Kafka, see Brook Henkel, "Animistic Fictions: German
Modernism, Film, and the Animation of Things" (PhD diss., Columbia
University, 2013).

22. Musil, "Toward a New Aesthetic," 197.

23. Musil, "The German as Symptom" (1923), in *Precision and Soul*, 186.

24. Friedrich Nietzsche, "On Truth and Lies in a Nonmoral Sense" (1873), in
The Nietzsche Reader, ed. Keith Ansell Pearson and Duncan Large (Oxford:
Blackwell, 2006), 119. Bernd Hüppauf first drew attention to this passage
in "Über das Mästen von Begriffen und die Furcht vor der Erfahrung: Be-
merkungen zur Sprache in Robert Musils *Nachlass zu Lebzeiten*," in *Die
Fremdheit der Sprache: Studien zur Literatur der Moderne*, ed. Jochen C.
Schütze, Hans-Ulrich Treichel, and Dietmar Voss (Hamburg: Argument
Verlag, 1988), 26–47.

25. Nietzsche, "On Truth and Lies," 116.

26. See the Nazi film *The Eternal Jew* and its equation of Jews with mice and
rats. It is the genius of Art Spiegelman to have taken up this Nazi discourse
and turned it critically against its ideologically loaded genealogy in *Maus*.

27. Musil, "The Serious Writer in Our Time" (1934), in *Precision and Soul*, 251.

28. Musil, "Helpless Europe: A Digressive Journey" (1922), in *Precision and Soul*,
117.

29. Ibid., 121.

30. On the desire for immediacy (*Unmittelbarkeit*) in the discourses after 1900,
see Tobias Wilke, *Medien der Unmittelbarkeit:Dingkonzepte und Wahrneh-
mungstechniken 1918-1939* (Munich: Wilhelm Fink Verlag, 2010).

31. Helmuth Lethen, "Eckfenster der Moderne. Wahrnehmungsexperimente
bei Musil und E. T. A. Hoffmann," in *Robert Musils 'Kakanien': Subjekt und
Geschichte*, ed. Josef Strutz (Munich: Fink Verlag, 1987), 195–229.

32. Musil, *Tagebücher*, ed. Adolf Frisé (Reinbek: Rowohlt, 1976), 309, my translation. An even earlier and much longer entry from November 1913 already
has the outline and much of the phrasing of what was to become the miniature in *Posthumous Papers of a Living Author*. See ibid., 284ff. It was first
published in 1914 in *Die Argonauten* under the title "Römischer Sommer"

and republished several times in other papers and magazines after 1918. See Arntzen, *Musil Kommentar*, 148.

33. Some of these images are already present in the November 1913 version, but they assume a different connotation in the context of war, including the phrase "or like sleepers," which may well refer to Rimbaud's poem "Le dormeur du val," which conjures the dead soldier's body lying in a meadow as if he were sleeping.

34. See Helmut Arntzen, *Musil Kommentar* (Munich: Winkler Verlag, 1980), 148.

35. Franz Kafka, *The Trial*, trans. Breon Mitchell (New York: Schocken, 1998), 227. This is a new translation based on the restored text.

36. Musil, *Tagebücher*, ed. Adolf Frisé (Reinbek: Rowohlt, 1976), 347. For the publication history of "Flypaper," see Arntzen, *Musil Kommentar*, 153.

37. Alpine warfare is again a theme in "The Blackbird," which at one point in the narrative tells the story of a near-mystical experience when an aerial dart, a special World War I weapon thrown from an Italian plane, barely misses the narrator on the ground, triggering a kind of out-of-body experience analogous to that described at the end of "The Mouse." Musil, *Posthumous Papers of a Living Author*, 136–138.

Coda. Diving into the Wreck: Adorno's Minima Moralia

1. This is not to say that certain aspects of Adorno's writing style in this work do not make cameo appearances in some of his other, more traditionally philosophical works and essays. Actually, the essay as form has definite affinities to the miniature and the aphorism. But then he never again wrote a work quite like *Minima Moralia*.

2. "So müsste ich ein Engel und kein Autor sein." *Adorno und seine Frankfurter Verleger. Der Briefwechsel mit Peter Suhrkamp und Siegfried Unseld*, ed. Wolfgang Schopf (Frankfurt am Main: Suhrkamp, 2003), 265, my translation.

3. Theodor W. Adorno, "Memento," in *Minima Moralia: Reflections from Damaged Life*, trans. E. F. N. Jephcott (London: Verso, 1974), 87, translation modified; I have changed the word "substance" to "object." Page numbers for all further quotes from *Minima Moralia* will be given in the text.

4. Edward Said, *Reflections on Exile and Other Essays* (Cambridge, Mass.: Harvard University Press, 2000), 186. See also Elisabeth Bronfen, "Exil in der Literatur: Zwischen Metapher und Realität," *Arcadia* 28 (1993): 167–183.

5. Bertolt Brecht, *Flüchtlingsgespräche*, in *Gesammelte Werke 14. Prosa 4* (Frankfurt am Main: Suhrkamp, 1967), 1462, my translation.

6. Said, *Reflections on Exile*, 184.

7. One exception is Alexander Düttmann, *So ist es: Ein philosophischer Kommentar zu Adornos Minima Moralia* (Frankfurt am Main: Suhrkamp, 2004). The reception of *Minima Moralia* has been thoroughly documented in Alex Demirović, *Der nonkonformistische Intellektuelle: Die Entwicklung der Kritischen Theorie zur Frankfurter Schule* (Frankfurt am Main: Suhrkamp, 1999), 525–555.

8. On the "foreign" and foreign derivation in Adorno's understanding of language politics, see the incisive chapter on Adorno in Yasemin Yildiz, *Beyond the Mother Tongue: The Postmonolingual Condition* (New York: Fordham University Press, 2012), 67–108, esp. 84ff.

9. Raymond Williams, "When Was Modernism?" In *The Politics of Modernism: Against the New Comnformists*, ed. Tony Pinkney (London: Verso, 1997), 31–35.

10. Andreas Bernhard and Ulrich Raulff, eds., *Theodor W. Adorno Minima Moralia—Neu gelesen* (Frankfurt am Main: Suhrkamp, 2003).

11. Of course his pre-California work with Paul Lazarsfeld and the Princeton radio project should be mentioned here as well.

12. Letter of December 19, 1939, in Theodor W. Adorno, *Letters to his Parents 1939–1951*, trans. Wieland Hoban (Cambridge, Mass.: Polity Press, 2006), 26.

13. Letters of November 30, 1941, and May 20, 1940, in ibid., 69 and 50, respectively.

14. See especially the letter of November 30, 1941, in ibid., 69ff.

15. Ibid., 70.

16. Actually, the German term *"Verblendung"* implies both deception and delusion. Being deceived creates delusion in the subject.

17. On the rhetoric of exaggeration, see esp. Alexander Garcia Düttmann, *Philosophy of Exaggeration*, trans. James Philips (New York: Continuum, 2007).

18. "Lexical Note," ibid., vii.

19. Theodor W. Adorno, *Gesammelte Schriften*, Band 10, Teil 2 (Frankfurt am Main: Suhrkamp, 1977), 622, my translation.

20. See for instance the anthology *Mass Culture: The Popular Arts in America*, ed. Bernhard Rosenberg and David Manning White (New York: The Free Press, 1957).

21. Theodor W. Adorno, "What Does Coming to Terms with the Past Mean?" in *Bitburg in Moral and Political Perspective*, ed. Geoffrey Hartman (Bloomington: Indiana University Press, 1986), 128.

22. Theodor W. Adorno, *Ästhetische Theorie* (Frankfurt am Main: Suhrkamp, 1973), 201.

23. Adorno, "Was bedeutet: Aufarbeitung der Vergangenheit," in *Erziehung zur Mündigkeit* (Frankfurt am Main: Suhrkamp, 1972), 13. This "horrifying spectre" haunts not only German developments after 1945 but is identified here with the "historical blindness of American consciousness" in the wake of Henry Ford's quip that "history is bunk." This phrasing, part of the radio lecture version, does not appear in the version published in Adorno's *Eingriffe*, which in turn served as the source for the English translation in *Critical Models: Interventions and Catchwords*.

24. "Asylum" would be the better translation for the German *"Asyl."* "Refuge" just sounds too optimistic.

25. Theodor W. Adorno, *Negative Dialectics*, trans. E. B. Ashton (New York: Seabury Press, 1973), 363.

26. See Harro Müller's analysis of Nietzsche's writing strategy in *Genealogy of Morals* in "Genealogie als Herausforderung: Anmerkungen zu Friedrich

Nietzsche und ein Seitenblick auf Michel Foucault," in *Literaturwissenschaft heute: Gegenstand, Positionen, Relevanz*, ed. Susanne Knaller and Doris Pichler (Göttingen: Vandenhoeck & Ruprecht Unipress, 2013), 125–143.

27. Thomas Mann, *Tagebücher 1944–46*, ed. Inge Jens (Frankfurt am Main: Fischer, 1986), 282, my translation.

28. Ibid., 257, my translation.

29. See Thomas Mann, *The Story of a Novel: The Genesis of Doctor Faustus* (New York: Alfred A. Knopf, 1961), 42–48, 154–156. On the somewhat fraught relationship between Mann and Adorno, see Klaus Harprecht, *Thomas Mann: Eine Biographie* (Hamburg: Rowohlt, 1995), esp. 1540–1549.

30. Theodor W. Adorno, *Philosophy of New Music*, trans. and ed. Robert Hullot-Kentor (Minneapolis: University of Minnesota Press, 2006), 30.

31. Thomas Mann, *Doctor Faustus: The Life of the German Composer Adrian Leverkühn as Told by a Friend*, trans. H. T. Lowe-Porter (New York: Random House, 1948), 239.

32. For an excellent critique of that older consensus of exile Germanistik, see Bettina Englmann, *Poetik des Exils: Die Modernität der deutschsprachigen Exilliteratur* (Tübingen: Max Niemeyer Verlag, 2001).

33. Letter of February 12, 1940, in Adorno, *Letters to His Parents*, 66.

34. Letter of May 20, 1940, in ibid., 80.

35. The translation reads: "Wrong life cannot be lived rightly" Adorno, *Minima Moralia*, 39.

36. In Theodor W. Adorno, *Critical Models: Interventions and Catchwords* (New York: Columbia University Press, 1998), 239.

37. See, for instance, Claus Offe, *Selbstbetrachtung aus der Ferne: Tocqueville, Weber und Adorno in den Vereinigten Staaten* (Frankfurt am Main: Suhrkamp, 2004), 101.

38. Theodor W. Adorno, "On Jazz," in *Essays on Music*, selected with introduction, commentary, and notes by Richard Leppert, new translations by Susan Gillespie (Berkeley: University of California Press, 2002), 470–495. He repeated his condemnation of jazz in 1953 in "Perennial Fashion Jazz," published in *Prisms*, trans. Shierry Weber Nicholsen and Samuel Weber (Cambridge, Mass.: MIT Press, 1981), 119–132.

39. Theodor W. Adorno, Else Frenkel-Brunswik, Daniel J. Levinson, and R. Nevitt Sanford, *The Authoritarian Personality* (New York: Harper & Brothers, 1950).

40. See David Jenemann, *Adorno in America* (Minneapolis: University of Minnesota Press, 2007) and the Adorno chapter in Amy Villarejo, *Ethereal Queer: Television, Historicity, Desire* (Durham, N.C.: Duke University Press, 2014), 30–65.

41. Claus Offe in *Selbstbetrachtung* faults him for not having reflected enough on the postwar shift in his views on America.

42. Theodor W. Adorno, *Introduction to the Sociology of Music*, trans. E. B. Ashton (New York: Seabury Press, 1976), 36.

43. Theodor W. Adorno, "Scientific Experiences of a European Scholar in America," in *Critical Models: Catchwords and Interventions*, trans. Henry Pickford (New York: Columbia University Press, 1998), 239–240.

44. "Im Flug erhascht," in Theodor W. Adorno, *Gesammelte Schriften*, Band 2 (Frankfurt am Main: Suhrkamp, 1986), 548, my translation.
45. See Miriam Bratu Hansen, "The Mass Production of the Senses" in *Reinventing Film Studies*, ed. Christine Gledhill and Linda Williams (New York: Oxford University Press, 2000), 332–350.

Index

absence: absent presence, 53, 96, 276; in Benjamin, 121, 142, 144, 153, 186, 196; of the city, 52, 57, 96, 138, 274–276, 295; of ekphrastic description, 142, 275; of emblematic picture in Benjamin, 147, 149; of empirical reference, 99, 144, 275–276; in Kafka, 52, 57, 61, 65, 69, 137; of language, 257; of photographs, 153, 196; structure of, 57, 144, 147–149, 274; of visual, 69, 121, 148, 162, 196

abstraction, 15, 28, 132, 154, 156; abstract regime of visuality, 134, 136; of urban space, 38, 54, 83

acceleration, 6, 10, 71; accelerated style in Keun, 171, 176–177; of fall in Jünger, 19, 231; of modernization, 5; of modern life, 2–5, 65; speed of film, 2, 62, 125; speedup & slowing down in Kafka, 65, 73, 80

Adorno, Theodor W., 2–4, 15, 20–21, 64, 66, 117–118, 131, 190, 193; and Benjamin, 58–59, 119–120, 184, 197, 199; on Benn, 91; correspondence with parents, 276, 280, 283; correspondence with Thomas Mann, 230; on Jünger, 222; on Kafka, 58, 63; *Introduction to the Sociology of Music*, 293; *Minima Moralia*, 1, 13, 208, 270–296; *Negative Dialectics*, 287; "Second Harvest," 273

Adorno, Theodor W. Horkheimer: Max: *Dialectic of Enlightenment*, 116, 235, 259, 274–275, 281

advertising, 67, 143–145, 163, 168–169; electric, 16, 138–139, 171, 229–230

affirmative sabotage, 30, 169

Agamben, Giorgio, 184

Alciati, Andrea, 141

alienation, 74, 98, 107, 248, 290; alienated seeing, 40; alienated self, 39, 53, 96; alienated space, 38, 139; of exile, 273; of modern life, 47; of perception, 116; urban, 49, 53, 59, 137, 228

allegory: in Baudelaire, 29, 37, 41, 50, 183; in Benjamin, 202, 204, 208; in Höch, 168; in Jünger, 235, 238; in Keun, 173; in Kracauer, 119, 124, 134–135, 140, 168; in Musil, 250, 259, 262–264, 269. *See also* emblem

Altenberg, Peter, 6, 57

Andersch, Alfred, 218

Anderson, Mark, 81

Andreas-Salomé, Lou, 34, 39

animal, 7, 50, 149; in Benjamin, 182; in Benn, 100–101, 104–105; in Jünger, 227, 240; in Kafka, 105, 245; in Musil, 105, 250–251, 256–269

anthropocentrism, 7, 257, 259, 269

Aragon, Louis, 3, 23, 92, 250; and Benjamin, 149, 181–217; *Le Paysan de Paris*, 181–217